IN RWANDA in 1994, up to one million people were killed in a planned public and political campaign. For six years Linda Melvern has worked on the story of this horrendous crime, and this book, a classic piece of investigative journalism, is the result. Its new and startling information has the makings of an international scandal.

A People Betrayed contains a full narrative account of how the genocide unfolded. It describes its scale, speed and intensity. It is a terrible indictment, not just of the UN Security Council, but of governments and individuals who could have prevented what was happening but chose not to do so.

Drawing on a series of in-depth interviews, the author also tells the story of the unrecognized heroism of those who stayed on during the genocide: volunteer UN peacekeepers; their Force Commander, the Canadian Lt-General Romeo A. Dallaire; and Philippe Gaillard, the head of a delegation of the International Committee of the Red Cross, helped by medical teams from Médecins Sans Frontières.

The international community, which fifty years ago resolved that genocide should never happen again, failed to prevent it happening in Rwanda. Moreover, as this book shows, international funds intended to help the Rwandan economy actually helped to create the conditions that made the genocide possible. Documents held in Kigali, the Rwandan capital, and hitherto unpublished evidence of secret UN Security Council deliberations in New York reveal a shocking sequence of events.

What happened in Rwanda shows that, despite the creation of an organization to prevent a repetition of genocide – for the UN is central to this task – it failed to do so, even in the face of indisputable evidence. At a time when increasing attention is being given to the need for UN reform, this book provides evidence to accelerate and focus that process. Only by understanding how and why the genocide happened can there be any hope that this new century will break with the dismal record of the last.

About the author

Linda Melvern is an investigative journalist and writer. For four years she was a reporter with the *Sunday Times*, including as a member of their award-winning Insight Team. Since leaving the paper to write her first book, she has written widely for the British press and also lectures on international issues. She is a visiting fellow in the Department of International Politics, University of Wales, Aberystwyth. Her books include:

The Ultimate Crime: Who Betrayed the United Nations and Why (1995)

The End of the Street (1986)

Techno-Bandits (1984) (co-authored)

A People Betrayed

The Role of the West in Rwanda's Genocide

Linda Melvern

NAEP
CAPE TOWN

Zed Books
LONDON • NEW YORK

A People Betrayed: The Role of the West in Rwanda's Genocide was first published by Zed Books Ltd, 7 Cynthia Street, London N1 9JF, UK and Room 400, 175 Fifth Avenue, New York, NY 10010, USA in 2000.

Published in South Africa by New Africa Education Publishing, PO Box 23317, Claremont 7735, Republic of South Africa

Distributed in the USA exclusively by Palgrave, a division of St Martin's Press, LLC, 175 Fifth Avenue, New York, NY 10010, USA

Second impression, 2000

Cover designed by Phillip Green
Front cover map reproduced by courtesy of the US National Imagery and Mapping Agency
Set in Monotype Dante by Ewan Smith, London
Printed and bound by Bookcraft, Midsomer Norton

A catalogue record for this book is available from the British Library

Library of Congress Cataloging-in-Publication Data
Melvern, Linda
A people betrayed: the role of the West in Rwanda's genocide / Linda Melvern.
p. cm.
Includes bibliographical references and index.
ISBN 1-85649-830-1 (cased) – ISBN 1-85649-831-x (pbk.)
1. Genocide–Rwanda. 2. Rwanda–Ethnic relations. 3. Rwanda–History–Civil War, 1994–Atrocities. 4. Rwanda–Foreign relations. I. Title.
DT450.435.M426 2000
967.57104–dc21

00-032070

ISBN 1 85649 830 1 cased
ISBN 1 85649 831 x limp

In South Africa
ISBN 0 620 26654 6 limp

Contents

To the memory of
Raphael Lemkin

Acknowledgements

Interviews were indispensable in the writing of this book. I made every effort to interview as many people as possible. I would like to thank all those who contributed to my knowledge and understanding of what happened.

Many people who were present in Rwanda during the genocide allowed me the opportunity to talk with them and very often at great length, giving me important information. Some of them gave me documents. I thank you and I apologize for anything that I may have got wrong.

I thank Jeremy Harding, a senior editor of the *London Review of Books*, who, in December 1996, enabled me to publish 'The UN and Rwanda', my first account of the Security Council's informal meetings in 1994. I also thank Anthony McDermott, editor, *Security Dialogue*, who published 'Genocide Behind the Thin Blue Line' in September 1997.

I thank Nicholas J. Wheeler of the University of Wales, Aberystwyth, for his encouragement. I was fortunate to have benefited from the knowledge of Daniela Kroslak, a research student, University of Wales, Aberystwyth, an expert on the French involvement in Rwanda, and whose reading of an early draft made important differences to the text.

I thank most sincerely the staff in the library of the Royal Institute of International Affairs, and particularly Sue Franks. I thank Anne Cecilie Kjelling, head librarian, Nobel Institute Library. Alexandra McLeod, UN librarian, was invaluable. Her knowledge of the UN system is second to none, and she was indefatigable. I thank Marilla B. Guptil, chief, Archives and Records Management Section at the UN. I thank Michael Melvern, my nephew, who was generous with his considerable computer skills. I thank Stephanie Woolf Murray and Maria-Teresa Garrido for their belief in the project.

The support and encouragement of friends was crucial. I thank Lisa Chakowa, Lizzie Cox, Julian Fraser and Isabelle Fraser Cox, Simon Cox, Polly Low, Tony and Margaret Grimes, Granville Fletcher, Cynthia Jabs, Iain and Paulli Joyce, Geoff and Carol Kremer, Florence and Bertrand Mary, Daphne Norman, Susie Morgan, Michael Pye, Jane Rackham, Sue Snell and Francis Vande Putte. I thank S. J. Taylor for her continuing support.

I thank publisher Robert Molteno. My agent Michael Shaw was supportive over a very long haul. It was a stroke of good fortune that I met Peter

Greaves. A dedicated internationalist, his enthusiasm for the book was inspiring. He provided much practical help. Magnus Linklater, who edited the manuscript, is generous and brilliant. He gave crucial professional guidance. He is a wonderful journalist, and I owe him a debt greater than he realizes.

The love and support of my family was unfailing. My son Laurence showed extraordinary forbearance and good nature. I owe a special debt of gratitude to my parents, Mavius and Jim Melvern, and my partner Phill Green. Without them, I could not have written this book.

Linda Melvern, London

Abbreviations

ADL	Association Rwandaise pour la défense des droits de la personne et des libertés publiques
APC	armoured personnel carrier
BACAR	Banque Continentale Africaine Rwanda
BBTG	broad-based transitional government
CDR	Coalition pour la Défense de la République
CHK	Centre Hospitalier de Kigali
CND	Conseil National pour le Développement
DAMI	Détachement d'Assistance Militaire et d'Instruction
DGSE	Direction Général de la Sécurité Extérieure
DMZ	de-militarized zone
DPKO	Department of Peacekeeping Operations
DSP	Division Spéciale Présidentielle
ESM	Ecole Supérieure Militaire
ETO	Ecole Technique Officielle
EW	early warning
FAO	Food and Agriculture Organization (UN)
FIDH	International Federation of Human Rights
ICRC	International Committee of the Red Cross
ICTR	International Criminal Tribunal for Rwanda
IMF	International Monetary Fund
MDR	Mouvement Démocratique Républicain
MRND	Mouvement Révolutionnaire National pour le Développement
MRNDD	Mouvement Républicain National pour la Démocratie et le Développement
MSF	Médecins Sans Frontières
NGO	non-governmental organization
NMOG	OAU Neutral Military Observer Group
NRA	National Resistance Army
OAU	Organization of African Unity
ONUSAL	UN Observer Mission in El Salvador
ORINFOR	Office Rwandais d'Information

Parmehutu	Parti du mouvement de l'émancipation des Bahutu
PDC	Parti Démocrat Chrétien
PDD	Presidential Decision Directive (USA)
PL	Parti Libéral
PSD	Parti Social Démocrate
QRF	Quick Reaction Force (UN)
RANU	Rwandan Alliance for National Unity
RGF	Rwandan Government Forces
ROE	rules of engagement
RPF	Rwandan Patriotic Front
RRWF	Rwanda Refugees Welfare Association
RTBF	Radio Télévision de la Communauté Française de Belgique
RTLMC	Radio-Télévision Libre des Mille Collines
SAP	structural adjustment programme
SRG	Service Général du Renseignement de l'Armée (Military Intelligence, Belgium)
UNAMIR	United Nations Assistance Mission for Rwanda
UNAR	Union Nationale Rwandaise
UNCIVPOL	United Nations Civilian Police
UNDP	United Nations Development Programme
UNESCO	United Nations Educational, Scientific and Cultural Organization
UNHCR	United Nations High Commissioner for Refugees
UNICEF	United Nations Children's Fund
UNOMUR	United Nations Observer Mission Uganda–Rwanda
UNOSOM	United Nations Operation in Somalia
UNPROFOR	United Nations Protection Force
UNREO	UN Rwanda Emergency Office
UPR	Union de Peuple Rwandais
WFP	World Food Programme
WHO	World Health Organization

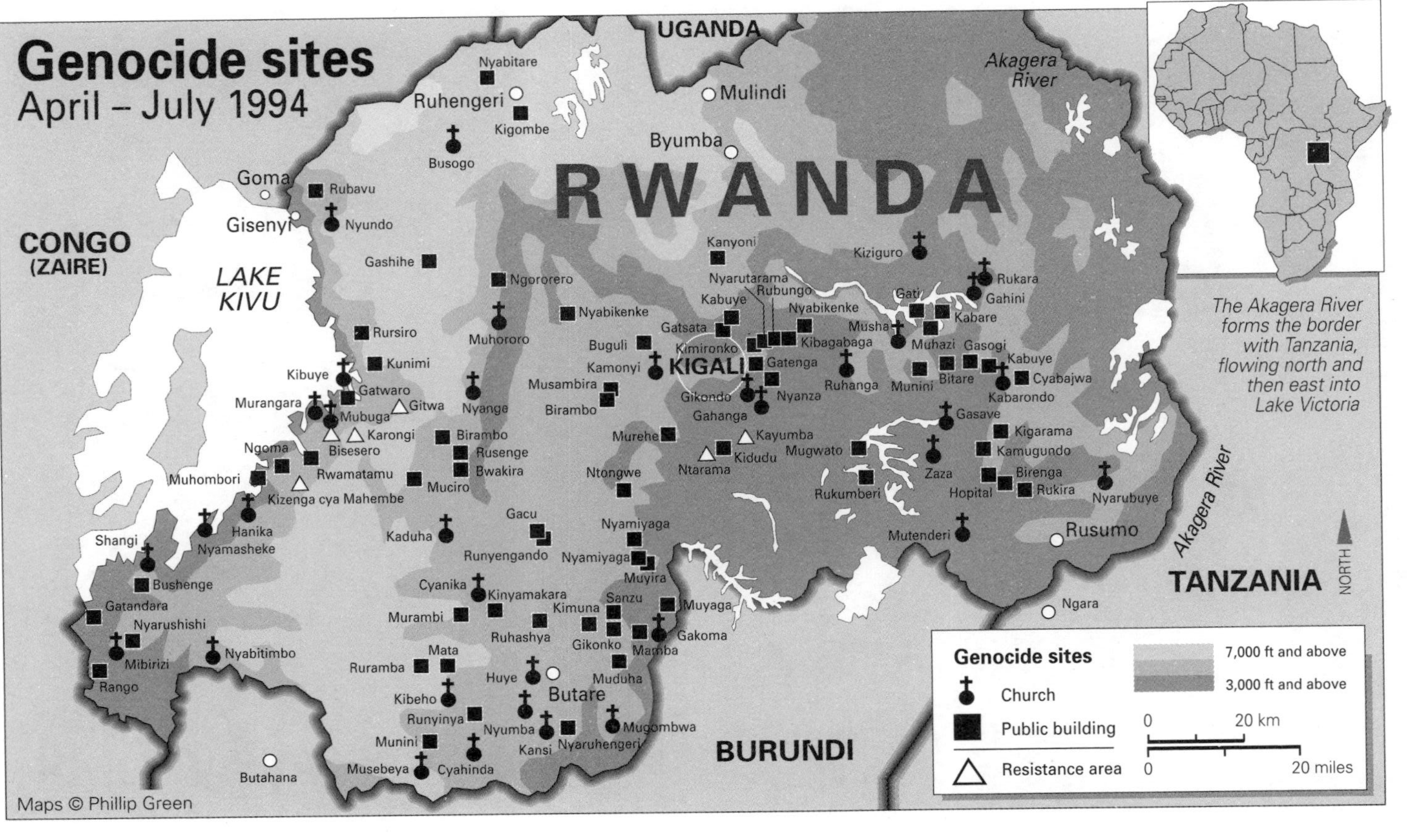

Genocide sites
April – July 1994
CONGO
(ZAIRE)
LAKE
KIVU
UGANDA
RWANDA
BURUNDI
TANZANIA
KIGALI
Akagera River
Akagera River
The Akagera River forms the border with Tanzania, flowing north and then east into Lake Victoria
NORTH
Goma
Gisenyi
Ruhengeri
Nyabitare
Kigombe
Busogo
Rubavu
Nyundo
Gashihe
Mulindi
Byumba
Kanyoni
Kiziguro
Rukara
Gahini
Gati
Kabare
Ngororero
Muhororo
Nyabikenke
Rursiro
Kunimi
Kibuye
Gatwaro
Murangara
Mubuga
Gitwa
Nyange
Karongi
Bisesero
Ngoma
Rwamatamu
Muhombori
Kizenga cya Mahembe
Birambo
Rusenge
Bwakira
Muciro
Hanika
Nyamasheke
Shangi
Bushenge
Gatandara
Nyarushishi
Mibirizi
Rango
Nyabitimbo
Butahana
Kaduha
Gacu
Runyengando
Cyanika
Kinyamakara
Murambi
Ruhashya
Mata
Ruramba
Kibeho
Runyinya
Munini
Musebeya
Cyahinda
Huye
Butare
Nyumba
Kansi
Nyaruhengeri
Mugombwa
Muduha
Mamba
Gikonko
Kimuna
Sanzu
Muyaga
Gakoma
Muyira
Nyamiyaga
Nyamiyaga
Ntongwe
Murehe
Musambira
Birambo
Kamonyi
Buguli
Gatsata
Kabuye
Nyarutarama
Rubungo
Nyabikenke
Kimironko
Kibagabaga
Gatenga
Gikondo
Gahanga
Nyanza
Kayumba
Ntarama
Kidudu
Mugwato
Ruhanga
Musha
Muhazi
Gasogi
Kabuye
Munini
Bitare
Cyabajwa
Kabarondo
Gasave
Kigarama
Kamugundo
Zaza
Rukumberi
Birenga
Hopital
Rukira
Nyarubuye
Mutenderi
Rusumo
Ngara
Genocide sites
Church
Public building
Resistance area
7,000 ft and above
3,000 ft and above
0
20 km
0
20 miles
Maps © Phillip Green

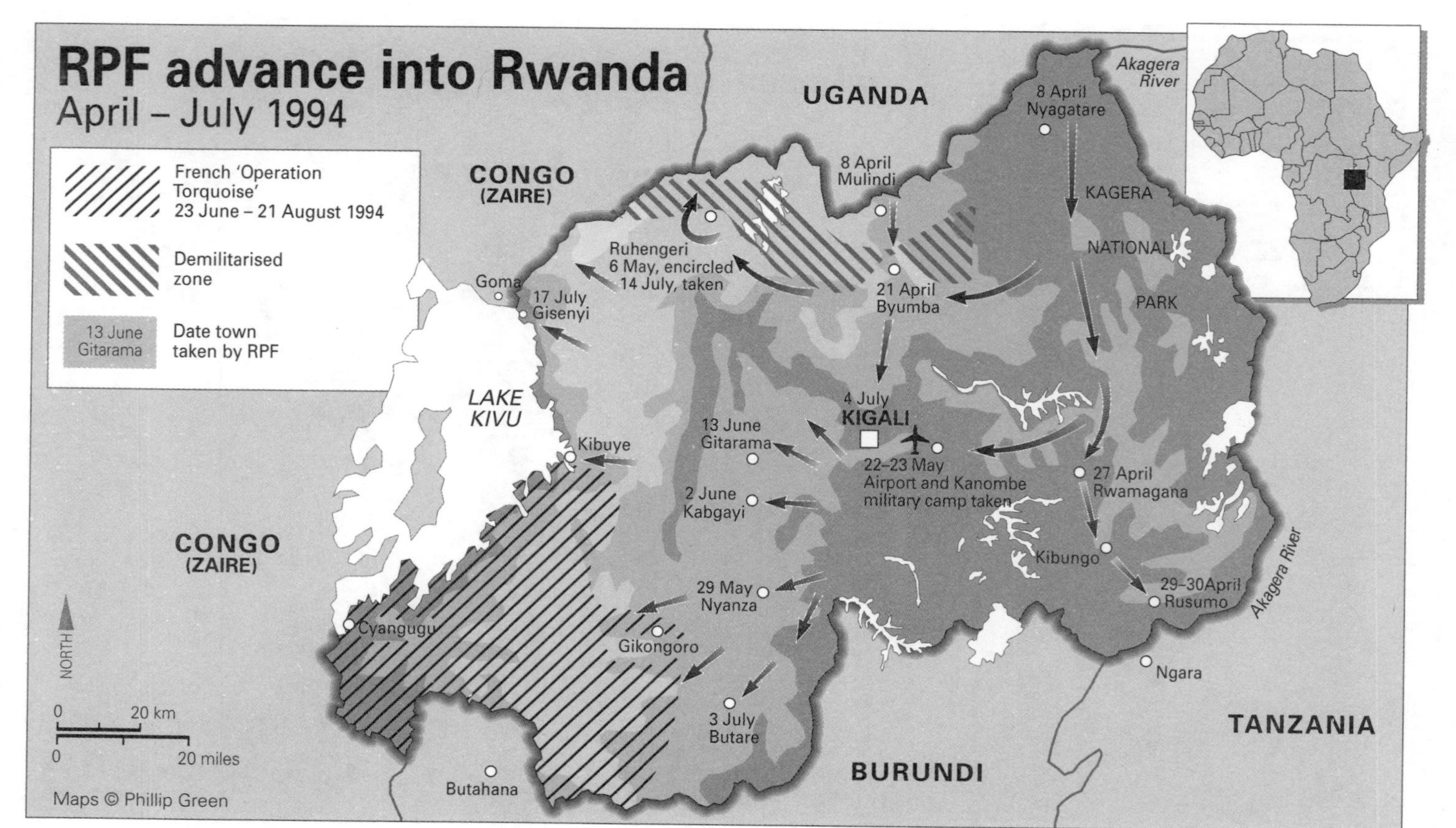
RPF advance into Rwanda
April – July 1994
French 'Operation Torquoise' 23 June – 21 August 1994
Demilitarised zone
13 June Gitarama
Date town taken by RPF
UGANDA
CONGO (ZAIRE)
CONGO (ZAIRE)
BURUNDI
TANZANIA
Akagera River
Akagera River
8 April Nyagatare
8 April Mulindi
KAGERA
NATIONAL
PARK
Ruhengeri 6 May, encircled 14 July, taken
21 April Byumba
Goma
17 July Gisenyi
LAKE KIVU
4 July KIGALI
22–23 May Airport and Kanombe military camp taken
13 June Gitarama
2 June Kabgayi
Kibuye
27 April Rwamagana
Kibungo
29–30April Rusumo
Ngara
29 May Nyanza
Gikongoro
3 July Butare
Cyangugu
Butahana
NORTH
0
20 km
0
20 miles
Maps © Phillip Green

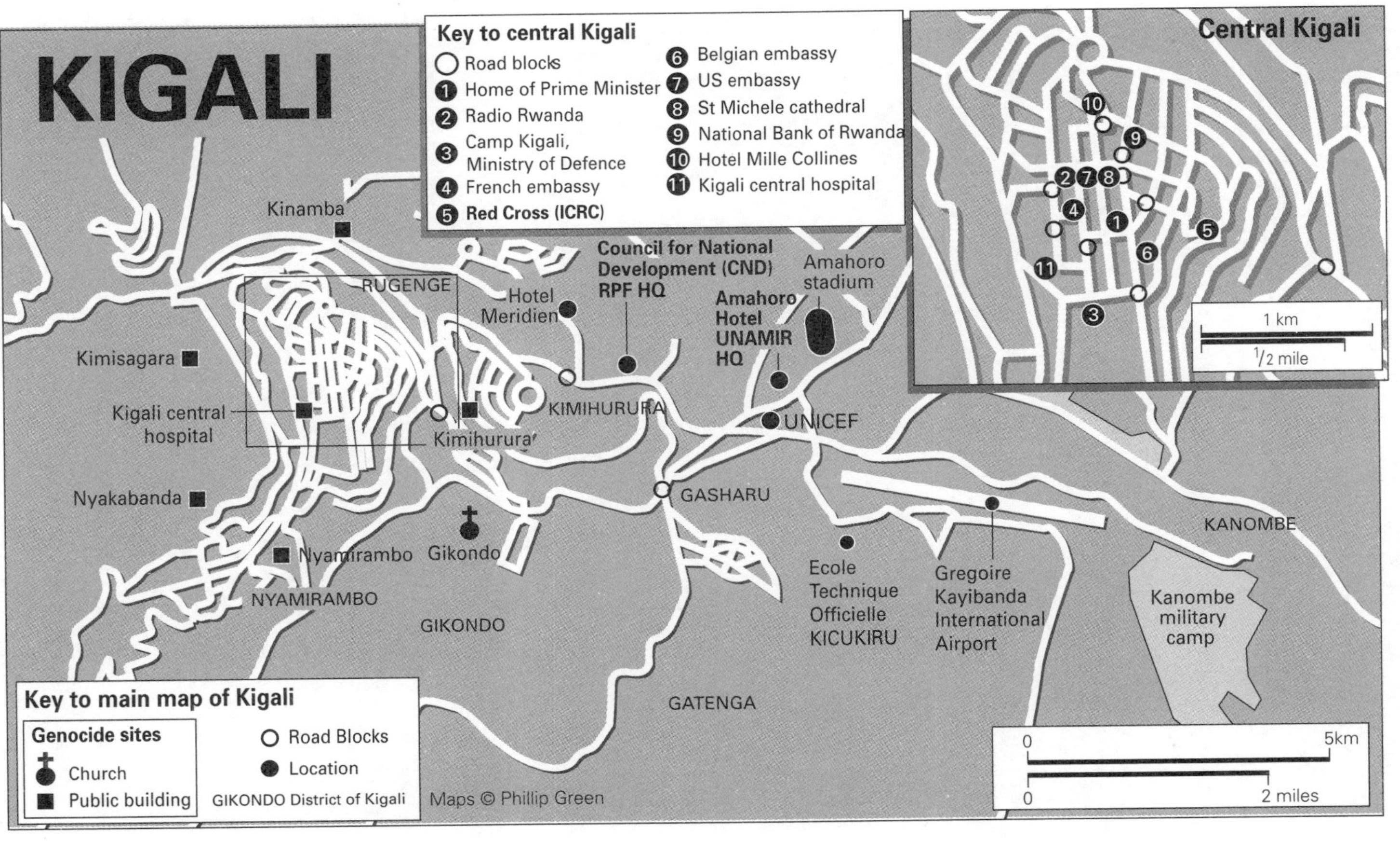
KIGALI
Key to central Kigali
Road blocks
1 Home of Prime Minister
2 Radio Rwanda
3 Camp Kigali, Ministry of Defence
4 French embassy
5 Red Cross (ICRC)
6 Belgian embassy
7 US embassy
8 St Michele cathedral
9 National Bank of Rwanda
10 Hotel Mille Collines
11 Kigali central hospital
Central Kigali
1 km
1/2 mile
Kinamba
RUGENGE
Hotel Meridien
Council for National Development (CND) RPF HQ
Amahoro Hotel UNAMIR HQ
Amahoro stadium
Kimisagara
Kigali central hospital
KIMIHURURA
Kimihurura
UNICEF
GASHARU
Nyakabanda
Gikondo
Nyamirambo
NYAMIRAMBO
GIKONDO
Ecole Technique Officielle KICUKIRU
Gregoire Kayibanda International Airport
KANOMBE
Kanombe military camp
GATENGA
Key to main map of Kigali
Genocide sites
Church
Public building
Road Blocks
Location
GIKONDO District of Kigali
Maps © Phillip Green
0
5km
0
2 miles

1 · Genocide, April 1994

THE people had turned up in small groups, emerging from the eucalyptus trees at the back of the school. There was a girl, aged about six, with a machete wound in her head and a boy with a gaping hole in his shoulder from a bullet. He did not cry. One man had a hand almost severed from a machete blow.

Soon families were camped out in the classrooms, and when these became overcrowded people huddled together in groups on the playing field. Outside the gates of the school the militia brandished their machetes and hand-grenades. They cruised around in jeeps drinking beer, hurling vulgarities and chanting '*Pawa, pawa*' 'power', for Hutu Power.[1] The notorious Café de Gatenga, where the militia congregated, was nearby.

It was Friday 8 April 1994. Here in Kicukiro, and all over the city, people were fleeing in terror to churches, to schools, to hospitals and to wherever they saw the UN flag. The UN had peacekeepers in Rwanda, the UN Assistance Mission for Rwanda (UNAMIR), and 450 of them came from Belgium. These peacekeepers were spread out in fourteen different locations and the largest group was billeted at this technical school, the Ecole Technique Officielle, run by Salesian Fathers. There were ninety peacekeepers, part of the southern group, from the 14th company of Flawinne. The school went under the codename 'Beverly Hills'. The commander was Lieutenant Luc Lemaire. He had been in Rwanda for two weeks.

Lemaire welcomed the people although he wondered how, with so little ammunition, he could protect them.[2] There were explosions nearby and the sound of grenades and shooting. There were roadblocks. Then came the news that ten Belgian peacekeepers had been murdered by Rwandan soldiers. They could all be targets now. Lemaire had tried to reassure the younger members of his contingent.

Lemaire told his commanding officers by radio about the people at the school and he estimated their number at about 2,000. He ordered defensive positions built around the perimeter fence.

The food provided by the priests soon ran out. There was not enough water. There were insufficient medical supplies. Lemaire telephoned the local offices of Médecins Sans Frontières (MSF) and the International Committee of the Red Cross (ICRC). He was told that it was impossible for anyone to get through the roadblocks.

Then Lemaire heard that the Belgian government had decided to pull out its soldiers. It was unbelievable. The Belgians were the backbone of the mission. And what would happen to the people they were protecting? No one had an answer. Lemaire asked a bourgmestre to assemble the crowd and he stood on a chair to explain to the people that while the UN flag flew over the school they were safe, but that would not last. The politicians in Brussels were withdrawing the soldiers. Lemaire advised them to disperse, to slip away under cover of darkness. Several people approached him later and asked if, in the event of a pull-out, he would shoot them first, telling him that a bullet was preferable to being cut to pieces with a machete.

Lemaire spoke with a senior officer in the Rwandan army, Colonel Leonidas Rusatira, who came to the school. Lemaire asked Rusatira if, when the Belgians withdrew, he would make sure that Rwandan soldiers looked after the people. 'I thought this man might be enough of a human being to protect them,' said Lemaire. Rusatira was the director of a military academy and said he had no soldiers at his command. Nevertheless, he brought them sacks of rice, although there was only enough for the children.

Lemaire considered escorting everyone to the headquarters of the UN mission, but he wondered if there were enough peacekeepers to look after them even there. To move the people in small groups would require more than ninety soldiers. They risked attack en route.

On Sunday 10 April Lemaire was relieved to see French troops, but they had flown to Rwanda only to evacuate expats. The French soldiers chose from the crowd three French and several Italian nationals. This approach angered Lemaire and he told them that they could at least take all the Europeans. Some 150 people were prepared for departure.

That day Lemaire was ordered to send soldiers to Gitarama, a town some forty miles away, to escort Belgian nationals to Kigali airport. He argued that this would diminish the security of the Rwandans he was protecting. The mission was cancelled, but for other reasons.

Lemaire's final evacuation order came on Monday 11 April and he faltered. He wanted the order confirmed. He contacted headquarters to be sure sure that his commanders knew the consequences. The log of the battalion records: 'leave 2000 refugees at "Beverly Hills?"'[3] He knew there were people in the crowd at risk.

'I did not want to leave,' he said some years later. 'But I did not think there was any other solution.'[4]

All that was left was to plan the departure. If the people found out what was happening there might be a riot so Lemaire planned for the peacekeepers to leave quietly, as though going out on a mission. By chance a French jeep was passing, and as it drove on to the playing field its soldiers were applauded by the crowd. One by one the UN vehicles left the school grounds. But it was soon obvious what was happening, that the peacekeepers were sneaking away. 'We could not believe what they were doing … just abandoning us when they knew the place was surrounded … There were thousands of unarmed refugees … it seemed unthinkable.'[5]

People tried to hang on to lorries. The Belgian soldiers brandished their weapons, and fired into the air. The French soldiers prevented others from getting too near to the peacekeepers. The French promised the people that they would stay. At 13.45 the last Belgian soldier pulled out of the school. Then the French soldiers left. People started to cry. The bourgmestre, a member of Rwanda's Parti Social Démocrate (PSD), the centre-left opposition party, tried to calm everyone, and told them that they must defend themselves. 'But we had no weapons, not even a stick,' someone said.

Soldiers and militia started firing at the people and throwing grenades into the crowd. Some people recognized as Hutu were put to one side. The vice-president of the national committee of one of the militia groups, an agricultural engineer, Georges Rutaganda, was in a jogging suit, standing guard at a small entrance located on the side of the athletic field. He was carrying a gun.[6] In the crowd were pro-democracy opposition politicians and human rights activists but the vast majority of people carried identification cards with the designation Tutsi. There were both young and old people, and some who could barely walk.

Most of the people decided to try to escape to UN headquarters but instead they were herded along the road by militia and soldiers. 'As we walked … the soldiers and militia terrorized us with their grenades and guns … they slapped and beat people up, stealing their money … it was a long walk and the militia were everywhere.'

At one moment the Presidential Guard ordered the people to sit down and cursed and insulted them for being Tutsi, telling them they were going to die. Then the convoy moved on again. 'As we walked along, the militia were hitting people with machetes. Some of the people who were wounded fell down and were trampled upon.'

They came to a crossroads that led to Nyanza-Rebero and when they reached a gravel pit near the Nyanza primary school they were told once more to sit down. A witness said that Rutaganda was instructing the militia how to proceed; there were militia coming from different directions and they had machetes. 'The Presidential Guard were watching us from a place that was higher than where we were.' Then the soldiers started firing and threw grenades. Some people tried to break through the militia but were struck down with machetes. 'We were so stunned that no one cried out … it was only afterwards that you heard the voices moaning in agony ... then the Interahamwe [militia] came in and started with the machetes, hammers, knives and spears.' People in pain were told that they would be finished off quickly with a bullet if they paid money. There were children crying over the bodies of their dead parents.

The next morning militia came back to kill anyone still alive. Survivors of Kicukiro were mostly children who hid under the bodies.

In the next few days Lemaire and his men were deployed helping to escort Europeans to the airport. Told that their UN mission was over, they were the first to fly home. On the tarmac and in front of television cameras, one of them slashed his blue beret with his combat knife. Lemaire wore his beret. He still believed in the UN ideal.

In the course of a few terrible months in 1994, 1 million people were killed in Rwanda in circumstances similar to these.[7] It was slaughter on a scale not seen since the Nazi extermination programme against the Jews. The killing rate in Rwanda was five times that achieved by the Nazis.

The killing in Rwanda was vicious, relentless and incredibly brutal. The stories of betrayal, of insensate cruelty, of human suffering, are reminiscent of stories of Treblinka or Babi Yar. But, unlike the Holocaust, far from trying to conceal what was happening, the killing took place in broad daylight. The incitement to genocide was broadcast via a radio station and the people were psychologically prepared for months, and were ordered and coerced to carry out the extermination. In Rwanda, the perpetrators and organizers of genocide were secure in the knowledge that outside interference would be at a minimum.

The international community, which passed laws fifty years ago with the specific mandate of ensuring that genocide was never again perpetrated,[8] not only failed to prevent it happening in Rwanda but, by pumping in funds intended to help the Rwandan economy, actually helped to create the conditions that made it possible. The whole of the international community was involved while genocide was being planned: the United Nations and many of its agencies, independent aid groups, and two of the most powerful international institutions, the World Bank and the International Monetary Fund.[9]

The Holocaust in Europe was a unique historic event and to some people to make a comparison is insulting to the memory of its victims. Yet when it comes to Rwanda the comparison is impossible to resist, for the central purpose was the elimination of a people. Every Tutsi was targeted for murder.

To the outside world, however, the genocide would be portrayed as something very different: a senseless civil war, a tribal conflict between Hutu and Tutsi, in which old conflicts and bitter rivalries led to an almost primitive savagery. The images of crude barbarity relayed across the world, the machete attacks, the bodies floating down rivers, corpses piled by the roadside, seemed only to confirm the atavistic nature of the killing. True, there was a civil war, but preoccupation with that blinded most commentators, governments, the UN Secretariat and Security Council to the fact of the genocidal killing perpetrated by one of the parties to the civil war. But a genocide does not take place in a context of anarchy. Far from being a chaotic tribal war, what happened in Rwanda was deliberate, carefully planned and clinically carried out by an extremist group using army units and gendarmes to drive people systematically from their homes and assemble them at pre-arranged places of slaughter. A militia of the mainly unemployed, the Interahamwe, those who work together, and the Impuzamugambi, those with a single purpose, were trained to kill 1,000 human beings every twenty minutes. Local administrators organized the disposal of bodies in garbage trucks. The slaughter continued unhindered for three months.

Nor was the massacre a remote African episode, beyond the control of the outside world. Arms, from machetes to rocket launchers, were supplied by France, South Africa, Egypt and China. The governments of both France and Egypt were intimately involved in arms deals with the extremists in Rwanda. In order to pay for them, money was taken from funds supplied by the international financial institutions. In the year in which the genocide was planned, Rwanda, a country the size of Wales, became the third largest importer of weapons in Africa. World Bank officials were fully aware of the militarization of Rwanda, but failed to share their knowledge even with the UN Security Council.

With the help of individuals who know the truth (and have found it very hard to live with), it has been possible to piece together the facts. Documents held in Kigali, the Rwandan capital, as well as hitherto unpublished evidence of UN Security Council deliberations in New York, reveal a sequence of events that is as agonizing as it is shocking. There is evidence, too, of a more sinister dimension. There are those who were all too aware of the situation in Rwanda, and who nevertheless failed to take action. There are those whose actions contributed directly to events. There are others who helped conceal the reality of what was taking place. And there are some who covered it up. There is evidence that points not just to negligence, but to complicity.

What happened in Rwanda showed that despite the creation of an organization set up to prevent a repetition of genocide – for the UN is central to this task – it failed to do so, even when the evidence was indisputable.

The combination of revelations about the scale and intensity of the genocide, the complicity of western nations, the failure to intervene, and the suppression of information about what was actually happening, is a shocking indictment, not just of the UN Security Council, but even more so of governments and individuals who could have prevented what was happening but chose not to do so. It is a terrible story, made worse because its true nature has been deliberately distorted and confused.

Notes

1. Hutu Power is the name given to an ideology whose adherents were rabidly anti-Tutsi. Racist and nationalistic, they were opposed to democracy. Hutu Power sought the elimination of all Tutsi and all pro-democracy Hutu.

2. Lemaire believed that he had just enough ammunition – nine machine guns, a grenade per soldier – to get his men to the airport. Interview, Lieutenant Luc Lemaire, November 1996.

3. Astri Suhrke, 'Facing Genocide: The Record of the Belgian Battalion in Rwanda', *Security Dialogue*, Vol. 29, No. 1, 1998: 37–48, p. 45.

4. Interview, Lieutenant Luc Lemaire, December 1999.

5. African Rights, *Rwanda. Death, Despair Defiance*, London: African Rights, 1995, pp. 567–71. The quotes of the survivors of the genocide are taken from this book unless otherwise stated.

6. ICTR case number ICTR-96-3–1. Witness statements attached to the indictment of Georges Rutaganda, 12 January 1996. Rutaganda was charged with eight counts including genocide. He was a shareholder of RTLMC, the hate-radio.

7. The death toll is provided by Philippe Gaillard, chief delegate, International Committee of the Red Cross (ICRC), Rwanda, 1993–94. It was confirmed by Charles Petrie, deputy co-ordinator of the UN Rwanda Emergency Office (UNREO). Some UN reports quote a lower figure. This is discussed later in the book.

8. Article 1 of the Convention on the Prevention and Punishment of the Crime of Genocide states: 'The Contracting Parties confirm that genocide, whether committed in time of peace or in time of war, is a crime under international law which they undertake to prevent and to punish.'

9. At the end of the 1980s, Rwanda was the largest recipient of aid from both Belgium and Switzerland. It had the highest density of technical assistants (foreign experts) living in the country per square kilometre in Africa. See Peter Uvin, *Aiding Violence: The Development Enterprise in Rwanda*, West Hartford, CT: Kumarian Press, 1998.

2 · The Past is Prologue: Rwanda 1894–1973

EUROPEAN involvement in Rwanda began exactly one hundred years before the genocide in 1994. The kingdom of Rwanda had been entirely shut off from the world, and even from the African world, until 4 May 1894 when the first European, a German count, Gustav Adolf von Götzen, was received at court by a king called Rwabugiri, who claimed that his dynasty stretched back hundreds of years. The king welcomed the count but was unaware that ten years earlier, at the Berlin Conference of 1885, the European super-powers, knowing nothing at all about Rwanda, had divided the African continent and given Rwanda to Germany. Von Götzen became Governor of German East Africa, which included Rwanda. For the time being the Rwandan monarchy was allowed to continue. Germany kept only twenty-four military officers and six administrators in Rwanda.

Rwanda was a mountain kingdom in the heart of Africa. The descriptions of early travellers suggest a tropical Switzerland; one colonial official called it 'the pearl of Africa'.[1] A small country, Rwanda was poor, overwhelmingly reliant on agriculture, landlocked and remote. Sometimes referred to as the 'Land of a Thousand Hills', it had few exploitable natural resources and was of little interest to the outside world.

Pre-colonial Rwanda remains largely a mystery, for its history was recalled only in poems and in myths. These told of Rwandan kings who ruled the earth's most powerful kingdom. The king, the Mwami, owned everything: the land, the cattle and all the people. One myth told how the first king of all the earth had three sons, Gatwa, Gahutu and Gatutsi, and to test them he entrusted to each a churn of milk. Gatwa quenched his thirst, Gahutu spilt the milk but Gatutsi kept his intact and so he was entrusted to command the others.[2]

The first explorers immediately noticed how in Rwanda the population divided into three groups, the Hutu, the Tutsi and the Twa. These groups were not tribes, for the people shared the same religion, told the same ancestral stories, and spoke the same language, Kinyarwanda. Long before Rwanda became a state, people were speaking variants of the language and were widely settled in the area.[3] There were no distinct areas of residence. The Twa, less than 1 per cent of the population, were pygmies and lived as hunter-gatherers. The Hutu, the vast majority, were peasants who cultivated the soil and resembled most of the people living in the neighbouring countries of Uganda and Tanzania with typical Bantu features. The Tutsi were usually taller, thinner and with angular features and were cattle-herders. The word Hutu means subject or servant and the word Tutsi means those rich in cattle. But the differences were not solely based on wealth or class; there were Hutu and Tutsi in the same class. Tutsi pastoralists were as poor as their Hutu neighbours.

There is no consensus among historians or anthropologists on the origins of these divisions so crucial to Rwanda's history. In fact, many anthropologists contest the notion that Hutu and Tutsi are distinct groups and maintain that the distinction is more one of class or caste. Others maintain that what is now Rwanda was inhabited by the hunter-gatherers, the Twa, who were displaced by agriculturalists migrating northwards, and supposedly the ancestors of the Hutu. The Tutsi were said to have originated in the Horn of Africa, migrating south, and they gradually achieved dominance over the other two groups. It was this theory which led eventually to the view that the Tutsi were somehow a 'superior race', a lethal interpretation of history and one that would seriously affect the views and the attitudes of Europeans.[4]

The idea that Hutu and Tutsi were distinct ethnic groups appears to have originated with the English colonial agent and celebrated explorer John Hanning Speke, who 'discovered' and named Lake Victoria in 1859; the year in which Darwin published *On the Origin of Species*. Speke visited the states of Karagwe and Buganda (part of what is now Uganda, on the border with Rwanda), and thought that there was a natural explanation for the divisions in the society that he observed. Speke would theorize that in this part of central Africa there was a superior race, quite different from the common order of natives.[5] It became widely believed that so superior was the culture in central Africa that it must have come from somewhere else; it was impossible that 'savage negroes' could have attained such high levels of political and religious sophistication. The Tutsi ruling classes were thought to have come from further north, perhaps Ethiopia, and were more closely related to the 'noble Europeans'. They were superior and too fine to be 'common negroes'; they were taller and their noses were thinner. They had an intelligence and a refinement of feelings which was 'rare among primitive people'. Some missionaries thought that the Tutsi were descendants of ancient Egyptians: 'their … delicate appearance, their love of money, their capacity to adapt to any situation seem to indicate a semitic-origin.'[6]

The first European visitors to Rwanda were amazed at the intricate social order, which was basically feudal, with aristocrats and vassals. There was an administrative structure radiating from the centre which was organized on four levels: province, district, hill and neighbourhood. The provinces were managed by high chiefs although borders of the country were the responsibility of army chiefs. Each district had two chiefs appointed by the Mwami, the king. There was a land chief in charge of agricultural levies and a cattle chief who collected cattle taxes. The hills were administered by hill chiefs who were responsible for landholdings, taxation, grazing rights. The power radiated from the capital to the provinces. Each layer of the hierarchy was linked in a relationship of mutual dependence based on reciprocal arrangements regarding goods and services. This was known as *ubuhake* and it referred to a contractual service in which a more powerful person could provide protection in exchange for work. Most often the patron was Tutsi, but not always.

In this strictly controlled society the neighbourhoods were generally headed by Hutu who obeyed orders from above, and most above this level were Tutsi; the monarchy was Tutsi and the king's army was mostly Tutsi, and Tutsi were favoured for political offices.

The Germans ruled through this existing power structure. Count von Götzen believed that German policy must be to support the chiefs in such a manner that they would be convinced that their own salvation and that of their supporters depended on their faithfulness to the Germans. But the Germans also favoured expansion and in 1912 helped the Tutsi monarchy to subjugate the areas to the north.

After the First World War the western provinces of German East Africa, Rwanda (Ruanda) and neighbouring Burundi (Urundi), were given to Belgium to administer as Ruanda-Urundi under a League of Nations mandate. The greater part of the territory, Tanganyika, was given to the British. The Covenant of the League of Nations was to herald a new phase of human evolution, to offer a framework for practical and effective co-operation between nations for their common good. The Covenant stipulated that the tutelage of the peoples in the colonies should be entrusted to advanced nations who, by reason of their resources, their experience or the geographical position, could best undertake this responsibility. The character of the mandate would differ according to the stage of the development of the people. In the mandated territories there was to be 'fair and humane conditions of labour ... just treatment of the native inhabitant ... the prevention and control of disease'.

Ruanda-Urundi was placed under a category reserved for those countries for which self-determination was considered unfeasible. Belgium was pledged to the League to assure administration and promote development, free speech and freedom of religion.

In a remarkable report from the colonial archives, written in 1920, the

Belgian minister of colonies outlined the Belgian policy towards Rwanda. The European, he wrote, must be the guide and teacher. There would be no direct administration. Belgium could use the existing institutions. 'We have a certain responsiblity to the WaHutu', the report disclosed. 'We have to protect them against the injustices they often face ... but we will go no further. We find the Watutzi established since ancient time, intelligent and capable, we will respect that situation.'[7] A priest who arrived in Rwanda in 1907 and who stayed until 1945, Monsignor Léon Classe, wrote in 1930: 'The biggest mistake the government could make would be to do away with the Tutsi caste. This would lead the country to anarchy and communism, and to be viciously anti-European.'[8]

What in fact happened was that a policy of indirect rule under the Germans was gradually changed by the Belgians to one of direct rule, and in the years to come the power of the king was eroded by Belgian administrators. In 1922 the king was obliged to be assisted by Belgian representatives of the colonial resident, and in 1923 he was forbidden to appoint regional chiefs. In November 1931 the king, Mwami Musinga, who was against colonization, was deposed by the Belgian administration with little objection from the League of Nations. The king was replaced with one of his more pliant sons, Mutara Rudahigwa. Rudahigwa became known as the king of the whites. He wore western suits. He drove his own car. His conversion to Christianity in 1943 was part of a Belgian policy for encouraging mass conversions. Christianity became a prerequisite for membership of the Tutsi elite.

Belgium also interfered in local administration and by the Second World War Rwanda was divided into chiefdoms with Belgian administrators involved at every level of society. Money was introduced and so was education, although the latter was reserved for the sons of chiefs.[9]

The Belgian administration created an African civil service within the Rwandan bureaucracy composed of the members of the Tutsi oligarchy. Belgian rule was harsh and, as Belgian rule consolidated, hundreds of thousands of Hutu peasants fled to neighbouring Uganda to become migrant labourers. The chiefs on each hill were used by the colonial administration to requisition forced labour from the Hutu masses, particularly for road building, and routine beatings and corporal punishment were administered on behalf of the colonial masters. Forced labour was customary and strictly enforced; the chiefs were under the direct supervision of a Belgian colonial administrator responsible for a particular portion of territory.

In 1933 the Belgian administration organized a census and teams of Belgian bureaucrats classified the whole population as either Hutu or Tutsi or Twa. Every Rwandan was counted and measured: the height, the length of their noses, the shape of their eyes. Everyone was classified: the Tutsi were the taller, the Hutu were shorter and broader, although for many Rwandans it was not possible to determine ethnicity on the basis of physical appearance. Rwandans in the south were generally of mixed origin and most Rwandans of mixed origin were classified as Hutu.[10] Yet many of them looked typically Tutsi – tall and thin. In the north mixed marriages were rare. Some people were given a Tutsi card because they had more money or possessed the required number of cows. Every Rwandan was classified and given an identity card. Although the Tutsi monarchy had initially opposed missionary schools because of the imposed conversions to Christianity, by 1946 King Mutara was persuaded to dedicate Rwanda to Christ the King and there were three days of celebration. Catholic missions sprang up everywhere in Rwanda. And with education, the divisions in society became more pronounced. When a school was opened – the Groupe Scolaire, in Astrida (now Butare) – to give administrative training, it was mainly for the Tutsi elite, producing agronomists, doctors and vets, and between 1945 and 1954 out of 447 students only sixteen were Hutu.[11] Most of the Hutu students who did acquire education found there were fewer jobs for them and those who did eventually graduate from mission schools and seminaries took up posts in the lower administration, or became tradesmen and shopkeepers. Hutu women were not allowed an education at all.

The United Nations was involved in the affairs of Rwanda from its creation in 1945, when the UN Charter – in many ways similar to the Covenant of the League of Nations – promised the colonized peoples of the world freedom, justice and protection. A special council was created, the Trusteeship Council, which was to oversee the transition to independence of the world's colonized peoples. Rwanda was transferred from its League of Nations mandate and became a UN trusteeship territory.

Among the powers accorded the Trusteeship Council was the right to visit the territories placed under trusteeship and in mid-July 1948 the first UN trusteeship visiting mission went to Africa. A group of four ambassadors visited Rwanda and Burundi, officially known as Ruanda-Urundi, and Tanganyika, which was under British rule.[12]

The four ambassadors found Rwanda densely populated, with poor and difficult land and inadequate soil suffering erosion and drought. The rainfall was irregular and the basic problem was how to feed all the people. The ambassadors noted the strange feudal system, which appeared to be based on cattle. Cattle seemed to be the pivot in an extremely complicated series of civil contracts and political relationships. 'The pre-eminence of man over the cow is still far from being established,' the ambassadors reported. 'All, even the most humble peasant, have but one desire; to own cows, no matter what the quality ... better two poor beasts than one good one.' The people of Rwanda counted their wealth in the number of their cattle but most of the cows in Rwanda were of poor quality and of little use economically. Because of their high social value, cattle were not used as regular food and cattle demanded a greater area of pasture land than the country could afford. The ambassadors described 'rigid ethnic, linguistic and territorial lines of demarcation'.

These ambassadors came back from their visit and wrote reports for the other government members of the UN Trusteeship Council. The reports were critical and castigated Britain and Belgium for their policies. Believing in the noble principles of the Charter, the authors pointed to the colonial powers' great material success, obtained at the expense of the people. 'The African's economic and social world is still separated from that of the European by a wide gap.'

There was uproar, particularly when one of the reports blamed Britain for allowing the poverty of the black Africans in Tanganyika, and advocated that education and health care be provided for these people and paid for using a tax to be put on the export of African diamonds. In London the Foreign Office was indignant, for Britain did not accept the right of the UN to tell it how to discharge its responsibilities, and the report was considered no more than mischievous political propaganda. At the time, the issue of colonialism was dominant in the UN and some member states were becoming increasingly vociferous about how slowly the great powers were applying Charter principles in the colonies. There was an increasingly effective anti-colonial block built around Egypt, India and Pakistan, a group beginning to enjoy support from the Soviets. As for the Americans, who rejected colonialism, they were torn by their close alliance with European countries. Washington was none the less worried about the radical nature of the department of trusteeship at the UN, and particularly about the influence of certain secretariat officials within it.[13]

Critical of Belgium, the visiting mission laid particular emphasis on the lack of education in Rwanda and there was criticism about the practice of whipping, which was 'all too prevalent', especially during forced labour. Although it was illegal, the Belgian authorities apparently condoned it. What surprised these ambassadors, like most visitors to Rwanda, was the level of social and political control in the country. The ambassadors pointed out that the system in place contained all the elements necessary for democratic development. Each sub-chief had a council composed of representatives, from all the hills and all the social groups, appointed by selection with the consent of the family groups on each hill. In spite of the absence of a proper electoral system, this was a fairly democratic representation through which the desires of the lowliest person could be expressed. It was a mechanism enabling contacts between the native leaders and the masses. The councils met frequently and dealt in the main with local matters.[14]

In the General Assembly of the UN, Belgium was criticized for the subservient status of the Hutu masses who were subjected to forced labour and discrimination in all walks of life.

The UN Trusteeship Council in New York sent five visiting missions to Rwanda between 1948 and 1962, and each report was more critical than the last. Each time the UN paid Rwanda a visit, the Belgians responded with a gesture towards the creation of democracy. In 1952 the Belgians introduced electoral procedures for advisory councils at four administrative levels. The Tutsi won the seats. The Tutsi administration remained entrenched and Tutsi won again in 1953 when elections were held at chiefdom level, but with the vote restricted.

In 1954 the visiting mission urged the Belgian administration to give serious attention to the political education of the people. Belgium should recognize the growing forces of nationalism in Africa. But with sparse natural resources, Rwanda was never a high priority for the international community. Little was changed. In an election in September 1956 when men only were allowed the vote, it was only for sub-chief level. Only in the north of Rwanda, in Gisenyi and Ruhengeri, did the Tutsi incur electoral losses, for here there was aggression against Tutsi. The northern Hutu were independent until the first decade of the century when they were militarily defeated by German and Tutsi-led southern Rwandan troops. It had taken several military expeditions by the German Schutztruppe between 1910 and 1912 to subdue them. In spite of being incorporated into the Rwandan state, the northern Hutu, the Kiga, formed a distinct Hutu culture, representing an independent Hutu tradition. There was considerable bitterness towards both the Tutsi and southern Hutu about the subjugation.[15] It was in the north that Hutu Power, the racist anti-Tutsi ideology underpinning the genocide, was conceived.

The first serious political challenge to the Tutsi oligarchy came in 1957, when, in anticipation of another visit from the UN, a group of Hutu published a manifesto which demanded their emancipation and majority rule. This was the start of political struggle. The Hutu had the support of many Belgian priests who worked in Rwanda, one of whom had helped to write the manifesto. Many of these priests had come to identify with the Hutu masses; their own country was divided along ethnic lines between the francophone Walloon community and the Flemish. The priests understood the Hutu demand for liberty of expression, and an end to ethnic discrimination in the public service. A key ideological ingredient of this emerging Hutu revolution was the belief that Rwanda had been overrun by Tutsi invaders who had enslaved the Hutu. This was an effective appeal to Hutu solidarity, a rallying point for revolution.

In 1957, the report of the visiting trusteeship mission was pessimistic; it found 'little hope for a rapprochement between the races' and called on Belgium to accelerate efforts to emancipate the Hutu. But when, in the late 1950s, Rwanda's first political parties were created, they were established along ethnic lines. The Parti du Mouvement de l'Emancipation Hutu (Parmehutu) was a Hutu party and called for an end to Tutsi colonization, before freedom from the Belgians. The opposition party, created on 3 September 1959, was mainly a Tutsi party, the Union National Rwandaise (UNAR), which was pro-monarchist and anti-Belgian. Another party was the Rassemblement Démocratique Rwandais (Rader), founded by two moderate Tutsi, with the objective of economic and cultural development for both Tutsi and Hutu.

On 24 July 1959, Rwanda's forty-six-year-old Tutsi King Mutara III Rudahigwa died in suspicious circumstances. He had been given an antibiotic injection while in hospital. Belgian doctors maintained that he died from an allergic reaction but there were rumours and suspicions. Among the Tutsi elite were those certain that the king had been killed by the Belgians, with the Hutu in on the plot. In the royal court an extremist group sought to destroy the Hutu leadership and there were brutal political assassinations. The political tensions increased but the fuse was said to have been lit on 1 November 1959 when a group of young UNAR militants had attacked the Parmehutu leader Dominique Mbonyumutwa on his way home from mass at a Catholic mission in Gitarama. Violence spread like wild-fire from hill to hill and, according to the UN visiting mission report of 1960, some 200 people died. Dozens of petitions were sent to the Trusteeship Council in New York from threatened Tutsi pleading for help. One of them read:

> the officials report that the fighting is between two groups of inhabitants which is not true ... for a long time they have been living together, mixed up ... still burning, killing etc ... are being done during the daylight sometimes in the presence of so-called police ... how can people with no proper communications have organised such a thing ... please help innocent people from this destruction.[16]

Hutu started to attack the Tutsi authorities, burning Tutsi homes, and large numbers of Tutsi fled the country. The Hutu had huge numerical predominance, a sense of injustice and of inferiority. The Belgians portrayed the violence as a problem of race between Hutu and Tutsi, and on 11 November 1959 Belgium placed Rwanda under military rule, its fortunes entrusted to a Belgian colonel, Guy Logiest, who immediately began to replace Tutsi chiefs with Hutu and announced to Belgian administrators that in future the Hutu would be favoured within the administration. It would be called a social revolution, but it was not.

A UN Commission of Inquiry arrived in April 1960 and called for a conference in Brussels to reconcile the political parties. In May the Belgians set up a territorial guard of 650 men, the vast majority Hutu. In June and July there were the first direct communal elections and as predicted the Parmehutu won 71 per cent. The UNAR party claimed the vote was rigged and that the Parmehutu could not fail to win owing to the support of the Belgian adminstration. In June the new Tutsi king, Kigeli V, left Rwanda, never to return, and tens of thousands more Tutsi were forced into exile into neighbouring countries.

There followed several UN-sponsored reconciliation conferences, and lobbying of the member states of the Trusteeship Council by the monarchists. In January 1961, while a UN reconciliation conference was taking place in Belgium, and a UN trusteeship commission was due in Kigali, Gregoire Kayibanda, a former school teacher, one of the original signatories of the 1957 Hutu manifesto and a founder of Parmehutu, organized a mass rally of communal councillors and bourgmestres at Gitarama and a vote was taken to abolish the monarchy. Rwanda was declared a republic. Kayibanda wanted no more tinkering in Rwanda affairs by the UN.[17]

At this direct challenge, the UN sent another mission to Kigali and a referendum was organized to decide upon the principle of the monarchy, to run simultaneously with direct elections for a national assembly. The UN tried to supervise these elections, but there was intimidation and violence. Kayibanda, with Belgian help, had built up a network of cells; the most influential Hutu on each isolated hillside was made responsible for the people around him. In September 1961 Kayibanda's Parmehutu party won massively and the monarchy was abolished. The UNAR wanted fresh elections. There was a new wave of violence against Tutsi and another exodus. The UNAR petitioned the UN to contest the fairness of the elections.

In December 1961, Kayibanda's government began the rapid expansion of the Belgian-trained National Guard, to double its size from 1,300 soldiers to 3,000. The National Guard was responsible for the maintenance of internal security. Units were stationed in each of the nine prefectures. They were commanded by Belgian officers.

It was the escalating refugee crisis caused by Tutsi exiles, and the continuing violence in Rwanda, which prompted the UN General Assembly in February 1962 to establish a special commission of five member states to ensure that Rwanda acceded to independence as soon as possible and that the refugees would be able to return. There were by now an estimated 135,000 refugees in four neighbouring states, the Kivu Province in the Congo, in Burundi, in Uganda and Tanganyika. Temporary camps had been set up and the refugees were dependent on government assistance. Their situation was precarious. There was an acute shortage of food. In Kivu, people in the camps were dying from hunger at a rate of fifty a day and the number of refugees was growing; on average, 1,000 people were crossing into Uganda every week.

The UN commission, mandated to try to ensure human rights in Rwanda, the maintenance of law and order, and the withdrawal of Belgian military forces, discovered during a visit to Rwanda in March 1962 that the Tutsi ethnic minority had been brutally expelled from the social and political scene. The UNAR party leaders told the commissioners of the mass arrests of their members. The UNAR complained of acts of brutality against its officials and of torture and murder. The killing seemed to be systematic and seemed designed to eliminate the UNAR. The UNAR wanted the UN to set up an immediate judicial inquiry.[18]

During their visit the commission members saw roadblocks everywhere. There were roadblocks at the entry to each prefecture where the identity of travellers was checked. Travel permits were required for every Rwandan to go from one prefecture to another. The permits were not granted to members of the opposition. There was a curfew from 6 p.m. The government, under the pretext of combating the terrorist bands known as Inyenzi, had taken extreme security measures which brought it close to a police state, if not a reign of terror. The commission was told that the racism in Rwanda bordered on 'Nazism against the Tutsi minorities' and that this was the work of the government, backed by the Belgian authorities. The hostility between the different ethnic groups had been artificially engendered in the last few years. The number of victims was estimated in the region of 2,000 people.[19]

Kayibanda assured the UN commissioners that stability had been restored and that the recent violence in Rwanda was because the colonialists were creating a problem where none existed. He assured them that his government wanted to see the return of the refugees. From the report produced by the commissioners, it is clear that they did not believe him.

Before leaving Kigali, the UN commission told Kayibanda of the vital importance which the international community attached to fundamental human rights. In the eyes of the civilized world, that principle constituted the very basis and justification of a people's right to independence. The termination of trusteeship was set for July 1962, in three months' time. Unless there was national reconciliation, the commission concluded in a report, then the outlook for Rwanda was bleak. Thirty-two years later, in 1994, there would be a similar warning and with similar results.

It was to prevent any further UN interference in Rwanda's affairs that, on 1 July 1962, the monarchy was formally abolished and an independent republic was proclaimed by Kayibanda who was inaugurated as president. The racial dictatorship of one party had been replaced by that of another one.

The ex-Mwami, Kigeli V, had gone to live in Kampala in neighbouring Uganda and from there he called for the formation of a government of national unity. The king also asked the UN for help for the refugees. And in Kampala a group of monarchists formed a secret organization which recruited about 1,500 men from refugee camps, and they gave themselves the name Inyenzi, or cockroach, a word which would be picked up and taken over by their enemies.[20] On 14 November 1963 these men invaded Rwanda from

Burundi. They brought three truckloads of arms; they had sold food supplied by voluntary agencies to pay for these weapons. But they were intercepted by the Belgian-commanded National Guard. Then at 4.30 a.m. on 21 December a group of about 200 men, armed with bows, arrows and home-made rifles, crossed the border with Burundi at Nemba. With local Tutsi joining their ranks, and reaching about 600 in number, they attacked a military camp at Gako; taking weapons and vehicles, they drove towards Kigali.

Some twelve miles from the capital they were intercepted and at Kanzenze bridge on the river Nyabarungo they were decimated by units of the Gendarme National Rwandaise, who were commanded by Belgian officers and were armed with semi-automatic weapons and mortars. The invaders were overwhelmed with the superior fire-power.

Kayibanda's reaction to the invasion was immediate. It began with the elimination of the internal opposition and the murder of the most prominent political opponents. The murders would mark the end of the role of Tutsi in public life. Three days later, two days before Christmas, an organized slaughter of Tutsi began. When, some four weeks later, journalists from the western press arrived, so outraged was western public opinion at what had happened that some would recall the Holocaust. How could it happen that people who had shared the history of the same state, and who could be distinguished neither by culture nor language, could behave in such a way? The British philosopher, Lord Bertrand Russell, broadcast on the Vatican Radio that it was the most horrible and systematic extermination of a 'people' since the Nazi's extermination of the Jews.[21] The element of planned annihilation links the killings in 1963 to the genocide in 1994. The planning and the methods used, thirty years apart, are similar.

In 1963 a minister was assigned to each of the nine prefectures, the name given to the former provinces, and they were turned into what was called emergency territories. Each government minister worked with local prefects, sub-prefects and elected bourgmestres and there were roadblocks everywhere, manned by civilians. Kayibanda organized 'self-defence' groups. And Kigali Radio repeatedly broadcast emergency warnings that the Tutsi were coming back to enslave the Hutu.

The killing began on 23 December in Gikongoro, where the prefect was said to have understood that the Tutsi must be killed before they killed the Hutu. Armed with spears and clubs a group of Hutu started to kill every Tutsi in sight – men, women and children. Some 5,000 people were killed.

The people who died in the massacres were killed in the most atrocious and cruel circumstances by the local population, using whatever arms were available, mostly hoes and the *panga*, the long knife for cutting grass. Hutus carried out the most hideous mutilations on their Tutsi neighbours. Bodies and body parts were dumped in piles at the side of the road. At Shigira near the border with the Congo, some hundred Tutsi women and children committed mass suicide by drowning themselves in the river to escape attack by Hutu mobs.[22]

The government version was that the Hutu population had run amok and that the local authorities had lost control. The official Rwanda government figure was 350 Tutsi invaders killed, and 400 civilian deaths. The exact number of people who died will never be known. The World Council of Churches estimated between 10,000 and 14,000. The UN estimate was 1,000–3,000.

There were few witnesses to what had occurred. *Le Monde* carried a story in January that the Tutsi were being arrested and in some places were being exterminated. Thousands had sought refuge in churches.[23] Another account was published in *Le Monde* in February. A Swiss professor in the southern Rwandan town of Butare named M. Denis Vuillemin, who worked for UNESCO, had written to the newspaper to castigate publicly the Belgian government for its role in Rwanda. Under a headline, 'L'Extermination des Tutsi', Vuillemin's article was given two columns and in detail he explained that he was resigning his job because he refused any longer to represent Belgium, whose government, he said, was responsible for complicity to genocide. Vuillemen described how in Rwanda most Europeans working for aid agencies had been indifferent and impassive to the massacres and thought that the persecution of the Tutsi was proof of the 'savagery of the negro'. Vuillemin described how Rwanda was under totalitarian rule, and no foreign news media maintained a regular correspondent there.

Vuillemin described the Kayibanda regime as increasingly bigoted and racist. The government, instead of organizing development programmes, was doing nothing more than encouraging racial hatred. In the December massacres, Vuillemin described how educated Tutsi had been arrested and thrown in prison and were beaten and left without food. In Cyangugu some eighty Tutsi were put on lorries and taken to a forest, thrown into a ravine and then shot. In Gikongoro it was a 'veritable genocide' where the prefect, the bourgmestres and party officials from Parmehutu had encouraged bands of killers to undertake a systematic extermination of Tutsi. The killing lasted for four days. Women and children were killed with clubs or they were speared. Clothes were taken from corpses and the corpses thrown into the river. These events were no accident. They were the product of carefully nutured racial hatred. 'How can I teach under a UNESCO aid programme in a school where pupils are killed for the sole reason they were Tutsi? How can I teach pupils who will perhaps be assassinated in several months or several years?' Vuillemin asked.[24]

The UN Secretary-General, U Thant, asked Max Dorsinville, a UN official from Haiti, his chief UN official in the Congo, to visit Rwanda and undertake a special mission to report on what was happening. Dorsinville spent several days in Kigali, arriving on 30 December, and was assured by Kayibanda that all local authorities were being ordered to avoid 'reprisals'. The failure of Dorsinville to protest strongly what was happening allowed the killing to continue until mid-January. Dorsinville made another visit in February. Dorsinville reported to the UN Secretary-General that the estimates of the dead varied between 3,000 and 45,000 but Dorsinville called the later figure 'fantastic' and told New York that whatever the number of victims, the Rwandan government did not deny that there had been 'excesses'. The government had promised an investigation and assured Dorsinville that the culprits would be severely punished.[25]

The accusation of genocide against the Kayibanda regime was unproven. The killings were widely accepted to have been the result of an extreme interpretation by local officials of the order to take 'all measures to defend the country' against external attack. Further proof that this was not a genocide was that 6,000 Tutsi refugees were allowed to cross into Uganda; if this were genocide then these slow-moving and defenceless people would have been killed. Within Rwanda the Tutsi who sought shelter at Catholic mission stations suffered no reprisals. A report some six months later in the *Atlantic Monthly* described how the invasion in December had caused panic in government. The National Guard with 1,000 members was hard pushed to defend the borders. It had been decided that the defence of the country would have to rely on the civilian Hutu population. A minister had been sent to each of the prefectures but the worst slaughter had been in Gikongoro, where the word spread that the Tutsi had taken Kigali and that the Mwami had been restored. In Kibungo the Catholic White Fathers had prevailed upon the local authorities not to excite the Hutu population. Rwanda was now in a state of constant military alert with roadblocks everywhere. The effect on the economy was disastrous and malnutrition was widespread. The presence of Tutsi refugees on the border made life impossible for those Tutsi inside the country who were regarded as suspect.[26] It was difficult to know how many Tutsi were left in Rwanda; those who remained were not allowed to leave, were branded as traitors and were subject to intimidation. By early 1964 there were a quarter of a million Rwandans living in camps with a bare subsistence and inadequate medical services.

In April 1964, the Fabian Society in London published a pamphlet, *Massacre in Rwanda*, pointing out that whatever their past conduct and attitudes the Tutsi did not merit annihilation as a people. It had taken organized massacres to bring tiny Rwanda to the attention of the outside world, but Rwanda had more to contribute to the world than stories of mass slaughter.

Gregoire Kayibanda, Rwanda's first president, was the founding father of Hutu nationalism. He was authoritarian and secretive and he had total control, making appointments and nominations from the highest to the lowest level. He ruled through a small group of politicians who came from his home town of Gitarama. There was favouritism, corruption and censorship.

Rwanda was a Christian country. The second largest employer, after the state, was the Church. Around the churches there grew schools, health clinics and printing presses for religious tracts. Church attendance was high. Contraception was banned and so was prostitution. Not less than 90 per cent of the population was Christian, and more than half of those were Catholic. The Hutu were told to be proud to be Hutu. The poor were told to bear their poverty with dignity.

The links between Church and state were close because the Hutu nationalists were part of a small elite educated at Catholic schools. President Gregoire Kayibanda was linked closely with Monsignor André Perraudin, a Swiss Catholic who arrived in Rwanda in 1950 and who taught and later was rector at the Grand Séminaire of Nyakibanda. He became the archbishop of Kabgayi and Kigali and leader of the Catholic Church in Rwanda in November 1959. Perraudin was said to have influenced Kayibanda and supported the Hutu revolutionary movement. The Church had financed a bi-monthly newsletter, the *Kinyamateka*, with Kayibanda for some years as its editor-in-chief.[27]

So overt was the Catholic support for Hutu nationalism that, when the 1994 genocide happened, the archbishop of Kigali, Vincent Nsengiyumva, was on the central committee of the ruling party, and closely linked to the inner circle of Hutu Power which organized the genocide. Not all members of the Church were as close to the regime and some priests preached in favour of reconciliation.[28]

The Parmehutu, Kayibanda's party, was the only party to submit candidates for legislative elections. But with rule by the majority Hutu, to the outside world Rwanda was widely considered to be a democracy. And the president lived modestly. His behaviour contrasted well with that of other African leaders. Rwanda continued to be supplied with technical and military aid by Belgium. Rwanda was supposedly stable.

That this was an apartheid system was conveniently overlooked. There were vigilante groups created to ensure that Tutsi were not acquiring more than their fixed quotas in schools and employment; according to the calculations of Hutu officials, the Tutsi counted for 9 per cent of the population, a figure which was contested, and so would be represented in Rwanda accordingly.[29]

Kayibanda's reliance on regional power was his great weakness. There was discontent in the army about the large percentage of senior posts given to southerners. To deflect criticism, Kayibanda would mount ferocious anti-Tutsi campaigns.

Because Rwanda and Burundi were administered as a joint colonial territory, and because there was violence between Hutu and Tutsi in both countries, the two were often linked. They are actually two distinct and self-contained states although sometimes the events in one country triggered a reaction in the other.

Burundi reached independence in 1962, with Tutsi, a minority, dominating the majority Hutu. Then in April 1972 there was an abortive coup by Hutu and there followed massacres of Hutu of unprecedented magnitude. An estimated 200,000 Hutu were killed in a systematic slaughter which led to accusations of genocide, although one academic called it a 'selective genocide' to emphasize that the educated, the semi-educated, the schoolchildren, the employed, that is the actual or potential Hutu leadership, were special targets.[30] In the State Department it was estimated that an attempt had been made to kill every Hutu male over the age of fourteen; every Hutu member of the cabinet had been killed, all the Hutu officers, half the country's school teachers, thousands of civil servants.

In special a report produced by the Carnegie Endowment for International Peace,[31] a congressional aide was quoted: 'By the end of May we knew it was genocide from officially classified information from the State Department.' Journalists started to write about what was happening in Burundi. In June news stories prompted congressional interest. Senator Edward M. Kennedy told the Senate that the Hutu were being killed at the rate of 3,000 a day. 'Should not governments condemn the killings?' he asked.

The Belgian government called what had happened a 'veritable genocide'.[32] The French National Assembly urged action. The United States made diplomatic representations. No other government raised the issue in the UN or in any other forum. In August, an official from the State Department explained: 'Genocide is a specific, legal term with a precise meaning. It boils down to trying to kill a whole people. The Burundi government didn't try to do that; they couldn't. You can't kill off 80 percent of your population. Perhaps they engaged in mass murder; they weren't guilty of genocide.'

At its meeting in 1973 the sub-commission on the prevention of discrimination and protection of minorities forwarded to the Commission of Human Rights in Geneva a complaint against Burundi for gross violations of human rights. But when the commission met in 1974 the only action was a working party established to communicate with the government of Burundi.[33] After a few days in the headlines, Burundi sank back into obscurity and the killing continued.

At least two hundred thousand people fled into Rwanda as a result of the massacres in Burundi and for Rwanda's President Gregoire Kayibanda the events in Burundi were considered something to be exploited and manipulated for political advantage. He initiated a further crack-down against the Tutsi and started a campaign to 'purify' the country, setting up committees of public safety to make sure that in education and employment the 9 per cent

Tutsi quota was strictly enforced.[34] In Butare, Hutu students formed tribunals to check the bloodlines of students to determine who was pure Hutu. Tutsi fled the campus and some of them were beaten by Hutu students with iron bars.

In charge of the nationwide anti-Tutsi campaign was the army chief, Major Juvenal Habyarimana. He was a northerner and for years northern Hutu had been complaining that the southern-led government was not doing enough to keep Tutsi down. It was Habyarimana who, in July 1973, ousted Kayibanda in a bloodless coup and declared himself president. Twenty-one years later Habyarimana would be ousted too, and in more dramatic circumstances.

Notes

1. *Encylopaedia of Africa South of the Sahara*. Vol. 4. John Middleton (editor-in-chief), New York: Simon and Schuster, 1997.

2. Antoine Lema, *Africa Divided: The Creation of 'Ethnic Groups'*, Sweden: Lund University Press, 1993, p. 43.

3. David Newbury, 'The Invasion of Rwanda; The Alchemy of Ethnicity', mimeo, Chapel Hill: University of North Carolina, November 1995.

4. Gérard Prunier, *The Rwanda Crisis 1959–1994. History of a Genocide*, London: Hurst and Company, 1995, p. 12.

5. Lema, *Africa Divided*, p. 43.

6. J.-B. Piollet, *Les Missions catholiques françaises au X1Xe siècle*, Les Missions d'Afrique, 1902.

7. Lema, *Africa Divided*, p. 59. He sources this to a confidential memorandum of the Ministère des Colonies, dated 15 June 1920 from Archives Africaines, AE/II no. 1849 (3288).

8. Belgian Senate, *Commission d'enquête parlementaire concernant les événements du Rwanda*, Raport, 6 December 1997, p. 107.

9. René Lemarchand, *Rwanda and Burundi*, London: Pall Mall, 1970, London. p. 73.

10. In the genocide in 1994, physical traits rather than an identity card could spell the difference between death and survival.

11. Lemarchand, *Rwanda and Burundi*, pp. 74–5 and 137–9.

12. They were Henri Laurentie, France, E. W. P. Chinnery, Australia, Lin Mousheng, China, and R. E. Woodbridge, Costa Rica. They were accompanied by the distinguished American anthropologist Jack Harris, political affairs officer, territorial research and analysis section of the UN Division of Trusteeship.

13. Linda Melvern, *The Ultimate Crime. Who Betrayed the UN and Why*, London: Allison and Busby, 1995, pp. 52–61.

14. UN Trusteeship Council, *Report of the Visiting Mission to the Trust Territory of Ruanda-Urundi under Belgian Administration* (T/217), 31 October 1948.

15. Lemarchand, *Rwanda and Burundi*, p. 106.

16. Petition from B. K. Kavutse from Kigeri High School, Kigezi, Uganda (T/PET.3/107).

17. Kayibanda was born in 1924 and educated in a seminary at Nyakibanda. He had been the chief editor of a Catholic magazine and ran TRAFIPRO, a coffee co-operative.

18. UN General Assembly, *Question of the Future of Ruanda-Urundi. Report of the UN*

Commission for Ruanda-Urundi established under General Assembly resolution 1743 (XVI) (A/5126) 30 May 1962.

19. Ibid.

20. Aaron Segal, *Massacre in Rwanda*, Fabian Society, April 1964. The origin of the name is also in Lema, *Africa Divided*, p. 71.

21. *Le Monde*, 6 February 1964.

22. Lema, *Africa Divided*, p. 72. See also Lemarchand, *Rwanda and Burundi*, p. 224.

23. 'De sanglants incidents auraient lieu au Ruanda', *Le Monde*, 17 January 1964.

24. 'L'Extermination des Tutsi', *Le Monde*, 4 February 1964.

25. Max Dorsinville, *Report of the Officer-in-Charge of the UN Operation in the Congo to the Secretary-General*, 29 September 1964 (declassified UN Archives, 11 November 1999).

26. 'The Atlantic Report. Rwanda', *Atlantic Monthly*, June 1964.

27. Guy Theunis, 'Le rôle de l'église catholique dans les événements récents', in André Guichaoua (ed.), *Les Crises Politiques au Burundi et au Rwanda (1993–1994)* Université des Sciences et Technologies de Lille, Karthala, 1995, p. 289.

28. Ibid.

29. Middleton (ed.), *Africa South of the Sahara*, Regional Surveys of the World, has the percentage of people with Hutu identity cards in Rwanda as 85 per cent.

30. Leo Kuper, *The Prevention of Genocide*, New Haven, CT and London: Yale University Press, 1985, p. 154.

31. Michael Bowen, Gary Freeman and Kay Miller, *Passing By. The United States and Genocide in Burundi*, Special Report. Humanitarian Policy Studies, Carnegie Endowment for International Peace, 1972.

32. Kuper, *The Prevention of Genocide*, p. 161.

33. Ibid., p. 162.

34. Prunier, *The Rwanda Crisis*, p. 60.

3 · The Involvement of France, Egypt and Uganda

RWANDA'S violent divisions might have been easier to heal and its tragic history somewhat different had it not been for the involvement of outside interests. None had more dramatic effect than that of France, for without France the dictatorship of Juvénal Habyarimana would never have lasted as long as it did. Two years after Habyarimana took power, in 1975, a military co-operation and training agreement was signed with Paris and, over the next fifteen years, France slowly replaced Belgium as the foremost foreign ally, offering financial and military guarantees which Belgium could not provide. So staunch an ally was France that Habyarimana believed that French support for his regime was unconditional, no matter what military or political tactic he used to remain in power.

Rwanda was part of a family, Francophonie, a group of states linked to maintain the promotion and protection of the French language. Closely related to this obsession with French language and culture was a fear in France of an anglophone encroachment in Africa, nurtured by centuries of Anglo-French rivalry on the continent. Rwanda was important not because French was its second language,[1] but because Rwanda was located on a political fault-line between francophone and anglophone east Africa. After the end of the Cold War these divisions enjoyed a new lease of life. France was a major foreign military power-broker in Africa. Rwanda's neighbour was Zaire, a huge country with vast riches, and Rwanda, Burundi and Zaire were all in the Franco-African family.

The best way to maintain French influence in Africa was through a policy of close relations between the presidential palace in Paris, the Elysée, and African heads of state. President Habyarimana was close to President François Mitterrand, and considered him a personal friend.

At first, Habyarimana brought peace and stability to Rwanda but the price was a lack of freedom for the people. The regime was totalitarian. Although in July 1975 military rule was formally abolished, a new party had come into being, the Mouvement Révolutionnaire National pour le Développement (MRND). Only MRND candidates were allowed to run for office. Every

Rwandan, young or old, became a member. The party was everywhere, on every hill and every family unit. Members of the party were appointed to run local administrations and senior party officials were Habyarimana cronies from the north of the country. The one-party system ensured that Habyarimana was triumphantly elected president in December 1983 and again in December 1988. He was the sole candidate.

Habyarimana was clever, devious, double-dealing and brutal. There are varying theories about how he got rid of the previous president, Gregoire Kayibanda: some said the latter was refused medical treatment and others said he was starved to death. Habyarimana's opponents were arrested and tortured, and many were said to have been killed with hammer blows. There was racketeering and extortion. But most of the people were taught to adore him as the father of the nation. Internationally, Rwanda was portrayed as a democratic country with rule by the majority.

Among non-communist countries Rwanda was probably the most controlled state in the world. Every Rwandan carried a compulsory identity card showing his or her group, Hutu, Tutsi or Twa. Those who illegally changed this classification were subject to imprisonment or a fine or both.[2] No Rwandan could move from a prefecture without the appropriate authority.

In this strictly controlled society the Tutsi were marginalized. The Kayibanda quota system was retained by Habyarimana and under it only a certain percentage of Tutsi were allowed to attend schools and universities. There was one Tutsi in a nineteen-member cabinet, one ambassador in the foreign service, two deputies in a seventy-seat national assembly, and two members in the central committee of the ruling party.[3] In the army, Tutsi were disbarred from becoming officers, and soldiers were not allowed to marry Tutsi.[4]

One problem never seriously addressed by the regime was the plight of Rwandans living outside the country, refugees who had fled Rwanda during the anti-Tutsi campaigns which started in 1957 when what some Rwandan historians call the 'social revolution' occurred. These exiled Rwandans created Africa's largest refugee problem. Like the Palestinians, they were stateless. The regime in Kigali denied them the right of return and in Uganda they were not accorded full rights of settlement. In western Uganda the Rwandans were the subject of prejudice, discrimination and sometimes persecution.

In October 1982, after years of conflict over land and jobs, the refugee communities in Uganda were attacked and there was looting and rape. People were beaten up and some were killed. Some 35,000 head of cattle were stolen. More than 80,000 people fled towards the border with Rwanda and a few made it across before Rwandan guards closed the frontier. Some 10,000 people were then trapped, caught on a strip of land between the two countries barely two kilometres wide. People started to die and international agencies provided aid.

In March 1983, Rwanda agreed to resettle some 30,000 people but Ugandan persecution of Rwandan refugees continued. In December of that year thousands fled to Tanzania. With an announcement from Kigali in July 1986 that the refugees would not be allowed to return because the country was not big enough, there seemed to be little hope of settling the problem.

The total number of Rwandans living as exiles has always been a matter of debate. One estimate puts the figure at 2 million which includes all those living in other African countries, and those who were in Belgium and North America. The government in Kigali estimated some 200,000. The United Nations High Commissioner for Refugees (UNHCR) estimated that by 1990 there were 900,000 Rwandan refugees in Uganda, Burundi, Zaire and Tanzania.[5]

When the refugees had first fled Rwanda there were hopes for a quick return, but as the years went by the camps took on an air of permanency. The incursions into Rwanda had all failed. In Uganda, when President Milton Obote ordered the removal of non-skilled foreigners from public employment and a census was ordered, there were fears that the Rwandans might be expelled.

The UNHCR helped many of the exiles; the second generation and those who had fled Rwanda as children acquired education and many gained scholarships to study in Europe and North America. A diaspora was created. Like others with no country, the exiles set enormous store by education. The young and educated refugees kept in touch, forming clubs and associations. They lived in Quebec, in New York, Nairobi and Dakar, and were doctors, lawyers and social workers. They produced regular newspapers and magazines. Most of them had no memory of Rwanda – some had not been born there – but to them it was a land of milk and honey.

The first organized group established in the refugee community in Uganda was the Rwanda Refugees Welfare Association (RRWF), but in 1979 it evolved into the Rwandan Alliance for National Unity (RANU). RANU was more political and, as its name implied, was created to oppose the divisive politics of Hutu nationalism. It operated in exile between 1981 and 1986 in Nairobi and then in 1987, when it changed its name to the Rwandan Patriotic Front (RPF), it became an organization dedicated to the return of the refugees to Rwanda. It was more activist, half political party and half paramilitary group. It leaders denied that it was a Tutsi organization; its twenty-six-member executive committee was composed of eleven Tutsi and fifteen Hutu, and it claimed support from all those opposed to the repressive and backward Habyarimana regime. Its stated aim was to end the dictatorship for all Rwandans, but many were suspicious of RPF motives. There was criticism of its lack of effort in forging links with the opposition to the dictatorship within Rwanda.[6]

It is a truism that, if left unattended, refugee problems lead to conflict. In Kigali it was hoped that the refugee problem could be solved with the minimum repatriation because most refugees would want to stay in Uganda. In February 1988 Rwanda and Uganda formed a joint ministerial commission. The regime in Rwanda claimed that the RPF was 'encouraging' refugees to want to return home. It was decided in 1989 that the UNHCR should survey the settlements, beginning in October 1990. Talks were held about the refugees with the Organization of African Unity (OAU) and the UNHCR, but it was too little, too late.[7]

That an army would be created to force a refugee return was predictable for there was a widespread belief among the RPF leadership that, given the nature of the regime in Kigali, a return home could be achieved only through military means. The guerrilla army eventually created by the RPF, the Rwandan Patriotic Army, was unique: its recruits came from the armed forces of another country, Uganda. It was well-trained, disciplined and had a great deal of combat experience.

When Yoweri Museveni and his National Resistance Army (NRA)[8] took Kampala by force in January 1986, it was the first insurgent movement effectively to take power from an incumbent African government. Uganda was a country shattered by the brutal rule of Idi Amin and his successors. Museveni re-established an effective central government.

The original decision by Museveni to resort to guerrilla warfare against Amin's successor, Milton Obote, was taken in 1981 when, with only thirty-five men and twenty-seven weapons, known as the Popular Resistance Army, Museveni attacked the police military school at Kabamba.[9] There were two Rwandans in this small group. One of them was the popular and charismatic Fred Rwigyema, and the other, the secretive, sober and intelligent Paul Kagame. Both fighters would be instrumental in Museveni's ultimate success and both learned that it was possible for a small group of insurgents to launch an armed struggle with few resources and overthrow a government.[10]

The Rwandans were natural allies of Museveni. During the Obote regime the Rwandan refugees had been persecuted, a reason enough to help him. In 1982, when the refugee crisis occurred and Rwandans were trapped on the border between Uganda and Rwanda, many young Rwandans, rather than remain powerless and persecuted refugees, joined the ranks of the NRA. By the time Museveni took Kampala by force in January 1986, a quarter of the soldiers in the 14,000-strong NRA were Rwandan, up to 2–3,000 Tutsi fighters, the sons of exiles.[11] Many of Museveni's top commanders and officers were Rwandan, and during his campaign the regime of Obote had sought to discredit him by claiming falsely that he was Rwandan and was interfering in Uganda's affairs.

After his victory in 1986, Museveni consolidated his power, and his army and the NRA began a military recruitment campaign in western and southern

Uganda, from the Banyarwanda and Buganda areas. This increased still further the number of Rwandans in the ranks of the NRA as even more refugees took up the opportunity of military training. Thousands signed up hoping that what had successfully occurred in Uganda could now be repeated in Rwanda. Joining the NRA was a first step along the road leading home.

Over the next three years these recruits would gain much military experience for they took part in NRA campaigns to secure eastern and northern Uganda then in almost constant insurrection. There was fighting at Acholi, Teso, Lango, Kasese and West Nile. For the Rwandan recruits it was practical military training. The largest uprising against Museveni was led by a voodoo priestess, Alice Lakwena, whose supporters carried out suicide attacks. The atrocities committed by the NRA during these campaigns provoked resentment in Uganda and the Rwandans were blamed for crimes against civilians. There were said to be fears by people in Acholi and Lango that the intention was for the Rwandans to take their land.[12]

While the Rwandan officer corps was an asset for Museveni, the Rwandans themselves were a problem. There were increasing complaints among Ugandan officers that they were discriminated against in favour of Rwandans in the army. The most famous Rwandan, Rwigyema, was now a major-general and promoted to the NRA's deputy army commander-in-chief and deputy minister of defence in Uganda. Then in a reshuffle in November 1989, and perhaps to appease the anti-Rwandan camp, Rwigyema was removed from office. There was deep resentment among Rwandans and some of those who believed Rwanda to be an old story began to revise their opinion. In August 1990, two members of Rwanda's political elite fled to Kampala, Valens Kajeguhakwa, a Tutsi businessman, and Pasteur Bizimungu, a Hutu and relative of Habyarimana. These two described Rwanda as being on the edge of collapse, split north and south, drained by corruption and ready to welcome anyone who wanted to overthrow the regime.[13]

On 1 October 1990 Rwandan soldiers in the NRA invaded Rwanda taking their weapons and supplies. They had rallied round Rwigyema, 'Commandant Fred', created the Rwandan Patriotic Army,[14] and crossed the sparsely populated Mutara into Rwanda.

Museveni immediately denied supporting the invasion and claimed that the soldiers had stolen their Ugandan uniforms and equipment. International observers chose not to believe him. The soldiers in the RPF had almost unlimited access to NRA hardware and Museveni was accused of playing a double game, of professing friendship with neighbouring Rwanda while allowing the preparation of an invading army. The American-based Human Rights Watch Arms Project was told by a senior Ugandan officer that Uganda provided heavy weapons, including artillery, and a steady stream of ammunition, food and logistics for the RPF, and that the two armies shared intelligence.

According to senior RPF sources, Museveni had been told about the invasion plan but had rejected it, saying it would never work. Habyarimana was far too popular in the West and he warned that if the RPF *did* organize an invasion, Habyarimana would receive a great deal of outside help. Museveni promised the RPF that if they would wait he would see to it personally that Habyarimana would let the refugees return. According to the RPF leadership, they only ever mentioned the invasion once to Museveni. They did not share Museveni's certainties, and believed that the racist regime in Kigali would never allow the refugees home. 'There would never be a political settlement, we were in no doubt of that,' said Patrick Mazimhaka, vice-president of the RPF. 'We knew that the repression in Rwanda could only get worse.'[15]

The RPF published an eight-point programme that included an end to Rwanda's ethnic divide and the system of compulsory identity cards. The RPF wanted democracy for Rwanda, a self-sustaining economy, an end to the misuse of public offices, the establishment of social services, democratization of the security forces, a progressive foreign policy and the elimination of a 'system which generates refugees'. The RPF was a multi-ethnic movement seeking to depose a corrupt regime.

The invasion was a disaster. Nothing went to plan. Although the RPF managed to capture the tourist resort and barracks of Gabiro and the town of Nygatare, they were beaten back. Fred Rwigyema was killed on the second day, and so shocked were fellow officers that the news was not announced for two weeks. Rwigyema was known as a fearless fighter, a commander who always led from the front. His death caused immediate fears for the morale of the troops. On 7 October there was a counter-offensive by the Rwandan army. This army was only some 5,200 strong but, when the invasion occurred, it had received immediate help from France. At the end of October the RPF fell back to an area where the Rwandan army would not follow, into the Virunga, the heavily forested volcanic mountain range in the north-west. The soldiers were badly equipped and some of them died of cold.

It was Paul Kagame, one of Museveni's original 1981 guerrilla group, who saved the RPF. Kagame, who had fled Rwanda in 1959 as a young child, had become the NRA's deputy head of military intelligence, and when the invasion occurred he had been on a military training course at the US Army Command and General Staff College at Fort Leavenworth, Kansas. With Kagame as the RPF commander, Colonel Alexis Kanyarengwe, a northern Hutu and former Rwandan minister of internal affairs, was appointed president. Kanyarengwe had fled Rwanda in 1980 after accusations that he was plotting against Habyarimana and his appointment signified a link between the RPF and the Habyarimana opposition in Rwanda.

Kagame had combat experience dating back to 1981 and when he took control of the RPF he quickly realized that he would be fighting a protracted war. From a rag-tag band of fewer than 2,000 men, he created a 15,000-strong disciplined force. His soldiers had high endurance levels and strict discipline. If the RPF could manage to increase pressure points in the northern part of the country, Kagame believed, then the contradictions within Habyarimana's rotten regime would cause it to self-destruct.

President Yoweri Museveni's assessment was correct: the 1990 RPF invasion did cause international uproar and the amount of support given to the Habyarimana regime shocked the RPF leadership. Troops were sent from the Congo, Zaire and Kenya in support of Habyarimana. President Mobutu sent his Division Spéciale Présidentielle (DSP). Belgium sent 400 paratroopers to protect the 1,700 Belgian nationals living in Rwanda and the French sent troops. French spotter planes did much to locate the retreating RPF soldiers.

In Paris the RPF offensive was portrayed as an invasion by a neighbouring state, considered to be part of a Ugandan plot, which, in turn, was part of a larger post-Cold War attack by 'les anglo-saxons', whose eyes were on French interests in Africa. In French conservative, intelligence and army circles the RPF was anathema. To have abandoned Habyarimana would have been high treason, tantamount to handing Rwanda over to English-speaking rebels. In parts of the French military, Uganda was nick-named 'Tutsi-land'. It was taken for granted that what Museveni wanted was a Tutsi empire. There were policy-makers in France who believed that in Rwanda they were supporting a majority, the Hutu, against a minority, the Tutsi. For them, this justified calling Rwanda 'democratic'. That the majority was identified along ethnic lines did not seem to matter; majority rule legitimized French military and diplomatic support for the regime.

When the RPF invaded in October 1990, Habyarimana immediately telephoned the Elysée Palace in Paris, where Mitterrand kept African affairs a family matter: his son, Jean-Christophe, headed his Africa office.[16] There was a witness there that day. Gérard Prunier, a French political scientist, had gone to the Elysée Palace on another matter. He heard Mitterrand's son say that the crisis would be over in a few months.[17]

French troops were dispatched to Rwanda and on 4 October three days after the invasion took place, 300 French paratroopers, from the 2ème Regiment Etranger Parachutiste stationed in the Central African Republic, secured Kigali airport and within a few days more than 600 French troops were in the country to 'protect and evacuate French citizens'. There were also two companies of parachutists and paramilitaries from the French secret service, Direction Générale de la Sécurité Extérieure (DGSE), with combat helicopters. France installed soldiers next to the government troops in the north, although the

French soliders were not officially to use weapons. Secretly, the French had operational control of the counter-insurgency campaign. Later on in 1990, a pro-Hutu journal, *Kangura*, published a full-page photograph of President François Mitterrand. The caption, in Kinyarwanda, read: 'Great friends, they stand by you during difficult times.'[18]

One privileged insider at the time, a well-informed French colonel, René Galinie, who was present in Rwanda when the 1990 RPF invasion occurred, wrote a report to Paris stating that the Habyarimana government feared that the Tutsi were going to re-establish the monarchy in the north, and that if this was the case then it would lead to the elimination of all Tutsi everywhere.

From the moment the RPF invaded Rwanda there was panic in Kigali, while the Habyarimana regime made desperate efforts to increase the armed forces and to buy weapons. Rwanda relied on France but the government was desperate for other suppliers. Two weeks after the invasion, one was found.

On Monday, 16 October 1990, the Rwandan ambassador to Egypt, Célestin Kabanda, had gone to a meeting at the Ministry of Foreign Affairs in Cairo.[19] For seven years Egypt had refused to sell arms to Rwanda. Now there was added urgency.

Kabanda's meeting that day was with Dr Boutros Boutros-Ghali, who had not yet launched his campaign to become the sixth Secretary-General of the UN. He was for the time being an obscure professional diplomat, a lawyer and author of books and articles on international law and political science. He was a minister of state for foreign affairs and he had recently helped oversee a state visit to Cairo by Habyarimana. Kabanda said he desperately needed Boutros-Ghali's help and handed him a list of weapons. Egypt had mass-produced cheap weaponry for sale.[20] Buying weapons from Egypt, with its low production costs, showed a competitive advantage. Kabanda wanted Boutros-Ghali to intervene with the Egyptian government on Rwanda's behalf, saying that military aid from Belgium had just been cancelled.[21]

So desperate had Rwanda been in the past to get Egyptian arms that at one point it had even asked for weapons as gifts. Egypt, though, had always declined. The only gift so far was the statue of a pharaoh, placed with fanfare in the centre of one of Kigali's strategic roundabouts. During the recent head-of-state meeting in Cairo, Hosni Mubarak, Egypt's president, had told Habyarimana that Egypt could not supply the weapons that Rwanda wanted. Yet, when the meeting with Boutros-Ghali was over, Kabanda was optimistic. He telexed Kigali to tell the Foreign Ministry that Boutros-Ghali had promised his help and assured him that he personally would deal with the request.

Twelve days later, on 28 October, a first arms contract between Rwanda and Egypt was signed. It was for US$5.889 million. The weapons purchased included 60,000 grenades (weighed in kilos), some 2 million rounds of ammunition, 18,000 mortar bombs, both 82mm and 120mm, 4,200 assault rifles, rockets and rocket launchers. The Egyptian signature on the contract was that of Colonel Sami Said Mohamed, chief of the friendly countries branch in the Egyptian Ministry of Defence, and the deal proceeded quickly. The first consignment of weapons, described as 'relief materials', was loaded at Cairo international airport and was flown to Kigali on 28 October in a Boeing 707 by the Egyptian airline ZAS at a cost of US$65,000 for the round trip. Habyarimana gave authority for the money to be paid through the Commercial International Bank of Egypt.

It is not known whether President Mubarak was aware of the details of the arms deal but as a gesture of goodwill he gave Rwanda a gift of two field ambulances, later shipped by sea. There may have been other pressures elsewhere to persuade Egypt to sell arms to Rwanda. But Kabanda later wrote to thank Boutros-Ghali: 'Your personal intervention helped the conclusion of the contract. I thank you sincerely.' Kabanda wrote to his foreign minister, Casimir Bizimungu: 'the personal intervention of Boutros-Ghali with his colleague in the defence ministry was a determining factor in the conclusion of the arms contract for he was following closely the events on our borders.'

Bizimungu, wrote to Boutros-Ghali on 31 December 1990 to thank him for his help in hastening the arms deal. A year later, when Boutros-Ghali was selected Secretary-General of the UN, he received a telegram of congratulation from Bizimungu, who had unforgettable memories of their frank and profitable collaboration reinforcing the friendship between their two countries.[22]

The arms deal with Egypt was kept secret. It came at a time when strenuous international efforts had begun to prevent a civil war between the RPF and the Rwandan government forces. The Belgium prime minister, Wilfried Martens, had flown to Nairobi on 14 October to try to open negotiations between the Rwandan government and the RPF. Peace talks had begun on 17 October with Habyarimana, President Yoweri Museveni of Uganda and President Ali Hassan Mwinyi of Tanzania. The talks were facilitated by Mwinyi, who feared the creation of a larger refugee crisis. On 26 October, two days before the first arms deal between Egypt and Rwanda was signed, a ceasefire was agreed between the Rwandan government and the RPF following diplomatic efforts by the Belgian government.

Ceasefire or not, from now until the genocide began in April 1994, Rwanda would become the third largest importer of weapons in Africa, ranked behind Nigeria and Angola. An estimated US$100 million was spent on arms by this tiny African country. For the next three years, among the military hardware which entered the country, there was a seemingly unstoppable flow of small arms and light weapons.

Boutros-Ghali, when later interviewed about the arms sales, described his role as that of a 'catalyst'.[23] He was a minister of foreign affairs, he said, and it was his job to help to sell his country's weapons production; he would have helped any government wanting arms from Egypt. Egyptian arms were cheap and the Egyptians prided themselves on the speed of delivery. Kabanda made the approach, said Boutros-Ghali, because he would not have known who else in the Egyptian government to contact. About the wisdom of arranging an arms deal while international peace efforts were under way, Boutros-Ghali said that he did not think 'a few thousand guns would have changed the situation'.

We may never know the full facts of the sudden Egyptian change of heart in October 1990 and the reversal of its foreign policy not to sell weapons to Rwanda. The sales would undoubtedly have helped to boost foreign earnings. One important factor must have been Rwanda's sudden change in fortunes for, by the time Kabanda had requested Boutros-Ghali's help, some US$216 million of international funding had been earmarked for Rwanda, some of it from the European Union with sizeable bilateral contributions from France, Germany, Belgium, the EC and the USA. Rwanda's status had changed; the country's economy was now in the hands of the world's most powerful international institutions, the World Bank and the IMF. Rwanda was the subject of a structural adjustment programme (SAP) devised to try to prevent economic chaos; its perilous economy was going to be shored up and in exchange there was going to be fundamental reform – the creation of a sound, efficient financial system which envisaged low inflation.[24]

SAPs are economic reforms involving changes in pricing and trade policies, reductions in the size of government, and the regulation of production in order to integrate countries into the international market economy. Countries are required to make these economic changes in order to receive funding. The programmes are intended to rely on financial restraint to achieve their objectives. Yet evidence suggests that part of the money provided was not used productively as intended to prevent Rwanda's economic collapse, nor was it channelled to help Rwanda's famine and war victims.[25] It has since been discovered that sizeable portions of quick disbursing loans were diverted by the regime towards the acquisition of military hardware. And the military purchases of Kalashnikov assault rifles, field artillery – a powerful asset in the mountainous terrain – and mortars were made in addition to the bilateral military aid package provided by France.

From October 1990 the Rwandan army expanded virtually overnight from 5,000 to 28,000 men requiring, inevitably, a sizeable influx of outside money. Rwandan soldiers, who had only ever been equipped with light arms,[26] were now to have a wide range of light arms, heavier guns, grenade launchers, landmines and long-range artillery.

The close relationship between Dr Boutros Boutros-Ghali and the Rwandan regime had begun with his first official visit to Kigali in 1983. Most of the high-level Egyptian–Rwandan diplomatic dialogue went through him.[27] Boutros-Ghali knew Rwanda well. And everyone who knew Rwanda was aware that it was a single-party state based on nepotism and that the only opposition was mainly comprised of refugees in Uganda.

Rwanda is the source country of the Nile and Boutros-Ghali later described in his memoirs how he travelled southwards again and again, deep into the centre of the African continent to the source of this great river which had so impressed him as a child.[28] He learned that not only the source of the Nile but those of humanity itself lay deep in Africa: 'Africa is the mother of us all, and Egypt is the oldest daughter of Africa. This is why I have loved Africa and tried so hard throughout my life to help her.' When Boutros-Ghali first went to Rwanda on official business in the 1980s it had been Egyptian policy to create a friendly bloc of countries around the Nile basin. As deputy foreign minister he wrote to the Rwandan foreign minister offering closer co-operation, and the chance to attend a regional conference as a member of a group of central African states: Uganda, Sudan, Zaire and Egypt. One result of this initial diplomatic approach was an agreement that Egypt would train Rwandan soldiers, although the deal eventually faltered over which country should pay their living expenses. In 1985 a group of Rwanda army officers visited Cairo. They were given a tour of light arms factories, and watched the production of Kalashnikov assault rifles, made under Soviet licence, and heavy machine guns. A member of this mission, Lieutenant-Colonel Leonidas Rusatira, in a secret report to Habyarimana, complained bitterly there could be no arms deal.

A visit by Rwanda's foreign minister to Cairo in 1988 was equally disappointing. During this visit, Boutros-Boutros Ghali met Jean-Damascene Bizimana, secretary-general of the Rwandan Foreign Ministry. That year, Boutros-Ghali once again visited Rwanda.

The following year, in September 1989, the then foreign minister, Casimir Bizimungu, met President Hosni Mubarak. Mubarak told Bizimungu that Egypt would carefully examine Rwanda's request to supply arms but no deal was concluded. On 9 September an agreement for a programme of commercial, cultural and scientific co-operation was signed.[29] Among the provisions was an agreement by Egypt to provide twelve doctors and an electrical engineer to maintain hospital equipment. The co-operation agreement was negotiated and signed by Bizimungu and Boutros-Ghali. In 1990 President Habyarimana went to Cairo on a two-day official visit and Boutros Boutros-Ghali was the head of the delegation which accompanied the president.

Habyarimana met Mubarak and raised the issue of Egypt donating armaments to Rwanda. Rwanda asked for equipment for the 'maintenance and reestablishing of public order' – tear gas, truncheons, helmets with visors and gas masks. Once home in Kigali, Habyarimana received a detailed report about Rwanda's relations with Egypt from Colonel Rusatira, who thought that the Egyptians probably wanted to do a deal but they were distrustful. He believed the problem would be solved with the forthcoming visit to Kigali by Boutros-Ghali. The visit, however, was cancelled. It was August 1990. Iraq had invaded Kuwait. The Egyptian government needed Boutros-Ghali at home.

As though using a blueprint from 1963, the reprisals within Rwanda after the RPF invasion were swift and terrible. A curfew was imposed in Kigali which served to imprison people in their homes and an estimated 5,000 people said to be 'RPF supporters' were arrested. Hundreds of those arrested were detained in the Nyamirambo stadium in Kigali, where they were told that should the RPF get anywhere near Kigali, they would all be killed. In northern Rwanda, in Mutara, where some of the RPF were hiding, hundreds of Tutsi were killed and massacres were organized by local officials who told the peasants that the Tutsi were coming back to restore the king and turn them into slaves. To heighten fear of the RPF the Habyarimana regime staged a fake attack on Kigali. The gunfire and explosions heard during the night of 4 October were intended to encourage citizens to make arrests of 'Tutsi suspects'.

On 8 October there were reports of attacks on Tutsi in the sub-prefecture of Ngorolero in Gisenyi. On 11 October in Kibilira, also in the Gisenyi prefecture, local officials were instructed that the traditional communal work, a fact of life in Rwanda since before colonial times, was to get rid of the Bigogwe, poor and pastoral Tutsi who lived apart from Rwandan society in the Ruhengeri province.

> M ... saw his wife and six children killed. He hid because he thought it would be like 1959 and 1973 when everything was stolen and when only some of the men had been killed ... [this time] he saw his neighbour cut off the head of his wife with one machete blow, in front of his children, while the wife of his neighbour killed a child on the back of a victim ... this woman killed this child, while she herself was carrying a child of the same age on her own back.[32]

Another witness said: 'The old bourgmestre ... found a much more effective way of liquidating undesirables. He invited all the men from the area to a political meeting. Once arrived, the victims were given to the killers by the bourgmestre.' Rwandan soldiers also took part. Some soldiers brought victims back to their military camp at Gisenyi-Ville where the wives and children of the soldiers finished them off. Within the ranks of the gendarmerie, torture was described as endemic. Witnesses, fleeing the pogroms in the north, reported that government troops were killing people. Dozens of people living on cattle ranches in north-eastern Rwanda had been killed by Rwandan government soldiers. In early October, prisoners in Byumba prison who were being transferred were reported to have disappeared. All the victims were Tutsi. In a report by Amnesty International, the human rights abuses were said to have been carried out by government officials and the security forces. Amnesty International received numerous accounts of prisoners being tortured and of mass arrests. Most cases of torture occurred at detention centres in Kigali belonging to the gendarmerie.[31]

In two years from 1990, it is estimated that 2,000 people were killed and about 10,000 others were arrested and detained without charge.[32]

On 19 December 1990, in a report prepared jointly by the ambassadors of France, Belgium and Germany and the representative of the European Union in Rwanda, the following warning was issued: 'The rapid deterioration of the relations between the two ethnic groups, the Hutu and the Tutsi, runs the imminent risk of terrible consequences for Rwanda and the entire region.' In Brussels there was an outcry against the human rights abuses perpetrated by the Rwandan regime and, just days after the October invasion by the RPF, the Belgian government announced its intention to withdraw from Rwanda for good, citing a legal obligation to remain neutral in situations of war.

One other consequence of the invasion was the encouragement it gave to pro-democracy groups in Rwanda, supported in turn by the numerous human rights groups which had sprung up in Rwanda in particular and in Africa in general, where the role of such groups was expanding. At the end of the Cold War there had been hopes that the brutal and corrupt regimes in Africa, freed from the constraints of super-power rivalry, would change. Calls for democratization in Africa were echoed widely in Washington.

There was external and internal pressure for an end to the Habyarimana regime. In April 1990, Habyarimana had visited Paris, and later in June he attended a Franco-African summit at La Baule at which President Mitterrand had said he wanted to link economic aid with political democratization and advised Habyarimana to introduce a multi-party system. Habyarimana quickly complied and promised to liberalize, his keenness due partly to the visit to Rwanda in September 1990 of Pope Jean-Paul II. On 13 November, Habyarimana announced that a multi-party system would be created. Later that month, the first independent party was created, in exile: the Union du Peuple Rwandais (UPR). There was a wave of optimism and hope.

At the same time, Habyarimana was persecuting journalists deemed to have written subversive articles. The MRND continued to benefit from state resources and access to the media and when a coalition government was created it included only one opposition minister.

Notes

1. Unlike other African states in Francophonie, where French was the only common language, Rwandans have a common tongue, Kinyarwanda.

2. Gérard Prunier, *The Rwanda Crisis 1959–1994. History of a Genocide*, London: Hurst and Company, 1995, p. 76, note.

3. Catherine Watson, *Exile from Rwanda. Background to an Invasion*, US Committee for Refugees, Issue Paper. Washington, DC, February 1991.

4. Jean-Paul Gouteux, *Un Génocide secret d'Etat*, Paris: Editions Sociales, 1998, p. 104. While the percentage of Tutsi in Rwanda was officially 9 per cent, research by the UNDP showed this figure to be nearer 20 per cent. In some places the number of Tutsi was as high as 30 per cent, principally in the west, in Kibuye, there were just 5 per cent in other parts of Rwanda, most notably in the north-west, in Gisenyi and Ruhengeri.

5. Gérard Prunier, 'The Rwandan Patriotic Front', in Christopher Clapham (ed.), *African Guerrillas*, Oxford: James Currey, 1998, p. 121.

6. Dismas Nsengiyaremye, 'La Transition démocratique au Rwanda (1989–1993)', in André Guichaoua (ed.), *Les Crises Politiques au Burundi et au Rwanda (1993–1994)*, Université des Sciences et Technologies de Lille, Karthala, 1995 (2nd edn), p. 246.

7. *The International Response to Conflict and Genocide: Lessons from the Rwanda Experience*, Joint Evaluation of Emergency Assistance to Rwanda, Copenhagen, March 1996, Chapter 2, p. 19.

8. The National Resistance Army of Uganda was the military wing of the National Resistance Movement.

9. Pascal Ngoga Uganda, 'The National Resistance Army', in Christopher Clapham (ed.), *African Guerrillas*, p. 95.

10. Prunier, 'The Rwandan Patriotic Front', p. 125.

11. Watson, *Exile from Rwanda*, p. 11.

12. Ogenga Otunnu, 'An Historical Analysis of the Invasion by the Rwanda Patriotic Army', in Howard Adelman and Astri Suhrke (eds), *The Path of a Genocide. The Rwanda Crisis from Uganda to Zaire*, New Brunswick, NJ: Transaction, 1999, p. 33. Watson, *Exile from Rwanda*, p. 13.

13. Watson, *Exile from Rwanda*, p. 14.

14. Fred Rwigyema was elected president of the RPF.

15. Interview, Patrick Mazimhaka, London, September 1999.

16. Every president, from de Gaulle to Chirac, had retained a presidential prerogative in African policy-making. The president had the power to dispatch troops overseas without reference to parliament or ministers, advised only by the unelected head of the Africa Unit attached to the Elysée Palace.

17. Prunier, *The Rwanda Crisis*, p. 100. Jean-Christophe acquired his knowledge of Africa while a correspondent for Agence France-Presse. He is the oldest of Mitterrand's children. He was appointed to his father's Africa Unit in October 1986, having been deputy in the office since August 1982. He left this office in July 1992, handing over to Bruno Delaye, a career diplomat whose previous posting had been in Togo.

18. *Kangura*, No. 6, December 1990.

19. The letters, contracts and minutes of meetings concerning Rwanda's arms deals with Egypt were abandoned in the Rwandan embassy in Cairo when the genocide was over. Copies of all these documents are in the possession of the author.

20. Minister of Defence Abu Ghazala, a presidential adviser, had built up a network of

army enterprises in weapons and had recently been made responsible for selling off some of these to the private sector. Egypt ranked fifteenth in the league of world arms exporters (1989) and exported arms essentially to make domestic defence industries less of a financial drain.

21. On 3 October, President Habyarimana had appealed to Belgium for help and 500 para-commandos had been sent to Kigali. Troops witnessed brutality and massacres committed by the Rwandan army and this led to a parliamentary debate on 9 October. On 11 October military aid was suspended.

22. Casimir Bizimungu, a medical doctor from Ruhengeri in north-west Rwanda, was arrested in Nairobi on 11 February 1999 and is currently detained by the International Criminal Tribunal for Rwanda on charges of genocide and crimes against humanity in Rwanda in 1994. He was minister of health in the interim government that carried out the genocide.

23. Interview, Boutros-Boutros Ghali, Paris, December 1999.

24. There were seven bilateral donors, as well as the African Development Bank and the European Union in a co-financing arrangement.

25. Pierre Galand and Michel Chossudovsky, *L'Usage de la Dette Extérieure du Rwanda (1990/1994). La Responsabilité des Bailleurs de Fonds*, Brussels and Ottawa, 1996. Copy in possession of author.

26. The Rwandan army's most significant weaponry had included eight 81-mm mortars, six 57-mm anti-tank guns, French 83-mm Blindicide rocket launchers, twelve French armoured cars and sixteen French M-3 armoured personnel carriers.

27. Diplomatic relations between Rwanda and Egypt were opened in May 1975.

28. Boutros Boutros-Ghali, *Unvanquished. A US–UN Saga,* London: I.B.Tauris, 1999.

29. Programme Executif de l'Accord de Cooperation Culturelle, Scientifique et Technique.

30. ADL, *Rapport sur les Droits de l'homme au Rwanda*, Kigali: Association Rwandaise pour la défense des droits de la personne et des libertés publiques (ADL), December 1992. See also Amnesty International, *Rwanda: Amnesty International's Concerns since the Beginning of an Insurgency in October 1990*, March 1991.

31. Amnesty International, *Rwanda: Persecution of Tutsi Minority and Repression of Government Critics, 1990–1992*. May 1992.

32. Human Rights Watch, *World Report, 1994*. December 1993.

4 · Akazu: The Oligarchy Ruling Rwanda

AFTER their disastrous invasion in October 1990, the RFP had sufficiently regrouped, rearmed and recruited by January 1991 to attack a prison in a northern Hutu stronghold, Ruhengeri. It held some 1,000 prisoners and the attack led to an immediate order from Kigali to kill the inmates before the RPF released them, but a Rwandan army officer had refused to obey and the prisoners were freed. In retaliation, a new wave of massacres of Tutsi started in north-west Rwanda.

There were three years of sporadic fighting between the RPF and the Rwandan government army and in those three years the RPF did not broaden its political base, nor did it rally large numbers of Hutu to its side. The civil war divided society and it created political instability and near economic collapse.

What the RPF did achieve was a transition from rebel group to legitimate participant in the political process. This transition was recognized internationally when the RPF had talks with the US assistant secretary of state, Herman Cohen, and with the OAU's secretary-general, Ahmed Salim Salim, in Kampala in May 1992. There were even preparatory talks with the French government in Paris in June.

There were ceasefires between the RPF and the Rwandan government in October 1990, and in November and February 1991, each renewed after violations. The civil war had a devastating effect on Rwanda, displacing thousands of people, and having an impact on tea and coffee production. The war cut the road to the Kenyan port of Mombasa – Rwanda's main overland route to the outside world. It destroyed the fledgling tourist industry, which had become the third largest earner of foreign exchange.

Although in Rwanda the levels of poverty remained high, during the 1970s and the early 1980s economic and social progress had been made. The real gross domestic product (GDP) growth was of the order of 4.9 per cent per annum (1965–89), school enrolment increased and inflation was among the lowest in sub-Saharan Africa, less than 4 per cent per annum.[1] There was local self-sufficiency and the development of an export economy. Coffee was cultivated by approximately 70 per cent of rural households, although it constituted only a fraction of total monetary income. And 75 per cent of Rwanda's export earnings came from coffee. All coffee producers in Rwanda were smallholders and the government assured them a guaranteed price which made the government a profit.

A Belgian academic and expert on the region, Professor Filip Reyntjens of Anvers University, says that towards the end of the 1980s corruption was limited and human rights were more or less respected. Compared with other African countries, Rwanda was not so bad.[2] Imports of cereals including food aid were minimal and the food situation started to deteriorate only in the early 1990s with a marked decline in the per capita availability of food.

The Habyarimana years began with a period of development. Rwanda was richly endowed with one of the best road systems in Africa, post and telephone services, and there was an expansion of the electricity supply. It was a popular country for aid workers. Rwanda was beautiful and well-organized. It was 80 per cent Christian, with 62 per cent Catholic and 17 per cent Protestant. The Church controlled 80 per cent of health clinics and contraception was forbidden. Until the late 1980s Rwanda had been a small and poor but self-sufficient country with an average annual inflation rate not higher than 4 per cent. There were improving standards of public health and education and Belgium, France and Switzerland poured money in. There were also fault-lines. Rwanda had the highest, and growing, population density of any African country. In 1989 there was drought and famine in the south, and when the RPF invaded in October 1990 there was further loss of food production in the north, and the creation of 300,000 refugees.

A lethal blow to Rwanda's economy had come in June 1989 when the International Coffee Agreement (ICA) had fallen apart, as a result of political pressure from Washington, acting on behalf of the large US coffee traders. World prices plummeted. In Rwanda, the Fonds d'égalisation – the state coffee stabilization fund, which purchased coffee from Rwandan farmers at a fixed price – started to accumulate a sizeable debt.[3] Revenues decreased drastically and foreign earnings diminished by 50 per cent. Poverty increased. Very few countries had experienced such a rapid decline. Rwanda was a desperate case.

International financial institutions had concluded that with the imposition of an SAP the levels of consumption would increase markedly and there would be recovery of investment, and an improved balance of trade leading to lower levels of debt. These outcomes depended on the speedy implementation of trade liberalization and currency devaluation and the lifting of all subsidies to agriculture, the privatization of state enterprises and the dismissal of civil servants.

The first devaluation of the Rwandan franc was carried out in November 1990, barely six weeks after the RPF invasion. Intended to boost coffee exports, the devaluation was presented to the public as a means of rehabilitating a war-ravaged economy. But the fall in the currency contributed to inflation and a decrease in real earnings. There were large increases in the prices of fuel and consumer essentials. Soon the state administration was in disarray; the biggest employer was the government, with 7,000 employees in central government and some 43,000 in local administration. State enterprises were pushed into bankruptcy and health and education services collapsed. The incidence of severe child malnutrition increased dramatically, as did the number of recorded cases of malaria. The economic crisis reached its climax in 1992 when Rwandan farmers in desperation uprooted some 300,000 coffee trees, for the government had frozen the farm-gate price of coffee at its 1989 level. A significant profit was appropriated by local coffee traders and intermediaries serving to put further pressure on the peasantry.

In June 1992, a second devaluation was arranged by the IMF leading to further escalation in the prices of fuel and consumer essentials. Coffee production tumbled by another 25 per cent. The loan co-operatives which provided credit to small farmers disintegrated. The Food and Agriculture Organization (FAO) warned of the existence of widespread famine in the southern provinces. By early 1994 coffee production had collapsed. Rwandex, the mixed enterprise responsible for processing and exporting of coffee, had become largely inoperative. Rwanda was descending into poverty and destitution.

President Juvénal Habyarimana lived in a large villa in Kigali between an army barracks and the airport. There was no visible sign of his wealth although there were tennis courts and a swimming pool. The house was filled with white and gold French furniture. There was a simple and unadorned private chapel but although the president and his wife were ostentatiously Catholics, and the word God figured largely in Habyarimana's speeches, in reality they consulted soothsayers and clairvoyants.

Habyarimana, a tall man, walked with a limp from an old injury received when he first joined the military academy in the days before Rwanda's independence. Educated by a French-speaking religious order, he was fluent, and eloquent, in French. His links with France were well known and he had stayed with the Belgium royal family in Brussels. Habyarimana was closest to President Mobutu in neighbouring Zaire and Mobutu was particularly close to Habyarimana's wife, Agathe.

Although Habyarimana was considered the Mwami (King) of the Hutu, the real power in Rwanda resided with Agathe. She was so conniving and influential that the Rwandans nicknamed her in memory of a terrible character from Rwandan history, Kanjogera. Kanjogera was the former King Musinga's mother.[4] In pre-colonial times, Kanjogera played a vital role as manager of the royal household, and was the focal point of all court intrigue. She held the reins of power in the shadow of the throne. Agathe Habyarimana came from a powerful and well-known northern family but her husband had no such power base; there were even rumours that he may have been not from Rwanda at all, but from Uganda.

Born Agathe Kaziga, Habyarimana's wife had a strong and forceful personality. She was proud of her ancestral roots. It was with the support of her family that Habyarimana ousted the former president, Gregoire Kayibanda. Agathe, the daughter of Gervaise Magera, a Hutu from Bushiru, like most northerners loathed all Tutsi and southern Hutu, blaming them for the subjugation of the north. Few northerners married Tutsi. In the north there was great awareness of pre-Tutsi history when the northern people were ruled by kinglets, lineage heads and landowners.[5] With the 1990 RPF invasion, the Hutu in the north came to dread an alliance between the Tutsi, non-northern Hutu and the pro-democracy politicians.

With Habyarimana as president, the north had been favoured for state-sponsored rural investment.[6] Access to power was granted only to those from northern prefectures. Some speculated that had the RPF not invaded, there might have been a different civil war, north against south.

Agathe Habyarimana surrounded herself with ruthless northerners, a tightly knit mafia which was was given the name Akazu, meaning 'little house', a pre-colonial name to describe the circle of courtiers around a king. Agathe's personal network comprised her three notorious brothers: Protais Zigiranyirazo, alias Monsieur Z, former prefect of Ruhengeri, who was responsible for widespread killings, Colonel Pierre-Célestin Rwagafilita, and Séraphin Rwabukumba, a prosperous businessman who ran La Centrale, an import company and quasi-monopoly, and who owned a large house in Belgium. Rwabukumba would eventually help to divert funds to enter into arms deals. The Akazu had its own death-squad, recruited from the French-trained Presidential Guard. Akazu had contacts everywhere: in local councils and prefectures; it had representatives in all of Rwanda's embassies; and its richer members kept bank accounts abroad (the National Bank of Rwanda was under the direction of Séraphin Rwabukumba).

The existence of Akazu was no secret. In August 1992 a defector, Christophe Mfizi, went public to reveal how Rwanda was being ruled by an oligarchy from the north.[7] Mifizi warned that until this oligarchy was destroyed, there was no chance of creating democracy in Rwanda. For fourteen years Mfizi had run the Office Rwandais d'Information (ORINFOR), which controlled Rwanda's press. He had been a senior official of the MRND from 1976 to 1991 and had resigned from the party on 15 August 1992 writing an open letter, published in Paris. There was what he called *Le Réseau Zéro* (Network Zero), a group of people who had successfully infiltrated all areas of Rwandan society: politics, the army, finance, agriculture, science and religion. These people treated the country like a private company from which a maximum profit could be squeezed. The president and the leaders of the MRND were enmeshed by this group and unable to escape. In order to retain power, the group was encouraging racism and regional division.

There were more specific and terrifying warnings about Akazu. In the spring of 1992 the Belgium ambassador in Kigali, Johan Swinnen, reported to Brussels: 'This secret group is planning the extermination of the Tutsi of Rwanda to resolve once and for all, in their own way, the ethnic problem and to crush the internal Hutu opposition.'[8] Swinnen had been leaked a list of the members of this secret group: Protais Zigiranyirazo, the president's brother-in-law; Elie Sagatwa, a colonel in the army, another brother-in-law, head of the secret service and the president's secretary; François Karera, deputy prefect in Kigali, in charge of the logistics of a recent massacre of civilians in Bugesera; Pascal Simbikangwa, captain; Jean-Pierre Karangwa, commander; Justin Gacinya, captain, head of the communal police in Kigali; Anatole Nsengiyumva, lieutenant-colonel, head of army intelligence; Tharcise Renzaho, lieutenant colonel, prefect of Kigali. In Rwanda there existed a group of professional killers whose role was to do away with liberals and pro-democracy politicians. Later in 1992 Swinnen was given a document from within the Rwandan Ministry of Defence which had been sent to all sector commanders of the army and which described all Tutsi, in Rwanda and living outside it, as the 'principal enemy'.

An earlier but similar warning about what was going on in Rwanda had been sent to the French government. In June 1991, an intelligence assessment written by a French agent identified an inner circle of power in Rwanda, dominated by Agathe Habyarimana and her family. This group was using ethnic hatred to increase its power and was determined to resist democracy. Knowing that it would be suicidal to oppose reform directly, the group relied on propaganda to instil fear among the people about an invasion by the Ugandan army supporting the RPF. In Rwanda huge amounts of money were being spent to strengthen the army, and independent political parties were being sabotaged. While this group maintained its grip on power the creation of democracy never stood a chance. The report warned that if anyone tried to impose democracy, it would serve only to provoke resistance. The moderate members of the military, the cabinet, the young educated officers and the intellectuals were powerless.[9] In France the scholar Jean-Pierre Chrétien warned that the racist ideology had not just erupted as a consequence of the RPF invasion but had been nurtured for decades. Chrétien wrote in 1991 that if the importation of arms into Rwanda did not stop then the country would become a powder keg.[10]

The situation in Rwanda was no secret. In the Paris-based *Libération*, on 9 February 1993, a journalist wrote:

> In the far hills of Rwanda ... France is supporting a regime which for two years, with a militia and death squads, has been trying to organize the extermination of the minority Tutsi ... the death squads, organized in a Réseau Zéro [Network Zero] by the President's clan, are operating a genocide against the Tutsi, as though it were a public service.

In a report of the Rwandan human rights group ADL, for the years 1990–92, the word 'genocide' was used to describe massacres of Tutsi in the northern prefectures of Gisenyi and Ruhengeri.[11]

On 9 October 1992, in the Belgian Senate in Brussels, Professor Filip Reyntjens organized a press conference, with the help of Senator Willy Kuypers, at which Reyntjens described how a death squad was operating in Rwanda. Reyntjens said the squad was similar to those operating in Latin America. In Rwanda the membership of the death-squad included off-duty soldiers and militia. He named the leaders including Agathe Habyarimana's three brothers, the commander of the Presidential Guard, the head of G2 military intelligence, and Colonel Théoneste Bagosora.[12] Murder in Rwanda and immunity for killers was taken for granted.

Like the Hitler Youth, the militia, attached to political parties, comprised the uneducated and unemployed of the country's youth, taken from the streets and from local football teams and given rudimentary training in the use of weapons. [13] The militia contained delinquents and petty criminals, experts in thuggery who disrupted political meetings and terrorized anyone who criticized the government.

When the 1994 genocide began, the militia was estimated at some 30,000-strong. There were two groups, one of them attached to the extremist Hutu Power Coalition for the Defence of the Republic (CDR) and named Impuzamugambi, 'those with a single purpose', and the other named Interahamwe 'those who work together'. The Interahamwe would become the most 'effective', the largest and the best-known. This was the group formed as the youth wing of the ruling party, the Mouvement Révolutionnaire National pour la Développement (MRND).

The militia was organized nation-wide; they were disciplined, and had leaders at neighbourhood level. Not just recruits but their families were looked after and given food, beer and clothing.[14] The Interahamwe had committees in every one of Rwanda's 146 communes. In each commune there were 200 militia members – one man for ten families. Some of them were issued AK47s, although these required requisition forms. The Interahamwe had supporters in the Rwandan gendarmerie, in the Presidential Guard and the army.[15] In Rwanda, when people talked about the third force, it was this network they were referring to.

There was one training camp for the militia in an army installation not far from the airport in Kigali. There were also training camps in Mutara, Bugesera and in the forest of Nyungwe and in Gishwati. The recruits were taught to handle weapons and use explosives. Later they were taught to kill, with the emphasis on killing at speed, cutting the achilles heel in order to prevent escape.[16] There was never any serious investigation into killing in Rwanda, and no attempt made to apprehend those responsible for murder.

Two men ran these camps: a Belgian-trained former Presidential Guard chief, Colonel Leonard Nkundiye, and the American-trained Lieutenant-Colonel Innocent Nzabanita, who was nicknamed Gisinda (wild animal). One witness said: 'Two French instructors took part in our training … during several weeks, a total of four months training between February 1991 and January 1992.'[17] French ministers have strenuously denied any accusations that French troops trained the militia, but there were French army instructors working with the Rwandan government army, where they may have been lax in screening the candidates they accepted, or may have deliberately turned a blind eye to the standards of the recruits.

Many soldiers turned up in the ranks of the militia, which kept growing. The Bigogwe army commando camp was notorious for its violence and anti-Tutsi racism. The militia was an open secret and everyone knew that militia members were protected by the army, and were said to have infiltrated every prefecture.

The very first time that militia took part in the killing of Tutsi will probably never be known, although Tutsi were attacked and killed in November 1991 in the commune of Murambi, east of Kigali.[18] The organized killing of Tutsi became more evident in March 1992 in the Bugesera, a region in the southern part of Kigali prefecture where there was a higher percentage of Tutsi than anywhere else. The homes of Tutsi were looted in the communes of Kanzenze, Gashora and Ngenda. An estimated 300 people died in the Bugesera but the exact number cannot be known. People were thrown in the rivers or were burned in their homes. Tutsi who tried to defend themselves were disarmed by government soldiers. There were reports that thousands of people had taken refuge in the Nyamata Roman Catholic church, and that the church was surrounded. Many people died from hunger and exposure and from harassment from local security forces.

In a telex to Brussels, Johan Swinnen reported that the Interahamwe, recruited outside the Bugesera, had taken part in the killings. A local group of Interahamwe was ordered to pillage and set fire to homes to allow the killing to be explained as local ethnic disturbances, whereas in fact what had happened in the Bugesera was well planned. Swinnen also discovered that a group of professional killers had played a role. A local commando group had been recruited at the national gendarmerie school, Ecole Nationale de la

Gendarmerie, in Ruhengeri. Dressed in civilian clothes these recruits had killed members of the local Parti Libéral (PL) and the Mouvement Démocratique Républicain (MDR).[19]

There were public accusations about what had happened. On 10 March in Kigali a group of five Rwandan human rights groups held a press conference to reveal that the massacres were the work of local officials determined to ruin the 'new politics'. The deaths in the Bugesera were directly linked to news broadcasts on Radio Rwanda, at peak times, which claimed that an unknown group in Nairobi, associated with the Parti Libéral, intended to kill twenty-two prominent Hutu. The PL was known in Rwanda as a Tutsi party; the core of its support were businessmen. Some of the peasants had taken part in the killing, told that there was going to be a special collective work session. When local officials ordered the people to 'clear the bush', everyone knew by then they must clear their hill of Tutsi. The slaughtering of women and children was called 'pulling out the roots of the bad weeds'. More than 3,000 people fled the area, their homes razed to the ground.

The killing in the Bugesera bore all the hallmarks of the genocide to come.[20] It lasted from 4 until 9 March 1992. After Bugesera, similar incidents occurred in the Kigali prefecture, in Kibuye, in Cyangugu and in Gisenyi.

The government explained the killings in Bugesera as 'self-defence', and although 466 people were arrested, they were later released. The regime blamed the president of the Parti Libéral, Justin Mugenzi.[21] A report of the Fédération International des Droits de l'Homme blamed the government, stating that Habyarimana's entourage was involved.[22] The US and Canadian ambassadors[23] went to see President Habyarimana to express concern at the violence, although the French ambassador, Georges Martre, refused to join this *démarche*.[24]

Rwanda became more violent. A series of terrorist attacks took place, and grenades were thrown into crowds in Kigali and a bomb exploded in a taxi, killing five people. All attacks were attributed by the government to the RPF or their supporters. In the countryside there were reports of Tutsi killed in Gisenyi and of MRND officials threatening those attempting to register opposition political parties. With every move towards the building of democracy, there was violence.

To appease his western backers, on 6 April 1992 Habyarimana formed a new government. It looked as though for the first time the ruling MRND party would be sharing power, for it was given nine ministries from a total of twenty.[25] For the first time there were women in government; one of them, Agathe Uwilingiyimana, a moderate Hutu, was given the Ministry of Education.[26]

Bombings were reported throughout the country, particularly in Ruhango, south west of Kigali, and in Butare. On 8 May Uwilingiyimana, trying to end the quota system for Tutsi in schools, was attacked in her home in Kigali by twenty armed men. Later that month, some 3,000 women demonstrated in Kigali in support of her. In May here was more violence. At the end of the month, the RPF met with members of Rwanda's political opposition in Brussels and a communiqué was signed calling for political reform and for all parties to work together to expose the misdeeds of the Habyarimana regime. America, by now committed to peace in Rwanda, sent the US Assistant Secretary of State for African Affairs, Herman Cohen, to try to contribute to peace talks between the government and the RPF In August 1992, talks between the two sides began in Arusha, Tanzania.

By now the country was in chaos. Military spending increased and the government was relying upon food aid.[27] There was an epidemic of bacillary dysentery spreading through Byumba, and, in Rwanda, 500,000 cases of AIDS.

A ferocious anti-Tutsi campaign was launched on 22 November 1992. In a land mark speech, Leon Mugesera, the vice-president of the MRNDD in the northern stronghold of Gisenyi, and a political science professor, addressed party militants in a rabble-rousing, racist speech which quite clearly incited the murder of Tutsi:

> what about those accomplices here who are sending their children to the RPF ... we have to take responsibility in our own hands ... the fatal mistake we made in 1959 was to let them [the Tutsi] get out ... they belong in Ethiopia and we are going to find them a shortcut to get there by throwing them into the Nyabarongo River. We have to act. Wipe them all out.[28]

Members of the Interahamwe militia later chanted his words.

Mugesera was one of the intellectual architects of the genocide, a man who could portray the Tutsi as evil and clever, turning them all into permanent threat. At the time, Rwanda's minister of justice was a member of the opposition, a man called Stanislas Mbonampeka, of the Parti Libéral. A lawyer and human rights advocate, he charged Mugesera with inciting racial hatred. A warrant was issued for Mugesera's arrest but he took refuge in a military camp and the police were too frightened to arrest him. Mbonampeka resigned. He was not replaced.

International pressure continued for Rwanda to democratize. A communiqué of the US State Department issued in early 1993 maintained that the continuation of US bilateral aid meant progress with reform and the pursuit of democracy. There would later be criticism of this policy. The objective of installing a multi-party coalition government, under the trusteeship of Rwanda's external creditors, was considered by some to be impossible.[29]

In spite of Rwanda's ever-worsening situation, the regime in Kigali received ever-increasing support from France. And while propping up the regime France managed successfully to leave the French public and the rest of the world in the dark about the extent of its help and interference. It continues to do so to this day. France armed, financed and trained the Presidential Guard, the elite force which comprised northern Hutu recruited from the president's home region of Bushiru. It was French technical and military training that allowed the Rwandan army to increase from 5,000 to 28,000, equipping it with modern weaponry. France tripled finanacial aid to Rwanda.[30] And all these decisions concerning Rwanda were secret; the French remained unaccountable for them.

French African politics were quite peculiar, and such anomalies were not exclusive to Rwanda. French policy on Africa emanated from different centres of power in Paris but was decided primarily by Mitterrand advised by his unelected African Unit which, between 1986 and 1992, was headed by his son Jean-Christophe. It was located in the Elysée Palace and there grew around it a charmed circle of Franco-African political leaders and businessmen. The decisions taken by this unit were often made on the basis of good-will towards favoured clients or personal friends. There was also input from the French foreign ministry, the ministries of co-operation, of defence, of finance, and the French intelligence service (DGSE). Thus, African policy was the preserve of a small and powerful elite. In the case of Rwanda, apart from the African unit in the Elysée, those with the strongest voices in favour of Habyarimana came from the ministry of cooperation and the DGSE.[31]

During 1991–92 at least US$6 million of arms from France was sent to Rwanda: mortars, light artillery, armoured cars and helicopters. By 1993 Rwanda was receiving US$4 million military aid from France. All this was under the terms of an amended 1975 military technical assistance accord which had entailed an initial modest annual transfer of arms.[32] The accord had been signed by President Valéry Giscard d'Estaing two years after Habyarimana seized power. Sometimes knows as 'Giscard the African', Giscard wanted to expand France's African sphere to include Belgian and French-speaking colonial territories, including neighbouring Zaire, where France became a principal arms supplier. France justified its intervention in Rwanda to be no more than honouring a treaty obligation to an ally. In 1992, the agreement was amended to an 'Accord de défense'.

The full story of French involvement will never be known. Five days after the 1994 genocide began, the French embassy in Kigali was abandoned. Left behind was a huge pile of shredded documents, almost filling a room. But some documentary evidence about French military involvement has survived, found in a military archive in Kigali. There is letter from Colonel Déogratias Nsabimana, commander-in-chief of the army, dated 9 December 1992, paying tribute to French soldiers helping to improve the defences against the RPF in the north. 'The French work has been good but they must be more discreet,' Nsabimana wrote to his minister of defence. Successive ministers in the French government have denied that French paratroopers were directly participating in the civil war against the RPF, but there was evidence to the contrary. Aid workers saw French soldiers manning artillery positions during the fighting with the rebel RPF in January 1991. A French mercenary, Paul Barril, would later claim proudly that he knew a member of the French secret services who had single-handedly stopped an RPF advance in 1992.[33]

French soliders were seen controlling check-points in Kigali, demanding to see identity cards, arresting Tutsi and passing them over to the Rwandan army. There were complaints about the anti-Tutsi behaviour of the French soldiers. When, in October 1992, the supporters of an extremist Hutu party took to the streets to demonstrate against a peace agreement with the RPF, they were chanting, 'Thank you, Mitterrand. Thank you, people of France.' In Kigali the French president was laughingly called 'Mitterahamwe'.

There was a credibility gap between the officially recognized co-operation with France and the reality. Colonel Cussac, French military attaché and head of the French military assistance mission to Rwanda, once explained: 'French military troops are here in Rwanda to protect French citizens and other foreigners. They have never been given a mission against the RPF.'[34] But while claiming that there were only 600 French soliders in Rwanda, with a creative manipulation of rotas it was possible to keep 1,000 soldiers there.[35]

The RPF commander, Major-General Paul Kagame, told the French newspaper *L'Humanité* on 13 March 1992: 'We were fighting to give negotiations a chance, and up against a power which refused any chance for democracy ... by its presence the French army prolonged the conflict, they should realise that.'

Notes

1. Michel Chossudovsky. 'Les Fruits empoisonnés de l'adjustement structurel', *Le Monde Diplomatique*, November 1994.

2. Belgian Senate, *Commission d'enquête parlementaire concernant les évenéments du Rwanda*, Report, 6 December 1997, p. 82.

3. According to the World Bank, the growth of GDP per capita declined from 0.4 per cent in 1981–86 to –5.5 per cent in the period immediately following the slump of the coffee market (1987–91).

4. Gérard Prunier, *The Rwanda Crisis 1959–1994. History of a Genocide*, London: Hurst and Company, 1995, pp. 23–5.

5. René Lemarchand, 'Rwanda: The Rationality of Genocide', *Issue: A Journal of Opinion*, Vol. XXIII, No. 2, 1995.

6. Filip Reyntjens, L'*Afrique des Grands Lacs en crise. Rwanda, Burundi: 1988–1994*, Paris: Karthala, 1994.

7. Christophe Mfizi, *'Le Réseau Zéro', Lettre Ouverte à Monsieur le Président du Mouvement Républicain National pour la Démocratie et le Développement (MRNDD)*, Editions Uruhimbi, BP 1067, Kigali, Rwanda, 1992.

8. Belgian Senate, *Commission d'enquête* , p. 493.

9. *Evaluation of Emergency Assistance to Rwanda*. Study 2: *Early Warning and Conflict Management*, Copenhagen, 1996, p. 28.

10. Jean-Pierre Chrétien, *Le Défi de l'Ethnisme. Rwanda et Burundi, 1990–1996*, Paris: Karthala, 1997, p. 136.

11. ADL, *Rapport sur les Droits de l'homme au Rwanda. September 1991–September 1992*. Kigali: Association Rwandaise pour la défense des droits de la personne et des libertés publiques (ADL), December 1992. There had been killing of Tutsi by now in Kibilira, Mutara, Nasho, Bigogwe and Murambi.

12. Prunier, *The Rwandan Crisis*, p. 168.

13. The most notorious being the Mukungwa team in Ruhengeri.

14. Interviews, Kigali, October 1997.

15. In 1990, there had been 2,000 gendarmes, increasing to 6,000 by the time the genocide started.

16. One of the camps was at Gabiro, near a hotel in the Akgagera game park, and another was in the north-western Gishwati forest, near the Hôtel Mont Muhe, which belonged to the Akazu. The youths lived in tents in the forest near Gabiro.

17. Interview with Janvier Africa, *Courrier International*, 30 June–6 July 1994.

18. Filip Reyntjens. 'Akazu, "escadrons de la mort" et autres, "Réseau Zéro": un historique des résistances au changement politique depuis 1990', in André Guichaoua (ed.), *Les Crises Politiques au Burundi et au Rwanda (1993–1994)* Université des Sciences et Technologies de Lille, Paris: Karthala, 1995 (2nd edn), p. 265.

19. Belgian Senate, *Commission d'enquête* , p. 495.

20. In the Bugesera, Hassen Ngezethe, editor-in-chief of the extremist journal *Kanguara*, was seen distributing copies of anti-Tutsi leaflets. Colette Braeckman, *Rwanda, Histoire d'un Génocide*, Paris: Fayard, 1994.

21. The Parti Libéral had the largest Tutsi membership. The Parti Social Démocrate, recruited from among Hutus from the south, was more intellectual. The oldest opposition party was the Mouvement Démocratique Republicain.

22. Fédération International des Droits de l'Homme, *Rapport sur la Commission d'enquête sur les violations des droits de l'homme au Rwanda depuis le 1er October 1990*, March 1996, Paris and New York

23. Lucie Edwards, the Canadian ambassador, operated from the Canadian embassy in Kenya.

24. Martre served from September 1989 until March 1993 and was replaced by Jean-Michel Marlaud.

25. The MRND, the Mouvement Révolutionnaire National pour le Développement, changed its name in April 1992 to the Mouvement Républicain National pour la Démocratie et le Développement (MRNDD).

26. Uwilingiyimana eventually became prime minister in a coalition government and while holding this office she was shot the night the genocide began. Belgian peacekeepers died trying to protect her.

27. The International Development Agency contributed $19 million as part of a co-ordinated relief programme with the UNDP. The UNDP pledged $3.1 million and the World Food Program $16 million.

28. The complete text of the Mugesera speech can be found in Guichaoua (ed.).

29. Interview, Michel Chossudovsky, Professor of Economics, University of Ottawa, December 1999.

30. Chrétien, *Le Défi de l'Ethnisme*, p. 143.

31. Daniela Kroslak, *Evaluating the Moral Responsibility of France in the 1994 Rwandan Genocide*, paper presented at the 23rd Annual Conference of the British International Studies Association, 14–16 December 1998.

32. Mel McNulty, 'France's Rwanda Débâcle', *War Studies*, Vol. 2, No. 2, Spring 1997, p. 10.

33. McNulty, 'France's Rwanda Débâcle', p. 12. Paul Barril, former head of the GIGN (Groupe d'intervention de la gendarmerie nationale) and currently director of the private security firm SECRETS (Société d'études de conception et de réalisation d'équipements techniques et de sécurité), one of five constituent companies of Groupe Barril Sécurité.

34. Human Rights Watch Arms Project, *The Arms Trade and Human Rights Abuses in Arming Rwanda*, Vol. 6, No. 1. January 1994.

35. Prunier, *The Rwanda Crisis*, p. 164.

5 · Peace in Rwanda? The Arusha Accords

IT was thanks only to international pressure that negotiations began between the government of President Habyarimana and the RPF, pressure which came from Belgium, the USA and the Organization of African Unity (OAU). The negotiations opened in Arusha, Tanzania, in July 1992. They were the only hope for a peaceful resolution of the civil war.

It took thirteen months of talks to get the Rwandan government and the RPF to sign a peace agreement; without international pressure, given their differences and the problems, an agreement would never have emerged. So happy were they with the outcome, the diplomats concerned called the eventual agreement, known as the Arusha Accords, one of the best deals negotiated in Africa. It was a truly international effort with the involvement of delegations from five African states: Burundi, Zaire, Senegal, Uganda and Tanzania. The negotiations were organized by the OAU with leadership provided by President Ali Hassan Mwinyi of Tanzania, whose government acted as facilitator. Four western countries had observer status: France, Belgium, Germany and the USA. The talks were monitored by Britain, Canada, the Netherlands and the European Union from their local embassies.

The OAU secretary-general, Salim Ahmed Salim, a Tanzanian and one-time front-runner for the job of UN Secretary-General, had a high profile at these talks.[1] The OAU had been involved from the start of the civil war and its leadership had seen the RPF invasion of Rwanda not as aggression by a neighbouring state, but as an attempt by the children of exiled refugees to go home. One of the ceasefires that followed the outbreak of fighting in 1990 had provided for the presence in Rwanda of a fifty-member Neutral Military Observer Group (NMOG), provided by the OAU, to monitor the border between Uganda and Rwanda in order to prove that Uganda was not helping the invaders. A group of fifty officers was provided but it was plagued by serious logistical and financial shortages.[2]

The Arusha Accords provided for radical change. The triumphant signing ceremony came in August 1993 and the agreement was comprehensive and wide-ranging, providing for political, military and constitutional reform.

Rwanda was to have a broad-based transitional government until a democratically elected government was installed. The presidency was to become largely ceremonial, with the president wielding less power than most constitutional monarchs. A neutral international force was to be deployed, to be followed by the withdrawal of French soldiers. The RPF and the Rwandan army would integrate; there would be disarmament and demobilization. The refugees would be allowed home. As a first step, a battalion of RPF soliders would be stationed in Kigali.

The transitional government was to hold power for no more than twenty-two months until free elections, and it would contain representatives of the three political blocs: President Habyarimana's political party and its allies, the internal opposition parties, and the RPF. The accords named Faustin Twagiramungu of the Mouvement Démocratique Républicain (MDR), the largest internal opposition party, as prime minister during the transition.[3]

Some thought that the Arusha Accords were the best that would ever be achieved. Eric Gillet, a human rights lawyer who helped to write a landmark report on Rwanda, said that he thought that all that could be done was done at Arusha. The trouble stemmed not from the accords themselves but from the fact that Habyarimana and his entourage did not want them to work, and did everything possible to prevent agreement. Gillet said: 'The human rights workers, whether Rwandan or international, were not fooled. We did not think that someone capable of organizing massacres would suddenly turn into a democrat. We saw what was happening. We kept telling the Belgian authorities.'[4]

There are critics of Arusha who claim that the accords served only to back the extremists into a corner, taking away their power. The hardliners in the MRND party, the northern clique in the military and in the ruthless new grouping, the Coalition pour la Défense de la République (CDR), were denied power in the transitional institutions. The ruling party was reduced to five seats in the transitional government. If a newly independent judiciary were to be installed, then the culture of impunity would end. The corruption could be exposed as would be the murders carried out by the Akazu members grouped around Agathe, the president's wife. Under Arusha there was no amnesty for political, economic or human rights crimes. Any government figure, from the president down, could have been investigated and charged. All that was left to the extremists was their ideology of Hutu nationalism, and the means to attract sympathy to their cause.

The vice-president of the RPF, Patrick Mazimhaka, who participated in the negotiations in Arusha, says that no one in the RPF leadership believed for one minute that Habyarimana was sincere when he negotiated and signed the accords. Mazimhaka tells a story about Colonel Théoneste Bagosora, a Hutu army colonel who had provided a direct link between Arusha and the extremists in Kigali. At one point during negotiations, Bagosora, a fervent anti-Tutsi, had packed his bags. Mazimhaka saw him standing in a hotel lift surrounded by suitcases and asked why he was leaving. Bagosora said he was going back to Rwanda to prepare 'apocalypse deux', the second apocalypse.[5]

The RPF put its faith in the international community, said Mazimhaka, hoping that if neutral peacekeepers were provided then this would stop the worst from happening. Major-General Paul Kagame had received assurances: 'The whole world will be watching,' Kagame says he was told by western diplomats.[6] 'We thought Habyarimana would be isolated,' said Mazimhaka.

Whether or not to include extremists in negotiations and in government is an issue that bedevils peace agreements. A flash-point during the Arusha negotiations was the exclusion from the process of the extremist CDR. The RPF would not countenance the CDR in government, arguing that it was an offshoot of the president's party, the MRNDD, a crypto-fascist gang that would not even allow anyone with a Tutsi grandparent to join. Habyarimana wanted inclusion of the CDR and he was supported in this by French diplomats who argued that it was better to have the CDR in government where it could be controlled than out of government where it could not. The Tanzanians said the same. The obstinacy of the RPF leadership over this issue sent western diplomats, both British and American, urgently seeking meetings with Kagame to persuade him to let the CDR take part. The US ambassador to Rwanda, David Rawson, was forceful over the issue. According to the State Department desk officer for Rwanda, an inter-agency meeting to discuss Rwanda agreed as early as March 1992 that the CDR must be included.[7] Western governments saw the exclusion of the CDR as a departure from constructive negotiations, insisting that a more substantive role should be given to those who stood to lose power.

The RPF delegates told everyone that the founder of the CDR, Jean-Bosco Barayagwiza, who worked as director of political affairs in the Rwandese Ministry of Foreign Affairs, was a fascist thug and that the CDR was the above-ground official incarnation of the 'underground forces' murdering the opposition and the Tutsi, and running the country. The RPF was blamed for intransigence for not accepting the CDR. Overall, the RPF achieved a high level of success in Arusha and proved superior in negotiation. Critics of the Arusha Accords describe the Arusha deal as a veritable coup for the RPF and Rwanda's internal pro-democracy opposition. The RPF prevailed over the CDR issue and the transitional institutions were to give equal representation for the RPF and the ruling MRNDD, at five members each. The balance of power would be shared between eleven members of the National Assembly, representing five of the smaller parties established since 1991. The prime minister and the minister of foreign affairs were to be drawn from the minor parties, with defence going to the MRNDD and the Ministry of the Interior to the RPF.

Just how sincere the Habyarimana regime was came to light only afterwards when it emerged that while negotiations were taking place in Arusha, the regime entered into the largest of all the arms deals with a French company called DYL Investments for US$12 million, involving the purchase of 40,000 grenades, 29,000 bombs, 7 million rounds of ammunition, 1,000 truncheons, 1,000 pistols and 5,000 AK 47s, the money to be paid in million-dollar instalments. Transport was in the hands of the OGA (Office Général de l'Air) and East African Cargo, a Belgium company.[8]

Soon after the deal was signed, the manager of Rwanda's bank, Jean Birara, took the risky and exceptional step of privately warning diplomats from western embassies about the purchase. But by late December 1993, so openly distributed were weapons in Rwanda that the Bishop of Nyundo, from north-western Rwanda, issued an unprecedented press release asking the government why arms were being handed out to certain civilians. The government's answer was that the locals had to defend themselves against rebel and guerrilla forces because there were not enough troops.

In the years immediately before the 1994 genocide there was a bewildering array of aid agencies involved in Rwanda and most of them were fully aware of the overt system of apartheid operated against the Tutsi. In 1993 there were thirty-eight non-governmental organizations (NGOs) in Rwanda. There was a plethora of information but nothing exists to show that any of the knowledge, even that which the Bretton Woods institutions possessed, was ever shared with the western diplomats negotiating the peace deal in Arusha. The Americans were actively involved in the peace process from 1991, lending weight to the talks with the involvement of a deputy assistant secretary. For several months in 1991 a series of French and American meetings with the government and the RPF ran in parallel, while each kept the other informed. In early 1992, in the African Bureau of the State Department, the assistant secretary of state for Africa, Herman Cohen, convened an inter-agency forum which continued to meet for the next two years to co-ordinate American efforts.[9]

There were human rights groups, too, gathering information and becoming increasingly active in Rwanda. They reported extensively on the Bagogwe massacres in January 1991 and the February 1992 massacre at Bugesera, describing the involvement of military and local government officials. In some communes Tutsi had been repeatedly attacked, and the military had distributed arms to civilians who supported Habyarimana. In one case, Tutsi victims were buried in the backyard of a local government official.

So bad did the situation in Rwanda become that, in January 1993, a group of international human rights experts from ten countries collected testimony from hundreds of people, interviewed witnesses and the families of victims, and reviewed numerous official documents. In March 1993 a report was published revealing that in the previous two years those who held power in Rwanda had organized the killing of a total of 2,000 of its people, all Tutsi, singly, or in small or large groups. Some 10,000 Tutsi and members of the political opposition had been arrested or detained without charge. Many people had been tortured or badly beaten; some were held incommunicado in military camps rather than in prison. The report made clear that those in power were guilty of serious, and systematic, human rights abuses. The authorities in Rwanda, at the highest level, including the president, were responsible for the violence and murder committed by civilians, soldiers and increasingly, militia. The militias operated with impunity. Rwanda's judicial system was paralysed by political interference.[10]

The word genocide was not used in the report, being considered too highly charged by some of the group's authors, but a press release distributed with the report carried the headline: 'Genocide and war crimes in Rwanda.' This was written by William Schabas, a Canadian lawyer from the International Centre for the Rights of the Person and Democratic Development, Montreal, and a member of the investigating commission. Schabas was convinced that the fact of genocide in Rwanda was undisputable, citing its definition in the 1948 Genocide Convention: 'acts committed with the intent to destroy a national, ethnical, racial or religious group.' Those acts were killing, causing mental harm, inflicting conditions of life calculated to bring about the group's destruction, imposing measures to prevent birth and transferring children from one group to another (see Appendix 2). In Rwanda the intent to destroy the Tutsi as a group was evident because of the hate propaganda; with genocide a pervasive racial ideology and propaganda are essential.

In response to the damming human rights report, Habyarimana promised a ten-point set of reforms. His chief propagandist, Ferdinand Nahimana, who helped to provoke the massacres at Bugesera, was on a tour of Europe and the USA, trying to convince the press and public that the international commission had been misinformed. There had been an internal Rwandan inquiry, Nahimana claimed, which found that local officials were responsible for the violence.

There was little international concern when the human rights report came out. Only the Belgian government recalled its ambassador from Kigali for consultations, and the Rwandese ambassador in Brussels was told that Belgium would reconsider its economic and military aid unless steps were taken to rectify the situation. The French ambassador dismissed the massacres as rumours.

From 8 to 18 April 1993, the Special Rapporteur for the Commission on Human Rights for Extrajudiciary, Summary or Arbitrary Executions, Bacre Waly Ndiaye, visited Rwanda. He had received allegations of grave and massive violations of the right to life in Rwanda. His report was published on 11 August, and in the report the word genocide was used in relation to Rwanda.

The victims of violence in Rwanda, Ndiaye reported, were in the overwhelming majority of cases Tutsi, and so the Convention on the Prevention and Punishment of the Crime of Genocide, 1948, was applicable.

The UN Commission on Human Rights was set up in 1946 to filter and consider human rights complaints.[11] There are fifty-three member states and the commission is a subsidiary of the UN General Assembly. It meets annually, from February to mid-March. In 1992 and in 1993, the commission discussed Rwanda; both times, the confidentiality clause was used, a way to avoid embarrassment for the state concerned, and a way to allow the commission to approach the government in closed session.[12] These confidential discussions were conducted by a committee of five.[13] This was the first step in a process which could lead to the serious and public step of appointing a Special Rapporteur.

In his report Ndiaye accused the Rwandan government of using propaganda to create a situation in which 'all Tutsi inside the country were collectively labelled accomplices with the RPF'. He described an elite which, in order to cling to power, was fuelling ethnic hatred. Concerning massacres, he wrote: 'such outbreaks were planned and prepared, with targets being identified in speeches by representatives of the authorities, broadcasts on Rwanda radio, and leaflets ... [and] the persons perpetrating the massacres were under organised leadership.' Local government officials were found to have played a leading role in most cases.[14]

Ndiaye said later that for all the attention his report achieved he might just as well have thrown it into the sea. At the time of its publication the RPF and the Habyarimana regime signed the Arusha Accords and from then on all efforts were concentrated on a rushed and desperate effort to implement them.

In early 1993, while the protocol which dealt with the distribution of seats in a transitional government was being negotiated in Arusha, there were violent demonstrations against the peace process organized by the MRNDD. The opposition parties launched counter-demonstrations. Three hundred Tutsi civilians were killed. At the negotiations in Arusha, Kagame was insisting that the whole issue was about fundamental change. What they were dealing with was a dictatorship that killed its own people.[15]

On 8 February 1993, the RPF breached the ceasefire agreement, ostensibly to stop the killing.[16] A massive offensive was launched, driving back government troops and creating a wave of terrified people fleeing south, adding to the misery of those already displaced by civil war. By now in Rwanda one million people were homeless – one-seventh of Rwanda's population – and huge camps were created, with children dying of starvation and dysentery.[17] These people were dependent on massive food aid for their survival. As a result of the exodus from fertile land, and fears that the next harvest could be down by 40 per cent, there were predications of famine. Ndiaye's report had described the problems of the large number of displaced people as a 'time bomb with potentially tragic consequences'.

In Arusha there was speculation among the negotiators that the massive RPF invasion had been launched because the next item on the agenda was the integration of the two armies. The RPF offensive was launched to prove how strong the RPF was militarily, in order to get more of a share in the new Rwandan army.[18] If this was the intention then it succeeded. The invasion proved that the RPF, while less well equipped than the Rwandan army, was a superior fighting force. The RPF doubled the territory it controlled, reaching Rulindo, 50 kilometres from Kigali.

Once again it was France to the rescue and the RPF fought helicopters, artillery fire and radio-jamming by the French. Without the French, the RPF could easily have taken Kigali, and Kagame said later he wished he had carried on and taken the capital. In this event the genocide would have been avoided. The OAU accused the French government of prolonging the conflict by supporting the Rwandan military, and for firing upon RPF positions in Ruhengeri. Undeterred, on 20 February, Paris had announced that two more companies of French troops would be sent.

The RPF invasion had disastrous effects. From now on all Tutsi inside the country were labelled RPF accomplices and Hutu members of the opposition were branded traitors. The invasion damaged the fragile relationship which existed between the RPF and the opposition parties. There was speculation about whether the RPF really wanted a negotiated settlement. The opposition split into two groups, pro- and anti-RPF. According to the International Federation of Human Rights, the RPF had violated human rights. Ndidaye's report pointed to reliable sources who claimed that the RPF had executed at least eight local officials, supporters of the MRNDD, and civilians. Because of the inaccessibility of the area where these events took place, Ndiaye said it was difficult for him to form an opinion, but the events must be investigated by an international team of experts. He reported that the RPF was willing to co-operate with an investigation.[19]

In the Ministry of Defence in Kigali the idea was gaining ground that, in order to defend the country, a civilian self-defence network must be created. Habyarimana told his army sector commanders on 11 March that the population must begin to organize to defend itself. And in a press release dated 25 February 1993, the CDR announced that the real RPF plan was to kill all the Hutu. The government 'must provide the people with the means' to defend themselves.

A nucleus of Hutu extremists was now promoting the idea that in order to destroy the RPF something must be done about the Tutsi in Rwanda. Most of these conspirators came from the north-west of Rwanda. Their names are known.[20]

Notes

1. In June 1992, Salim Ahmed Salim had presented a proposal to create an OAU Mechanism for Conflict Prevention, Management and Resolution, and a year later this was established by the Assembly of Heads of States and Government. A peace fund was launched in 1993 to pay for it but African funding was not available. The OAU was not provided with enough money by its member states to finance military operations.

2. NMOG had a mandated strength of fifty-five soldiers from Mali, Nigera, Senegal and Zimbabwe.

3. Twagiramungu lacked the support of the majority of his party, which was badly divided. A pro-reform Hutu, he was accused of having sided with the RPF and therefore seen by the extremists as corrupted.

4. Testimony of Eric Gillet. Belgian Senate, *Commission d'enquête parlementaire concernant les evénéments du Rwanda*. Report, 6 December 1997. p. 193.

5. Interview, Patrick Mazimhaka, London, September 1999.

6. Interview, Mahjor-General Paul Kagame, Kigali, October 1997.

7. Bruce D. Jones, 'The Arusha Peace Process', in Howard Adelman and Astri Suhrke (eds), *The Path of a Genocide. The Rwanda Crisis from Uganda to Zaire*, New Brunswick, NJ: Transaction, 1999, p. 141.

8. Contrat pour la fourniture de matériels techniques militaires. Contrat No. 01/93 Dos 0384/06.1.9 Pour l'acheteur: le Ministre de la Défense, Dr James Gasana. Le Ministre des Finances, Marc Rugenera. Pour le vendeur: Dominique Lemonnier. Copy in possession of author.

9. Jones, 'The Arusha Peace Process', p. 135.

10. International Federation of Human Rights (FIDH), Africa Watch, InterAfrican Union of Human Rights, and International Centre of Rights of the Person and of Democratic Development. *Report of the International Commission of Investigation of Human Rights Violations in Rwanda since October 1, 1990 (January 7–21, 1993).*

11. A sub-commission on Prevention of Discrimination and Protection of Minorities was created in 1946 to undertake studies to make recommendations to protect racial, national, religious and linguistic minorities. This sub-commission meets at least once a year. Members are nominated by governments and elected by the Commission on Human Rights but serve in a personal capacity.

12. The USA, UK, France and Canada were members of the commission. Belgium was not.

13. In the first set of confidential discussions with the commission in 1992, the Rwandan judge who appeared for the government was notable for his incompetence. In 1993, the Rwandan government sent a member of the democratic opposition, Agathe Uwilingiyimana, minister of education, who was one of the first politicians to die on the night the genocide began. She gave evidence on 8 March 1993 in Geneva telling delegates that her government was trying its best to rectify the situation.

14. UN Commission on Human Rights, *Report by Mr. B.W. Ndiaye, Special Rapporteur, on his mission to Rwanda from 8–17 April, 1993* (E/CN.4/1994/7/Add. 1) 11 August 1993.

15. Interview, Paul Kagame, Kigali. October 1997.

16. The peace agreement was concluded on 12 July 1992 during the Arusha peace negotiations.

17. Jean-Hervé Bradol, 'Rwanda, Avril–Mai 1994. Limites et Ambiguités de l'Action Humanitaire. Crises Politiques, Massacres et Exodes Massifs', *Le Temps Modernes*, No. 583, 1995, p. 126.

18. Jones, 'The Arusha Peace Process', p. 141.

19. *Report by Mr. B.W. Ndiaye.*

20. Immediately after the genocide, the RPF gave the Special Rapporteur for the UN Commission on Human Rights, René Dégni-Ségui, the names of fifty-five people considered to be the core group of genocidaires. The International Criminal Tribunal for Rwanda later prepared an unofficial list of some 500 people involved. See paragraph 144, Report of the Special Representative of the Commission on Human Rights, 17 September 1999. A provisional list of 220 people who organized the genocide, published by the RPF in July, is reproduced in Guichaoua 1995, pp. 723–7.

6 · Preparing the Genocide

WE may never know the exact moment when the conspirators first conceived the genocide: the moment when a group of ruthless and opinionated people plotted to wipe out entirely those who stood in the way of their power and privilege.

In order to commit genocide, a group of people must make an agreement; this constitutes conspiracy. In the case of the military defendants now awaiting trial in the International Criminal Court in Arusha, the prosecutor appears to have traced the roots of an agreement to December 1991 when President Juvénal Habyarimana set up a commission to identify the enemy, and to advise on what had to be done to defeat it militarily, in the media and politically.[1] A report was produced and extracts from it were circulated among the troops. In one extract the main enemy was defined as follows: 'The Tutsis from inside or outside the country, who are extremists and nostalgic for power; who do not recognize and have never recognized the realities of the Social Revolution of 1959, and are seeking to regain power in Rwanda by any means, including taking up arms.' The secondary enemy was defined as: 'Anyone providing any kind of assistance to the main enemy.' The document specified that the enemy was recruited from within certain social groups, notably: 'The Tutsis inside the country, Hutus who are dissatisfied with the present regime, foreigners married to Tutsi women.' The report was said to have been written by Colonel Théoneste Bagosora.

Bagosora hated Tutsi. He was firmly of the view that the invasion by the RPF had been an attempted take-over by Tutsi and that there was a danger that the RPF would have the support of everyone excluded from power in Rwanda – all Tutsi, as defined by their ID cards, the political opposition and the regime's critics. These people, he warned, were an inherently disloyal 'fifth column'.

The drawing up of lists was an on-going process and was organized immediately after the RPF invasion of October 1990. Later, the army, gendarmerie and local authorities were given orders to prepare new lists or update the existing ones. For the hardliners, the logic and the dynamic of the genocide must have been apparent, even then.

Bagosora epitomised Hutu extremism. He zealously held the view that the struggle in Rwanda was not political but between the Hutu and the Tutsi. Rwanda, he believed, belonged to the Hutu. The Tutsi were invaders, they were naturalized immigrants trying to impose their will. Moreover, all Tutsi were dictatorial, proud, cruel, arrogant, clever and sneaky. Bagosora still defends these views and has written a document to explain them: 'The Tutsi are the masters of deceit, even going as far as comparing themselves with the Jews of Europe to gain the sympathy of this powerful lobby ... but the Tutsi have never had a country of their own ... with their arrogance and pride they are trying to impose their supremacy in the region.'[2] When the Tutsi first arrived in Rwanda, he wrote, they deceived the Hutu, who realized the true nature of the Tutis only when it was too late. Bagosora's version of history involved a Hutu King called Mashira, killed by the Tutsi along with his whole family. The Tutsi had cut off Mashira's genitals and hung them on a drum, the Kalinga, a way of signifying the wiping out of the Hutu rival. Bagosora believed that most of the Hutu kings in the region had died this way. The two 'protagonists' in the 'Rwandan drama' were different people; Bagosora said that, in contrast to the Tutsi, the Hutu were modest, open, loyal, independent and impulsive.

Bagosora comes from a northern middle-class Hutu family from Gisenyi, in the commune of Giciye (the neighbouring commune to Habyarimana's birthplace). The son of a teacher, he was the eldest of six children and went to school in the Petit Séminaire St Pie X in the diocese of Nyundo. The army became his life; on 1 August 1962, he joined the school for officers in Kigali. He made several visits to Belgium for training and, on 11 December 1981, had the singular honour of being chosen to attend the Etudes Militaires Supérieures de l'Ecole de Guerre Française, the first Rwandan to do so. On his return from France, he commanded the Kanombe military camp outside Kigali. Bagosora was ambitious but his rise was far from meteoric. For a time he was out of favour with the Habyarimana entourage for marrying Isabelle Uzanyinzoga, a woman from southern Rwanda. Habyarimana wanted to appoint Bagosora chief of staff but the oppostion members in a coalition government objected to the influence of the northern hardliners in the army and Habyarimana was forced to remove several colonels from the army command. Bagosora was due to retire. Instead, he entered the Ministry of Defence as *directeur de cabinet*, the administrative head.

There are clues to the genesis of a plot in the military intelligence archives in Kigali. It can be traced to two people: Lieutenant-Colonel Anatole Nsengiyumva, the chief of army intelligence (G2) and Colonel Théoneste Bagosora. In July 1992, an extraordinary series of secret reports were written by Nsengiyumva and sent to both the army command and President Habyarimana warning of dire consequences should the RPF (or, as he sometimes writes, 'cockroaches') be allowed to share power. Nsengiyumva informed the president that people were so terrified of Tutsi domination, there was talk of a mass exodus if the Tutsi were allowed to share power.[3] 'Before the people leave the country,' warned Nsengiyumva, 'they will massacre all the Tutsi.' It was a chillingly accurate prediction.

Nsengiyumva warned of dissatisfaction in the army: 'Certain officers are asking whether or not civilians in the government are really capable of taking decisions in the national interest.' The president was advised that he should only pretend to be enthusiastic for the process towards democracy. In a letter copied to Habyarimana there is a warning that army officers would never accept a merger with the RPF; some of the soldiers on the front line were thinking of giving up the fight because the country was being sold out. The nation must prepare for the resumption of hostilities. It must be explained to the allies – France and the USA – that Rwanda was a special case and that the enemy's intention was to seize the power they had lost in 1959 and re-establish the monarchy. Nsengiyumva reported that Tutsi had infiltrated Kigali and that there was a network of saboteurs in place passing counterfeit money.[4]

Bagosora, Nsengiyumva and others set about creating a secret Hutu Power society within the army called Amasasu (the Alliance of Soldiers Provoked by the Age-old Deceitful Acts of Unarists, i.e. monarchists). Amasasu is also the Kinyarwanda word for bullets. In January 1993, as the Arusha peace negotiations progressed, an open letter was sent to Habyarimana by Amasasu, accurately predicting that the RPF was preparing a major attack.

By February 1993 Bagosora was arguing that there must be a plan for civil defence, though his plan bore a startling similiarity to one devised by President Gregoire Kayibanda in 1963. It involved the creation of local 'self-defence' groups, a move which preceded the genocide of Tutsi in December that year. Bagosora was familiar with what had happened, including in his curriculum vitae the fact that in December 1963 he had taken part in 'campaigns' in the Bugesera against 'Inyenzi' (cockroaches).[5] Now, some thirty years later, he was proposing that a 'popular' army be created of local men. They were to be given military training either by the communal police or the military itself. Each cell and each sector must elect men to be responsible for defence; sixty trained men in each commune. There must be co-ordination between the military authorities and the local administration, communal councillors and local police. In a diary found in his house and given to Human Rights Watch, there are details of how many weapons will be needed for this plan. An entry in late February 1993 mentions ordering 2,000 Kalashnikovs to 'bring to 5,000 the number for the communes'. Three to five weapons were to be distributed to each cell, and 'hand-grenades' is written next to a list of six communes. Bagosora was obtaining vehicles and finding storage for weapons. He refers to 'organizing information', and notes that a propaganda campaign, aimed at human rights organizations and the diplomatic corps, is assigned to a former

Rwandan diplomat. He proposes that radio programmes should include the songs of Bikindi, a singer of anti-Tutsi songs.[6]

As we have already seen, Bagosora was a member of the Akazu, the extremist entourage surrounding Agathe Habyarimana, and he had links with members of the French secret service (Direction Générale de la Sécurité Extérieure, DGSE).[7] His brother, Pasteur Musabe, was a director of the Banque Continentale Africaine Rwanda (BACAR).

The idea of arming the population was nothing new. It had already been suggested in 1991 in letters from Colonel Laurent Serubuga, the president's brother-in-law, then in charge of military intelligence. When arming the population, he advised that only people approved by the local authorities should receive arms, warning that army officers were sickened by the creation of political parties and the proliferation of the private press. The enemy was hiding behind freedom of expression as a means to gain power, and the officers wanted a law to stop such abuse of the press.[8]

In January 1993, weapons were distributed to communal police in certain communes in Rwanda. In the Ngoma, for instance, in the prefecture of Butare, eight new Kalashnikovs were added to a supply of twenty-six rifles as part of the civil defence network. By the end of the year there were hidden stockpiles of brand-new machetes, hoes, axes and picks in most communes, and each commune contained members of the Hutu Power militia. The communes were divided into quartiers, each containing a representative of the MRNDD, responsible for ten houses. In the hills of Rwanda, there was constant surveillance by neighbours.

The militia was expanding. There were new recruits from the ever-increasing ranks of the unemployed, and thousands of delinquents were drafted. Some of the weapons purchased in the spending spree on light arms were passed by the armed forces directly to the militia. Some militia leaders were issued with AK47s, after filling out requisition forms; the distribution of grenades did not require paperwork.

From information later acquired by UN peacekeepers, arms had been stockpiled in secret locations in Kigali by senior figures in the Ministry of Defence, eventually to be distributed to the Interahamwe in Kigali. In Gitarama, a town with 150,000 inhabitants, there were 50,000 pistols and rifles, machetes and other arms. By the time the genocide began, 85 tons of munitions are thought to have been distributed.[9] There are documents, discovered in the Banque Nationale du Rwanda, which prove that this was the result of careful advance planning. There are invoices, bank statements, arms contracts, faxes and telexes showing that the most intensive preparations took place in 1993, when half a million machetes and other agricultural tools were purchased and distributed throughout the country, including hundreds and thousands of hoes, axes, hammers and razor blades. Documents prove that this equipment was purchased using quick disbursing loans from western donors who entered into agreements with the regime that the funds should not be used for military or paramilitary purposes.

The machetes came from China, supplied between 1992 and 1994 by a company called Oriental Machinery. The invoices are filed under the heading 'eligible imports'. According to bank records, US$4.6 million was spent on agricultural equipment in 1993 by Rwandan companies not usually concerned with agricultural tools.[10] A significant importer of machetes was Félicien Kabuga, a relation of Habyarimana, whose wealth came from coffee exports and the import of household goods and clothes. Invoices show that most commercial concerns in 1993 imported machetes. A total of US$725,669 was spent on 581,000 machetes; one machete for every third adult Hutu male. All imports to Rwanda had been made easier because the World Bank/IMF had insisted on the liberalization of the import licence system.[11]

Michel Chossudovsky and Pierre Galand, who made a study of bakning records, concluded that without international finance the money would not have been available for the purchase of tools to be distributed to the militia, or for expanding the army, or for substantial arms deals, or for the beer, petrol, clothes and food given to the armed forces, the militia and their families. Simultaneously, the public services collapsed and there was famine and a rise in unemployment.

Despite President Habyarimana's assurances that he was rearming to protect the country, the purchases of weapons entered into by the regime in the two years prior to the genocide included a substantial amount of low-intensity weapons. Small arms – automatic weapons, machine guns, grenades and landmines – are less expensive to buy and maintain and easier to conceal. These weapons contributed to the huge numbers of victims in the genocide, and to the speed of the killing. Although the total arms purchases between 1990 and 1994 were in the region of US$83 million, it is estimated that military expenditure was higher, for many of the purchases were hidden in the government budget.

The first arms deal with Egypt in October 1990 for US$5.889 million was followed by another in December for US$3.511 million. By April 1991, the Rwandan government had spent US$10.861 million on Egyptian weapons. In June 1992, a further US$1.3 million was given to Egypt for weapons. In November 1992, 250 Kalashnikov assault rifles and 25,000 rounds of ammunition were purchased; in February, 1993, 3,000 automatic rifles, AKM guns, each worth US$250 were purchased; later, another deal was signed to include 100,000 rounds of ammunition, and thousands of landmines and grenades.

In December 1991, with a contract in the pipeline worth US$1 million for 82mm bombs, fuses and charges, Egypt felt it necessary to remind the

Rwandans of the importance of keeping the deals secret. Colonel Sami Said told the regime in Kigali that were these arms deals to be made public, Egypt's relations with its allies would be compromised. In order to camouflage the deals, it was proposed that commercial trading should start and Egypt would buy Rwandan tea and coffee. The links between Egypt and Rwanda were strengthened and a military attaché was appointed to Rwanda's embassy in Cairo, which, by 1992, had become increasingly important.[12]

The largest arms deal between Egypt and Rwanda came in March 1992 and was for US$6 million of light weapons and small arms. The deal included 450 Kalashnikov rifles, 2,000 rocket-propelled grenades, 16,000 mortar shells and more than three million rounds of small arms ammunition.[13] This time Rwanda asked if it would be possible to pay in instalments. Egypt expressed reservations, insisting there be a guarantee of payment, and the French state-owned bank, Crédit Lyonnais, agreed to act as guarantor.[14] An arrangement was made for the money to be paid in $1 million cash instalments in London, deposited by the Rwandese government into a Crédit Lyonnais bank in Regent Street, into the account of the office of the Egyptian defence attaché in London. The payments were spread over four years. A further million dollars was accounted for in the delivery of Rwandan tea which was to arrive in Cairo at the end of 1993.

Six weeks before the genocide, in February 1994, another contract was concluded between the Ministry of Defence in Cairo and the Rwandese government for $1 million of mortars and ammunition. Rwanda asked for urgent delivery. For the regime in Kigali, the Rwandan embassy in Cairo was pivotal. During the genocide, some US$1.4 million were transferred there, the money coming from the Banque Nationale du Rwanda, passing through the Rwandan embassy in Nairobi, then on to Cairo where it was paid into the Commercial International Bank of Egypt. Whether or not this money was to pay for weapons has never been ascertained.[15]

South African dealers sold arms worth US$56.263 to Rwanda between 29 October 1990 and 29 May 1991. In 1991, substantial international financial aid had been promised under the structural adjustment programme (SAP) amounting to more than US$170 million, including US$46 million from the European Community, $41 million from the IMF, $25 million from the USA and $17 million from Belgium.[16] The weapons imports from South Africa included 20,000 R-4 rifles and 10,000 hand-grenades, machine guns, and 1.5 million rounds of ammunition for R-4 rifles. The money for these arms was paid into banks in Brussels, the Belgolaise, the Banque Nationale de Paris, and an account in the Volkskas Bank in Pretoria. The Chinese also provided weapons, but under a credit scheme of US$1 million for mortars, machine guns, multiple rocket launchers and grenades.

For three years, the Hutu Power regime used every accounting trick in the book to get enough money to pay for weapons. In bank records there are flagrant manipulations of funds; sometimes the same invoices are used two or three times to get at money from different donors. The Rwandan government's auditor, in a secret report to the Rwandan government, later complained: 'On several occasions double payments have been made into Rwandese commercial banks for the same import.' The regime even sold petrol on the open market to get money for the armed forces. Experts who studied the paper trail conclude that to arm and equip the people of Rwanda cost US$112 million.

It is a mystery why the five missions sent by the World Bank to follow and supervise the SAP between June 1991 and October 1993 apparently failed to notice all this activity. Only in December 1993 did the World Bank suspend payment of a tranche of money because 'certain objectives had not been met', but even then it had already deposited, in a special account in the Banque Bruxelles Lambert, funds which would continue to be used by regime until 31 May 1994 while the genocide was carried out.

Whatever the procedures in place, the unprecedented purchases of weapons, of machetes and other tools, using money provided under quick disbursing loans, seem to have passed through the system unnoticed. The arms purchases are a different matter. Several times World Bank officials raised the issue of the militarization of Rwanda with the regime. Indeed, the President of the World Bank, Lewis Preston, wrote to Habyarimana to raise the matter of military spending at a time when there was famine in the south and warnings from the International Committee of the Red Cross and the Food and Agriculture Organization that health and welfare provision in Rwanda were collapsing. This letter was sent out in April 1992, one month after the Rwandan government had concluded the $6 million deal with Egypt that had benefited from a guarantee from Crédit Lynonnais. In his reply, Habyarimana wrote that the increase in military expenditure was due to the civil war with the RPF and the need to defend the country from aggression from Uganda. One fatal blow from the RPF and all the efforts and sacrifice made by the Rwandan people to adhere to the World Bank programme would be ruined. Habyarimana assured Preston that his aim was progressively to reduce military expenditure. In his reply, Preston reminded Habyarimana that the World Bank had agreed a safety-net for the first stage of the SAP in order to protect those who were the most disadvantaged in the short term and to help ease poverty. 'I take note of your intention to reduce military expenditure and I encourage you to do it urgently,' he wrote.

The IMF seems to have been aware of military spending and a confidential briefing paper from 1992 betrays a sense of hopelessness about the continuing ethnic conflict, for it did not look as though the objectives of the IMF mission could be achieved. Even if hostilities ceased, it would take a long time to demobilize military personnel. The IMF mission decided to examine how to improve control over the government's spending.

At the end of 1992 the World Bank stopped negotiating with the regime.[17] At a hastily convened government meeting in Kigali, it was decided to cancel the latest arms deal and look for helpful gestures. The government decreed a reduction in the food rations given to soldiers and to their families, and a lowering of the salaries of civil servants. The money saved was channelled to the military and the militia; even lorries, purchased as agricultural imports, were diverted to the army. In Kigali, the militia used hospital vehicles, filling them with petrol at the Ministry of Health's expense.

Although the SAP was based on the assumption that military spending would be kept under control, the budget of the minister of defence steadily increased. Yet in Paris in June 1993, during a World Bank conference, a further US$120.3 million for Rwanda was agreed. Because the global financial institutions operate in secrecy we may never know what was said about Rwanda at this conference. It would appear that a plea was made in favour of the regime by a World Bank official who reminded the other delegates that in Rwanda at least the government was in control of the country.[18]

Notes

1. Document from Case no. ICTR 96.7.D. The Prosecutor of the International Criminal Tribunal for Rwanda against Théoneste Bagosora.

2. Col. BEM Théoneste Bagosora, 'L'Assassinat du President Habyarimana ou l'Ultime Opération du Tutsi pour sa reconquête du pouvoir par la force au Rwanda', unpublished. In possession of the author.

3. The letters: Ministère de la Défense Nationale. Armée Rwandaise. Etat-Major. G2 Secret. Note au Chef. EM AR Objet: Sûreté Intérieure de l'Etat. Letter dated 2 July 1992; Objet: Etat d'esprit des militaries et de la population civile. 27 July 1992. Signed: A. Nsengiyumva Lt. Col. Copie: SEM le Président de la Republique. In possession of the author.

4. Nsengiyumva was arrested in Cameroon in March 1996. He is awaiting trial.

5. Bagosora, 'L'Assassinat du Président Habyarimana'.

6. Human Rights Watch/Fédération Internationale des Ligues des Droits de l'Homme, *Leave none to tell the story. Genocide in Rwanda*, 1999, p. 107.

7. Interview with witnesses by ICTR investigator, Kigali, 1997.

8. Letters dated 29 November 1991 and 12 October 1991. Copies in possession of the author.

9. Jacques Castonguay, *Les Casques Bleus au Rwanda*, Paris: Editions l'Harmattan, 1998, p. 68.

10. Pierre Galand and Michel Choussudovsky, *L'Usage de la Dette Extérieure du Rwanda (1990/1994) La Responsabilité des Bailleurs de Fonds. Analyse et Recommandations*. Preliminary report. Brussels and Ottawa, November 1996, unpublished. In possession of the author. A list of machete and agricultural tools importers is listed in this report together with invoice amounts. Most companies imported no tools at all until 1993, when they became involved in importing huge amounts.

11. IMF Rwanda. Briefing Paper – 1992 Article IV Consultation and Discussions on a Second Annual Arrangement. May 14, 1992.Confidential. In possession of the author.

12. In December 1991, Colonel A. Ndindiliyimana went to Cairo. In February 1992, President Habyarimana visited Cairo on a two-day official visit. Documents Cairo Embassy. In possession of the author.

13. United States Congress, Committee on International Relations, House of Represententives, Rwanda: Genocide and the Continuing Cycle of Violence. Hearing before the Subcommittee on International Operations and Human Rights, 5 May 1998. Addendum, *The Nature of the Beast – Arms Trafficking to the Great Lakes Region of Africa*, Kathi Austen.

14. See Gérard Prunier, *The Rwanda Crisis 1959–1994. History of a Genocide*, London: Hurst and Company, 1995, p. 148. In France, after the legislative election of March 1993, the new conservative majority in the French parliament started to investigate the operation of Crédit Lyonnais and found it to have undertaken a number of operations which were politically motivated and without justifiable business reasons. Accounts were in the red for over $9 billion. Its general manager, Jean-Yves Haberer, was dismissed. (See *Le Nouvel Observateur*, 29 September–5 October 1994.)

15. During the genocide, Cairo airport was used as a staging post for arms deliveries to Rwanda; a Boeing 707, registered in Nairobi and chartered by the British company Mil-Tec, called in at Cairo.

16. Regional Survey of the World, *Africa South of the Sahara*, 1994.

17. Funds were blocked for some months between 1992 and 1993 and resumed after signing of the Arusha Accords.

18. Interview, Washington, January 1998.

7 · The Hate Radio: Radio-Télévision Libre des Mille Collines

JUST one month before the triumphant signing ceremony for the Arusha Accords on 8 July 1993, a new radio station called Radio-Télévision Libre des Mille Collines (RTLMC) began broadcasting in Rwanda. It was quickly dismissed as a joke by the diplomats in Kigali. The station was rowdy and used street language, there were disc jockeys, pop music and phone-ins. Sometimes the announcers were drunk, particularly Noël Hitimana, whose jokes became offensive, vulgar and crude.[1] RTLMC was designed to appeal to the unemployed, the delinquents, and the gangs of thugs in the militia. It broadcast mainly in Kinyarwanda and it revolutionized Rwandan broadcasting.

Using the FM frequency, the radio station carried no factual reports but there were commentaries and lengthy interviews. Its style was in direct contrast to that of the only other station in Rwanda, the government-owned Radio Rwanda, which favoured a formal approach.

The planning for RTLMC started in November 1992, when Ferdinand Nahimana, the propagandist and historian, and Joseph Serugendu, the technician responsible for Radio Rwanda, travelled to Brussels to look for equipment. It was Nahimana who inspired the style of RTLMC, planning news bulletins to instil fear and to incite to murder during the massacres in Bugesera in 1992. Eight journalists went to work for RTLMC, all of whom had previously worked for pro-MRNDD newspapers or for the government. Not all programmes were in Kinyarwanda: there was a French-language programme presented by former teacher George Ruggiu, a Belgian citizen.[2]

The broadcasting studios of RTLMC were connected to the electric generators of the presidential palace[3] and programmes were relayed to all parts of the country via a network of transmitters on two frequencies, the transmitters owned and operated by the government's Radio Rwanda. RTLMC began broadcasting at a time when transistor radios suddenly became cheap and available in Rwanda. In a largely illiterate population, the radio station soon had a very large audience who found it immensely entertaining. The documents of incorporation for RTLMC contain a most extraordinary clause stating that the radio station was set up 'to create harmonious development in Rwandese society', to contribute to the education of the people and to transmit true, objective information. The founders of RTLMC were apparently 'encouraged by progress towards democracy'.[4] Nothing could have been further from the truth. RTLMC was financed by Hutu extremists. Its list of shareholders, some twenty-five pages, starting with Habyarimana, contain all the members of the Akazu.[5] There were 20,000 shares at 5,000 Rwanda francs each. No one could own more than 1,000 shares and the largest shareholder was the president. The radio was incorporated on 8 April 1993 as a jointly funded company with fifty original shareholders. The list of shareholders contains the names of businessmen, bank managers, journalists, army officers and government officials. All of them played a significant role in the genocide. One shareholder was a singer, Simon Bikindi, known for his anti-Tutsi songs played during pro-Hutu rallies.

The purpose of the new radio station was to prepare the people of Rwanda for genocide. A propaganda weapon unlike any other, its campaign was to demonize the Tutsi, and to circumvent key clauses in the Arusha Accords that barred both sides from incitement to violence and hate.

The pro-Hutu message of RTLMC was anti-Arusha and anti-Tutsi. RTLMC would eventually broadcast the names of certain government opponents, individuals who 'deserved to die'. Its announcers told the people that all supporters of the Tutsi RPF were traitors, the Tutsi were lazy foreign invaders who refused to work the land. 'I listened to RTLMC', said a survivor, 'because if you were mentioned over the airways, you were sure to be carted off a short time later by the Interahamwe. You knew you had to change your address at once.'[6] On 26 November 1993 an announcer called for the assassination of Agathe Uwilingiyimana, the pro-democracy opposition politician and prime minister in the coalition government.

It was impossible to persuade diplomats in Kigali to take RTLMC seriously. The French and American ambassadors were against taking action to stop its broadcasts. David Rawson, the US ambassador, said that its euphemisms were subject to various interpretations. The USA, he said, believed in freedom of speech.[7] The human rights community was aware of the role of RTLMC: when, on 6 August 1993, Habyarimana went to Brussels for the funeral of King Baudouin, a human rights group issued a press release saying that Habyarimana was playing a double game and that while ostensibly supporting the peace deal he was in fact a shareholder in a radio station inciting racial hatred.

The president of the board of directors of RTLMC was Félicien Kabuga, industrialist and financial adviser to Habyarimana, who helped to finance the Interahamwe. His import company was used to purchase machetes from China. He also financed *Kangura*, a weekly newspaper with a relatively small circulation but which had the support of powerful government and military figures. *Kangura* carried hate-propaganda about Tutsi who 'owned a disproportionate amount of wealth', and its editorials promised 'the defence of the majority people'. When the Arusha Accords were signed, Kangura warned its readers that the agreement was a Tutsi plot. For those who found themselves denounced in its pages, the consequences could be fatal: 'Let us learn about the Inkotanyi (Tutsi) plans and let us exterminate every last one of them' (*Kangura* 9, February 1991).[8] In December 1990, *Kangura* published the famous Hutu Ten Commandments which were instructions to mistreat and discriminate against Tutsi.[9] Copies of *Kangura* were read aloud at public meetings and at the rallies of the Interahamwe who, wearing their black and yellow pyjama-suits and chanting 'Pawa, Pawa', blew whistles and unfurled giant banners bearing the face of Juvenal Habyarimana.

The Belgian ambassador in Kigali, Johan Swinnen, warned Brussels several times about RTLMC destabilizing the country and admitted later that not enough was done to try to neutralize the broadcasts.[10] He knew of the extremists' involvement and, in January 1994, three months before the genocide started, he informed the Foreign Ministry. Swinnen wanted the broadcasts of RTLMC to be translated from Kinyarwanda (there were only two hours of French programmes every day), but there were too few embassy staff to translate and analyse all the transmissions. One Belgian military intelligence officer, Lieutenant Mark Nees, remains convinced that if RTLMC had been prevented from broadcasting the genocide could have been limited, if not avoided.[11] Swinnen raised the issue of the radio station when he met Habyarimana on 3 March just over a month before the 1994 genocide began. He told the president that action against RTLMC was essential if the Arusha Accords were to succeed.

According to RTLMC, the final war could not be won by the army alone; it required the participation of the entire Rwandan population. In one telling broadcast after the genocide had started, an announcer said: 'Stand up, take action ... without worrying about international opinion.'[12]

Notes

1. *Broadcasting Genocide: Censorship, Propaganda and State-sponsored Violence in Rwanda 1990–1994*, Article 19, pp. 85–6, International Centre Against Censorship, London, October 1996.

2. In June 2000, the International Criminal Tribunal for Rwanda sentenced Ruggiu to twelve years on two counts of directly and publicly inciting people to commit genocide.

3. Frank Chalk, 'Hate Radio in Rwanda', in Howard Adelman and Astri Suhrke (eds), *The Path of a Genocide. The Rwanda Crisis from Uganda to Zaire*, New Brunswick, NJ: Transaction, 1999, p. 96.

4. Radio-Télévision Libre des Mille Collines Société Anonyme (RTLMC SA), Statutes.

5. Liste des Actionnaires de la Radio-Télévision des Mille Collines (RTLMC), unpublished. In possession of the author.

6. Reporters sans Frontières, 'Rwanda: Médias de la haine ou presse démocratique?' Rapport de mission, 16–24 September 1994.

7. *Evaluation of Emergency Assistance to Rwanda: Lessons from the Rwanda Experience.* Joint Evaluation of Emergency Assistance to Rwands. Copenhagen, 1996, Chapter 2, p. 19.

8. In December 1993 *Kangura* predicted that President Habyarimana would be assassinated, not by a Tutsi but by a Hutu. 'There is no one more worried than Habyarimana himself,' *Kangura* told its readers. *Kangura*, No. 53, December 1993. See Guichaoua, *Les Crises Politiques au Burundi et au Rwanda (1993–1994)*. Université des Sciences et Technologies de Lille. Paris: Karthala, 1995.

9. The first three commandments referred to Tutsi women; the first commandment forbade marriage between Hutu and Tutsi because every Tutsi woman was a traitor and Hutu girls made more suitable mothers. There was enormous propaganda against Tutsi women in the build-up to genocide and the hatred mobilized allowed the most inhumane acts of sexual violence to take place. In Rwanda, women could not inherit land or take out a loan and a wife could not work without the authorization of her husband.

10. Belgian Senate, *Commission d'enquête parlementaire concernant les événements du Rwanda*, Report, 6 December 1997, p. 607.

11. Ibid., p. 599.

12. *Broadcasting Genocide*, p. 114.

8 · The New World Order and High Hopes for a UN Success

THE New World Order which was to be created at the end of the Cold War was publicly envisioned by presidents Bush and Gorbachev as being founded on the rule of law and the principle of collective security enshrined in the UN Charter. The use of military force by the Security Council, foreseen by the founders of the UN, was to be an essential element. So enthusiastic was the international community about the New World Order that the UN was given ambitious new tasks: nation building and peace enforcement, often popularly lumped together under the heading 'peacekeeping'.

In January 1992, the UN Security Council held its first meeting at summit level, a meeting billed as 'an unprecedented recommitment ... to the purposes and principles of the Charter'. It was claimed as a British initiative. Britain held the council presidency and Prime Minister John Major faced an election at home. The French delegation said the meeting was President Mitterrand's idea.

'Now that the Cold War is over,' British Foreign Secretary Douglas Hurd had written on 13 January in the *Guardian*, 'the UN, and particularly the Security Council, is working as the founding fathers intended.' Major spoke grandly of a reaffirmation of the principles of collective security and the need for preventive diplomacy. 'The aim must be to equip the UN to lead in crisis prevention,' he said. The only concrete suggestion was a request to the new Egyptian UN Secretary-General, Boutros Boutros-Ghali, to formulate some ideas to expand peacekeeping, peace enforcing and preventive diplomacy.

No Secretary-General had ever taken the helm of the UN at a more propitious time than Boutros Boutros-Ghali – not even the first in 1945. For years the Secretary-General had been obliged to act in the face of Council paralysis and ill-will, but now, in the post-Cold War world in January 1992, the Security Council was unified at last. This presented a number of opportunities. Boutros-Ghali said that if he had been offered the job five years before, he would have turned it down: 'The UN then was a dead horse, but after the end of the Cold War, the UN has a special position.'[1] He displayed great ambition for this newly relevant world organization and said that it was time to shift the UN's emphasis from world development to human rights. Boutros-Ghali had been one of the leading advocates in 1978 for an African Charter of Human Rights, a proposal which was adopted with the specific inclusion of the rights of peoples as well as of individuals. He also wanted an expansion of peacekeeping and for the UN to play an enhanced role in the creation of democracy around the world. The UN must become involved in national reconciliation processes, the restructuring and the rehabilitation of governments.

Some UN colleagues were sceptical about Boutros-Ghali's vision of global leadership. His style was forthright, outspoken and confrontational. Some thought that he should rather have pursued a role complementary to that of the Security Council; instead, he began to compete with it, leading to a falling out with the organization's most powerful member state, America.[2] The USA had abstained on the vote for him in the Security Council as President George Bush had wanted Prince Sadruddin Aga Khan to be the next Secretary-General. Boutros-Ghali, though, had the support of another permanent member of the Security Council, France. He was a personal friend of President François Mitterrand.[3] On the day of his selection – 21 November 1991 – Boutros-Ghali was in Bonn. After telephoning President Mubarak he had telephoned Mitterrand to thank him. 'He seemed to feel a personal victory in my election,' Boutros-Ghali later wrote about this moment.[4]

For France, there was no better outcome. It was looking for a greater role in the newly revitalized post-Cold War Security Council, and the appointment of a francophone as Secretary-General was something of a coup. Of the five permanent members in the Security Council, only France had actively supported his candidacy. Boutros-Ghali could rely on French support, not just because of his friendship with Mitterrand, but because he had facilitated Egyptian entry into Francophonie, the world-wide association of nations which share the French language, an organization allowing France to pursue its interests and influence via a cultural and linguistic crusade.

To the rest of the world, Boutros-Ghali would be portrayed as a neutral, a man of the Third World, an African Arab, a Coptic Christian married to an Egyptian Jew, a man who spoke French. At sixty-eight his age was against him, but doubts were dismissed after President Bush's White House doctor gave him a clean bill of health.[5]

Boutros-Ghali had begun his campaign for the job of Secretary-General in 1991 with a tour of Africa. It was familiar territory. As the president of Egypt's Society of African Studies, he had known African leaders for fifteen years and had created a special fund for co-operation in Africa under his direction, with a budget of millions of Egyptian pounds which enabled him to send hundreds of Egyptian experts to African countries.[6] Even so there was an undercurrent of resentment among some diplomats from sub-Saharan African countries because Boutros-Ghali was the only light-skinned Arab African on the list of African candidates and he lacked the whole-hearted support of the Organization of African Unity (OAU), which had failed to make a choice from among seven other African candidates. There was the complication, too, of the rivalry between two of the five permanent members of the Security Council, France and Britain, specifically over which region of the African continent – Francophone or Anglophone – should provide the candidate. Four of the seven African candidates for the job were from English-speaking Africa, but Boutros-Ghali also had the backing of the Arab League, which had twenty-one seats in the General Assembly. By August 1991, he had the promise of support from at least eighty-six assembly votes, quite clearly a majority, a factor which the Security Council would take into account when it made its selection. President Mubarak gently reminded the Bush administration that Egypt had been a leading ally during the Gulf War. For Egypt, the candidature of Boutros-Ghali was a matter of national pride.

Boutros-Ghali, described as a radical anti-colonialist, is a French-educated intellectual and scholar. He studied at the Sorbonne in Paris, receiving a doctorate in international law in 1949. He had been brought into government in 1977 as an international relations expert when he was a professor at Cairo University. He was a Fulbright research scholar at Columbia University and director of the research centre at The Hague Academy of International Law. Boutros-Ghali was one of the few Egyptian officials who accompanied President Sadat on his historic trip to Jerusalem.

After the assassination of Sadat in 1981, Boutros-Ghali transferred his loyalty to his successor, Hosni Mubarak, and was minister of state for foreign affairs for fourteen years but, as a member of the country's influential Coptic Christian minority, he could go no higher. The Islamic lobby would not tolerate a Coptic Christian historian as prime minister. In 1991, the year he was lobbying to become UN Secretary-General, Mubarak appointed him deputy prime minister for international affairs. Boutros-Ghali's nomination as Secretary-General was, according to the president of the Chamber of Deputies, Fathi Sorour, 'an honour for each Egyptian, each Arab, each African'.

Boutros-Ghali promised that because of his decades of involvement with the economic, political and diplomatic problems of Africa, he would try to advance the cause of the continent throughout his term in office. Without development, conflict in Africa would become endemic. He would preside over the UN's fiftieth anniversary in 1995, by which time he wanted the UN to have undergone a fundamental renewal: there was 'a fervent desire to raise the banner of peace'. He said that the course now decided would determine the UN's future for the next generation. Not since the end of the Second World War had the expectations of the world's people depended so much upon the capacity of the UN. 'A better world is within our reach. It is time to move forward ... towards the realization of the vast potential of this organisation, and to bring new life to the world of the Charter,' he wrote.

After the new beginning, and the triumphant Security Council summit in January 1992, the five veto-wielding nations planned another Security Council summit for January 1995 to start the celebrations for the fiftieth anniversary year. However, events during the next three years ensured that this summit would never take place.

The request to the Security Council to provide peacekeepers for Rwanda was greeted with little enthusiasm. By March 1993, when France first suggested the idea, the UK and the USA were arguing that the UN was overstretched. There were then twelve UN peacekeeping missions world-wide,[7] and America was liable for 30 per cent of the UN's total peacekeeping bill. Congress was reluctant to appropriate money for the UN at a time when the cost of the UN Transitional Authority in Cambodia (UNTAC) was at issue. This proved to be the most expensive mission ever, with the UN assuming executive power for the country and overseeing elections. There had been 22,000 people serving in Cambodia – UN troops, police monitors, election officials and civilian administrators – at a cost of $2 billion. UNTAC's reputation for extravagance and corruption was so bad that a board of inquiry into its financial mismanagement had been set up.

The dramatic increase in calls for UN help was well known. The peacekeeping budget had gone from $600 million to $3 billion. In addition, the scope of missions had expanded from ceasefire monitoring and truce observations to include electorial support, human rights monitoring, military demobilization, de-mining, humanitarian support, and civilian police monitoring.[8]

Then there had been the historic precedent of intervention in Somalia, when the Security Council had invoked Chapter VII and created a military intervention for humanitarian purposes, the first time that all necessary means were given to establish a secure environment for the delivery of aid to the starving. This was the first time western powers were to intervene in an African state, justifying such action on humanitarian grounds. When on 9 December 1992 American troops stormed Somali beaches in the glare of television lights, there had seemed no limit to international humanitarianism. The outgoing President George Bush, who had decided this mission, had boasted: 'Only the United States has the global reach to place a large security force on the ground in such a distant place quickly and efficiently and, thus, save thousands of innocents from death.'[9] Bush sent 28,000 American soldiers to Somalia and a further 17,000 came from twenty other countries. An estimatated 1.5 million people were starving to death and some 4.5 million more were threatened with malnutrition. Suffering the effects of a barbaric civil war, Somalia was classified as the single worst humanitarian crisis in the world. There were warlords, wild marauding thugs, preventing the delivery of aid; youths with machine guns drove about in 'technicals' (jeeps and trucks armed with anti-aircraft guns and rocket launchers), in control of the streets as though in a *Mad Max* movie. There had been an unsuccessful UN peacekeeping mission in Somalia and Bush's Operation Restore Hope was planned to stabilize the situation quickly. It did not.

Always intended to be of limited duration, in March 1993, the American-led operation in Somalia was transferred to a multinational force under direct UN command. Unlike the previous American-led operation, the UN mission was much more ambitious and was mandated not only for the protection of relief supplies but, on the insistence of the Americans, it was also intended to compel the Somali militia to disarm. The mission was created with a Chapter VII mandate, the enforcement powers of the Charter, in resolution 814 of 26 March 1993. In this resolution the Council had determined that the UN mission would restore law and order.

So enthusiastic was the USA for resolution 814 that its ambassador to the UN, Madeleine Albright, said the UN was to 'embark on an unprecedented enterprise aimed at nothing less than the restoration of an entire country as a proud, functioning and viable member of the community of nations'. It was historic. The UN would be intervening without the consent of the parties.

In spite of the rhetoric, in reality the UN mission was desperately understaffed and ill-equipped. On 3 June 1993, twenty-three Pakistani peacekeepers lost their lives, and fifty more were seriously injured because of a lack of adequate equipment while trying to inspect a weapons dump. It was the highest peacekeeping casualty figure since the Congo. In response, and with the enthusiastic endorsement of Albright, the Council mandated that the warlord held responsible for these deaths should be arrested. On 3 October 1993, in an effort to do just that, eighteen US elite troops under US command, the Rangers, were killed in Mogadishu. Many more US troops were wounded and others were trapped by jeering and armed mobs. Their rescue was effected one by one, and only with the help of peacekeepers from Malaya and Turkey who were driving Pakistani tanks. The fiasco was the greatest military humiliation for America since Vietnam. Although this was an operation initiated and carried out without even informing, let alone consulting, the UN forces on the ground, the UN was blamed. The warlords were jubilant when America announced it was withdrawing all its forces from Somalia and urged all western nations to do the same.

Congress prepared a Peace Powers Act to make it impossible for the president to commit troops to UN operations. The administration was accused of turning US foreign policy over to feckless UN bureaucrats. 'We must stop placing the agenda of the UN before the interests of the US,' said the Senate Republican leader, Bob Dole. No American should be asked to sacrifice his or her life for a purpose not related to the defence, or in the interests of, the United States. The number of Somalis killed during US military operations in Mogadishu is unknown. 'It became', said one UN lawyer in New York, 'a rogue operation.'

The Security Council commissioned its own report into what had happened in Somalia, and when the report was finalized Council members tried to suppress it[10] for its conclusion was that the council had lost control of the mission.[11] There had been a false assessment of the capability of the Somali fighters, and a lack of intelligence-gathering capability. The Council report recommended that never again should the UN undertake enforcement action within internal conflicts of states; force should be applied only as the ultimate means after all peaceful remedies had been exhausted. The UN did not have the expertise, structure or resources to control forces in combat. 'The international community will be very careful in future,' said a peacekeeping official. 'We've learned ... that [troop-contributing] states don't want to take casualties ... you can't do coercive disarmament.'[12]

The American soldiers who died in Somalia were killed two days before the Council was due to vote on whether or not the UN would provide peacekeepers for Rwanda. It was a grave accident of timing.

Boutros Boutros-Ghali lobbied hard for a UN mission for Rwanda. He argued that what Rwanda needed was not peace enforcement, as in Somalia, but traditional peacekeeping. In a report to the Council, Boutros-Ghali outlined a concept of the operation and a deployment schedule, although this was much changed from the report prepared by the reconnaissance team in August 1993.[13]

Nevertheless, the report was welcomed as clear and realistic. There were passionate arguments in favour. Nigeria's ambassador, Ibrahim Gambari, said that Rwanda was small and pathetic, one of the poorest countries in the world. America had encouraged Rwanda to democratize and there was a moral obligation to see Rwanda through its transition.[14] The Arusha Accords were Rwanda's last, best hope.

The result was compromise. On 5 October the Security Council passed resolution 872, mandating a small and cheap peacekeeping mission for Rwanda. The decision was based on the assumption that both sides would hold to their side of the Arusha bargain. It was a half-hearted commitment. The Americans had wanted only a symbolic presence of 100 soldiers, arguing that there must be economy. The US government owed the UN $900 million in unpaid assessments for regular and peacekeeping expenses. Congress, approving the 1994 budget, had just killed off a proposed peacekeeping contingency fund that was intended to allow the USA to contribute emergency start-up funds for peacekeeping operations.[15] To cut costs further, the Americans argued for a reduction in role of the peacekeepers and, with the support of Russia and the UK, the

Arusha Accords were gutted. Under the terms of Arusha, the peacekeepers were to ensure security throughout the country but the Council decided that the peacekeepers should 'assist in ensuring the security of the city Kigali'. Under Arusha, the peacekeepers were to confiscate arms – 'the tracking of arm caches and neutralization of armed gangs throughout the country' – but the Americans would have none of it. The operation was strictly peacekeeping. Peacekeepers observe, they mediate. They do not seize weapons.

The Arusha Accords specified that the peacekeepers should assist in providing the security of the refugees returning home, yet the eventual mandate for the peacekeepers in Rwanda was 'to monitor the process of repatriation'. Secretariat officials said later it would have been useless at this stage to try to persuade the Council to approve a mandate more in line with the Accords.[16]

The UN mission was planned in four phases: phase one was the withdrawal of French troops and the installation of RPF soldiers in Kigali; phase two was the installation of a transitional government to last three months; phase three was disengagement, demobilization and integration of the armed forces; and phase four was to ensure a secure environment for national elections, an operation planned to last eleven months.

Both diplomats and officials at UN headquarters seem to have convinced themselves that Rwanda would be a success. So high were their hopes that some believed the mission for Rwanda would salvage the UN's battered reputation. It was an attitude that led to false political assumptions and unsound military decisions. The New Zealand ambassador, Colin Keating, who had a non-permanent seat on the Council, later blamed officials in the secretariat for their optimism and said they had been very discreet with their information about Rwanda. 'Perhaps they felt their hands were tied,' he said. The non-permanent members of the Security Council came to see Rwanda not as the smouldering volcano that it really was, but rather as a small civil war. The situation was much more complex and dangerous than was ever revealed to the Council whose non-permanent members, in ignorance, were completely won over by the Arusha process and even more convinced by the joint Rwandan government–RPF delegation that came to New York. They saw only the positive: the end of the civil war.[17]

After the Council's decision to create a UN mission for Rwanda, President Habyarimana expressed his gratitude in a speech to the UN General Assembly. 'My country's recovery', he said, 'depends on the generosity of the international community.' He was exactly right.

Notes

1. 'New Chief of UN Pyramid', Profile, Boutros Boutros-Ghali, *Observer*, 24 November 1991.

2. A former Assistant Secretary-General, Giadomenico Picco, wrote a strong criticism of Boutros-Ghali in *Japan Times*, 10 November 1996.

3. Boutros Boutros-Ghali, *Unvanquished. A US–UN Saga*, London: I.B.Tauris, 1999, p. 9.

4. Ibid., p. 23.

5. *Secretariat News*, September 1991.

6. Boutros-Ghali, *Unvanquished*, p. 7.

7. The missions were: UNPROFOR (former Yugoslavia); UNOSOM II (Somalia); UNOMOZ (Mozambique); UNIFIL (Lebanon); UNICYP (Cyprus); UNIKOM (Iraq Kuwait); UNDOF (Golan Heights); MINURSO (Western Sahara); ONUSAL (El Salvador); UNTSO (Israel Palestine); UNAVEM (Angola); UNMOGIP (India Pakistan).

8. UN General Assembly, *Effective planning, budgeting and administration of peace-keeping operations*. Report of the Secretary-General, A/48/1994, 25 May 1994. Nearly all post-Cold War operations concerned the transition from civil war to civil society: Namibia (UNTAG); Cambodia (UNTAC); El Salvador (ONUSAL); and Haiti (UNMIH). El Salvador, Mozambique and Namibia were successful although a peacful solution for Angola remained impossible because of the recalcitrance and the militarization, of one of the parties involved.

9. US Department of State Dispatch, Address to the Nation. Washington DC, 4 December 1992.

10. In October 1993, the non-permanent members of the Security Council were: Cap Verde, Djibouti, Japan, Morocco, Pakistan, Hungary, Brazil, Venezuela, New Zealand and Spain.

11. UN Security Council, *Report of the Commission of Inquiry Established Pursuant to Security Council Resolution 885 (1993)*, 4 February 1994.

12. Interview, Secretariat official, DPKO, July 1994.

13. Report of the Secretary-General on Rwanda, requesting establishment of a UN Assistance Mission for Rwanda (UNAMIR) and the Integration of UNOMUR into UNAMIR (S/26488) 24 September 1993. *The United Nations and Rwanda, 1993–1996*, UN Blue Book series, Vol. 10, 1996, New York: UN Department of Public Information, p. 221.

14. American diplomats in Rwanda funded conferences on constitutional reform and paid for printing the government's constitutional literature. The USA encouraged human rights groups.

15. Steven A. Dimoff, 'Congress's Budget-Cutting Fervor Threatens US standing at UN', *Interdependent* 19, Autumn 1993. United Nations Association of the USA.

16. Interviews, DPKO, March 1996.

17. Statement, 'The Security Council Role in the Rwanda Crisis', by Ambassador Colin Keating, Permanent Representative of New Zealand to the UN, at Comprehensive Seminar on Lessons Learned from UNAMIR, 12 June 1996. Unpublished. In possession of the author.

9 · Peacekeepers: the UN Arrives

IN peacekeeping, the transition from dictatorship to democracy is the most dangerous time. It is used by extremists to make the most of a vacuum. Any delay or any hint of a lack of commitment serves only to encourage the hardliners who do not want peace.

Under the Arusha Accords, a transitional government was to hold power in Rwanda until democratic elections, and during this period peacekeepers were to monitor compliance. Any delay in the arrival of the peacekeepers or failure to inaugurate the broad-based transitional government, and the peace agreement, planned to run to a strict timetable, could be derailed. Timing was crucial. Under the Accords a neutral force was to be established in Kigali by 10 September – just thirty-seven days after the Accords were signed. This defied all logic. The Security Council in New York had not yet decided to provide UN resources for Rwanda, had not even met to decide the issue. In any event, the average time for the UN to deploy a peacekeeping operation was about six months. Nor were individual governments keen to commit troops for Rwanda. Kofi Annan, Under-Secretary-General and head of the UN's Department of Peacekeeping Operations (DPKO), described as 'incessant' the problems of getting soldiers to serve in Rwanda.[1]

France offered soldiers, but the RPF was, naturally, opposed. In the end only Belgium, the former colonial power, came forward with a battalion of 400 of all ranks, and then Bangladesh offered 940 personnel, including soldiers, logisticians, military police and medical staff, and Ghana offered 800 soldiers. The force commander was Brigadier-General Roméo A. Dallaire, a Canadian.[2] He led a UN reconnaissance mission to Rwanda in August 1993 to examine the functions and resources needed. Initially Dallaire had gone to UN headquarters, where he discovered how low a priority this mission held: there was no paperwork available in the secretariat about the political and military situation in the country, and no reports on the Arusha Accords, although officials from the UN had been present during negotiations. There was more interest shown in Liberia, Somalia, former Yugoslavia, Cambodia, Mozambique and Georgia. Dallaire had suggested a reconnaissance mission and Boutros-Ghali had agreed. During his twelve-day mission to Rwanda, everyone Dallaire met, including representatives of the diplomatic community in Kigali, told him that the Arusha Accords were the last and best hope for Rwanda, stressing the urgency of implementation.[3] Dallaire visited the areas controlled by the RPF in the north and the government military positions, and he carried out a detailed survey of the forces, their structure and equipment. The Security Council created the UN Assistance Mission (UNAMIR) on 5 October.[4]

Dallaire was a patient and principled soldier who had trained in an army proud of its tradition of peacekeeping. He was dynamic and charismatic in command. He had risen through the ranks, commanding a troop, a battery, a regiment and a brigade. Raised in a working-class area in the east end of Montreal, Dallaire's father had been a sergeant in the premier French-Canadian regiment, the Royal 22nd. Both his parents had worked in a local military supply depot. Dallaire was a committed internationalist, and he had first-hand experience of UN missions. When he was brigade commander, two of his battalions had served, one in Cambodia and the other in Bosnia. Dallaire had the utmost dedication to the mission for Rwanda. He was a hard worker. And he was obstinate.

There was criticism afterwards that Dallaire was inadequately briefed about the realities in Rwanda[5] and Dallaire himself said later that had he known about the human rights reports then he would have insisted on a larger force. Others said that nothing could have prepared Dallaire, or anyone, for the reality to come. Some years later Dallaire speculated about whether or not it had been like a Greek tragedy on the grandest scale. 'You sort of wonder … when you look back at the whole thing, whether or not we were set up … whether or not the UN and myself fell into something that was beyond our ability to manage.'[6]

On the day before Dallaire arrived in Kigali as force commander came the terrible news of the assassination in neighbouring Burundi of the first ever elected Hutu president, Melchior Ndadaye, put to death by officers in the Tutsi-dominated army. Later, an expert on the region, a professor at the University of Anvers, Filip Reyntjens, would testify that with hindsight he considered that the assassination of Ndadaye had spelled the end of the peace process in Rwanda.[7]

The Ndadaye government had been unique. There had been elections in Burundi just four months earlier, and Ndadaye had symbolized unity between Hutu and Tutsi. A moderate, he had chosen a Tutsi prime minister and the progress in Burundi had heartened and encouraged democracts in Rwanda. Ndadaye left the mainly Tutsi army untouched within but the French began negotiations on a French military presence in the country. This had made his army officers, not consulted on the matter, suspicious of his links with France.[8] Although Ndadaye's murder was described as an attempted coup by senior officers, after the assassination soldiers returned to barracks and restored power to the civilian government. The retaliation was terrible: there were between 35,000 and 50,000 deaths, roughly evenly split between Hutu and Tutsi.[9]

The assassination gave a propaganda coup to the Hutu extremists in Rwanda. They gleefully capitalized on the tragedy, blaming the assassination on 'progressive politics', and on 'reconciliation with the Tutsi'. The broadcasts of RTLMC became inflammatory[10] with announcers claiming that the assassination was part of a wider plot to eliminate the Hutu completely so that the Tutsi could dominate the entire region.

Within two days of the assassination, at a rally in Kigali, politicians from the MRNDD and CDR, together with hardliners from opposition parties, claimed to the crowds that Major-General Paul Kagame, the commander of the RPF, had plotted the Ndadaye assassination. Kagame had lied in Arusha when he signed for peace and democracy. Froduald Karamira, once a moderate of the MDR, warned that 'the enemy' was among the people: 'We are not simply heating heads by saying we have plans to work ... We cannot sit down and think that what happened in Burundi will not happen here.' Karamira shouted: 'All Hutu are one power.'[11] 'Pawa, Pawa' was chanted over and over again. It was here that the Hutu Power movement is said to have been created.

The Security Council in New York decided not to intervene in Burundi, a decision greeted with considerable relief in the secretariat, particularly in the Department of Peacekeeping Operations.[12] There was mission overload. Nor was the western press interested in Burundi. The story never really made the news.[13] Later on there was speculation that the lack of reaction by the international community to the massacres in Burundi led Hutu Power extremists to take the view that, whatever they chose to do, outside interference and media interest would be at a minimum.[14]

Another consequence of the Ndadaye murder and ensuing violence was the flood of refugees it caused, and some 300,000 people fled to Rwanda from Burundi. Their only future was to live in misery. There was a dysentery epidemic and an estimated 9,000 people died. A doctor with MSF-France, Jean-Hervé Bradol, later described a general indifference to the plight of these people among Rwandan officials and diplomats. The food aid for them was diverted for profit, an operation organized by people close to the government. By January 1994, 40 per cent of children under five in a camp in the prefecture of Kigali, not far from the capital, were suffering severe malnutrition.[15]

The camps were fertile recruiting grounds for Hutu Power and large numbers of disaffected youth were recruited into the militia, promised a return to Burundi by force.

There was also a problem of refugees in the north of Rwanda. There were 600,000 people displaced, mostly Hutu, south of the demilitarized zone. Starting in February 1994, Tutsi refugees were returning to Rwanda, mostly men and boys of military age, and they were accompanied by large cattle herds, moving directly to the RPF zone and taking the land of the Hutus who had already fled. The RPF claimed not to be able to stem this flow of returnees, and yet it was clear that these people were being helped on their journey by the RPF. The UNHCR's regional representative told Dallaire that those returning to Rwanda should not be helped, for that would encourage an even greater movement of people. Aid for these people was eventually provided by independent agencies. The Rwandan army claimed that many of the displaced people were being recruited to the RPF.

Because of unmarked minefields north of the demilitarized zone, peacekeepers were unable to monitor effectively the movement of refugees and arms from the Uganda–Rwanda border. The mines allowed the RPF to funnel the refugees into its own zone. 'The war started', Dallaire would remember, 'before we had fully grasped the nature of these events.' Their worst and most crippling handicap was their late arrival. 'We were too little too late. It was a grave error.'[16]

How half-hearted was the UN's effort for Rwanda was plain to see. Dallaire lacked the barest essentials. He was reduced to borrowing petty cash from another UN agency. He lacked everything from ammunition to sandbags, fuel and barbed wire. The mission lacked essential personnel; there was no public affairs officer, legal adviser, humanitarian or human rights expert.[17] The majority of people in Rwanda had no idea why UN peacekeepers had arrived in their country, their only source of news being Rwanda's two radio stations, the government-controlled Radio Rwanda and RTLMC.

When Dallaire had first devised the mission, he had asked for a minimum requirement of 4,500 troops.[18] Yet this figure had been pared down by officials in the secretariat even before being submitted to the Security Council. In the end, a total of 2,548 was agreed. The Americans said that the operation must cost no more than US$10 million a month. The military component of UNAMIR was to comprise three infantry battalions, one engineer company, a transportation section (with four utility helicopters), one logistics company, one medical platoon, and 331 military observers, a force headquarters, a movement control unit and a field hospital. There were to be twenty-two armoured personnel carriers (APCs) and eight military helicopters to allow for a quick reaction capability. That was the plan. In fact, no military helicopters arrived. And only eight APCs were provided, of which five were serviceable. They arrived in early March 1994 without tools, spare parts, mechanics or manuals and with limited ammunition. Their main weapon had never been test-fired. They were Czech-made BTR-80s, on loan only, and worn out from use in the UN mission in Mozambique. Before long they were inoperable.

Hutu Power watched with fascination the slow build-up of UNAMIR. By the end of October 1993, only a nascent UN headquarters staff was in the country, and it was soon clear that the force structure given to the UNAMIR commander, in particular the equipment, and the readiness level of his force, bore no relationship at all to what was really needed.

The mission of the peacekeepers was to monitor the security of the city of Kigali within a weapons-secure area, monitor observance of the ceasefire and help with the formation of a new integrated army. UNAMIR was to train local people to remove landmines, monitor the repatriation of refugees, and assist other UN agencies in co-ordinating humanitarian assistance for the million refugees and displaced people. Dallaire said that it was not lack of effort or dedication and zeal that prevented the mission from ever achieving an effective state of operations or gaining the initiative from the belligerents in order to advance the peace process.[19]

The UNAMIR flag was raised for the first time in the northern town of Kinihira on 1 November when the UN mission officially integrated the UN military observer group. There was little to celebrate. Most of Dallaire's time and energy went into trying to sort out a logistics nightmare. He would spend more than 70 per cent of his time, and his principal staff's time, dedicated to battling with the UN's administrative and logistics structure, upon which his mission depended. Dallaire considered it a major achievement that UNAMIR was conducting any operational activities on the ground even six months after the mandate was approved. Apart from the 450 Belgian soldiers, all the contingents came from developing countries with their own weak logistics base at home. The Ghanaian battalion arrived without a single vehicle. The vehicles for UNAMIR were coming by sea and then being driven overland to Kigali. There was petty theft during shipment, rendering vehicles defective – mirrors, filters and maintenance tools were missing. In Kigali, the peacekeepers had to wait for radios, tents, flak-jackets and other material coming from the UN missions in Cambodia or Somalia. Dallaire said: 'I spent most of my time fighting the heavy mechanical UN system with all its stupidity … we would order torches, and after a long delay they arrived without batteries … Seeing to the most immediate needs stopped us from seeing what was reserved for us in the future.'[20]

In three separate incidents there were ceasefire violations along the border, and more than a dozen Rwandan government soldiers were killed. Rwandan army commanders told Dallaire that Ugandan battalions were crossing into Rwanda, although UN observers never reported any such occurrences. The phase one objective of UNAMIR's mission was to move an RPF battalion into Kigali, a move that was intended to counterbalance the Rwandan army and deter aggression against RPF political leaders. This was accomplished with Belgian peacekeepers providing the escort.

In December, most of the second half-battalion of infantry, a light unit from Bangladesh with some trucks, was deployed in Kigali. It became apparent that the Bangladeshis had had little operational experience; they were poorly trained and not a cohesive unit. They had no logistics, no engineer equipment, but they were intended to provide UNAMIR's quick reaction capability. Originally, this role was to have been given to the Belgian troops but Belgium had decided to send only 400 soldiers to Rwanda rather than a full battalion of 800. Dallaire began training some of the Bangladeshi troops to try to create a quick reaction force but they were below acceptable operational standards. The Bangladeshi troops had arrived in Rwanda without bottled water or food; instructions issued by the secretariat in New York that all contingents should be self-supporting for three months were simply ignored. The Bangladeshis were supposed to have provided a composite force of a medical company, an engineer squadron, a half-battalion of infantry, and a movement control platoon.[21]

There were also problems with the para-commandos from Belgium, who had come from the mission in Somalia and were conditioned to a peace-enforcement environment. Soliders were sent home for misconduct and lack of discipline. The briefing for their replacements stressed that they were in Rwanda because they had been invited to assist the implementation of the Accords. The key to success would be co-operation with and support of the locals assisting security. Dallaire was surprised that the Belgians had sent para-commandos. They were suitable for enforcement operations under chapter VII, but not chapter VI peacekeeping. In Canada they would have been considered unsuitable for this mission. He was concerned about their lack of peacekeeping training. In Canada a three-month peacekeeping training course would have been provided.

At the end of 1993, with the RPF battalion established in Kigali,[22] the French troops withdrew. The arrival of the UN peacekeepers marked the end of Operation Noroit, which had begun in October 1990, and now French TV news showed an exchange of presents between Rwandan and French soldiers. Some French soldiers stayed behind. French military personnel from the DAMI (Détachement d'Assistance Militaire et d'Instruction) were recognized in civilian clothes in Kigali. And the infamous French mercenary, Paul Barril, was there telling everyone he was an adviser to President Habyarimana.[23]

In spite of the failure to hold to the timetable agreed at Arusha, on 10 December the two sides met in Kinihira, on a hilltop from where the view extended over the whole country. There was a joint declaration that peace was possible, there was renewed optimism, and there were promises that every effort would be made to adhere to the peace agreement.

Events elsewhere were not so reassuring. A teacher who had lived for twenty-seven years in Rukara, a rural commune in Kibungo prefecture, in an area where Hutu and Tutsi had always lived together, noticed in December

1993 how the Hutu youth had started to withdraw and to drink beer by themselves, and some youth wings of the political parties were being taught to shoot. They were holding rallies, speaking against Tutsi and the Hutu opposition. Sometimes they roughed up Tutsi. A nun from a Spanish order at Rukara said she believed that the Hutu had been informed that they would have to kill the Tutsi, but that they did not know when.[24] And in a warning from the charity Oxfam, their specialist on the region, David Waller, said that Rwandan society was now more violently divided against itself than at any time since independence. The war had done incalculable damage to the economy and environment and the country stood on the brink of an 'unchartered abyss of anarchy and violence'. There were too many historical, ethnic, economic and political pressures that were likely to push it over the edge.[25]

As the UN mission was slowly becoming established, in November 1993 there was a series of killings in northern communes. The murders took place in Hutu Power strongholds in the Ruhengeri region. On 17 November thirty-six people were killed. Apparently all of them were Hutu and were members of local authorities. On 29 November in Mutara, north of the Gishwati forest, about twenty-five more people were killed, together with nine children. The children were murdered separately and their bodies found the following day by a UN patrol. The children had been mutilated and the girls raped. One of the girls survived but she died not long after arriving in hospital, and before being able to tell about those who had done it. A UNAMIR inquiry was established but it failed to discover the perpetrators.

These were the first murders to take place since the UN's arrival and, because the victims were Hutu, the RPF was blamed. The failure by UNAMIR to name those responsible led to a campaign against the peacekeepers, orchestrated over the airways of RTLMC. Dallaire's impartiality was questioned; he was said to favour the RPF.

Dallaire sent a code-cable to New York giving details of the UNAMIR inquiry into these massacres:

> The manner in which they were conducted, in their execution, in their co-ordination, in their cover-up, and in their political motives lead us to firmly believe that the perpetrators of these evil deeds were well-organised, well-informed, well-motivated and prepared to conduct premeditated murder. We have no reason to believe that such an occurrence could not and will not be repeated again in any part of this country where arms are prolific and ethnic tensions are prevalent.[26]

Dallaire asked for reinforcements, but at a meeting of the Security Council in New York he was given only a second half-battalion of infantry, the authorized phase two deployment of peacekeepers, which brought its strength up to the mandated 2,548.

At the end of November the extremist party, the Coalition pour la Défence de la République (CDR) issued a press release that the 'majority population' must be ready to 'neutralize its enemies and their accomplices'. The CDR, which liked to portray itself as a fringe party, was in fact a mafia of the powerful, created by senior government officials and businessmen. It included such Hutu Power luminaries as Ferdinand Nahimana, a former head of the Rwanda information bureau and who was held responsible for the inflammatory broadcasts on Radio Rwanda which led to the Bugesera massacres in 1992.

An anonymous letter written by a group of senior officers from the Rwandan army was sent to Dallaire on 3 December 1993. It was copied to all diplomatic missions. The letter warned of a 'Machiavellian plan' by the president. There were 'diabolic manoeuvres' to prevent the implementation of the Arusha Accords. Massacres would spread throughout Rwanda, starting in those areas where there were large concentrations of Tutsi. This was intended to convince public opinion that Rwanda's problems were ethnic. The RPF would be incited to break the ceasefire and the civil war would resume. Opposition politicians were going to be assassinated and two names were specified, the prime minister-designate under the Arusha Accords, Faustin Twagiramungu, and Félicien Gatabazi, the head of the Parti Social Démocrate (PSD), the second largest opposition party. The plot had been devised by Habyarimana, the letter went on, with the support of a handful of military officers from his home region. The anonymous authors of the letter maintained that they had written it because of 'revulsion against these filthy tactics'.[27]

There were other leaks from within the Habyarimana regime but these were reported only to Brussels. They came from a small intelligence unit attached to the Belgian contingent. An officer in this unit was told about a meeting in the Hôtel Rebero, chaired by Habyarimana, and at which it had been decided to distribute grenades and machetes to the Interahamwe.[28] By the new year the only hopeful sign was a peace march on 1 January with an estimated 6,000 people in Kigali with smaller numbers in Butare, Gisenyi, Gikongoro, in Kirambo, Biniga, and Ruhuha.[29]

A week later, on 8 January 1994, there was a violent demonstration by the Interahamwe in Kigali at which Rwandan gendarmes stood by helpless. They had no communications equipment, no appropriate vehicles, not even enough petrol. Nor did they have the will to act.

It was a turning point, certainly for the commander of the Kigali sector of UNAMIR, the Belgian Colonel Luc Marchal. It was a demonstration of strength by the Interahamwe and Marchal estimated how few options were available to the peacekeepers in the face of a serious crisis. Among Belgian officers there was a discussion about whether or not the peacekeepers should have gone to help the gendarmes, but throughout the riot there had been anti-UN slogans. Although the whole of UNAMIR was derided by the population, particular hatred was reserved for the Belgian peacekeepers. It seemed as though the intention of the rioting was to provoke the RPF battalion to break out of barracks; later the peacekeepers were told that this had indeed been the intention and that the demonstration had been pre-planned. Demonstrators and Interahamwe had turned up in lorries belonging to the Ministry of Public Works. Marchal was told by an informant that there had been grenades and guns distributed among the crowd. There was talk that Belgian soldiers would be killed.

The day before the demonstration took place, intelligence was received about a top-level meeting at the MRNDD headquarters with the president of the party, Mathieu Ngirumpatse, the minister of defence, Augustin Bizimana, the army chief of staff, Colonel Déogratias Nsabimana, the commander of the gendarmes, General Augustin Ndindiliyimana, and the president of the Interahamwe, Robert Kajuga. The meeting made plans to try to avoid future seizures, and decided that weapons would in future be stored in the homes of army officers. If the weapons locations needed protection from the peacekeepers, then the Interahamwe would fight them off, with stones if necessary. There was a plan devised to cause trouble between the peacekeepers, particularly the Belgian battalion, and the Rwandan people.[30]

Three times the inauguration of the transitional government was planned, and three times it was postponed. They were going round in circles. Dallaire believed that the Rwandan government was preventing implementation because the president wanted to keep control.

Boutros Boutros-Ghali says that he telephoned and wrote a letter to President Habyarimana on 13 January, telling him that the continuing delays were untenable and unless there was progress towards the installation of the government, then the international community would think again about its commitment to Rwanda. Habyarimana apparently told the Secretary-General that Rwanda's political parties were too divided to provide a stable government. It was true. By now the opposition parties were hopelessly split, torn between moderates who agreed to power-sharing with the RPF, and those who wanted power-sharing internally, but not with the RPF.

Throughout January, hostility towards Belgian troops worsened and in one incident the Interahamwe surrounded a minibus full of soldiers and chanted at them, calling them 'Tutsi'. Threats were made against the owners of bars and shops in Kigali frequented by Belgian soldiers. A grenade was thrown into Marchal's headquarters and throughout the night hundreds of grenades exploded all over Kigali.

Dallaire asked UN headquarters for an intelligence-gathering capability but his request was denied. He was told that such an operation was contrary to peacekeeping policy. Later on Dallaire described the effect of this decision: 'We were blind and deaf in the field. The five permanent members ... possess high-tech information capabilities ... yet the UN is expected to operate in an information void.' The subsequent deaths of his peacekeepers, says Dallaire, was a direct result of the failure to provide his mission with intelligence data.[31]

What intelligence collection there was in UNAMIR was conducted by Dallaire's Belgian military information office and two French-African military observers. This information was transmitted in the form of daily situation reports to Dallaire and then to New York. Only very occasionally was unofficial information provided to UNAMIR by local diplomatic or governmental sources. Dallaire was not to know how well informed US intelligence circles were; in January 1994 the CIA had given the State Department a desk-level analysis which warned that, if hostilities resumed, upwards of half a million people would die. The report analysed the Arusha Accords and concluded that they would fail, and that massive violence would result. It was not until the genocide was over that this analysis was passed to UNAMIR.

So concerned were they about the lack of intelligence-gathering that UNAMIR command circumvented UN headquarters and Marchal appealed directly to Belgian military intelligence, the Service Général du Renseignement de l'Armée (SRG). This resulted in the creation of a two-person cell to report to UNAMIR headquarters in Kigali as well as to the Belgian military headquarters in Evere, outside Brussels. Eventually the cell controlled a total of five informers thanks to a small sum of money to pay for information.[32] The network was run by Lieutenant Mark Nees.

At the end of December the intelligence cell was told that there were stocks of weapons stored at the homes of the militia leaders. A plan was being hatched involving MRNDD leaders, to try to undermine the credibility of the Belgian troops, using the Interahamwe. In January Dallaire was told the Interahamwe was receiving military training. Then on 10 January someone else came forward, this time from the heart of the Hutu Power network, who agreed to meet Marchal only at night, and alone. Marchal met the man by candlelight. They both laid their pistols on the table. The man's codename was Jean-Pierre and he had been introduced to the intelligence network by a senior politician.

Jean-Pierre had a most extraordinary story to tell. He was a former member of the president's security guard, who had worked as a chauffeur, and was now a senior trainer in the Interahamwe. His salary came from the ruling party, the MRNDD. He told Marchal that 1,700 Interahamwe had been trained in Rwandan army camps and these men were now scattered in groups of forty throughout the city. He said that since UNAMIR troops had arrived he personally had trained 300 men in sessions lasting three weeks. The focus of the training was discipline, weapons, explosives, close combat and tactics. Up until now Jean-Pierre had supposed that the Interahamwe had been created in order to protect Kigali from the RPF. But he said that since October he had been ordered to register all Tutsi in Kigali. He was certain that it was for their extermination, for the Interahamwe was now being trained to kill up to 1,000 people every twenty minutes. Jean-Pierre said he could not support the killing of civilians. The president, claimed Jean-Pierre, had lost control of the extremists. 'What he told me was so enormous,' said Marchal, 'it was so extraordinary. I was uneasy. I had not come to Rwanda to be James Bond. This was the work of a specialist intelligence officer.'[33]

Jean-Pierre described in detail how a demonstration, held on 8 January, had been organized, and he explained that the whole idea had been to trap Belgian peacekeepers and to kill them. Jean-Pierre said that there had been para-commandos and gendarmes in plain clothes in the crowd as agitators. He predicted that during the next attempt to inaugurate the transitional government, opposition politicians would be killed as they entered the parliament building. If Belgian peacekeepers reacted with force, then they would be killed too in order provoke a total withdrawal of UN troops from Rwanda. The people involved in these plans, from the Rwandan army and the Interahamwe, were in radio contact with each other. There was a direct link between the army chief of staff and the president of the MRNDD. Jean-Pierre was willing to tell the UN the location of secret weapons dumps. These included hundreds of AK47s, which were stockpiled throughout the city. In exchange for his information, Jean-Pierre wanted UN protection somewhere abroad for himself and his family. He would then go public and tell the press about what was being organized by Hutu Power extremists.

On Tuesday, 11 January 1994, Dallaire wrote a code-cable to New York to inform the Secretary-General's military adviser and fellow Canadian, Major-General J. Maurice Baril, of the details of Jean-Pierre's claims. Dallaire wanted to take action over the weapons cache in the next twenty-four hours and he recommended that the informant be given safe passage from Rwanda. Dallaire expressed reservations on the sudden change of heart of the informant, and he had not ruled out that this was a trap. In the meantime they would prepare a detailed plan for a weapons raid.

The cable caused alarm in New York and not only because of the startling claims from the informer. An immediate reply was sent telling Dallaire to stand by and await further instructions. There was alarm at the prospect of arms seizures. Only six months earlier in Somalia, twenty-three Pakistani peacekeepers had been killed during a weapons inspection, the incident that ultimately led to the deaths of the eighteen Americans in Mogadishu. Annan said later that given the circumstances it was reasonable to conclude that the

Security Council would not want aggressive force used in this peace mission. Annan was all too well aware of the restrictions on the budget of UNAMIR and on its mandate imposed by the Americans. UNAMIR was under a chapter VI mandate, nothing more, and under the UN Charter this concerned the pacific settlement of disputes.

A cable dated 11 January was sent from headquarters, from Annan, addressed to Jacques-Roger Booh-Booh, the Secretary-General's special representative for UNAMIR: 'No reconnaissance or other action, including response to request for protection, should be taken by UNAMIR until clear guidance is received from HQ.'[34] Booh-Booh cabled back to say that he had met with Faustin Twagiramungu, the Rwandan prime minister-designate, the person who had introduced Jean-Pierre to the intelligence network. Twagiramungu had told Booh-Booh that he had 'total, repeat total confidence in the veracity and true ambitions of the informant'. Booh-Booh told headquarters that Dallaire was prepared to 'pursue the operation in accordance with military doctrine with reconnaissance planning and preparation … if any possibility of an undue risk scenario presented itself the operation would be called off.' This time the reply came from the official concerned with the day-to-day running of the operation at UN headquarters, Iqbal Riza, an assistant secretary general in the Department of Peacekeeping Operations (DPKO). It was addressed to both Booh-Booh and Dallaire and it told them that arms seizures were beyond their mandate: 'The overriding consideration is the need to avoid entering into a course of action that might lead to the use of force and unanticipated repercussions.'[35]

Riza had himself run a chapter VI mission; he had been special representative with the UN Observer Mission in El Salvador (ONUSAL), from its inception until March 1993. The mission of ONUSAL was to monitor the end of a decade-long civil war, and the reform of the armed forces, the judiciary and the electoral system. Its focus was on human rights.[36] Both Annan and Riza were firmly of the opinion that in Rwanda only a political solution could minimize the violence. Dallaire had not ruled out that the informer might be part of a trap to lure the peacekeepers. 'Force Commander does have certain reservations on the suddenness of the change of heart of the informant to come clean with this information … Possibility of a trap not fully excluded.'

Some years later, interviewed for a US television programme, Riza said he regretted the failure to take more heed of the information in the 11 January cable: 'All of us deeply regret it, all of us are remorseful about it … yes, we failed.'[37] Annan and Riza were both criticized in a later UN report for failing to have briefed the Secretary-General and the Security Council about this telegram.[38]

In every UN mission the position of the Secretary-General's special representative is crucial. This post is intended to provide cohesive, consistent political leadership. In Rwanda, the job was given to a personal friend of Boutros Boutros-Ghali, a former foreign minister of Cameroon. The appointment of Booh-Booh was considered 'unfortunate'.[39] In his reconnaissance report, Dallaire had recommended a military special representative leading a French-language mission, but he got a civilian special representative leading an English-language mission in a French-speaking country. Both Booh-Booh and Boutros-Ghali were close to the rich elite in Cameroon and Booh-Booh, who arrived in Kigali on 23 Novemberm, was considered pro-Habyarimana from the outset. Booh-Booh, to the fury of the RPF, was intent on persuading them that they must accept a role for the extremist CDR.[40] In the months to come, Booh-Booh presented an optimistic assessment of what was happening.[41]

While refusing permission for arms seizures, Annan and Riza decided that the best way to handle the rest of Jean-Pierre's information was to tell President Habyarimana about it as quickly as possible. Dallaire and Booh-Booh met with the president and made it clear that the Security Council would hold him 'personally responsible' for any violence. On instruction from New York, they told him he must report within forty-eight hours of the steps taken to recover the arms that had been distributed.[42]

This diplomatic approach, devised by Riza and Annan, was a decision grounded in traditional peacekeeping. Their intention was to evaluate how far Habyarimana had progressed in disarming the population, and dismantling stocks of weapons. If this approach failed to have a result, then the Security Council must be informed. Riza said he was baffled why UNAMIR, with some 1,500 troops, should take responsibility for seizing weapons when in Rwanda there were 28,000 troops and 6,000 gendarmes under arms. Dallaire and Booh-Booh duly shared the information with the president. Booh-Booh cabled Annan that the president appeared alarmed by the tone of the démarche and he had denied the activities of the militia. They had also raised with the president the harassment of UNAMIR and the violence against one ethnic group during a demonstration on 8 January. Habyarimana said he had been unaware of the demonstration. Then Booh-Booh and Dallaire met the president and the secretary general of the MRNDD who both denied that the party militia was involved in violence. Booh-Booh reported to New York that the president of the MRNDD had seemed bewildered by how specific the information at their disposal was. 'The President of the MRNDD seemed unnerved and is reported to have subsequently ordered an accelerated distribution of weapons,' Booh-Booh cabled New York. Yet Booh-Booh also wrote that he thought the initiative to confront the accused parties with the information was a good one and might force them to decide on alternative ways of jeopardizing the peace deal.

Booh-Booh and Dallaire, on instructions from New York, met with three ambassadors in Kigali, from the USA, France and Belgium, and with the Papal

Nuncio, Monsignor Guiseppe Bertello, dean of the diplomatic corps, to tell them what Jean-Pierre had said. The three ambassadors expressed serious concern about the information and promised to consult their capitals. At a further meeting with these three ambassadors on 13 January, Dallaire presented a letter from Jean-Pierre containing more specific information. The following day the three ambassadors met with Habyarimana to express their concern that Arusha was being violated by his supporters.

It was left to Marchal to test Jean-Pierre's credibility. Marchal sent a Senegalese peacekeeper with the informer to find stocks of weapons and Jean-Pierre had gone straight to the headquarters of the MRNDD where in the basement were 137 Kalashnikov assault rifles and ammunition. Jean-Pierre showed the peacekeeper smaller caches of arms hidden in bushes and undergrowth at strategic cross-roads in Kigali. The fact that there were stocks of arms was an open secret. Marchal said that everyone knew and that everyone expected that the peacekeepers would do something about them. Marchal was stunned at the refusal of New York to allow weapons seizures. The whole point of their mission was to secure a weapons-free area in Kigali. 'It was the worst thing for us,' Marchal said later, 'just to stay, and to watch, without reaction.' Marchal asked himself how a transitional government was expected to be created in a country where there was a profusion of weaponry.

Dallaire tried on several occasions to persuade New York to plan seizures of weapons. Booh-Booh wrote to Annan to complain that each day of delay in authorizing arms recovery would result in an ever-deteriorating security. UNAMIR would soon be unable to carry out its mandate. So far, the only major weapons seizure by the peacekeepers had taken place at the airport when, on 21 January, in a DC 8 belonging to East African Cargo, a consignment of 40 tons of ammunition arrived to be immediately confiscated by peacekeepers.[43] UNAMIR did search aircraft coming into Kigali and tried to cover the land routes, although this was not in the mandate. Apart from this one airport seizure, only sixteen weapons and just over 100 hand-grenades had been seized.

Marchal told both his national authorities in Brussels and the Belgium ambassador in Kigali of the importance he attached to the information from Jean-Pierre. On 15 January, the Belgian ambassador in Kigali, Johan Swinnen, exerted his own pressure and told the government in Brussels that unless UNAMIR took action immediately, arms would be distributed to the Interahamwe. The ambassador believed that Dallaire's mandate certainly provide for weapons seizures. Boutros-Ghali did not agree. On 14 January he warned that arms seizures could cause serious political repercussions.[44] Habyarimana telephoned Boutros-Ghali that day. He told him that he needed all the help he could get, from the ambassadors in Kigali and from the UN. Boutros-Ghali told him that the UN trusted his leadership but that unless there was progress towards peace then the UN would be obliged to withdraw. A UN withdrawal would be a disaster for Rwanda, Habyarimana told Boutros-Ghali.[45]

On 16 January an estimated 5,000 MRNDD supporters held a rally at the Nyamirambo stadium in Kigali. It was calm, as Jean-Pierre had accurately predicted it would be, for its main purpose was to distribute grenades. Marchal, the very next day, warned his army command in Brussels that it was 'imperative' Dallaire be given permission to seize weapons; it was vital to support Dallaire in his request to the UN. On 23 January, during a demonstration in Kigali, forty-seven people were killed. Dallaire appealed to New York for a broader interpretation of his mandate. Three days later, on 26 January, gunmen shot at Belgian peacekeepers who were ensuring the security of Booh-Booh's residence. The following day the Belgian ambassador in Kigali told his foreign minister that either UNAMIR should be given a more forceful mandate, or the troops should be completely withdrawn.

At the end of the month, the Human Rights Watch Arms Project published a detailed report revealing that the Habyarimana regime had entered into arms deals with Egypt and South Africa. Rwanda was also getting arms supplies from France and the country was awash with weapons. The researchers obtained a secret Rwandan government document showing that the government had formed paramilitary 'self-defence' groups in select communities where human rights violations took place. The report noted:

> It is impossible to exaggerate the danger of providing automatic rifles to civilians ... In light of the widespread and horrifying abuses committed by Hutu civilian crowds and party militia armed primarily with machetes and spears, it is frightening to ponder the potential for abuses by large number of ill-trained civilians equipped with assault rifles.[46]

Notes

1. Assemblée Nationale, Mission d'Information Commune, *Enquête sur la Tragédie Rwandaise (1990–1994), Book III: Auditions*, p. 396.

2. Dallaire was the chief military observer of the UN Observer Mission Uganda–Rwanda (UNOMUR), established by the UN Security Council to help to bolster the Arusha Accords. This operation consisted of eighty-one military observers monitoring the 150-kilometre border and was intended to forestall the spread of the conflict and any accusations against Uganda of involvement in the internal affairs of Rwanda. The observers were to patrol, observe and make sure the buffer zone was not breached, although their activities were during daylight hours only. *The United Nations and Rwanda, 1993–1996*, Blue Book series, Vol. 10, 1996.The observers came from Bangladesh, Botswana, Brazil, Hungary, the Netherlands, Senegal, Slovakia and Zimbabwe.

3. Report of the Secretary-General on Rwanda, requesting establishment of a UN Assistance Mission for Rwanda, (UNAMIR) and the integration of UNOMUR into UNAMIR (S/26488) 24 September 1993, in *The Blue Helmets. A Review of UN Peacekeeping* (3rd edn), New York: UN Publications, p. 221.

4. Dallaire was appointed Force Commander on 18 October 1993. He was promoted to Major-General on 1 January 1994.

5. Paul LaRose-Edwards, 'The Rwandan Crisis of April 1994: The Lessons Learned', *International Human Rights, Democracy and Conflict Resolution*, Ottawa, 1994.

6. 'Remember Rwanda, Dallaire pleads', *Globe and Mail*, Toronto, 2 February 1998.

7. Belgian Senate, *Commission d'enquête parlementaire concernant les événements du Rwanda.* Report. 6 December 1997. p. 194.

8. Interviews, Washington DC, January 1998.

9. Bruce D. Jones, 'The Arusha Peace Process', in Howard Adelman and Astri Suhrke (eds), *The Path of a Genocide. The Rwanda Crisis from Uganda to Zaire*, New Brunswick, NJ: Transaction, 1999, p. 153n.

10. *Broadcasting Genocide: Censorship, Propaganda and State-sponsored Violence in Rwanda 1990–1994*. Article 19, International Centre Against Censorship, London: October 1996.

11. Human Rights Watch/Fédération Internationale des Ligues des Droits de l'Homme, *Leave none to tell the story. Genocide in Rwanda*. 1999, p. 138. On 15 February 1997 Karamira was found guilty of genocide by a Kigali court. He was publicly executed on 24 April 1998.

12. Michael N. Barnett, 'The Politics of Indifference at the UN and Genocide in Rwanda and Bosnia', in Thomas Cushman and Stjepan Mesrovic (eds), *This Time We Knew: Western Responses to Genocide in Bosnia*, New York: New York University Press, 1996.

13. Susan D. Moeller, *Compassion Fatigue*. New York and London: Routledge, 1999, p. 286. Moeller quotes Steven Weisman, the *New York Times* deputy foreign editor, who said Somalia had used up a lot of the news resources.

14. Guy Theunis, 'Le Rôle de l'église catholique dans les événements recents', in André Guichaoua (ed.), *Les Crises Politiques au Burundi et au Rwanda, (1993–1994)*. Université des Sciences et Technologies de Lille. Paris: Karthala, 1995, p. 289.

15. Jean-Hervé Bradol, 'Rwanda, Avril–Mai 1994. Limites et Ambiguïtés de l'Action Humanitaire. Crises Politiques, Massacres et Exodes Massifs', *Le Temps Moderne*, No. 583, 1995.

16. Interview, General Roméo A. Dallaire, London, November 1994.

17. Roméo A. Dallaire, 'End of Innocence: Rwanda, 1994', in Jonathan Moore (ed.), *Hard Choices: Moral Dilemmas in Humanitarian Intervention*, Oxford: Rowman and Littlefield, 1998.

18. In Kigali during the reconnaissance mission, a French attaché had argued for only 500 UN observers.

19. Dallaire, 'End of Innocence'.

20. Jacques Castonguay, *Les Casques Bleus au Rwanda*, Paris: Editions l'Harmattan, 1998.

21. The best the Bangladeshi troops managed was to construct a volleyball pitch and a soccer field for themselves in Byumba. They were there because their government was paid $1,000 a month for each solider by the UN (the Bangladeshi government paid their troops $10 a month).

22. UNAMIR observers were with the battalion and observers were also alongside the RPF and Rwandan government army in outlying areas.

23. Mel McNulty, 'France's Rwanda Débâcle', *War Studies*, Vol. 2, No. 2, Spring 1997, p. 12.

24. *Genocide in Rwanda. Documentation of Two Massacres during April 1994*. Issue Brief, US Committee for Refugees, November 1994, p. 11.

25. David Waller, *Rwanda: Which Way Now?* Oxford: Oxfam, 1993.

26. UNAMIR, Code-cable, 6 January 1994.

27. Guichaoua (ed.), *Les Crises Politiques au Burundi et au Rwanda*, pp. 653–4.

28. The small unit was run by the Belgian Lieutenant Mark Nees. It may have been infiltrated; during the genocide the hate-radio RTLMC targeted Nees by claiming that he had prepared lists of members of the Interahamwe.

29. Guy Theunis 'Le rôle de l'église catholique'.

30. Human Rights Watch/Fédération Internationale des Ligues des Droits de l'Homme, *Leave none to tell the story*, p. 149.

31. Major-General Roméo Dallaire. 'Military Aspects', in Dick A. Leurdijk (ed.), *A UN Rapid Deployment Brigade*, The Hague: Netherlands Institute of International Relations. Cligendael, 1995.

32. The force commander did not know of this slush fund. He knew only that one request for cash had been denied.

33. Interview, Colonel Luc Marchal, December 1999.

34. UN Security Council, *Report of the Independent Inquiry into the Actions of the UN during the 1994 Genocide in Rwanda*, 15 December 1999, p. 10.

35. Ibid., p. 11.

36. The UN Observer Mission in El Salvador, ONUSAL, ran from July 1991 to April 1995. See *The Blue Helmets* (3rd edn), p. 737.

37. Frontline Transcript. http://www.pbs.org/wgbh/pages

38. UN Security Council, *Report of the Independent Inquiry*, December 1999. p. 26.

39. Ingrid A. Lehmann, *Peacekeeping and Public Information. Caught in the Crossfire*. London: Frank Cass, 1999, p. 101.

40. Interviews, Paul Kagame and Claude Dusaidi, Kigali, October 1997; Patrick Mazimhaka, London, 1999.

41. Under J.-R. Booh-Booh were four subordinate commands: Mission HQ, Military Division, Police Division and Administration and Management Division. In his reconnassance report, Dallaire had recommended that they be under military command in accordance with the principle of unity of command.

42. The cable: Annan, UNATIONS, New York to Booh-Booh/Dallaire, UNAMIR, Kigali, No. 100, 11 January 1994 (see Castonguay, *Les Casques Bleus*).

43. Human Rights Watch/Fédération Internationale des Ligues des Droits de l'Homme, *Leave none to tell the story*, p. 156.

44. Ibid., p. 154.

45. UN Security Council, *Report of the Independent Inquiry*, p. 11.

46. Human Rights Watch Arms Project, *Arming Rwanda. The Arms Trade and Human Rights Abuses in the Rwandan War*, Vol. 6, No. 1, January 1994.

10 · Peacekeepers in Trouble: February–April 1994

MAJOR-General Roméo Dallaire never gave up hoping the peace plan would succeed. 'Once ministers were round a cabinet table, I thought they would be able to reach compromises,' he said.[1] He held meetings to try to break the political deadlock and get the agreement back on track. Once the broad-based government was established and the moderates were in charge of key ministries and once a national army was created, phase two of the mandate, then the extremists would be subdued and even marginalized.

Colonel Luc Marchal, commander of the peacekeepers in the Kigali sector, believed there was no better solution than the Arusha Accords. After all, although much criticized later, they had stopped the war. In the first weeks of 1994, however, there was political stagnation and a series of postponements of the swearing-in of the transitional government. The security situation deteriorated.

Marchal had previous experience in Africa, having served for five years, as a para-commando, for Belgian technical military co-operation in Zaire. In Rwanda he liaised on a daily basis with Dallaire. There was mutual respect. Dallaire considered Marchal a remarkable officer, and was certain that one day he would be promoted to general. By early February both men were seriously worried. On 3 February Dallaire warned New York in the strongest terms:

> We can expect more frequent and more violent demonstrations, more grenade and armed attacks on ethnic and political groups, more assassinations and quite possibly outright attacks on UNAMIR installations. Each day of delay in authorising deterrent arms recovery operations will result in an ever deteriorating security situation and may, if the arms continue to be distributed, result in an inability of UNAMIR to carry out its mandate in all aspects.[2]

Dallaire and Marchal both reached the conclusion that determined and selective deterrent operations were needed to target confirmed arms caches and those individuals known to have weapons in their possession. Marchal had come up with a plan to enlist the gendarmes in arms recovery and was proposing that if the gendarmes took the lead in these operations then UN military observers could monitor and advise. He had already begun to train gendarmes. But UN headquarters questioned even this and asked for further clarification. On 15 February Annan sent a cable to remind Dallaire that his mandate authorized UNAMIR only to contribute to the security of the city, 'within a weapons secure area by the parties'. Two days later another warning went to New York in which Dallaire told headquarters that he had heard of a plot to kill opposition politicians. Dallaire ordered UNAMIR soldiers to guard the homes of the prime minister, the president of the Assembly and the homes of moderate opposition politicians who requested protection.

Towards the end of February there was a sudden deterioration in security, and so serious was the violence that it seemed at times as though it would spiral out of control. On Sunday, 20 February, during a demonstration, there was looting of shops and six people died. At the Nyamirambo stadium during a meeting of the MDR, Belgian peacekeepers, providing an escort for Prime Minister Agathe Uwilingiyimana, had stones thrown at them by an angry crowd and they fired shots in the air. That night assassins tried to kill the prime minister-designate, Faustin Twagiramungu, and killed one of his body guards. On Monday, 21 February extremist Hutu blocked the centre of town and demonstrators burst into a government building and took hostages, releasing them later. Then, at around 11 p.m., the prominent opposition politician Félicien Gatabazi was shot dead.

Gatabazi, a moderate Hutu from the south, was to be the minister of public works in the transitional government and was the secretary-general of the PSD. He had recently revealed where militia training was taking place and he had accused the Presidential Guard of training militia at Kanombe barracks in Kigali. The killing of Gatabazi postponed the installation of the transitional government, scheduled for the following day. That morning Kigali was a ghost town. The only people outdoors were groups armed with machetes at the principal road junctions, watched over by peacekeepers and gendarmes.

On the road south to Butare roadblocks were erected. In Butare, Gatabazi's home town, there were huge demonstrations. That afternoon, near Butare, the national head of the CDR, Martin Bucyana, was lynched. In the next four days, thirty people were murdered and more than a hundred were wounded.

On the day Bucyana was killed, the Interahamwe together with Presidential Guard in civilian clothes waited in ambush to attack a convoy supposed to carry the RPF leadership from their northern base, a tea plantation factory in in Mulindi, north of Byumra. In this convoy were UN military observers, Belgian peacekeepers and an armed RPF escort travelling in Toyota Landcruisers. Dallaire's order that the convoy should stay overnight had been ignored. The ambush took place on the outskirts of Kigali and the Belgian peacekeepers and the military observers left the RPF guards to their fate. In order to rescue them, and in spite of repeated orders from Dallaire not to do so, RPF soldiers broke out of their CND base and raced to their trapped commrades. They returned to the CND with one dead and two wounded. No Belgians responded to the call for help and Dallaire said that the shame this incident brought on UNAMIR forces was never expunged. The best equipped and trained peackeepers had left the RPF to fend for itself. 'This was a disgusting situation,' he said later. It lowered his poor assessment of that contingent even further.

None of the RPF leadership was on board the convoy. Kagame was suspicious and had forbidden them to travel that day. From now on, says Kagame, he realized how little help the UN peacekeepers would provide in an emergency.[3] Kagame secretly reinforced the battalion in Kigali with arms and ammunition, smuggled in from the northern headquarters during troop rotation. If there were renewed fighting, the RPF leadership let it be known, there was an excellent chance of victory.

On the day of the ambush, the US State Department issued a travel advisory for Rwanda.[4] In the days to follow there was militia-inspired rioting in Kigali, and thirty-five people were killed and 150 wounded. In Gikondo, a parish in central Kigali, and a CDR stronghold, the militia killed thirty Tutsi and dozens more were forced from their homes.

Dallaire cabled headquarters to tell them the time for political discussion was running out: 'Information regarding weapons distribution, death squad target lists, planning and civil unrest and demonstrations abound ... any spark on the security side could have catastrophic consequences.'[5] Booh-Booh wrote to headquarters that there were reports that one of the demonstrations might have been ethnically motivated and directed against the Tutsi minority.

The creation of a new national army was a crucial part of the Arusha Accords, intended to reunite the country and to symbolize a new Rwanda without ethnic or regional divides. Yet the issue of a combined army had almost collapsed the negotiations. The regime's initial negotiating position had been to offer the RPF a 15 per cent share of army command, to correspond to the percentage of Tutsi in Rwanda. The eventual deal was to create an army with troop numbers shared 60:40 between the RPF and the Rwandan government forces, the majority for the government.[6] There would be 13,000 soldiers in the new army, and a 50:50 joint command, down to field commanders. The Presidential Guard would be abolished. The deal was widely considered a victory for the RPF. Herman Cohen, who was the American under-secretary of state for African affairs until 1993, said he was shocked when told of the deal reached at Arusha; it was too favourable to the RPF. Cohen said that the international community's obsession with getting a peace agreement led to a lack of analysis and a failure to consider whether or not the Accords could be implemented. The idea of stationing RPF soldiers in Kigali, Cohen thought, was folly. It would cause hysterical reactions among the Hutu. But Kagame did not trust the safety of any RPF officials in Kigali without soldiers to protect them, arguing that they were dealing with a regime that routinely killed people.[7] Diplomats who took part in Arusha warned that so advantageous was this deal to the RPF that the hardliners would never accept it.[8] Fear of the future of the Rwandan army soldier fuelled support for the extremists.

The role of the peacekeepers in the creation of the new army was to assist with the disengagement, demobilization and integration of the armed forces and gendarmerie. This would mean that 16,000 soldiers would have to be demobilized. No provision was made for their pensions or plans made for retraining and employment. Nor was any assistance offered by headquarters, in spite of the considerable expertise which existed after successful demobilization under UN supervision in central America and Cambodia.

The reports arriving at the small intelligence unit were increasingly alarming. Informers provided details of two meetings. One took place on 25 February when Robert Kajuga, head of the Interahamwe, met local militia leaders and a system of communication was devised allowing the Interahamwe to keep in touch through telephones, whistles and runners. The second meeting was on 27 February, this time in the offices of the MRNDD, during which the compilation of lists of Tutsi was discussed.[9] Some Tutsi planned an emergency evacuation. Others left the country.

The Hutu Power press was predicting that 'something big' was about to happen. Diplomats from African countries heard boasts that soon there would soon be no Tutsi left in Rwanda. Announcers on RTLMC warned that RPF soldiers, stationed in Kigali, were planning to kill all the Hutu. The newspaper *Kangura* claimed that the UN peacekeepers were in Rwanda to help the RPF take power by force, and that the RPF was planning to kill the president.

In spite of the increasing violence, the public warnings and the publication in January 1994 of Human Rights Watch's exposure of the regime's arms deals, the press paid little attention.[10] *Le Monde* carried a small story about the Egyptian arms deal and in London, the *Guardian*, in a short story on 23 February, reported the failure to implement the peace deal with a warning of 'a new wave of tribal killings' in Rwanda.[11] Dallaire and Marchal held press conferences in Kigali to try to explain the role of the UN in Rwanda. The local press was hostile and the international press, at a time when exposing what was going on could have made a decisive difference, was not interested at all.

The problems of Rwanda were hardly a secret. All aid workers were aware of how tense the situation was. An emergency plan was devised by the

International Committee of the Red Cross (ICRC) and MSF-France, together with other groups. They stockpiled medicine and water and installed four huge tents in the court yard of the Centre Hospitalier de Kigali (CHK), a pavilion-style 200-bed hospital. There were discussions held to decide which agency, in the event of large numbers of casualties, would collect the wounded from the streets and which agency would provide emergency medical care. The head of MSF-France in Rwanda, Eric Bertin, an expert logistician, described the plan in a fax to MSF-France headquarters in Paris, explaining that local clinics had been assessed for their capacity to treat wounded people. The ICRC had a surgical team kept in reserve for Kigali. Bertin was in Rwanda helping to provide sanitation, water and medical help for the refugee camps in the Bugesera for those people who had fled from Burundi and who were living in misery and squalor. In these camps children and old people were dying from starvation. The security situation worried Bertin. He wrote to Paris: 'It is beginning to be fearful ... we must respect our rules of security.'[12] During the week of violence at the end of February, all aid workers had stayed at home and it had not been possible to go to the refugee camps. In despair, some of the refugees had returned to Burundi and were murdered after crossing the frontier.

In testimony to the Belgian Senate some years later, Willy Claes, the Belgian foreign minister, claimed that on 11 February he told Boutros-Ghali that unless the peacekeepers took firmer action, UNAMIR might soon find itself unable to continue at all.[13] Claes, who had been warned by Foreign Office officials that the peace process in Rwanda was being sabotaged, visited Kigali at the end of the month. He was shocked. The regime did not even bother trying to disguise the stockpiling of weapons, and arms were openly distributed to civilians. Booh-Booh told Claes that he no longer believed that the Accords could be implemented. Dallaire told Claes that he had not found in Rwanda the courage and determination necessary to get through the transition. The mission could not stay indefinitely and his lack of resources was causing him serious concern. Marchal asked Claes for munitions better suited to the situation and for the means to resolve the problem of having Belgian peacekeepers spread out in fourteen different locations in Kigali. At a press conference, Claes says that he told Boutros-Ghali of his fears.

Before Claes returned from Rwanda, a telex was sent from the Belgian Ministry of Foreign Affairs to the Belgian permanent representative at the UN in New York. Dated 25 February, it warned that UNAMIR was in very serious trouble. The peacekeepers were incapable of keeping public order.

> It would be unacceptable if Belgian troops were to find themselves as passive witnesses to a genocide about which the UN would do nothing.

> If the conditions deteriorate further, the UN and the Belgians can hardly, in reality, withdraw. UNAMIR must play a more active role ... and reinforce the credibility of the international community.[14]

Claes says he warned Boutros-Ghali that Dallaire was achieving nothing practical because he was continually having to await instructions from New York. Dallaire needed a stronger mandate. Claes also says he warned the Americans, telling them of the double-game which Habyarimana could be playing. Claes argued that it was in everyone's interests to avert a resumption of the civil war. The Americans were well informed. The American embassy's deputy chief of mission, Joyce Leader, was trusted and respected by Rwandan human rights activists, and well-informed about the extremists.[15]

For the peacekeepers there was no increase in the mandate and no increase in troop numbers. When Belgium's UN ambassador, Paul Noterdaeme, met Boutros-Ghali, it was to be told that the USA and the UK were opposed for financial reasons. This was a low-budget mission. Noterdaeme subsequently met with British and American diplomats[16] whom he found to be unenthusiastic about UNAMIR. At a forthcoming Security Council meeting, the Americans were intending to argue that unless the peace agreement was back on track in a matter of weeks, UNAMIR should pull out. There were already warnings to this effect. Booh-Booh gave a speech in which he said unless there was progress there was every possibility that the UN would pull out.

At a meeting in Kampala on 8 March, Kagame told a group of ambassadors that the regime was continuing to rearm and Hutu Power militia members were spreading across the country.[17] Kagame pointed to the increasing violence against RPF supporters, members of the opposition parties and southerners. The CDR party, which promoted Hutu Power, rejected the idea of national unity, for it wanted identity cards and the institutionalized discrimination against Tutsi to be retained.

Three days later the Belgian minister of defence, Leo Delcroix, visited Kigali. He too was appalled and he publicly called for UN officers to take the initiative and order weapons seizures.

In what turned out to be one of her last appeals for her country, on 12 March the prime minister of Rwanda, Agathe Uwilingiyimana, asked for more time. A democrat, she had been chosen as a compromise candidate and appointed prime minister in a government that under the Arusha Accords was planned to last thirty-seven days and to be replaced by a broad-based transitional administration. Habyarimana had thought she would be easy to manipulate. She was not.

In a moving interview, with Belgian journalist François Ryckmans, parts of which were broadcast in Belgium on 15 March, Uwilingiyimana said she could not believe that the international community would even think of abandoning Rwanda. 'Almost every day people are killed, assassinated, whether they are poor peasants or political leaders,' she told him. 'Famine is raging in the country. People die of diseases, dysentery, malaria ... you see we do not have institutions capable of negotiating with our donors in order to solve these problems.' Ryckmans, who had slipped away from the organized Delcroix press itinerary, was a specialist in central Africa working for Radio Télévision de la Communauté Française de Belgique (RTBF).

Uwilingiyimana, aged thirty-eight and a former chemistry teacher, had been one of the first female members of the Mouvement Démocratique Républicain (MDR) founded in 1991 as the successor to Gregoire Kayibanda's MRD-Parmehutu party. Politics was at the heart of everything, she said: someone had to speak for the poor people, as they were the ones who suffered.[18]

Uwilingiyimana told Ryckmans:

> When you have a dictatorial regime ... for twenty years how do you expect the officials of this dictatorship to give up power without any pressure? The international community really helped us to persuade the president that the war could end through negotiations ... in all his speeches he said he would fight the war to the end ... but the international community helped us change this. Why doesn't the international community go the last step? We have put pressure on ... but we think you must go slowly otherwise you will endanger lives. If we are abandoned the Rwandan people will be left to their fate ... What will happen? ... but this is not the moment for pulling out. One last time we must make an effort ... to take the last step.

The people of Rwanda wanted peace, she said, but political leaders were showing a lack of good-will, even irresponsibility. Ethnic differences were being used to sow confusion and division and she blamed Habyarimana for encouraging the divisions in the opposition parties. Who would benefit from these divisions? Ryckmans asked her. 'The President,' she replied. 'He has all the territorial power ... with all the bourgmestres, all the prefects, the sous-prefects and the MRNDD, and in three months, under the Arusha Accords, all this [power] was to have been wiped away.' The Rwandan people were not ready to give themselves over to extremism: 'Extremists will always be wrong, whatever their ethnic origins.'

By the time of the interview her party was hopelessly split into pro- and anti-Hutu Power. She was ridiculed on RTLMC, accused of collaboration with the RPF and one broadcast called for her assassination. She had received death threats.[19] Uwilingiyimana openly denounced Habyarimana. She spoke about how 'those people from the north' were too greedy. Several times she had questioned Habyarimana as to why civilians were issued with arms. In her speeches she reassured the Rwandan people of every effort at dialogue with the RPF. A few days before the Ryckmans interview, she had made a speech in which she said that the only thing in the way of peace was the will of the president.[20] Some thought she was politically naive and immature and that only ambition drove her forward.

It was the refusal to allow the extremist CDR a part in the transitional institutions that was widely perceived to be holding up the peace agreement. And it was in an attempt to push the process further that, on 28 March, a joint communiqué was issued by Kigali's diplomatic community, led by the dean, Monsignor Guiseppe Bertello, and signed by all ambassadors and the Secretary-General's special representative. It urged acceptance of the CDR and contained a guarantee from the diplomats that a commission on national unity and reconciliation would be created to ensure that every political party respected the principles of political ethics, the violation of which would lead to exclusion. If the CDR were accepted, there would be no further cause for delay.[21]

With increasingly violent demonstrations in the streets of Kigali, and with roadblocks, assaults on civilians and murders, at the end of March Dallaire requested more civilian police. There was only a small UN civilian police unit in UNAMIR, consisting of sixty officers under an Austrian police commissioner, Colonel Manfred Bliem. They came from Austria, Bangladesh, Belgium, Mali, Senegal and Togo. There was a special investigations team, a liaison section and six police monitoring teams. These officers were to work with the Gendarmerie Nationale and the Police Communale in Kigali. Since its creation in January, the special investigations team had dealt with fifty-four serious crimes and allegations of human rights violations. Since the civilian unit had become operational in January there had been thirty-six deaths in riots. The Rwandan national gendarmerie and commune police were handicapped in terms of personnel, equipment and training. Intended originally to have been country-wide, a further forty-five police officers were needed if this were to be achieved.

Dallaire suggested the redeployment of 250 peacekeepers from the demilitarized zone in the north to Kigali to free Belgian troops from static guard duty so that they could provide a mobile force for foot patrols, checkpoints, escort duties and reserve tasks. Dallaire and Marchal were increasingly worried about the security of Kigali and wanted better defences at the airport. At this stage Dallaire had 2,539 soldiers from twenty-four countries. Each week UNAMIR carried out ninety foot patrols, 220 mobile patrols and twenty patrols by air, and provided twenty-five escorts; the peacekeepers guarded the houses of the prime minister and some of the opposition politicians, the residence of the Secretary-General's special representative, UN headquarters, food stocks and the airport.

Dallaire sent weekly reports to New York, each one giving considerable detail about violence and the problems of creating the transitional institutions. Some sentences he repeated week after week. The phrase, 'The situation is deteriorating significantly and all our resources are used to the full', is used seven times between 24 February and 5 April. Dallaire's cables leave no doubt that a serious crisis threatened.[22] In his daily reports to New York and in his more frequent telephone calls he made it abundantly clear that genocide was looming. He continued to press for more forceful action over the weapons issue.[23] But an operation to seize weapons with the assistance of the Rwandan gendarmerie was not approved by headquarters until after Dallaire went to New York at the end of March. On 1 April an operation did take place, carried out by gendarmes, with peacekeepers providing the outer cordon. But no weapons were found. The gendarmes had proved to be inept and news of the raid was leaked. The gendarmes would have to be better trained and more use made of UNAMIR's civilian police.

According to Lieutenant Luc Lemaire, a Belgian peacekeeper billeted with his men in a school in Kicukiru, nothing had gone right from the beginning: 'It was obvious to us that the gendarmes were playing around with UNAMIR … in the end we stopped telling them the details of our patrols.'[24]

On 1 April a telegram from Foreign Minister Claes to Ambassador Swinnen in New York said: 'Given all that we are doing for Rwanda, it is incomprehensible that this radio station [RTLMC], and we are well aware where the finance for this station comes from … is conducting a scandalous anti-Belgian campaign.'[25]

On 2 April, a UN pull-out was again threatened when Radio Rwanda broadcast an interview with Booh-Booh, who said that in a few days time the Security Council in New York was going to 'review' UNAMIR. Booh-Booh said it was normal for the Secretary-General of the UN to have to account to the Security Council on how UN resources were used and said the progress towards peace had been 'rather pathetic'. The current problems had their 'origin in the history of the country', he said.[26]

In New York, the RPF representative there, Claude Dusaidi, met with the president of the Security Council for the month of April, the New Zealand ambassador, Colin Keating. Dusaidi told Keating that the peace process was in danger of collapse.[27] Dusaidi was concerned that Booh-Booh was urging acceptance of the CDR and, indeed, Booh-Booh had recently allowed the CDR to take part in discussions about the broad-based transitional government, which had infuriated the RPF. Booh-Booh had approved a list of deputies for the National Assembly, a list which included members of the CDR.

A jokey item was broadcast on 3 April on RTLMC when an announcer revealed that a 'little something' was to happen in Kigali city, but that this would be camouflage for the final attack, or 'simusiga'. Some Tutsi began to sleep in church compounds for fear of being killed. 'Genocide', recalled a Polish peacekeeper, 'hung in the air.'[28] Some Rwandese army officers were boasting that if Arusha went ahead they were prepared 'to liquidate the Tutsi'.[29]

In the Belgian military intelligence (SGR) headquarters in Evere, Brussels, an official analysing the intelligence data warned that there could be thousands of victims in Rwanda if the Arusha Accords collapsed. This official would later testify that no one, not even with the information available, could ever have imagined the scale of what was to come.[30]

On 4 April Uwilingiyimana held a reception for local administrators and army officers, including the head of the gendarmerie, Major-General Augustin Ndindiliyimana, a fellow southerner who came from the same commune, Nyaruhengeri. The following day, 5 April, RTLMC broadcast the news that the prime minister had held this reception to raise her objections to the power of the northerners in the army. Secretly, claimed RTLMC, Uwilingiyimana was planning a coup d'état and she was going to get rid of the president.

Dallaire also met Ndindiliyimana on 4 April, at which meeting it was decided to proceed with an operation of search and disarmament in the Nyakabanda part of the city. This fresh attempt was due to start at 4.30 p.m. on 7 April. On the morning of Wednesday, 6 April, a co-ordination meeting was held by the commanders of the gendarmerie. The operation was to be provided with UNAMIR soldiers and some logistics.[31] By now, an internal UNAMIR assessment estimated that there were 85 tons of munitions spread throughout the country.[32]

That same morning, a Belgian peacekeeper noted how Rwandans and a few Europeans living near Kanombe were leaving, whole families carrying heavy bags. Someone else saw the Rwandan army setting up machine-gun posts at the military camp at Kanombe. In the afternoon there was reportedly heavy-weapons fire around the airport[33] and roadblocks were erected in the Kimihurura area. At around 3 p.m., guns were distributed from the back of a van in Nyarugenge commune, central Kigali.[34] Someone noticed the Presidential Guard building roadblocks. Near the Hôtel Méridien, military families evacuated.[35] At about 4.30 p.m., shopkeepers and traders in Kigali were told by the Presidential Guard to close their doors.[36]

At 6.30 p.m. at the airport, a Belgian peacekeeper in the control tower saw with surprise an old Nord-Atlas, usually parked near the airport building, preparing to take off. Black limousines drove on to the tarmac, and dozens of cases, trunks and even safes were unloaded and put on the plane. Some rather well-dressed men boarded the plane. It took off.

Notes

1. Interview, Major-General Roméo Dallaire, London, November 1994.

2. This cable is General Dallaire to UN New York, Code-cable, MIR 267, 3 February 1964. See Human Rights Watch/Fédération Internationale des Ligues des Droits de l'Homme, *Leave none to tell the story. Genocide in Rwanda*, 1999, p. 160.

3. Interview, Major-General Paul Kagame, Kigali, October 1997.

4. The State Department report for 1994 noted that in January and February government militiamen killed several dozen citizens, blocked streets, searched cars, beat perceived opposition supporters and damaged property. (US Department of State, *Country Reports on Human Rights Practices for 1994*. (Washington, DC: US Government Printing Office, 1995.)

5. UN Security Council, *Report of the Independent Inquiry into the Actions of the UN during the 1994 Genocide in Rwanda*, 15 December 1999, p. 12.

6. The Rwanda government forces numbered 28,000 soldiers, with some 6,000 gendarmes, while the RPF was estimated at some 20,000 strong.

7. Interview, Major-General Paul Kagame, Kigali, October 1997.

8. Bruce D. Jones, 'The Arusha Peace Process', in Howard Adelman and Astri Suhrke (eds), *The Path of a Genocide. The Rwanda Crisis from Uganda to Zaire*, New Brunswick, NJ: Transaction, 1999, pp. 142–3.

9. UN Commission on Human Rights, *Report on the situation of human rights in Rwanda submitted by Mr. René Dégni-Ségui, Special Rapporteur, under paragraph 20 of resolution S-3/1 of 25 May, 1994*. (E/CN.4/1995/7) 28 June 1995, p. 9.

10. Human Rights Watch Arms Project, *Arming Rwanda. The Arms Trade and Human Rights Abuses in the Rwandan War*, Vol. 6, No. 1, January 1994.

11. Lindsey Hilsum, 'Fears of new wave of tribal killings', *Guardian*, 23 February 1994.

12. Eric Bertin, unpublished report, Kigali, 28 February 1994.

13. Belgian Senate, *Commission d'enquête parlementaire concernant les événements du Rwanda*. Raeport, 6 December 1997, p. 242. In the UN Independent Inquiry the date is given as 14 February.

14. Ibid., pp. 392–3. The telex was sent by the chef de cabinet, M. Willems.

15. Holly J. Burkhalter, 'The Question of Genocide. The Clinton Administration and Rwanda', *World Policy Journal*, Vol. 11, No. 4, Winter 1994–95, p. 45.

16. Belgian Senate, *Commission d'enquête*, p. 394.

17. Present were the regional ambassadors of Belgium, France, Germany, the United Republic of Tanzania, the USA and representatives of the OAU and the UN.

18. François Ryckmans, *Chapeau Magazine*, Rwanda, 15 March 1994. Broadcast. Radio Télévision de la Communauté Française de Belgique (RTBF).

19. *Broadcasting Genocide: Censorship, Propaganda and State-sponsored Violence in Rwanda 1990–1994*. Article 19, International Centre Against Censorship, London, Ocotber 1996.

20. André Guichaoua (ed.), in *Les Crises Politiques au Burundi et au Rwanda (1993–1994)*. Université des Sciences et Technologies de Lille. Paris: Karthala, 1995, p. 694.

21. The communiqué was signed by Dr Jacques-Roger Booh-Booh, Monsignor Giuseppe Bertello, Dean of the Diplomatic Corps; the US Ambassador, David Rawson; the French ambassador, Jean-Michel Marlaud; the Belgian ambassador, Johan Swinnen; the German ambassador, Dieter Holscher; the Zaire ambassador, M. Kokule; the Ugandan ambassador, Ignatius B. Katetegirwe; the chargé d'affaires from Burundi, Severin Mfatiye; and the representative of Tanzania and the facilitator to Arusha, Saleh Tambwe. Copy in possession of author.

22. Jacques Castonguay, *Les Casques Bleus au Rwanda*, Paris: Editions l'Harmattan, 1998. p. 140.

23. Interview, Major-General Roméo A. Dallaire, 23 September 1994.

24. Testimony of Captain Luc Lemaire, in Belgian Senate, *Commission d'enquête*, p. 267.

25. Belgian Senate, *Commission d'enquête*, p. 595.

26. Summary of World Broadcasts. AL/1962 A/3. 4 April 1994.

27. Interview, Claude Dusaidi, Kigali, October 1997.

28. Interview, Stefan Stec, The Hague, October 1995.

29. Belgian Senate, *Commission d'enquête*, p. 334.

30. Ibid., p. 345.

31. There are claims that Ndindiliyimana had ordered all gendarmes to barracks for the night of 6–7 April. See Filip Reyntjens, *Rwanda. Trois Jours qui on fait basculer l'histoire*. Paris: L'Harmatttan, 1995, p. 34.

32. Castonguay, *Les Casques Bleus*, p. 68.

33. Vénuste Nshimiyimana, *Prélude du Génocide Rwandais. Enquête sur les Circonstances Politiques et Militaires du Meutre du Président Habyarimana*, Belgium: Quorum (SPRL), 1995.

34. Indictment against Georges Rutaganda, 12 January 1996.

35. African Rights, *Rwanda. Death, Despair and Defiance*. London: African Rights, 1995. p. 574.

36. Alain Destexhe, *Qui a Tué Nos Paras?* Brussels: Editions Luc Pire, 1996, p. 33.

11 · The UN Security Council: 5 April 1994

THE presidency of the Security Council changes monthly, by alphabetical rotation. In April 1994 it was the turn of New Zealand. The ambassador, Colin Keating, said later it was a bad time for the Council; there was a crowded agenda with renewed chaos in Bosnia and US forces departing Somalia.[1]

During the Easter weekend, on Saturday 2 April, Keating was telephoned at home and told that the Serbs had begun a massive attack on the so-called safe haven of Gorazde. This issue alone would have dominated the Council. The indiscriminate shelling of the town and of the outlying villages had led to considerable casualties among civilians. The UN peacekeepers there were in danger, and commanders had requested NATO close air support. On 31 March the Council had extended the mandate of the United Nations Protection Force (UNPROFOR) for an additional six months and decided to increase its strength by an additional 3,500 troops.

Rwanda seemed quiet in comparison with other trouble spots, but Keating was unhappy about an American idea to impose a time limit on UNAMIR. There was no evidence that this tactic worked; on the contrary, there were situations where it would be in the protagonists' interests to secure UN withdrawal. Such tactics risked playing into the hands of one of the parties and destabilizing the situation. Only later would Keating realize that the Council had not been adequately briefed about Rwanda. Few member states had independent sources of information about what was going on there and relied on the reports prepared by officials in the secretariat. There was no mechanism at UN headquarters to quickly provide information to members of the Council.

It is customary for the management of peacekeeping operations to be handled by officials in the secretariat, in the same way governments delegate responsibility for a complex operation to its public service. Certainly the officials in the secretariat were of the view that it was their prerogative to manage UN missions. What bothered Keating was that any request by a member state for information was resented in the secretariat, where officials seemed to believe that it was not the business of states to micro-manage.[2] Keating believed there had to be detailed political oversight over all UN missions. A classic recipe for disaster was for those politically accountable to lose control of an operation. This was what had happened over Somalia. There was urgent need for the Security Council to be reformed, making it more transparent and accountable. Its legitimacy and credibility were being eroded.[3] When it came to Rwanda, said Keating, the non-permanent Council members should have been exposed to the realities, and should have been informed of the extensive information which existed certainly among the intelligence services of the permanent five – most notably France – and among the secretariat's own experts.

'We were kept in the dark,' said Keating. 'The situation was much more dangerous than was ever presented to the Council.'[4] There was no mention of the UN Commission on Human Rights report which revealed that the 1948 UN Convention on the Prevention and Punishment of the Crime of Genocide was applicable to Rwanda, and which blamed the Rwandan government for human rights abuses.[5] The author of this report, Special Rapporteur on Extrajudicial, Summary or Arbitrary Executions Bacre Waly Ndiaye, says that if he had been consulted by the Council he would have said that the mission created for Rwanda was too weak to make any difference. Habyarimana had no intention of sharing power. Ndiaye would have recommended effective measures to protect civilians against organized massacres which, he said, had been described by the authorities in Kigali as 'spontaneous acts of anger' and 'self-protection'. 'With better information,' said Keating later, 'the council might have proceeded quite differently.'

On 5 April, the Security Council met to discuss what to do about the mission in Rwanda, established under resolution 872 on 5 October 1993. Peacekeeping operations are given six-month operating periods and after that the Security Council has to decide the conditions for extending or even ending the mandate.

There are fifteen members of the Security Council. Five of them – Britain, the USA, France, China and the Russian Federation – are permanent and they wield a veto on all substantive decisions. Ten come from countries that are elected by the General Assembly to sit on the Council for two years. In April 1994 they were the Czech Republic, Djibouti, New Zealand, Nigeria, Oman, Pakistan, Spain, Argentina, Brazil – and Rwanda, recently voted a seat. The extremists in Kigali were well informed, with access as privileged insiders, while their Hutu ambassador, Jean-Damascène Bizimana, sat in the Council.[6]

Some members of the Council were impatient with the Rwanda problem. American diplomats argued that unless the broad-based transitional government was established immediately, the UN's operation should close. The Clinton administration was determined to demonstrate a tough policy to an anti-UN Congress and to show that the UN could be selective. Some non-permanent members did not agree. Nigeria thought that Rwanda should be given a reasonable time to achieve democracy and should receive the resources and attention given by the UN elsewhere, particularly in the former Yugoslavia, where there were more UN peacekeepers stationed than in any other region in the world.

A written report on Rwanda had been prepared for the Security Council by Boutros Boutros-Ghali in which he gave an account of the delays in the peace process. His report described how most violent incidents in Rwanda could be attributed to armed banditry. It was optimistic in tone and claimed that, through their respect for the ceasefire, the parties had 'demonstrated that they remained committed to the peace process'. The peacekeepers continued to play a stabilizing role: 'I am encouraged by the fact that in spite of increasing tensions, the parties have maintained the process of dialogue.' There was a brief mention of ethnic crimes, but the report did not include the critical new intelligence from the informer. Afterwards, Boutros-Ghali maintained that he had been away from New York in January and not in close touch with the Rwandan situation, and that he did not learn about the informer's claims until three years later.[7] Also missing from Boutros-Ghali's report were details of a ten-page military assessment prepared by Dallaire which highlighted his serious deficiencies in capability and equipment; only later did Dallaire realize that the details of his assessment given to the Council had been watered down somewhere in the process of drafting the report.

With a coercive response ruled out, one strategy, already suggested by America, was to threaten that, unless the peace agreement was implemented, the peacekeepers would withdraw. From this point on, most of the debate was about how long to keep the mission going.

At 7. 10 p.m on Tuesday, 5 April, the ambassadors filed from the room at the back of the council chamber where their secret deliberations are held. In a formal and open meeting they unanimously agreed a compromise, resolution 909, which extended the mandate of UNAMIR until the end of July, but subject to a review in the next six weeks. Unless the transitional institutions provided for under the Arusha Accords were established by then, UNAMIR would pull out completely.[8] In a speech in French to the Council, only moments before the vote was taken, Rwanda's UN ambassador, Jean-Damascène Bizimana, said that like the Secretary-General he was optimistic about the peace process. He praised the observance of a ceasefire by the parties who were 'demonstrating their unwavering commitment to the peace process'.

Perhaps at this juncture the extremists determined that with only six weeks to go, they must prepare their plans even faster.[9] Perhaps at this moment some people concluded that the interests of Hutu Power and that of the great powers coincided. We may never know. But what does seem to have happened is that, with this vote, the Council played straight into the hands of the extremists. Within hours, the genocide had begun.

The day following the crucial Security Council meeting, Wednesday, 6 April, President Habyarimana and other regional heads attended a one-day sub-regional summit meeting in Dar-es-Salaam, invited by the President of Tanzania, Ali Hassan Mwinyi, the facilitator during the Arusha negotiations who was now concerned that the peace process was in jeopardy.[10] At the meeting, at the Kilimanjaro Hotel, President Mwinyi was in the chair. Also present were President Yoweri Museveni from Uganda, the vice-president of Kenya, George Saitoti (President Arap Moi had turned down the invitation at the last moment), President Cyrien Ntaryamira of Burundi and Salim Ahmed Salim, the OAU secretary-general.[11] The meeting reportedly turned into a humiliating experience for Habyarimana, for he was told that the delay in implementing the peace agreement was threatening the entire region. A renewed civil war would mean international isolation, and with international isolation would come empty bank accounts. Habyarimana was apparently shaken and agreed that power-sharing with the RPF was inevitable. He would not insist on the CDR taking part in government.

Habyarimana was never given another chance to establish the transitional government. At this point events conspired to remove him from the scene and to this day there is still no adequate explanation for what happened next.

Notes

1. Statement, 'The Security Council Role in the Rwanda Crisis', by Ambassador Colin Keating, Permanent Representative of New Zealand to the UN at Comprehensive Seminar on Lessons Learned from UNAMIR, 12 June 1996. Unpublished.

2. Interview, Colin Keating, New York, 13 September 1994.

3. Address to the UN General Assembly by the Rt Hon. Don McKinnon, Deputy Prime Minister and Minister of Foreign Affairs and Trade of New Zealand, 27 September 1994.

4. Interview, Colin Keating, New York, December 1996.

5. UN Commission on Human Rights, *Report by Mr. B.W. Ndiaye, Special Rapporteur, on his mission to Rwanda from 8–17 April, 1993.* (E/CN.4/1994/7/Add. 1) 11 August 1993, p. 22.

6. Rwanda's candidacy for a non-permanent seat was put forward to the General Assembly in October 1993. Its candidacy was endorsed at the summit meeting of the Organization of African Unity held in Cairo at the end of June 1993.

7. Boutros Boutros-Ghali, *Unvanquished. A US–UN Saga*, London: I.B.Tauris, 1999, p. 130.

8. As of this date, UNAMIR had a strength of 2,539 military personnel from twenty-four nations: Austria (15), Bangladesh (942), Belgium (440), Botswana (9), Brazil (13), Canada (2), Congo (26), Egypt (10), Fiji (1), Ghana (843), Hungary (4), Malawi (5), Mali (10), Netherlands (9), Nigeria (15), Poland (5), Romania (5), Russian Federation (15), Senegal (35), Slovakia (5), Togo (15), Tunisia (61), Uruguay (25) and Zimbabwe (29).

9. Interview, Claude Dusaidi (RPF Representative), New York, Kigali, October 1997.

10. In early April, President Juvénal Habyarimana made a series of visits to neighbouring states. On the day before the crucial Security Council meeting, Monday, 4 April, he was in Zaire, at Gbadolite, visiting President Mobutu.

11. Summary of World Broadcasts. AL/1966 A/3. 8 April 1994.

12 · Four Days in Kigali: 6–9 April 1994

HABYARIMANA rarely travelled anywhere at night; it was a rule imposed by security. However, he was kept waiting in Dar-es-Salaam, and the summit was delayed. Afterwards, the president had insisted on flying home. His jet, a Mystère Falcon 50, was waiting for him at the airport. It was a present from President François Mitterrand. It was four years old and it was spotless, its maintenance paid for by France as was its crew, three former French military officers, a pilot, chief mechanic and a navigator. Apparently, President Ntaryamira of Burundi asked Habyarimana for a lift. Ntaryamira was tired and his own propeller-driven plane was slower and less comfortable. Ntaryamira's wife was in Kigali. His Air Burundi Fokker 28 could fly on later, fifteen minutes behind the Falcon. Some people speculated that Habyarimana, not unaware that his life was in danger, wanted Ntaryamira on his plane for extra protection.

On board the Falcon were Habyarimana's closest advisers: Juvénal Renzaho, former ambassador to Rome and now the president's political counsellor; his private doctor, Dr Emmanuel Akingeneye; his private secretary, Colonel Elie Sagatwa, in charge of Habyarimana's personal security; the chief of the army, Major-General Déogratias Nsabimana; and Major Thaddée Bagaragaza, who commanded the Presidential Guard. Also on the plane were two Burundi government ministers, Bernard Ciza and Cyiaque Simbizi. Left behind in Dar-es-Salaam was the Foreign Minister, Anastase Gasana, who was obliged to travel home by car because, said Habyarimana, he did not want an opposition minister in his airplane.[1]

It was dark when the Falcon approached Kigali airport. The plane was cleared to land by the control tower. It was beginning its approach when the airport was suddenly plunged into darkness.[2] The plane circled once and then at 8.23 p.m., as it came towards the airport, rocket fire lit up the sky. There was a flash and a streak of light. Two ground-to-air missiles had been launched. The second blew the plane apart. All on board were killed and in the strangest irony the wreckage fell directly into the garden of the presidential palace nearby.

Within minutes the palace perimeter and that of the airport were sealed by an impenetrable cordon of troops from the Kanombe barracks. Then the airport lights came back on.

At the airport, Belgian peacekeepers, on their way to meet the regular Belgian transport plane C-130 carrying supplies from Nairobi, were prevented from entering the northern gate by Presidential Guards who took their weapons and the keys to their vehicles. They became hostages.

The news of the president's assassination was broadcast on RTLMC within half an hour. Almost at once, a series of roadblocks were put in place. A rural capital spread over many hills, Kigali consists of a maze of tree-lined roads which connect at strategic roundabouts.

'I ran as fast as I could,' said a survivor. 'Even before the President died, the consciousness of the Hutus in our area had already been awakened … they had been given a very clear idea. Hutus on our hill were always being called to secret meetings with the bourgmestre, councillors and other officials.'[3] Another remembered: 'No civilians or cars were on the street. Only military vehicles could be heard and seen.'

There was sporadic gunfire and explosions.

At Kigali airport a Belgian captain whose group patrolled the interior and who had spoken with Rwandan air-traffic control confirmed by radio that the president's jet had crashed.

Dallaire was at home. He called the prime minister, Agathe Uwilingiyimana, and she told him that with the death of the president she was now the titular head of the country. She wanted to broadcast to the people and make an appeal for calm. She would need a military escort to take her to the studios of Radio Rwanda. Uwilingiyimana said there should be a meeting of the Council of Ministers but she was worried about how ministers would get through the roadblocks.[4]

Dallaire issued a red alert, ordering the peacekeepers to barracks, doubling security and making the wearing of flak-jackets compulsory. More than an hour after the downing of the jet, he received a telephone call requesting his presence at a meeting of army officers at the Etat Major des Force Armées Rwandaises, the Rwandan army headquarters. On his way Dallaire noticed that members of the Presidential Guard had been deployed.

Elsewhere, in Kicukiro, a known critic of the government saw a checkpoint erected near his home: 'The checkpoint had been reinforced by people armed to the teeth … cars were passing by full of people with machetes. Some even had guns … my telephone was cut shortly after midnight … It was clear massacres were about to begin.'

Dallaire's deputy, Brigadier Henry Kwami Anyidoho, making his way to the Amahoro stadium from the Hôtel Méridien took a circuitous route because of roadblocks. He remembers that there was firing all over the city and particularly in the Kimihurura district where many politicians had their homes. 'Things happened very rapidly, as if they had been rehearsed,' he wrote later.[5]

At Kigali's five-star hotel, the Hôtel des Mille Collines, owned by the Sabena Belgian World Airways, the staff discovered at the end of a shift that roadblocks prevented them from going home. They stayed put.[6]

The meeting of army officers began at 10.30 p.m. There were ten officers quietly taking stock. There was a power vacuum. The head of the army, Major-General Déogratias Nsabimana, was dead. The minister of defence, Augustin Bizimana, and the head of G2 (Military Intelligence), Colonel Aloys Ntiwiragabo, were in Cameroon. The head of G3 (operations), Colonel Gratien Kabiligi, was in Egypt.

Colonel Luc Marchal arrived after the meeting began. He remembers it quite clearly and wrote an account of it later in his diary. No one seemed to be in charge. There was an exchange between General Augustin Ndindiliyimana, the commander of the gendarmes, and Colonel Théoneste Bagosora; each was urging the other to take the chair. Ndindiliyimana argued that Bagosora, as directeur du cabinet in the Ministry of Defence, had a duty to replace the minister of defence. Marchal thought that Bagosora's behaviour was strange. A few days earlier, in an extraordinary outburst, Bagosora had publicly advocated the extermination of Tutsi, arguing that so bloody and tragic had been the history of his country that this was the only 'solution'. Although Bagosora was known for openly expressing his views, this particular incident had taken place at a diplomatic dinner given by the Senegalese. Bagosora was quiet now, and guarded. He seemed genuinely shocked by the death of the president. He wanted Colonel Augustin Bizimungu, commander of the barracks in Ruhengeri, to take command of the army. There were objections.

Writing later about these events Bagosora described 6 April as a 'fateful' day, remarking how extraordinary it was that so many people responsible for state security were either dead or out of the country.[7] Before this night-time meeting had concluded, Ndindiliyimana assured both Dallaire and Marchal that what had happened was not a coup d'état. The military was keen to get the Arusha Accords back on track and ensure the creation of a transitional government. It was suggested by Dallaire that peacekeepers should patrol the streets accompanied by gendarmes, and these patrols would be allowed through army roadblocks. Dallaire asked that the militia be kept under control, and that the Presidential Guard return to barracks. He was assured of co-operation, and was asked to keep watch on the RPF battalion housed in the Conseil National pour le Développement (CND), the parliament building. Dallaire suggested that Bagosora should make contact with Uwilingiyimana but Bagosora replied that she was inept and untrustworthy and that not even her own party trusted her. Several officers suggested that Bagosora ask the MRNDD to find someone to replace the president. It was eventually decided to appoint Colonel Marcel Gatsinzi, a moderate, as interim chief of staff; he was a member of the High Council of the army command, established under the Arusha Accords.

Dallaire later accompanied Bagosora to the residence of Jacques-Roger Booh-Booh. Booh-Booh asked Bagosora if a coup d'état had taken place and Bagosora assured him that it had not, adding that every effort would be made to adhere to the Arusha Accords. Bagosora again objected to any contact with the prime minister. Booh-Booh said that he would arrange a meeting for nine o'clock the next morning with the American, French and Belgian ambassadors.

For the rest of the night Bagosora's movements are not known, but at some time during the early morning of 7 April, he signed the first official announcement of the president's death. It began: 'The Ministry of Defence has the profound sorrow in announcing to the people of Rwanda the death of their chief of state.' The statement, later read over Radio Rwanda and RTLMC, ended with advice that the population stay at home and 'await further directives'.[8]

At 1 a.m. on 7 April, Marchal drove through Kigali. It was quiet, quieter than other evenings at this hour. Some of the roadblocks erected earlier had been dismantled. (There were always roadblocks whenever the president travelled anywhere.) This did not seem like a coup d'état: there was no great military presence on the streets, no immediate military presence at the radio station, nor did it seem as though the reins of power been seized in a carefully planned military operation.

At 3 a.m., a Belgian peacekeeper found himself stuck at a roadblock manned by Rwandan soldiers, trying to negotiate his way through. He heard talk about how the president's plane had been shot down by Belgians who were going to help the Tutsi seize power.[9] Only three hours later did Marchal learn that the Belgian peacekeepers were being blamed for the assassination.[10]

At 2.38 a.m., Marchal ordered Lieutenant-Colonel Joe Dewez, commander of the 2nd battalion of Belgian troops, to send peacekeepers to the studios of Radio Rwanda where the prime minister was to broadcast her appeal for calm. At 3.10 a.m., a group of Belgian peacekeepers was ready to depart but the centre of the city, known as the 'presidential district', normally protected by numerous Rwandan army posts, was sealed by strategic roadblocks reinforced with light tanks belonging to the Rwandan army. Another Belgian platoon of peacekeepers was ordered to escort Agathe Uwilingiyimana from her house to the radio station. Ten Belgian para-commandos, travelling in four jeeps, set out. They had been in Rwanda for ten days.

Uwilingiyimana, at home when the plane crashed, had received telephone calls from friends telling her to go into hiding immediately. She refused. She had to take over the running of the country and ensure that there was calm. One kilometre away from her house, at the intersection with Avenue Paul VI and the Grands Lacs, a short distance from the St Michel cathedral, the UN escort was stopped at a roadblock. In accordance with peacekeeping policy, the escort radioed for gendarmes to negotiate their passage. No gendarmes turned up. A Belgian peacekeeper, a captain, intervened and took them via a back road, further up the hill. As they neared the house there was the sound of intense gunfire.

Uwilingiyimana was at home with her husband and her five children. She was interviewed by Monique Mas of Radio France Internationale: 'There is shooting, people are being terrorized, people are inside their homes lying on the floor. We are suffering the consequences of the death of the head of state, I believe. We, the civilians, are in no way responsible for the death of our Head of State.'[11] She telephoned the Belgian command at 3.40 a.m. to ask what had happened to her UN escort. She was told to stay put. The peacekeepers were on their way. And they were. It had taken three hours to make a journey which normally took fifteen minutes. Nearing the house they were met by five Ghanaian peacekeepers assigned to nightly guard duty outside her gate. Their arrival was timed at 5.20 a.m. The officer in charge of the UN escort, Lieutenant Thierry Lotin, saw an armoured car belonging to the Presidential Guard. There was the sound of gunfire and grenades exploding nearby.[12]

Uwilingiyimana was not ready to leave. She wanted her escort reinforced and had tried unsuccessfully to get hold of the Rwandan army command. She assumed that it was members of the military who were firing in the streets.[13] She received a call from Booh-Booh who told her that the army commanders would not talk to her. Lotin wanted her to hurry. He could see armed men crouched on roof tops. At 5.49 Lotin radioed that shots were being fired at the prime minister's house. Near the studios of Radio Rwanda, the peacekeepers were stuck at a roadblock manned by gendarmes and reinforced by tanks. They decided to park in a side road to sit it out, and the Rwandan gendarmes put planks full of nails across the road to prevent their departure. It was 6 a.m.

In northern Kigali, in Kacyiru, someone recalled: 'When we looked outside immediately after the 6 a.m. news bulletin … we saw the place crawling with Interahamwe. They had already erected barriers …and they were already killing people in the open.' This bulletin was the official announcement on Radio Rwanda that the president had been assassinated.

Witnesses in Byumba prefecture driving towards Uganda described endless roadblocks manned by well-armed Interahamwe. Identity cards were being checked. In the prefecture of Cyangugu, in a parish called Gisuma, a survivor said that gendarmes had turned up at around 5 a.m. and were killing with machetes and looting, and that the gendarmes were using explosives to break down doors.

At the home of the prime minister at 6.10 a.m., Lieutenant Thierry Lotin noticed a tank had been parked in the road by the house. Lotin sent a message to the Belgian command at 6.44 to tell them that he was under fire. Inside the house, Uwilingiyimana was trying to contact ministers in the government but those she managed to get hold of feared for their lives. There was nothing but bad news. The minister of information, Faustin Rucogoza, had been taken away by the Presidential Guard. There were by now fifteen peacekeepers guarding her – ten Belgian, five Ghanaian – and ten Rwandan gendarmes. In such situations a directive provided for the Belgian officer to take command.

Lotin radioed again at 6.55 to say that the prime minister's house was surrounded by perhaps twenty soldiers armed with guns and grenades. There were Presidential Guards on the roof. The Rwandans had ordered him to disarm. Lotin and his men were still inside the house and virtual prisoners. The next message from Lotin came at 8.17: 'They have weapons we do not have, grenades, bombs … we will never hold out.'[14]

There was a sudden explosion outside and Uwilingiyimana took flight with her husband, Ignace Barahira, a lecturer at the University of Butare, and the children.[15] The youngest was three years old. They clambered over the bamboo fence at the back of the house, the children still in their pyjamas. Momentarily confused, Lotin radioed UN headquarters, and spoke to his Belgian commanding officer and was told to follow her. He said that if he did this he would lose radio contact, for the only communications equipment was in the jeeps. Lotin was told to remain with the jeeps. There was the sound of tyres screeching to a halt and Lotin and his men, and the five Ghanaians, were surrounded by Presidential Guard. An officer told Lotin that he must give up all weapons and all the peacekeepers would be escorted to UN headquarters. Lotin kept his head. He radioed again from the jeep. 'What shall I do?' he asked. His soliders had the capacity to resist; each had an automatic rifle, half of had them revolvers and there were two semi-automatics in the jeeps. Lotin was told by the battalion commander, Lieutenant-Colonel Joe Dewez, not to disarm and that he must negotiate.[16]

Lotin was twenty-nine years old with a pregnant wife back home. He had two years' peacekeeping experience. He radioed back: four of his men were disarmed and on the ground. Dewez told him it was better to do as he was asked. Lotin reflected, then decided to disarm. He and his men were led to a minibus parked nearby. A Rwandan major, Bernard Ntuyahaga, who worked for G4 (logistics) in the Rwandan army, told the peacekeepers that they would be escorted to UN quarters. The peacekeepers believed this assurance. With a Rwandan driver, Ntuyahaga accompanied them in the minibus. The peacekeepers clearly did not feel threatened; one of them had kept his pistol hidden but did not use it.

The peacekeepers were taken a short distance to the Camp Kigali army barracks where there was a UN military observer post at the entrance. Arriving at around 8.30 a.m,. Lotin and his men and the five Ghanaian peacekeepers left the minibus and, hands in the air, walked into the camp. An eyewitness noticed an adjudant who worked for the G2 intelligence section in the army tell soldiers at the camp entrance that these were the Belgian peacekeepers responsible for the assassination of the president. The fifteen peacekeepers were immediately attacked with rifle butts and bayonets wielded by Rwandan soldiers. Only the quick thinking of a Togolese UN military observer managed to extricate the five Ghanaians, who were already injured. In vain, Rwandan army officers tried to stop the soldiers attacking the peacekeepers. It looked like a mutiny.

The next message from Lotin came at 9.06 a.m. He was communicating through a Motorola radio and he told Dewez that he had no idea where he was but that he thought that he and his men were going to be lynched. He did not ask for rescue. Dewez asked Lotin if he was not exaggerating slightly.[17] Dewez thought the peacekeepers were being 'roughed up' and telephoned a Rwandan army officer, his liaison with the force, to secure Lotin's release. Dewez trusted the Rwandan army: he had trained and had remained friends with some of its officers. He believed the assurances of co-operation given to Dallaire by the army high command. Dewez thought the trouble stemmed from the fact that the order to co-operate with the UN had not yet reached either the soldiers or the gendarmes. He called Marchal to tell him the men were prisoners. Marchal contacted senior officers in the Rwandan army headquarters to secure their release. 'Given the events in Kigali that morning,' one Belgian officer said, 'although the problems encountered by Lotin were serious, we did not think them exceptional, given what was happening elsewhere.'[18]

There were peacekeepers still held hostage at the airport and the rest of the Belgian contingent of 450 were located in small groups in fourteen different places, all of them isolated. The airways were jammed with pleas for help from UN staff, aid workers and diplomats. There were reports that the Rwandan army, 7,000 strong, had begun to prepare its heavy armaments, a flagrant breach of the rules of the weapons secure area. There were 600 Presidential Guard, some of them on the streets.

The only hopeful sign came later that morning from the airport, where after the intervention of the Belgian ambassador, the peacekeepers at the perimeter fence were released. They had been surrounded by Rwandan soldiers for seven hours and had sat it out, refusing to leave their vehicles.

At 7 a.m. Marchal met with a senior gendarmerie officer, Lieutenant-Colonel Innocent Bavugamenshi, who had sought him out to tell him that a systematic search and kill operation was under way aimed at opposition politicians. In the night Bavugamenshi had heard that the administrative head of the Ministry of Foreign Affairs, Déo Havugimana, had been killed. Bavugamenshi realized that Presidential Guards and gendarmes were evacuating MRNDD politicians and their families from their homes in Kimihurura. The Ministry of Defence had recently transferred responsibility for the security of MRNDD leaders from the gendarmes to a unit of the army. Bavugamenshi was the head of the gendarmes responsible for the safety of the other political leaders and he immediately tried to organize gendarmes to protect the opposition politicians left behind, but because of the lack of adequate equipment he could not locate the commander of the gendarmes, General Augustin Ndindiliyimana.[19]

Early that morning a report came into battalion headquarters from a contingent of Belgian peacekeepers in Kimihurura that Presidential Guards were carrying out systematic 'cleansing'. A unit of peacekeepers was living in the same street as Félicien Ngango, a lawyer and member of the Parti Social Démocrate (PSD) chosen to be the president of the transitional National Assembly. At 6.30 a.m. a firm response was ordered by Marchal, who wanted these peacekeepers reinforced and a platoon sent to the area. But the reinforcements were stopped at a roadblock by Rwandan soldiers. Ngango's entire family was killed. At 11.38 a.m. the report from Kimihurura was of a search and kill operation against civilians. Only Rwandans were targeted, no expats or UN personnel. A witness recalled: 'Very early on Thursday morning we began to receive news of killings on the telephone. We learned that whole families had been wiped out.'

At mid-morning on 7 April, Marchal received a call for help from the Canadian wife of a well-known opposition politician, Landoald Ndasingwa, known as 'Lando', a prominent member of the Parti Libéral (PL), the first vice-president of the party and minister of labour and social affairs. Lando was at home with his two children and his mother, a Tutsi. Five Ghanaian peacekeepers were protecting him. Presidential Guards had surrounded the house.[20] Lando's wife told Marchal they must have extra protection. Marchal doubted he could get any reinforcements to them because of the roadblocks. Then Lando himself came on the phone. Fifteen Presidential Guards were about to attack his home. Over the phone Marchal heard a loud explosion and shots. 'It's too late,' Lando had said. The family was killed.[21]

Marchal was later called to account by an American journalist, critical that he had not saved Lando and his family. Marchal quietly and patiently explained to the interviewer, 'We were a minority on the ground.'[22]

At 9 o'clock on the morning of 7 April, Dallaire was told that the prime minister had taken flight. He spoke over the phone to Iqbal Riza of the DPKO at UN headquarters, telling him that he might have to use force to protect the prime minister. Riza told him that he was not to fire unless fired upon.[23] Dallaire left UN headquarters to find the prime minister, but at a roadblock outside the Hôtel des Mille Collines he was ordered out of his jeep by Presidential Guards. He was obliged to walk, escorted by Rwandan soldiers. He was too late in any case. Uwilingiyimana and her husband were dead. Their children were gone, rescued by a UNDP employee, M. Le Moal, and a Senegalese military observer, Captain Mbaye Diagne, and taken to the Hôtel des Mille Collines where Presidential Guards would later come looking for them.[24]

Earlier that morning Bagosora apparently convened a meeting of the executive committee of the MRNDD to try to find a presidential successor, but the MRNDD was apparently not ready to nominate anyone without approval from the party's national congress. At 9 a.m. Bagosora, in his Audi 1000, travelled the short distance to the residence of the US ambassador, David Rawson. No other diplomats turned up. Bagosora was accompanied by Major-General Augustin Ndindiliyimana, the chief of staff of the gendarmerie. Rawson asked Bagosora why there was gunfire and Bagosora had replied that soliders were unhappy about the death of the president and were firing in the air.

Elsewhere in Kigali, in Nyamirambo, a witness recalled: 'By 9 a.m. on Thursday morning, the militia were everywhere in our area and had already started killing Tutsi.' Another witness said the sound of gunfire that morning was relentless.

Bagosora arrived at the Ecole Supérieure Militaire (ESM) at 10 a.m. and was met by its commander, Colonel Leonidas Rusatira. Rusatira had been Bagosora's predecessor in the Ministry of Defence and was the longest-serving officer, but recently he had been demoted and appointed director of the military academy. There were about a hundred people at the meeting, including all Rwandan army officers who commanded sectors in Kigali, the commanders of the military camps, the officers from the Etat-Major, the headquarters staff, the gendarmerie, and the liaison officers with UNAMIR. There were officers there from all over Rwanda and it was strange how quickly the meeting had been convened.

The meeting was chaired by Bagosora and Ndindiliyimana. Bagosora suggested that the army take control of the country but there was no agreement and it was decided to create a committee of public safety, a crisis committee, to re-establish stability and reunite members of the broad-based transitional government in order to accelerate the Arusha Accords. During the meeting there was the sound of gunfire and grenades exploding at the army barracks, Camp Kigali, next door. A Rwandan army officer interrupted the meeting, reporting that Belgian soldiers had been captured and taken to Camp Kigali. Other witnesses have said that the entire meeting knew that peacekeepers were being lynched not more than a hundred metres away.[25]

Dallaire had not yet arrived at the meeting, for it had taken him more than an hour to travel the short distance to the Ministry of Defence. Once he got there, a Rwandan officer had insisted on driving him to the ESM. Dallaire was accompanied by the senior Belgian duty officer, Major Peter Maggen. They passed Camp Kigali. Dallaire recounted later:

> I caught to my right side a brief glimpse of what I thought were a couple of soldiers in Belgian uniforms on the ground in the camp, approximately 60 metres. I did not know whether they were dead or injured; however, I remember the shock of realizing that we now had taken casualties. I ordered the RGF (Rwandan Army) officer to stop the car. The officer refused, saying that the troops in Camp Kigali were out of control and it was not safe for even RGF officers to go into the camp.[26]

Camp Kigali was a fortress; there were more than 1,000 Rwandan soliders there, plus the elite reconnaissance battalion.

As Dallaire arrived at the meeting, a Togolese UN military observer approached him in a nervous and excited manner and told him that a number of Belgian peacekeepers were being held at Camp Kigali and that they were being beaten up. After the meeting was over, and still under Rwandan army escort, Dallaire returned to the Ministry of Defence to find Bagosora. Bagosora had made a brief visit to the camp and Dallaire repeatedly and insistently asked Bagosora to allow him to go to Camp Kigali. Bagosora said that it was unsafe; the soliders were rioting because, he claimed, Belgian soldiers had fired on Rwandan soldiers. He promised Dallaire that he would ensure the camp was secure and would obtain the release of the peacekeepers. He also suggested that it might be advisable for the Belgian troops to be withdrawn from Rwanda because of the rumours that they were to blame for the president's murder, hence the violent reaction in the army camp next door. It was difficult, Bagosora told Dallaire, because he was not in command of all the elements in the army. Dallaire wanted Bagosora to talk to the RPF at the CND to preserve the peace and prevent a resumption of hostilities.

Dallaire remembers Bagosora briefing a senior officer about the release of the peacekeepers. That afternoon Bagosora spent much time in his office in the Ministry of Defence writing letters, answering the telephone, signing documents. He was working as though it was a day like any other.

Dallaire thought the peacekeepers were being kept in the barracks, and that they would be released, like those at the airport. His duty was to protect the ministers in the broad-based transitional government, but with peacekeepers prevented from moving freely about the city this was proving impossible. Dallaire wanted something done about the roadblocks, where people were at the mercy of the mood of the guards.

Some time that afternoon Bagosora wrote a communiqué that was broadcast on Radio Rwanda at 5.20 p.m. It announced the creation of the crisis committee and assured the people of Rwanda that the situation would rapidly return to normal. Calm would be restored and they must reject hate and violence. The young must guard against vandalism. The communiqué emphasized the necessity of accelerating the creation of transitional institutions in line with the Arusha Accords.

The weaknesses in the UN mission were now terrifyingly obvious. At 8.50 a.m. on 7 April, UNAMIR's Quick Reaction Force (QRF), with Bangladeshi soliders and three armoured personnel carriers, was turned back from a roadblock after being threatened with anti-tank weapons. Marchal and Dallaire had talked about the weakness of the QRF, wanting its soldiers to be replaced with troops from another country. Bangladesh, though, was one of the UN's most important troop contributors, with 15,000 soldiers serving the organization world-wide. Dallaire knew that in New York officials in the Department of Peacekeeping Operations had been asking other UN member states for more soldiers for Rwanda and for equipment but there had been no offers.

The sixty-strong Tunisian company, well-led, well-trained and disciplined, possessed no integral vehicles, communications equipment or logistics. The Belgians, already weakened by being scattered throughout the city, possessed only light arms. Under the guidelines for governments contributing military personnel to UNAMIR, written in the secretariat, 'mortars and other heavy crew-served weapons are not required' for Rwanda. They were now stuck with ammunition reserves 40 per cent below that required under standard military procedure. Marchal had asked Brussels for guidance about this fact several times but had never received a reply. No weapons he requested ever came – the anti-tank weapons, heavy weapons and mortar-bombs he needed if the airport was to be defended in a worst-case scenario. Dallaire and Marchal both knew that only Belgium would be likely to provide such equipment rapidly. Belgium did not. Had they been provided, the situation in which the peacekeepers now found themselves would have been different. They did not even have enough Motorola radios.

Dallaire located Lotin and his men at nightfall. It was almost dark but he could just make them out in the light of a 25-watt bulb. They were piled high, in a heap, like sacks of potatoes, in the courtyard of a Kigali hospital.[27] At first Dallaire and his aide-de-camp counted eleven bodies. Dallaire ordered photographs to be taken. He negotiated with the Rwanda gendarmerie for his men to be laid out with more dignity. A Rwandan colonel went to Camp Kigali and took money from the cash register behind the bar to pay somebody to wash the bodies. Ndindiliyimana, head of the gendarmerie, loaned Dallaire his escort to return to UNAMIR headquarters. No one wanted to leave the headquarters at night. Ndindiliyimana said afterwards he did not dare go home and spent the night at the Hôtel des Diplomates.

It took two days to get the bodies of the peacekeepers back to UN custody where they remained, under guard, in a lorry in a hotel carpark, and then a plane came to take them home. The peacekeepers had fought during six hours of combat, some of them managing to seize weapons from their aggressors, and the last surviving soldier had been killed sheltering behind the body of a dead comrade.

There was outrage in Belgium at the deaths of these men and the fact that in long hours of combat there had been no attempt to rescue them. The most senior Belgian officers in UNAMIR, Lieutenant-Colonel J. Dewez and Colonel Luc Marchal, came under a barrage of criticism. Marchal was made the scapegoat. When he returned to Belgium he was put through a court martial, accused of not taking adequate precautions, but the trial ended in acquittal; Marchal had not even been aware where Lotin was or that he and his men were in trouble.

Dewez, who had thought Lotin was exaggerating when he said he feared that the men would be lynched, would later explain in his testimony to an inquiry in the Belgian Senate:

> I had not come to Rwanda as a para-commando to fight but as a blue helmet, a symbolic presence to help the Rwandans … My perception of classic UN operations was that the UN does not fight … I believed in the assurance, the night before, of the command of the Rwandan army that they would help us to assure security and order … I was blinded by this logic, paralysed by it … the fact that my men had been taken prisoner by the Rwandan army assured me that they were safe.[28]

The Belgian press wanted to know why other soldiers had not gone to Lotin's rescue. There were thirty-six Belgians from Platoon B, 16th Company, and the command of the 16th Company of fifteen men in the city. These soldiers were only a kilometre away, separated by several roadblocks, but no one had known where Lotin was. Marchal tried to explain that even had they known where he was, the only way to liberate him would have been to negotiate with his captors. To have tried to fight the Rwandan army would have been suicidal. An attempted rescue would have drawn more peacekeepers into the army camp. It might have been a trap to drag them all in, and far more peacekeepers would have lost their lives.

'We had no armament, no equipment to face such a situation,' Marchal said. He had had every confidence in the Rwandan army, whose officers had, that morning, been co-operating with the peacekeepers. Marchal believed a great many soldiers in the Rwandan army had not wanted to take part in the violence and were looking for a sign from the international community that would enable them to keep the peace and avoid a war. In spite of the confusion and their lack of radio communications, there had been co-operation with the gendarmes. Only some gendarmes refused to take part in joint patrols with UNAMIR. At some roadblocks there had been arguments among the gendarmes about whether or not militia should be allowed through without being disarmed.

Marchal said Dallaire's actions that day were quite rightly tailored to keeping the town calm. They were all vulnerable, including the 331 unarmed UN military observers spread throughout the country with no protection.

Dallaire later explained just how vulnerable they were:

> Precipitous action in the context of the tense and uncertain security environment in Kigali that morning could have been the spark which would have ignited a wider conflict. This would have placed UNAMIR in an adversarial role ... Had either Colonel Marchal or Lt. Colonel Dewez requested authority from me to conduct an assault on Camp Kigali to rescue the detained group under the conditions of that time, my response would have been an outright refusal for such an armed intervention. The only solution reasonably available to us at that time was to continue to negotiate as a neutral force.

For the first two days Marchal thought that it would be possible to control the crisis, and that this was a situation similar to the one in February when there had been a sudden deterioration in security. Two days before the plane was shot down the army chief, Major-General Déogratias Nsabimana, had told Marchal about his fears of an imminent attack by the RPF. Of UNAMIR's serious deficiencies, Marchal believed that the most grave was a lack of intelligence analysis: 'With decent intelligence analysis it would not have taken long to tell us that the priority was to protect the Prime Minister and the President of the Constitutional Court.' But with the Rwandan army decapitated by the downing of the jet, there was confusion. 'We badly evaluated,' Marchal recalled later. 'We did not imagine the role of Bagosora in the shadows.'[29]

Later it was ascertained that everyone, whether Hutu or Tutsi, who wanted power-sharing, or who had spoken out against Habyarimana and Hutu Power were listed; every journalist, every lawyer, every professor, every teacher, every civil servant, every priest, every doctor, every clerk, every student, every civil rights activist were hunted down in a house-to-house operation. The first targets were members of the never-to-be constituted broad-based transitional government.[30] The lists of the victims included the names of Tutsi shopkeepers and business people, the lists prepared in the military intelligence office, from where Colonel Anatole Nsengiyumva had written his reports to persuade the president of the threat of 'the Tutsi' to the country. And while the pro-democracy politicians were being killed, the Hutu Power politicians, the leaders of the MRNDD and others, were whisked away under the escort of the Presidential Guard.

The new chief of staff of the army, Marcel Gatsinzi, arrived in Kigali from Butare during the afternoon of 7 April and was shot at when his convoy drove through the presidential district. Unharmed, he attended a scheduled meeting of the crisis committee at 7 p.m. Gatsinzi, Rusatira and Ndindiliyimana were in charge.[31] Rusatira commanded the Ecole Supérieure Militaire in Kigali, with only 100 soldiers at his command. Gatsinzi's battalion was in the south of the country, in Butare, and had been infiltrated by extremists.

Bagosora claims that he went to Kimihurura to evacuate his family to the Kanombe military camp that night. He then visited the family of Habyarimana, paying his respects to the dead president. But Bagosora had communications links with the best-trained units in the Rwandan army – the reconnaissance and para-commando battalions, some 800 strong. All were in Kigali. On 7 April, before dawn, the reconnaissance battalion had recalled to Kigali their armoured personnel carriers, which had been sent to Rambura, in the north, to evade UNAMIR control.

On Thursday morning, 7 April, there were massacres in Nyamata in the Bugesera. An accountant at the commune was seen to give beer to the Interahamwe in preparation for their 'work'. In the Kibungo prefecture early on Thursday morning, a 41-year-old cattle herdsman noticed wounded people fleeing from the direction of Murambe. They told him that Tutsi had been attacked all night long.[32] In Ntarama, about an hour and a half from Kigali going south, the militia had started to burn Tutsi houses, forcing them to flee to the local church where people thought they would be safe.[33] By nightfall on 7 April, the killing of Tutsi was taking place in the north-west in Gisenyi prefecture, in the south and north-east of Kigali prefecture, in Gikongoro prefecture and in the south-western town of Cyangugu. The next day the killing spread east and west.[34]

'I saw people running as their attackers ran after them with machetes ... I saw a lecturer from the University giving arms to the Interahamwe and telling them to do a good job.'

At roadblocks in Kigali the militia asked for identification cards at first, killing all those with the designation Tutsi, but this took too much time and became an irritation so the militia singled out those who were tall, with straight noses and long fingers. And then they killed those who looked educated and more wealthy than others.

Major-General Paul Kagame, commander of the RPF, was in his headquarters in Mulindi on 7 April. At around 1 p.m. he made a call to UN headquarters in Kigali. Kagame said he had just learned that the houses of some RPF supporters in Kigali had been surrounded by Rwandan government forces: 'I must inform you that we must act to protect our own.' He wanted Dallaire to know he was serious: this was advance warning.[35] A second message from

Kagame came fifteen minutes later: the peacekeepers must do all they could to protect the politicians who had been arrested.

In Kigali, stationed with the RPF soldiers, Tito Rutaremara, part of the political leadership, was warning both General Augustin Ndindiliyimana and Colonel Théoneste Bagosora that the RPF would attack if the slaughter of civilians did not stop. Rutaremara said that the RPF soldiers were being goaded. At 4.30 p.m. the RPF soldiers broke out of the CND and engaged the Presidential Guard. Witnesses testified to an attack, later that day, by the RPF on the Compagnie Territoriale de Gendarmerie in Remera during which civilians, including children, were killed.

On the night of 7 April, Dallaire was asked by Gatsinzi to establish contact with the RPF command in order to obtain a ceasefire. Kagame relayed a message to UN headquarters in Kigali that he was ready to send a battalion to assist government forces in preventing further civilian killings by 'renegade forces'.

Kagame says that he suggested that he secure some areas, creating safe havens; there was no mandate in the world that could stop their combined forces ending the bloodshed.[36] Dallaire did not trust the RPF offer. Both sides were by now killing non-combatants. 'I needed troops from a third party,' he said. 'A strong UN force to stop the killings was absolutely essential.' To have cooperated with Kagame would have guaranteed losses among his thinly spread out force. Dallaire told Kagame that he was doing all he could to secure a ceasefire.

On Friday morning, 8 April, Bagosora was to be found in the Ministry of Defence, where he was having a series of meetings with politicians. Armed escorts had been sent to collect various political figures and at 1 p.m. a group was assembled in the offices of the PSD party. A new president of Rwanda was chosen, Dr Theodore Sindikubwabo, a member of the MRNDD, who was elderly and in poor health. Over the next few hours an 'interim government', whose legitimacy apparently came from the 1991 Constitution, was set up.[37]

Later that same day the French ambassador, Jean-Philippe Marlaud, made a telephone call to the Belgian ambassador Johan Swinnen, to let him know the membership of the new government. Swinnen immediately realized that all the ministers came from the Hutu Power wing of the political parties, yet Marlaud was claiming that he thought the existence of this government would prevent a coup d'état.[38]

Marlaud then spoke with Bagosora. Both he and the deputy defence attaché at the French embassy, Lieutenant Colonel Jean-Jacques Maurin, claim that at four in the afternoon they tried to persuade Bagosora to take control of the situation, insisting that the army must cooperate with UNAMIR.[39]

The new government was announced on RTLMC by announcers Valérie Bemeriki and Noël Hitimana. After Bemeriki read out the names of the ministers she began to giggle and told her listeners that, for some reason, the opposition members in the previous government could not be found. Perhaps, she said, they had 'resigned or simply wandered off'.[40] She laughed again.

A first detailed assessment of the situation in Rwanda was sent to New York in a code-cable on 8 April in which Dallaire described a campaign of terror that was well-planned and organized, and led by the Presidential Guard. The violence was targeted against opposition leaders, the RPF contingent, the Tutsi ethnic group, the population in general, UNAMIR, and all UN offices, vehicles and personnel. His Belgian troops, the backbone of his operation, were isolated by roadblocks. They had no supplies of power or petrol. Ten peacekeepers were dead and he feared for the safety of the rest. They had food for less than two weeks, drinking water in some places for only one or two days and fuel for at most three days. He was critically short of ammunition and medical supplies. Although his primary task in Rwanda was the protection of politicians, given the murder of the prime minister and other ministers, this task was no longer possible.

Kigali was in a state of war. Roadblocks prevented any movement. The security of his troops could not be assured. The moment he took further casualties he would run out of medical supplies and would be unable to evacuate. He could not assure the safety of the airport.

Dallaire raised the possibility that the peacekeepers might have to evacuate their civilian personnel, in which case he would need a different mandate and reinforcements. He would try to regroup smaller and more isolated units. He was trying to bring about a ceasefire between some 200 RPF soldiers who had left the CND building and were fighting the Presidential Guard, but his telephone lines had been cut. He had a demoralized but brave Belgian battalion and an untrained, under-equipped, below-strength unit from Bangladesh. Dallaire assured New York: 'There must be no doubt, that without the presence of UNAMIR the situation here would be much worse.' He wanted to know if his mandate was still viable.[41] New York told him not to risk further losses or take action which might result in reprisals. Dallaire later commented:

> An operation should begin with the objective and then consider how best to achieve it with minimal risk. Instead, our operation began with an evaluation of risk and if there was risk, the objective was forgotten. You can't begin by asking if there is a risk. If there is no risk, they could have sent Boy Scouts, not soldiers.[42]

It was a conclusion also reached by Kagame, who asked why the UN had not sent Boy Scouts.[43]

In the first days, Dallaire thought this might be a power grab by the extremists, a military coup with the intention of eliminating all opposing politicians and ruining for ever the possibility of reconciliation with the RPF. The reply to his 8 April assessment came from the Department of Peace-keeping Operations. He was to negotiate a ceasefire.

For his part, Jacques-Roger Booh-Booh informed Kofi Annan that he was consulting with the crisis committee about security, and that the deaths of several ministers had created a power vacuum which could cause problems in the peace process.[44]

The official swearing-in of Rwanda's 'interim government' took place on 9 April. The new prime minister was Jean Kambanda.[45] An economist and banker, Kambanda later claimed to have been surprised by his appointment. In his inaugural speech as prime minister, Kambanda promised that his government would restore understanding between the people of Rwanda and provide security for them. The government would continue talks with the RPF and ensure compliance with the Arusha Accords.[46]

The members of the new government were presented to the crisis committee by Colonel Théoneste Bagosora, who was assisted by two other colonels, Laurent Serubuga and Pierre-Célestin Rwagafilita. Described as a coalition government, from now on it would portray the killing in Rwanda as the result of spontaneous Hutu grief due to the death of the president.

Some six days after the genocide began, Bagosora telephoned Gatsinzi, the Rwandan army officer summoned from Butare on 7 April to become, reluctantly and temporarily, the head of the Rwandan armed forces. Bagosora wanted Gatsinzi to prepare armed guards to escort the government's hard currency from the vaults of the Central Bank in Kigali to the interim government at Gitarama. Gatsinzi refused.[47]

The money was moved anyway. Bagosora organized a detachment of soldiers. There is only a rough estimate of how much it was, but it filled several trucks. The year's taxes had just been collected and the amount was later estimated to be 24 billion Rwandese francs (US$170 million). The Rwandan currency stolen is estimated at twice that in circulation at the time. There was also hard currency and gold in the vaults.[48]

The moderate army officers kept their distance from the interim government and on 12 April ten Rwandan officers published a communiqué in which they tried to short-circuit it. They proposed a meeting with the RPF command to examine how to put in place the institutions required in the transition to democracy. Nothing came of this. Gatsinzi was relieved of his command of the army on 17 April and replaced by Colonel Augustin Bizimungu, former commander at Ruhengeri, now promoted to major-general.

The first large massacre to be discovered by the peacekeepers was at Gikondo, a parish in the heart of Kigali and a CDR stronghold.[49] It was Saturday, 9

April, and they were answering a desperate call from two Polish military observers living there.

The investigating peacekeepers were two Polish majors, Stefan Stec and Marec Pazik, who had served in the UN mission to Cambodia. With them went Major Brent Beardsley, Dallaire's staff officer.[50] They took the one working Czech-made armoured personnel carrier (APC) and a three-man Bangaldeshi crew who warned that the APC could break down at any moment.

The APC slowly made its way through the streets. A group of people screamed at them to stop, but they drove on without speaking. The climb up the hill at Gikondo was laborious, for the road was steep and there were deep ruts made by the torrential downpours. At the top of the hill was a Catholic mission operated by Polish priests and nuns, set in terraced gardens surrounded by eucalyptus trees. It was a large mission, self-contained and dominated by a brick church.

They left the Bangladeshi crew with the APC, and walked into the church gardens. It was there they found the bodies. Whole families had been killed with their children, hacked by machetes. There were terrible wounds to the genitalia. Some people were not dead. There was a three-month-old baby, the mother raped and the baby killed with a terrible wound. There were children, some with their legs or feet cut off, and their throats cut. Most of the victims had bled to death. Steck returned to the APC. He wanted to get his camcorder to film it. There must be proof.

They found the two Polish UN observers huddled together in the church.[51] The observers said that the Interahamwe did the killing under the direction of the Presidential Guard. The priests were in the porch trying to stem the bleeding of the few survivors. The priests thought that the Rwandan army had cordoned off the parish. They said their parishioners did the killing. When the president's plane went down, there had been shooting all night long. The next day Tutsi had fled to the church for safety and some people were so afraid that they hid beneath floors, in cupboards or in the rafters.

On Saturday, 9 April, at about 9 a.m., the priests had organized a mass and around 500 people, sheltering in the compound, turned up at the church. While they were holding the mass there was shooting outside and grenades went off. There was a commotion and two Presidential Guards and two gendarmes burst into the church followed by Interahamwe. The Interahamwe wore their distinctive clothing, the *Kitenge*, multi-coloured trousers and tunics. 'The militia began slashing away,' a witness remembered. 'They were hacking at the arms, legs, genitals, breasts, faces and necks.' There was total panic. Some people were dragged outside and beaten to death. The killing lasted about two hours and then the killers had walked slowly among the bodies, looting them and finished off the wounded.[52]

One of the Polish military observers, Jerzy Maczta,[53] had watched the local police entering the buildings in the compound, followed by militia armed with machetes and clubs. One of the militia had what looked like a Kalashnikov. Maczta had seen militia climb over the fence and said he had tried to contact UNAMIR headquarters but the radio channels were jammed. Maczka helped the wounded and had noticed how ears and mouths were slashed, clothes had been pulled off and the genitals of men and women mutilated. Maczta took photographs.

There was a pile of identification cards with the ethnic designation of Tutsi burned in an attempt to eradicate all evidence that these people had existed. The next day the Interahamwe came back. They discovered that the survivors were hiding in a small chapel. When they failed to break down the door, the militia poured petrol in through the windows of the chapel and threw in hand-grenades.

Over the next three months, massacres like this became commonplace. But at Gikondo there was photographic proof. The Polish peacekeepers thought that Gikondo should alert the world, for they recognized what was happening as genocide.

Dallaire kept some convoys patrolling but after finding the mutilated bodies of Thierry Lotin and his men he pulled back and increased the size of the Belgian peacekeeping contingent at the airport. It was the only lifeline. His priority was the protection of the ill-equipped and poorly trained contingents, his civilian staff, and the people sheltering with them.

It took Dallaire more than two weeks to find out where all his troops were and gain access to them. Because of the constant pressure by the Americans in the Security Council, supported by Britain, to cut the costs and resources of the mission, most units in UNAMIR had one or two days' water, a maximum of two days' rations, virtually no stocks of fuel and about twenty rounds of ammunition for each soldier.[54]

From the balconies in the concrete-block hotel which served as UNAMIR headquarters, the peacekeepers watched. One peacekeeper remained haunted by a killing only yards away: 'he just held him by his shirt and started dragging him … and just raised his machete and hacked him on the head … he did that twice and we were standing there watching him … after that he just rubbed his bloodstained machete on his buttocks, and then searched the victim's pockets … we all screamed at this.' Not long afterwards a tipper truck came by with prisoners who had been detailed to collect bodies from the streets.[55] 'Someone flagged it down and dragged the body from under the tree and threw it into the tipper truck which was almost full and people were moaning and crying, you could see that some were not dead.'[56]

Notes

1. Lowell Blankfort, 'Almost a Million Dead, Rwanda Seeks Justice', *World Outlook*, 2 December 1995, UNA-US.

2. Some witnesses claim that only the lights of the runway went out.

3. Unless otherwise stated survivor statements are taken from African Rights, *Rwanda. Death, Despair and Defiance*. London: African Rights, 1995.

4. Interview, Major-General Roméo Dallaire, London, November 1994.

5. Henry Kwami Anyidoho, *Guns Over Kigali*. Accra: Woeli Publishing Services, 1997. p. 23.

6. André Guichaoua (ed.), in *Les Crises Politiques au Burundi et au Rwanda (1993–1994)*, Université des Sciences et Technologies de Lille. Paris: Karthala, 1995, p. 705.

7. Colonel Théoneste Bagosora, 'L'Assassinat du Président Habyarimana ou l'Ultime Operation du Tutsi pour sa reconqueste du pouvoir par la force au Rwanda,' Unpublished MS.

8. There are various rumours about Bagosora's night-time movements. He had his own communications network, a walkie-talkie which linked him to the army command, the Presidential Guard, the presidential palace and the executives of the extremist parties MRNDD and the CDR.

9. At the airport this rumour was in circulation earlier, about an hour after the crash occurred. The information was also given out by the Rwandan embassy in Brussels and by Rwanda's UN mission in New York. In Kigali the news that the Belgians were to blame for the crash was broadcast over Radio Rwanda at 23.04.

10. Interview, Colonel Luc Marchal, December 1999.

11. Summary of World Broadcasts. AL/1996. 8 April 1994.

12. Astri Suhrke, 'Dilemmas of Protection: The Log of the Kigali Battalion', *Security Dialogue*, Vol. 29, No. 1, March 1998, p. 40.

13. Summary of World Broadcasts. AL/1966 A/2. 8 April 1994.

14. Belgian Senate, *Commission d'enquête parlementaire concernant les événements du Rwanda*. Report, 6 December 1997, pp. 401–61.

15. The children were Théophile Umuhire, aged three, Michel Hirwa, aged five, Christine Gasare, aged thirteen, Marie-Christine Umuraza, aged fifteen, Aimé Barahira, aged nineteen. They escaped and were granted asylum in Switzerland.

16. Suhrke, 'Dilemmas of Protection'.

17. Belgian Senate, *Commission d'enquête*, p. 437.

18. Testimony of Major Timsonet during the courts martial of Luc Marchal (unpublished).

19. Interview, Colonel Luc Marchal, December 1999.

20. Anyidoho, *Guns Over Kigali*, p. 27.

21. The Ghanaian peacekeepers were overpowered and were reported missing. They arrived back at headquarters later that morning.

22. Excerpt from the interviews on Frontline's website for 'The Triumph of Evil'. www.pbs.org/WGBH/Pages/Frontline/shows/evil. Copyright WGBH/Frontline, 1999.

23. UN Security Council, *Report of the Independent Inquiry into the Actions of the United Nations during the 1994 Genocide in Rwanda*, 15 December 1999, p. 20.

24. Memorandum. From Yvon Le Moal, Acting Designated Official, Rwanda. To Mr. Benon Sevan, UN Security Co-ordinator and Mr. G. Speth, the Administrator, the UN Development Programme. 20 April 1994. Unpublished.

25. Filip Reyntjens, *Rwanda. Trois Jours qui ont fait basculer l'histoire*. Paris: Editions l'Harmattan, 1995, p. 76.

26. Written answer to questions put to General Roméo Dallaire by the juge-avocat général of the Belgian military court. Belgian Senate, *Commission d'enquête*, p. 423

27. Interview, Major-General Roméo Dallaire, London, November 1994.

28. Belgian Senate, *Commission d'enquête*, p. 451.

29. Interview, Colonel Luc Marchal, November 1999.

30. The Parti Libéral lost nearly all its members, as did the Parti Social Démocrate. All MDR members who had advocated links with the RPF were killed, as were most of the militants in that party opposed to the dictatorship of the northern Hutu. See African Rights, *Rwanda*.

31. Interview, Marcel Gatsinzi, Kigali, October 1997.

32. *Genocide in Rwanda. Documentation of Two Massacres during April 1994*. Issue Brief, US Committee for Refugees, November 1994. p. 12.

33. Mahmood Mamdani, *From Conquest to Consent as the Basis of State Formation: Reflections on Rwanda*. Paper presented to the conference Crisis in the Great Lakes Region, organized by the Council for the Development of Social Research in Africa, Arusha, Tanzania, 4–7 September 1995.

34. Human Rights Watch/Fédération Internationale des Ligues des Droits de l'Homme, *Leave none to tell the story. Genocide in Rwanda*, 1999, p. 209.

35. Jacques Castonguay, *Les Casques Bleus au Rwanda*, Paris: Editions l'Harmattan, 1998, p. 145.

36. Interview, Major-General Paul Kagame, Kigali, October 1997.

37. Interview, Major-General Roméo A. Dallaire, London, November 1994.

38. Reyntjens, *Rwanda*, p. 89.

39. Assemblée Nationale, Mission d'Information Commune, *Enquête sur la Tragédie Rwandaise (1990–1994). Book III: Auditions*, Vol. 1, p. 296.

40. *Broadcasting Genocide: Censorship, Propaganda and State-sponsored Violence in Rwanda 1990–1994*. Article 19, 1996. pp. 110–11.

41. The text of the 8 April cable is published in Belgian Senate, *Commission d'Enquête*, pp. 508–15.

42. Human Rights Watch/Fédération Internationale des Ligues des Droits de l'Homme, *Leave none to tell the story*, p. 600.

43. Interview, Major-General Paul Kagame, Kigali, October 1997.

44. There were doubts expressed by almost everyone about John-Roger Booh-Booh's lack of impartiality. Before the genocide began he was considered too close a friend of Habyarimana for someone in his position and there was surprise when Booh-Booh was appointed by Boutros-Ghali. On 8 February 1994, Booh-Booh was seen with the president of MRNDD, Mathieu Ngirumpaste, together with the secretary-general, Joseph Nzirorera, in the café-restaurant Le Pêche Mignon. Four days before the plane crash, Booh-Booh passed the day at the presidential residence in Gisenyi. Also there were Bagosora and Joseph Nzirorera. Vénuste Nshimiyimana, *Prélude de Génocide Rwandais. Enquête sur les circonstances politiques et militaires du meutre du Président Habyarimana*, Brussels: Quorum, 1995, p. 76.

45. The International Criminal Tribunal for Rwanda. Case ICTR 97-23-S. Judgment and Sentence. 23 September 1998. Jean Kambanda received a life sentence for six counts including genocide, conspiracy to commit genocide, direct and public incitement to commit genocide, complicity in genocide, and two counts of crimes against humanity.

46. Radio Rwanda, Summary of World Broadcasts. AL/1968 A/2. 11 April 1994.

47. Interview, Marcel Gatsinzi, Kigali, October 1997.

48. For the duration of the genocide and some weeks after it, Hutu Power kept operational the world-wide government banking network and a total of US$17.8 million was spirited away with US$6.4 million taken out in travellers' cheques. 'Le financement de l'ancien régime après Avril 1994', in Pierre Galand and Michel Chossudovsky, *L'Usage de la Dette Extérieure du Rwanda (1990/1994) La Responsabilité des Bailleurs de Fonds*, Brussels and Ottawa, 1996.

49. In March, a Major Podevijn had reported to HQ that weapons had been distributed to the members of the Interahamwe militia there.

50. Interviews, Stefan Stec, The Hague, 10 April 1996; Major Brent Beardsley, Montreal, 20 March 1996; Marec Pazik, The Hague, 6 April 1996.

51. Military observers (MILOBS) consisted of commissioned officers from the rank of captain to lieutenant-colonel who were deployed around the country to monitor and ensure that all parties followed the peace agreement. There were officers from sixteen countries under the command of Colonel Tikoca from Fiji, and supported by operations officer, Lieutenant-Colonel Somalia Iliya from Nigeria. Some of them were evacuated when the genocide started but others stayed on and formed a team of liaison officers who were attached to the headquarters of the RGF and RPF. Others were formed into rapid reaction teams for information-gathering.

52. *Genocide in Rwanda, Documentation of Two Massacres during April 1994. Issue Brief.* US Committee for Refugees, November 1994, pp. 4–9.

53. Ibid., p. 9.

54. Jonathan Moore (ed.), *Hard Choices, Moral Dilemmas in Humanitarian Intervention.* Oxford: Rowman and Littlefield, 1998.

55. The bodies were taken to a mass grave at Nyamirambo.

56. Interview with Colonel Quist, transcript, tape 28. Twenty-Twenty Television, July 1994.

13 · The Genocide Exposed

TWO days after the attack on the church in Gikondo, the story of what had happened there appeared in the French newspaper *Libération*, written by Jean-Philippe Ceppi.[1] Ceppi described seeing mutilated bodies, with penises and breasts cut off. Only a dozen people had survived the massacre and they were not expected to live. In the roads around Gikondo, and all over Kigali, murder was being committed. Everywhere there were sounds of screams and gunfire. The Presidential Guard, carrying lists of victims, toured the city in APCs. The Interahamwe battered down doors, chasing Tutsi from house to house, and room to room. Nowhere was safe for Tutsi, not even the hospitals, where Rwandan soldiers were rampaging through the wards looking for them. There were so many bodies delivered to the city morgue that they had to be stacked outside.

The French daily *Le Monde* also published a story about Gikondo, on Tuesday, 12 April, by journalist Jean Hélène. Hélène described how the victims of the killing in Kigali were mostly Tutsi. According to the chief delegate of the International Committee of the Red Cross, Philippe Gaillard, who had organized vehicles and delegates to help the wounded of Gikondo, in the city of Kigali an estimated 10,000 people had already been murdered. Hélène speculated that by the time the RPF reached Kigali all the Tutsi would be dead.[2]

In the Ceppi article in *Libération* the word genocide was used. Ceppi wrote that the RPF was advancing on Kigali, and according to some reports was only 15 kilometres from the capital. 'But by the time they arrive,' Ceppi speculated, 'the genocide of the Tutsi would already have taken place.' This was the first mention of genocide, and then the word disappeared. For the next three weeks a fog of misinformation shrouded what was happening as the western press described the situation in Rwanda as 'chaos and anarchy', something which seemed pre-ordained, 'an orgy of ethnic violence'. Rwanda was described as a failed central African nation suffering from a centuries-old history of tribal warfare and a 'deep distrust of outside intervention'.[3] In the weeks ahead this view helped to bolster the arguments that nothing could be done.[4]

Roger Winter, director of the US Committee for Refugees, who had known the problems of Rwanda since 1983, had only just returned from Rwanda and was desperate to change this perception. He wrote an article explaining that the violence was political in nature, a plot by an extremist clique determined to cling to power, using ethnicity to achieve its ends. Winter's article was rejected by most American papers, including the *Washington Post* and the *New York Times*. It was eventually published in the *Toronto Globe and Mail* on 14 April.[5]

In a harsh rebuke to the media after the genocide was over an international inquiry concluded that, although the coverage had been handicapped by danger on the ground, the press, in characterizing the genocide as tribal anarchy, was fundamentally irresponsible. The media's failure to report that genocide was taking place, and thereby generate public pressure for something to be done to stop it, contributed to international indifference and inaction, and possibly to the crime itself.[6]

In the headquarters of the UN in New York, on Thursday morning, 7 April, Kofi Annan, Under-Secretary-General and head of the UN Department of Peackeeping Operations (DPKO), received a telephone call from Kigali. UNAMIR had suffered casualties. Three peacekeepers for certain, and probably more, had been murdered.[7] Annan met with the Belgian permanent representative to the UN, Paul Noterdaeme, later that morning. Noterdaeme was under instruction from his ministry to press for a stronger mandate for UNAMIR. Foreign minister, Willy Claes, thought that what had happened in Rwanda was probably a coup d'état, and that there would be widespread massacres. Claes was deeply worried about the 1,520 Belgian nationals in Rwanda and wanted to know if, under the present mandate, the peacekeepers could offer these people protection.

Annan told Noterdaeme that he had already asked Dallaire to get in touch with the Belgian ambassador in Kigali to see about co-operation should an evacuation of Belgian civilians be necessary. Annan said Dallaire was doing his best to protect Rwanda's politicians. UNAMIR would try to 'prevent or reduce the massacres', but it was up to Dallaire to see what was feasible. Dallaire's first duty was the security of his soldiers, and he must do nothing to encourage any reprisals. A more forceful mandate would require UNAMIR to be re-equipped and reinforced. Nothing was more dangerous than to ask a peacekeeping mission to use force when its composition, armament, logistical support, and rules of engagement denied it the capacity to do so. If UNAMIR were to take forceful action, then a decision would have to come from the Security Council. Three permanent members, America, Britain and Russia, were already reluctant about UNAMIR, and a more forceful mandate would require agreement from countries providing troops. Noterdaeme told Annan that if Belgians were going to be massacred, then Brussels had not ruled out flying in a another battalion.[8]

Willy Claes spoke on the telephone with the Secretary-General, Boutros Boutros-Ghali, who had just arrived in Geneva from Minsk, Belarus, at the start of a three-week tour of Europe. Claes asked Boutros-Ghali for an immediate change in the mandate of UNAMIR to allow for enforcement action. Boutros-Ghali, according to Claes, said that he needed time to consult his experts. The next day, Friday, 8 April, Claes again contacted Boutros-Ghali, who again made it clear that the mandate could not be changed immediately; no one knew whether or not the members of the Security Council would agree to such a change in the mandate.[9]

That day, writing from Geneva, the Secretary-General sent a letter to the president of the Security Council, Colin Keating, the permanent representative for New Zealand, in which he suggested the withdrawal from Rwanda of UNAMIR:

> It is quite possible that the evacuation of UNAMIR and other UN personnel might become unavoidable, in which event UNAMIR would be hindered in providing assistance under its present mandate and rules of engagement. The members of the Security Council might wish to give this matter their urgent attention. Should UNAMIR be required to effect such an evacuation, the Force Commander estimates that he would require two or three additional battalions for that purpose.[10]

Boutros-Ghali declined to return to New York and continued his scheduled European tour.[11] As the news from Rwanda worsened, in the secretariat in New York his decision was increasingly seen as inexplicable and irresponsible, and some said that it was a troubling abdication of leadership. Boutros-Ghali was an incessant traveller, and while he was abroad his officials found it hard to handle conflicts on a daily basis. This had been particularly true of the conflict in Bosnia. Boutros-Ghali later denied that his absence had made a difference and said that with secure coded telegrams he had kept in constant contact with headquarters. There were as many as eight conflicts which demanded his attention, he said.[12]

While the Belgians lobbied hard for a strengthened mandate for UNAMIR, Noterdaeme went directly to talk with British and American diplomats. He says that they told him that in the present circumstances the existing mandate for UNAMIR no longer made sense; indeed, both these countries were considering whether or not to pull out UNAMIR completely.[13]

By 7 April it was generally known that the USA was closing its embassy. The decision was communicated to Brussels late that day with a request from Washington for the Belgian government to exert pressure on the Security Council to allow Belgian troops in UNAMIR to protect all foreign nationals in

Rwanda, including the 240 US citizens present in the country.[14] In a strange coincidence of timing, an American military officer, Colonel Charles 'Chuck' Vuckovic, was already in Kigali and had an evacuation plan.[15]

Vuckovic had turned up at the five-star Hôtel des Mille Collines some six hours before the presidential plane was shot down.[16] He was an American operative based at the American embassy in Yaounde, Cameroon, and his beat included Rwanda and Burundi. His mission was successful; Vuckovic got all American citizens out of Rwanda by Saturday, 9 April. The civilian UN employees, some 150 people, who left in forty-two vehicles, got out first. The Americans travelled in a convoy of cars to Burundi protected by an armed escort of UN peacekeepers.

Claes considered instructing the Belgian troops in UNAMIR to abandon their peacekeeping and start to rescue Belgians. 'For your personal information,' Willy Claes wrote to Noterdaeme in New York, 'if it gets worse, we have not excluded that the Belgian commander, in order to protect Belgians, should receive his orders directly from the government.'[17] The priority was evacuation. Claes admitted as much. He said later that the preoccupation after the deaths of the ten peacekeepers was to avoid any more Belgian deaths at all costs. 'You could say that this is inadmissable,' Claes later told a Belgian Senate inquiry.[18]

The possibility of reinforcements for UNAMIR to take action against the increasing violence was hardly raised. Each time it was raised, it was in the context of rescuing expats.[19] According to a later Belgian Senate inquiry, one cabinet meeting discussed a plan to stop the massacres, but the idea was dismissed as it was deemed to constitute interference in Rwanda's internal affairs. Noterdaeme's deputy, Alexis Brouhns, said that once or twice the idea of reinforcing the peacekeepers was suggested to UN officials in New York but the officials were reluctant. Noterdaeme described how he was approached by a French diplomat who warned him that on no account should the Belgians think of reinforcing Rwanda for whatever reason. It was dangerous for Belgians in Rwanda because they were being blamed for the death of the president. The French diplomat said he had recently spoken with Rwanda's ambassador to the UN, Jean Damascene Bizimana, who thought that the Rwandans would probably adopt a more lenient attitude if the French wanted to intervene for 'humanitarian reasons'.[20] At a subsequent French parliamentary inquiry, General Christian Quesnot, the head of military affairs for the French presidency, would claim that help to stop the massacres was discussed by the French together with officials from Belgium and Italy, but that the idea came to nothing.

Troops were sent to Rwanda by, Belgium, France and Italy, but only to rescue expats. European troops were under orders to rescue only Europeans. Dallaire received a cable from Riza on 9 April to tell him to co-operate with the evacuation. 'You should make every effort not to compromise your impartiality or to act beyond your mandate,' he was warned. 'But you may exercise your discretion to do [*sic*] should this be essential for the evacuation of foreign nationals.' In other words, only in the rescue of expats could Dallaire take risks. 'This should not, repeat not, extend to participation in possible combat except in self-defense'.[21]

Dallaire discovered that some of the peacekeepers would no longer take orders, in particular not the soldiers from Bangladesh.[22] A further cable from Annan and Riza told Dallaire that if events moved in a more negative direction then it might be necessary to conclude that UNAMIR be withdrawn.

The evacuation began at dawn, on Saturday, 9 April, when a contingent of 190 French soldiers landed at Kigali and, with no warning to UNAMIR, took control of the airport, installing artillery and anti-aircraft weapons. Later that day, 400 French troops arrived. When the first French plane landed in Kigali at 3.45 a.m., a Senegalese peacekeeper saw several tons of ammunition unloaded; the boxes were picked up by Rwandese army vehicles, and taken to Kanombe camp where the Presidential Guard was quartered. The French strenuously deny this.

The French, having secured the airport and the road from the airport to the French embassy, began with the evacuation of the French embassy staff and Rwandan VIPs who were sheltering there. Among them were well-known Hutu extremists including Madame Agathe's brother, Séraphin Rwabukumba, and others central to Hutu Power including the ideologue Nahimana, who with his family had helped to create the radio station RTLMC.[23]

In the first French evacuation flight were Agathe Habyarimana, two of her daughters, one of her sons and two of her grandchildren. Later that day, some sixty children were evacuated from the Sainte-Agathe orphanage by the French and taken to the airport. They were accompanied by thirty-four 'helpers', all of them linked to Hutu Power.

The expats drove south to Burundi or took the road to Kigali airport. Some Tutsi who managed to board evacuation lorries were taken off at roadblocks and killed, under the eyes of French and Belgian soliders. A Russian woman, forced to abandon her Tutsi husband, argued on the tarmac to get her children on a plane. A survivor recalled: 'we were told they could not take us. We pleaded with them, pointing out the danger. Some of the children were screaming. But they told us that they were forbidden from taking Rwandese out of the country ... we were in so much fear that we were shaking and could hardly talk.'

In a matter of four days, almost all expats had left.[24]

Eric Bertin, the head of the MSF-France operation in Rwanda, made the decision to pull out his staff on Sunday 10 April after receiving a call from a colleague who told him that fifty wounded people waiting in the emergency tents in the Centre Hospitalier de Kigali (CHK) had been dragged from the courtyard by extremist Hutu. The killers had thanked MSF for providing a Tutsi collection point. Bertin said evacuation was the only option. What was happening was beyond the limits of humanitarian help. He spoke with MSF staff in Paris to say that a surgical team was needed. He was told that discussions were under way with the ICRC and that a convoy with doctors and medical supplies for Kigali was going to leave from Bujumbura, in Burundi.

Bertin and the MSF-France staff were evacuated on Sunday afternoon. It was a strange experience to be driven to the airport sitting in Rwandan army trucks driven by Rwandan soldiers but with an escort of French soldiers. Bertin said that quite clearly the French military had control over the Rwandan army and he still wants to know why French officers did not simply prevent the killing. While the UN peacekeepers wore bullet-proof vests, French soliders did not. They drove freely around Kigali. Bertin was certain that the killing was organized and pre-determined. A Hutu neighbour had told him how militia had come to the house looking for Tutsi, for Inyenzi, the 'cockroaches'.

Bertin heard about Bertrand des Moulins, a health officer with UNICEF living near the Hotel Méridien. Late in the morning of Thursday, 7 April, a member of the Presidential Guard had turned up at his house. Des Moulins had a Tutsi cook and a Tutsi nighwatchman. The Presidential Guard shot the first two people he found in the house, a couple in their early twenties. This couple were relatives of the cook who had fled to the des Moulins villa for safety early that morning. By then, said des Moulins, the Tutsi were quite sure they were targets. He buried the couple in his garden early on the third day and thinks that they were probably among the first of the non-political victims. Des Moulins was in no doubt about the nature of the killing. He had a secretary who lived in fear of her life for being a Tutsi. 'We did not use the word genocide but we knew that's what it was,' he said.[25]

For the French it was a Saigon-style departure, a humiliating and hurried exit after a period of total loyalty. When the French embassy closed on Tuesday, 12 April, there remained behind a room full of shredded paper. By now every UN agency, every aid agency, all the development and co-operation missions had closed their offices and shut the shutters. The vast majority of the Rwandan staff was abandoned; there were dreadful scenes with friends and employees pleading with the Europeans to be taken along. One woman who worked for the WHO saw twenty-eight people shot.[26] Every embassy, apart from that of the Chinese, had closed. No one has ever explained why there was such a speedy exodus from Rwanda. There was no such evacuation during other crises, no similar evacuation from Burundi after the assassination of the president.[27]

When the last evacuation plane took off only the peacekeepers and twenty-six delegates from the ICRC were left in Kigali.[28]

The head of delegation of the ICRC in Rwanda, Philippe Gaillard, had been in Rwanda for nine months. In that time he had built up a network of contacts and was trusted at the highest levels in the army command, the RPF, and the extremists groups, including the Interahamwe. Gaillard's presence was the deciding factor in the decision of the ICRC to stay. Only Gaillard stood any chance of negotiating the establishment of an area safe enough to run a hospital. Gaillard, as colleague Jean-Hervé Bradol, an MSF-France doctor, once described him, was unique. It was not only his steely determination; Gaillard possessed a personal philosophy and had tremendous intellectual strength, unusual in the field of humanitarian aid. For many years he had been a medieval scholar and he knew that genocide was not a new phenomenon: he said the apocalypse in Rwanda existed in the works of Bruegel, in the cast of monsters descending into the hell of Dante. He dismissed the fine words of politicians. For Gaillard, there was a stronger moral force in a poem of Federico García Lorca than in the Universal Declaration of Human Rights.[29]

Gaillard had joined the ICRC through a chance meeting and was immediately accepted for the induction course at its Geneva headquarters in March 1982. Before the Rwanda assignment he had worked for the Red Cross in Iraq, visiting Iranian prisoners of war, and had spent ten years in Argentina, El Salvador and Columbia. Rwanda was to have been an easier mission.

On the night when Habyarimana's plane was shot down, Gaillard had been in the parliament building holding meetings with RPF representatives to discuss the provision of food for the 600,000 people displaced in the north. The ICRC had mounted an operation there, and there were thirty-five expats and 130 locals employed in Rwanda. That first night Gaillard and two ICRC colleagues remained with the RPF battalion, sheltering in the damp basement of the parliament building. It was shelled all night. No one slept. They listened to RTLMC, and one of the announcers, Noël Hitimana, claimed that the Belgians had assassinated Habyarimana. Tito Rutaremara, an RPF official, did not believe that Habyarimana was dead and thought that the downing of the jet was only a pretext to start shelling the parliament and the RPF inside it. Rutaremara spoke with the prime minster, Agathe Uwilingiyimana, and she said she thought she was going to be killed.[30]

The next morning they watched in horror while people were killed with machetes in front of the building. People ran screaming in terror, chased by armed soliders and machete-wielding militia. A row erupted between enraged RPF officers desperate to intervene and a UN officer who told them they must not. Gaillard described the killing as 'instantaneous'.[31]

Gaillard's priority was to regroup the ICRC delegates and their families.

Some of them were pleading for rescue over the telephone and in one desperate call came the news of the murder by the Presidential Guard of an opposition politician. Gaillard and his colleagues left the building that morning against all advice. At the first roadblock Gaillard's car was stopped by Rwandan soldiers, some of whom were drunk. Gaillard was ordered out of the car. He approached a captain with his arm outstretched but received instead a blow to the stomach from a Kalashnikov assault rifle. Gaillard was told to hand over his car keys. Gaillard, small and skinny, said: 'My name is Philippe Gaillard. What's yours?' The captain did not answer. Gaillard told him that he was on his way home and that he lived near the Ministry of Defence. Colonel Bagosora was a neighbour and Gaillard said that he would report the state of these soldiers, and their lack of discipline. Gaillard was allowed through. 'Bluff ... game of poker,' Gaillard said later. He had been terrified.[32] That morning there was silence. He thought that everyone who had tried to run was probably dead.[33]

Gaillard regrouped all the delegates and the Rwandan staff and all their families into the Red Cross delegation and soon 500 people were crammed into a space where fifty people used to work. At a meeting he told them that there was no need for him to explain what was happening, for they all knew. Although there was a stampede to leave Rwanda, the Red Cross was staying on. Gaillard could not speak with them all individually, nor could he answer their questions. They must appoint a spokesperson.

Gaillard organized the evacuation of all non-essential staff. Remaining with him were twenty-six delegates, twelve of them medical personnel. He told them that if it became too hard for them, their duty was to tell him. One delegate, a strong man both mentally and physically, confided later that, even with years of service, he was trembling. Gaillard thanked him for his honesty and made arrangements for his evacuation.

'Everyone cracked up, at some time or another,' said Gaillard. 'Many of us not until it was over.'[34] After Rwanda a Swiss delegate, a male nurse who had worked for the Red Cross all over the world, never worked again. He told Gaillard that his mind had been macheted.

An ICRC convoy with a doctor, an anaesthetist and three nurses arrived late in the afternoon of 13 April, travelling by road from Bujumbura with 18 tons of medical supplies. A team of six from MSF-France also travelled in this convoy carrying 5 tons of medical equipment. The next day, Bradol, who entered Rwanda with this convoy, visited the CHK. Bodies filled the morgue. Patients told him how killers came at night to drag Tutsi from the hospital to kill them.[35] So the ICRC together with MSF-France created their own emergency field hospital in a convent adjacent to the ICRC delegation, at the Centre des Soeurs Salésiennes de Dom Bosco. It had 200 beds, two operating theatres and two rooms for minor surgery. The hospital was located in the

Avenue de Kiyovu, near a changing frontline between the RPF and the Rwandan government soldiers. It was shelled several times, but it was the safest hospital in the city.

Each morning a convoy of ambulances left the ICRC hospital to tour the streets of Kigali searching for wounded. The rescue teams included Rwandan volunteers, ICRC delegates and MSF medical staff. Bradol described searching through bodies tossed into ditches, deciding which of the wounded to lift into the ambulance. 'All the choices were difficult,' said Bradol. Only the most seriously wounded were taken to the hospital, only those who would die unless they received treatment. Children were a priority. It was pointless to rescue Tutsi men because they were bound to be killed at roadblocks. The Red Cross vehicles displayed special permits, signed by the army commander, Major-General Augustin Bizimana. Some of the militia could not read. Bradol would point to Bizimana's signature and the seal of the Ministry of Defence. He bought beer and cigarettes at roadblocks, and joked and laughed with the militia. One of them once asked Bradol if he could work for MSF because he did not like what he was doing.[36]

Bradol was in no doubt about the organized nature of the killing. 'There was no anarchy, no chaos,' he said. Although what was happening was described as a popular and sudden uprising, Bradol knew it was not. He had seen a popular uprising in Somalia. There was no comparison. If this had been a popular uprising, said Bradol, the Red Cross would not have been able to circulate at all. 'In Kigali, there was order.' he said. A Rwandan army officer had confided how every day a lorry full of arms and ammunition for distribution made a tour of the roadblocks.

Sometimes the Red Cross teams had to argue to stop the militia killing the wounded; one militia had wanted to throw grenades into the back of an ambulance. 'We tried to make contact with them,' Bradol said, 'to create relationships with them.' Each day the Red Cross visited the CHK where two Rwandan surgeons continued to carry out operations, mostly on wounded Rwanda government soldiers, and if the wounded were too numerous they would evacuate some of them to the ICRC hospital.

Bradol visited Gikondo. The parish was by now completely surrounded by roadblocks.[37] As he entered the parish, militia told Bradol that there was no point collecting the wounded because all the Tutsi were going to be killed. When Bradol left Gikondo the militia looked under his vehicle to see if anyone was hiding there.

The rescue teams made every effort to return to the ICRC hospital before 1 p.m. After that the militia were too drunk and high on drugs to make negotiation possible. 'When we got back to the hospital it was always a feeling of relief ... it was the only place where no one would be killed,' said Bradol. From the ICRC hospital the medical staff could see people being killed on the hill opposite. Once a group of people trying to reach the hospital was killed just yards from the door. Bradol particularly remembered one of their first casualties, a girl of six with a machete cut across her face. 'How could anyone look at a child of six, and lift a machete to her?' Bradol asked himself, and he worked out the angle at which the killer had wielded the blade.[38] The child was the same age as his daughter. Then after this, day after day, Bradol saw dozens and dozens of mutilated children. The word genocide did not enter his head. But he knew for certain that an extermination plan against the Tutsi was under way.

Three times Dallaire was told to plan an evacuation of the peacekeepers. The first occasion was when Booh-Booh ordered him to begin a withdrawal. Dallaire replied that Booh-Booh could issue all the orders he liked but that UNAMIR was staying put. 'I will not withdraw,' Dallaire had said. There were about 15,000 people under UN care. What would happen to them? On Sunday, 10 April, Dallaire received a telephone call from the Secretary-General's special political adviser, an Indian official called Chinmaya Gharekhan. Gharekhan told Dallaire to plan a withdrawal. Dallaire again said it was out of the question; if UNAMIR pulled out the situation would only get worse. Dallaire said that what he needed was a new mandate and that there should be a modest reinforcement of 5,000 soldiers to put an end to the massacres.[39]

On 12 April, Dallaire received a call from Boutros-Ghali in Bonn.[40] It was brief. The moment the Secretary-General came on the phone, Dallaire told him that a UN withdrawal could not be contemplated. Boutros-Ghali failed to persuade him otherwise. Later, Boutros-Ghali said that asking for a plan to be prepared did not necessarily mean that the plan would be carried out.[41]

No one could have been left in any doubt about the danger to people in UN care, or about the nature of the killings. New York was told in a cable from Dallaire on 8 April that there was a well-planned, organized, deliberate and orchestrated campaign of terror, with indications of large-scale massacres, and with the Tutsi as targets.[42] Dallaire started to formulate concrete proposals for the reinforcements needed to stop the killing. He believed that a show of force by the UN, with tanks and guns, would intimidate the gangs roaming the streets. Even taking into account the dangers of a renewed civil war between the RPF and Rwandan government soldiers, a modest expansion of UNAMIR of between 2,500 to 5,000 could knock out the radio station inciting the militia to kill. Protected sites could be set up for civilians. Dallaire wanted to make the most of what he called 'a balance of fear'.

Dallaire did not believe that his chapter VI mandate, dealing with the pacific resolution of disputes, prevented him from taking action. He had written his own rules of engagement in which it was quite clear that he could prevent crimes against humanity. Clause 17 specified:

> There may also be ethnically or politically motivated criminal acts committed during this mandate. I will morally and legally require UNAMIR to use all available means to halt them. Examples are execution, attacks of displaced persons or refugees, ethnic riots, attacks on demobilised soldiers etc. During such occasions, UNAMIR military personnel will follow the ROE outlined in this directive in support of UNCIVPOL and local authorities or in their absence UNAMIR will take the necessary action to prevent any crime against humanity.

Only a lack of means prevented him from taking action.

Some people have argued the validity of Dallaire's judgement about reinforcements, and claimed that this estimate is problematic given the determination of the extremists. But three years after the genocide the Carnegie Commission on Preventing Deadly Conflict, the Institute for the Study of Diplomacy at Georgetown University, and the US army undertook a project to assess it. An international panel of senior military leaders was convened. In a report to the Carnegie Commission based on the discussion at the conference, Colonel Scott Feil pointed to a consensus that a force with air support, logistics and communications would have prevented the slaughter of half a million people. The window of opportunity was between 7 and 21 April while the political leaders of the violence were still susceptible to international influence. This would have forestalled expansion of the genocide to the south; it was still relatively contained at this point. An intervention would have altered the political calculations of the extremists as to whether they could get away with it. A larger force was needed after 21 April because by then the genocide had spread. US forces, backed by air power, could have protected Rwandan civilians with little or no risk to US soldiers.[43]

Marchal is convinced that if the evacuation force which came to rescue the expats had not pulled out, then the killing could have been stopped. There were already 2,500 peacekeepers in Rwanda, 2,000 of whom would have taken part in an operation. There were 500 Belgian para-commandos, part of the evacuation operation, and 450 French and 80 Italians from parachute regiments. In Kenya there were 500 Belgian para-commandos, also a part of the evacuation operation. In Burundi there were 250 Rangers, elite US troops, who had come to help to evacuate American nationals. There were 800 more French troops on stand-by in the region. Together with Rwandan soldiers who wanted peace there would have been ample troops to restore calm. In this case there would have been no valid reason for the RPF to mount an offensive.

For the peacekeepers of UNAMIR, the pull-out of the troops that came to rescue the ex-pats was an affront to their mission. It was unbelievable that these troops could leave, knowing the dangers. Dallaire said that it was inexcusable by any human criteria. 'We were left to fend for ourselves,' he said, 'with neither mandate nor supplies – defensive stores, ammunition, medical supplies or water, with only survival rations that were rotten and inedible – is a description of inexcusable apathy by the sovereign states that made up the UN, that is completely beyond comprehension and moral acceptability.'

In the UN Secretariat in New York, on Monday morning, 11 April, senior officials from the Department of Peacekeeping Operations (DPKO) held their daily meeting, known as morning prayers. The news was awful. The RPF battalion in Kigali had broken out of barracks and was fighting the Presidential Guard. The RPF had broken through the DMZ in the north and had begun an offensive. Ten peacekeepers were dead, and the rest of the Belgian force could be marked for assassination. There were reports of carnage. Access to the airport was increasingly precarious. The West was pulling out and the evacuation of expats was under way. That weekend, on 'Face the Nation', a CBS news programme, the republican leader in the Senate, Robert Dole, had said: 'I don't think we have any national interest here … I hope we don't get involved there. I don't think we will. The Americans are out. As far as I'm concerned in Rwanda, that ought to be the end of it.'

The position in Washington on Monday morning was camouflaged in news spin. At a daily press briefing, when asked whether or not the USA, the only super-power, had a responsibility to lead an international effort to restore order in Rwanda, Michael McCurry, the State Department spokesman, answered that the situation would be under review at the UN, the appropriate place for such discussions. Other officials, off the record, were letting it be known that the American strategy on Rwanda was to keep expectations as low as possible, a decision rooted in the appalling peacekeeping mission in Somalia.

The next day, Tuesday 12 April, at a meeting between Boutros-Ghali and Willy Claes in Bonn, Claes announced that Belgium was pulling its soldiers out of UNAMIR. Claes said that the situation was deteriorating drastically and would grow rapidly worse. All the troops were at risk. The whole of UNAMIR should pull out. Claes claimed later that Boutros-Ghali agreed with this analysis.[44] Boutros-Ghali maintains that he argued with Claes against the Belgian pull-out.[45] From this moment, says Boutros-Ghali, he knew that the position of the remaining peacekeepers was untenable unless the Belgian troops were replaced with equally well-trained troops from somewhere else.

After the Bonn meeting the Belgian government launched a furious diplomatic campaign to try to persuade everyone else of the wisdom of a total UNAMIR withdrawal. Claes telephoned his counterparts in Washington, London and Paris to argue for it, and explained that the Belgian press was in an uproar because of the deaths of the Belgian soldiers and that public opinion was demanding that the troops come home. Claes said the reaction was similar to that in America after the deaths of the American soldiers in Somalia.[46] When asked later why the Belgian government had made such strenuous efforts to achieve a total withdrawal of UNAMIR, Claes replied: 'The fear of losing face ... did play a role.'

After the meeting in Bonn, Boutros-Ghali wrote a letter to the president of the Security Council, the New Zealand permanent representative Colin Keating, to inform him officially of the Belgian decision. It was dated 13 April. 'I have asked my Special Representative and the Force Commander to prepare plans for the withdrawal of UNAMIR, should this prove necessary.'[47]

Notes

1. Jean-Philippe Ceppi. 'Kigali livré à la fureur des tueurs Hutus', *Libération*, 11 April 1994.

2. Jean Hélène, 'Le Rwanda a feu et a sang', *Le Monde*, 12 April 1994.

3. Elaine Sciolino, 'For West, Rwanda is not worth the political candle', *New York Times*, 15 April 1994.

4. The international reporting of Rwanda has been the subject of a number of studies which have shown that the coverage of these crises was ambiguous, unclear and often misconstrued. Ingrid A. Lehmann, *Peacekeeping and Public Information. Caught in the Crossfire*, London: Frank Cass, 1999.

5. Roger Winter, 'Power, not tribalism, stokes Rwanda's slaughter', *Globe and Mail*, Toronto, 14 April 1994. The *New York Times* that day published: Frank Smyth, 'French Guns, Rwandan Blood'.

6. *The International Response to Conflict and Genocide: Lessons from the Rwandan Experience.* Joint Evaluation of Emergency Assistance to Rwanda. Copenhagen, March 1996, Chapter 2, p. 36.

7. Belgian Senate, *Commission d'enquête parlementaire concernant les événements du Rwanda.* Report, 6 December 1997, p. 523. Also interviews with UN officials in DPKO, New York, July 1994 and October 1996.

8. Ibid., p. 526.

9. Belgian Senate, *Commission d'enquête*, p. 536.

10. There are two versions of this letter. One, a copy of an original, and given to the author by the president of the Security Council, Colin Keating, and the second, a version printed in *The United Nations and Rwanda, 1993–1994.* The UN Blue Book Series, Vol. 10, p. 255. The former is used in this book. The difference between the two versions is that the letter in the Blue Book series does not mention the evacuation from Rwanda of UNAMIR. In the letter sent to the president a sentence reads: 'It is quite possible that the evacuation of UNAMIR and other United Nations personnel might become unavoidable, in which event UNAMIR would be hindered in providing assistance under its present mandate and rules of engagement.' The letter in the Blue Book series reads: 'It is quite possible that the evacuation of civilian staff from the United Nations system, as well as other foreign nationals, might become unavoidable, in which event UNAMIR would be hindered in providing assistance under its present mandate and rules of engagement.'

11. A list of the capitals visited by Boutros Boutros-Ghali, from April to June 1994, can be found in 'Travels of the Secretary-General', press information, 1 July 1994 (DPI/1557).

12. Interview, Boutros Boutros-Ghali, Paris, December 1999.

13. Belgian Senate, *Commission d'enquête*, p. 532.

14. Ibid., Chronology. p. 519.

15. Major Brent Beardsley, Dallaire's staff officer, had prepared a plan for total UN evacuation and an American special forces officer had requested certain details from him for their own plan.

16. Hotel records, Hôtel des Mille Collines, 5–12 April. Plan Hotel. Reservations. Photocopies in the possession of the author. Interviews, Brussels and Ottawa, September 1997.

17. Belgian Senate, *Commission d'enquête*, p. 535.

18. Ibid., p. 565.

19. Ibid., p. 535.

20. Ibid., p. 537.

21. UN Security Council, *Report of the Independent Inquiry into the Actions of the United Nations during the 1994 Genocide in Rwanda*, 15 December 1999, p. 16.

22. Ibid., p. 27.

23. A list of these people is provided in André Guichaoua (ed.), *Les Crises Politiques au Burundi et au Rwanda, (1993–1994)*. Université des Sciences et Technologies de Lille. Paris: Karthala, 1995, pp. 697–701.

24. The French evacuated 1,238 people by air and of these 454 were French, 784 were other nationalities and 394 were Rwandans. A further 115 French nationals were taken by road to Bujumbura in Burundi. Belgium evacuated 1,226 people of whom 1,026 were Belgian. Italy and Canada took out about 100 people.

25. Interview, Eric Bertin, December 1999. Also interview with Bertrand des Moulins, UNICEF, December 1999.

26. Interview, Gerry McCarthy (Consultant, UNICEF), December 1999.

27. The President of Burundi, Cyprien Ntaryamira, was killed with Habyarimana in the plane crash. In the days immediately following his death, local newspapers reported calm, allaying fears of further violence. The government took steps to strengthen national security. There was violence later in April but the situation was calm as the month ended.

28. A small UNICEF emergency operations team returned to Kigali on 22 April to distribute airlifted supplies. See UNICEF, *Rwanda Emergency Programme: Progress Report No. 1*, Kigali.

29. Interview, Philippe Gaillard, July 1998. In *Cycle des Conférences* Gaillard quotes Federico García Lorca's 'Enfance et Mort', García Lorca, *Poeta en Nueva York* (Poet in New York), English and Spanish. New York: The Monday Press, 1998, trans. G. Simon and S. F. White, ed. C. Maurer.

30. Interview, Tito Rutaremara, Kigali, October 1997.

31. Philippe Gaillard, *Rwanda 1994: La vraie vie est absente (Arthur Rimbaud) Cycle des Conferences les Mardi de Musée. M. Philippe Gaillard, délégué du CIRC, chef de délégation au Rwanda de Juillet 1993 à Juillet, 1994*, unpublished.

32. Gérard Delaloye and Elisabeth Levy, 'Philippe Gaillard, après Kigali, pouvez-vous encore croire en l'humanité', *Le Nouveau Quotidien*, 30 December 1994.

33. Gaillard, *Rwanda 1994*.

34. Delaloye and Levy, 'Philippe Gaillard, après Kigali'.

35. Interview, Jean-Hervé Bradol, November 1999.

36. Assemblée Nationale, Mission de'Information Commune, *Enquête sur la Tragédie Rwandaise (1990–1994)*, Paris.

37. On Friday, 15 April.

38. Jean-Hervé Bradol, 'Rwanda, Avril–Mai 1994. Limites et Ambiguïtés de l'Action Humanitaire. Crises Politiques, Massacres et Exodes Massifs', *Le Temps Modernes*, No. 583, 1995.

39. Interview, Major Brent Beardsley, December 1999, and Major-General Dallaire, November 1994.

40. 'Travels of the Secretary-General', press information.

41. Interview, Boutros Boutros-Ghali, Paris, December 1999.

42. The text of this cable is given in full in Belgian Senate, *Commission d'enquête*, pp. 508–15.

43. Colonel Scott R. Feil, *Preventing Genocide. How the Use of Force Might Have Succeeded in Rwanda*, pre-publication draft, December 1997, New York: Carnegie Commission on Preventing Deadly Conflict. This report contains a detailed description of Dallaire's plan, devised in three phases.

44. Belgian Senate, *Commission d'enquête*, p. 543.

45. Boutros Boutros-Ghali, *Unvanquished. A US–UN Saga*, London: I.B.Tauris, 1999, p. 132.

46. Doubts have been cast on this claim. Belgian opinion polls showed no overwhelming demand for withdrawal. See Human Rights Watch/Fédération Internationale des Ligues des Droits de l'Homme, *Leave none to tell the story. Genocide in Rwanda*, 1999, pp. 617–18.

47. *The United Nations and Rwanda, 1993–1996*, UN Blue Book series, Vol. 10, New York: UN Department of Public Information, p. 259.

14 · The Secret Meetings of the Security Council

THE meetings held by the Security Council to discuss what to do about the peacekeeping mission in Rwanda took place behind closed doors. Twenty years ago, when most Council meetings were held in public, it would have been possible to hear the options discussed, but nowadays most debates take place in a side room where the deals are concluded which make up 'UN policy'. This means that the policies of each member government are hidden from public scrutiny.

Throughout the genocide the Security Council was in almost constant secret session, meeting sometimes twice daily and long into the night. There were multiple crises and, in April 1994, the Security Council was preoccupied with a worsening Bosnia, where a Serb bombardment on the safe area of Gorazde was grabbing the headlines. However, having established the mission for Rwanda, the Security Council was now responsible for its future.

The meetings held to discuss Rwanda would usually have remained secret for ever, were it not for the leak from within the Council of a remarkable 155-page document containing an account of them.[1] This invaluable primary source gives a unique view of the Council's secret world and without it an account of the international failure over Rwanda would be incomplete. The document exposes some unpleasant truths – not least of which is the fact that the plans to try to prevent the organized killing of civilians using a modest reinforcement of troops were not discussed in the first few weeks of killing.

Those states which had advocated a tough line on compliance with Arusha a few weeks earlier – America and Britain – were now inclined to carry out their threat to withdraw the force, although the immediate reaction in the Council was to concentrate on whether or not it was possible to get a ceasefire in the renewed civil war. One of the ambassadors occupying a non-permanent seat, Karel Kovanda of the Czech Republic, recalled: 'No one was sure what, if anything, needed to be done. Into this absolutely bizarre situation came the big powers … who said they could do nothing.'[2]

At each of these informal meetings there were briefings from secretariat officials. One of these officials, Iqbal Riza, assistant secretary-general in the

DPKO and a member of Boutros-Ghali's inner cabinet, who had overseen the UN's successful mission in El Salvador, has said that later in the first week there was confusion. All the assessments coming from the field, apart from one, concerned the resumption of the conflict. Riza claims that only in one cable in the first week, on 8 April, was there any mention of organized killing.

This was the cable in which Dallaire described to New York the deliberate campaign of terror initiated principally by the Presidential Guard since the morning after the death of the head of state. But in the same cable a report from the Secretary-General's special representative, Jacques-Roger Booh-Booh, attributed the worsening of the security situation to the fighting between the Presidential Guard and the RPF.

Riza said that for the first week they were under the impression that they were dealing with a breakdown in a ceasefire, except for one sentence, in one cable. Later, Dallaire would query this reaction. In his daily situation reports and more frequent telephone calls he had made it abundantly clear that genocide was looming. Of the briefings given to the Council, Riza said: 'Possibly we did not give all the details ... And if we did not, I really can't tell you what happened then to prevent us from giving those details.'

At a meeting on Monday, 11 April, the Council was told about the thousands of people seeking safety wherever they could, in hospitals and in churches and wherever they saw the UN flag. The next day, 12 April, Riza told the Council of 'chaotic, ethnic, random killings' but most of his briefing concerned the activities of the interim government. In the days to come there would be requests from the non-permanent members for the views of both the force commander and the Secretary-General. The views of the force commander were never forthcoming. Complaints began to surface that no options for action had been presented and that the Secretary-General was absent from New York.

At this point, and while American diplomats were expressing doubts about the viability of the force, it was the British ambassador, David Hannay, who came up with four options. The first was to reinforce the troops and give the peacekeepers a stronger mandate to intervene to halt the bloodshed. But this, Hannay warned, would be a repetition of Somalia. Peacekeeping was not appropriate for civil war, for situations where there was no peace to keep and where fighting factions were unwilling to co-operate. Inadequate efforts were worse than no efforts at all.

Second, UNAMIR could pull out completely but the negative signal to public opinion would be damaging. Third, the troops could stay on, although he did query what they could effectively do, for there was no evidence that UNAMIR was in any position to protect civilians.

The fourth and last idea was to pull most of them out leaving behind 'some elements'. Although this might initially attract public criticism, it seemed to be the safest course. Hannay warned the Council that the decision could not be delayed.

The Americans agreed. No country should be expected to send soldiers into this chaotic environment. It was doubtful whether the peacekeepers could even be resupplied. If the UN failed to protect its own soldiers, then the Security Council would have serious difficulties obtaining any more troops for other UN operations. The USA did not want to be seen to be responsible for the gradual depletion of an isolated force, but the peacekeepers could be flown out and kept in a neighbouring country and then go back in at some later date. It was highly improbable that an outside force could halt the terror in Rwanda.

The Nigerian ambassador, Ibrahim Gambari, pointed out that tens of thousands of civilians were dying all the time.

The meeting adjourned. They decided to ask for the views first of the Secretary-General, and then of those states contributing troops to UNAMIR. The Council thought of one action: it urged a ceasefire. The African group at the UN was one step ahead. It urged the Security Council to take urgent action to protect the lives of civilians and reinforce UNAMIR.[3]

The RPF offensive had begun along an 80-kilometre demilitarized zone in three main axes, putting into place a plan long in preparation. Its aim was to defeat an army three times its size and with far superior weaponry. In a radio address on the RPF station, Radio Muhabura, people had been told that there had been a 'bloodbath' in Rwanda undertaken by the Presidential Guard that had wiped out almost the entire government. A new government had been formed of people who were opposed to the Arusha peace agreement. A military communiqué announced that the RPF was to fight the 'murderous clique' which had taken over in Rwanda; the RPF was willing to work with Rwandan government soliders in order to bring the murderers to book.[4]

The lead element of the RPF moved through the east along the border with Tanzania, a central axis of soldiers went through Byumba, and the western thrust advanced through Ruhengeri, where there was preparatory bombardment to draw out a large concentration of Rwandan army forces. Some soldiers on the central thrust also moved towards Kigali. In this way, Major-General Paul Kagame held down the Rwandan army on central and western fronts. Throughout the advance, the RPF used mortar fire to maximum advantage and, after a period of sustained fire, often succeeded in intimidating the government forces and cutting off supply lines.

The RPF advance on the east was amazing for its speed. The first battalion group from the brigade on the eastern front, some 1,500 soldiers, entered Kigali on 12 April, only four days after the start of the campaign and covering a distance of some 75 kilometres. The soldiers moved in small numbers during the night, infiltrating their heavy weapons and combat supplies and carrying out dawn attacks.

Kagame said he knew the genocide was under way in the first week because as his troops advanced they found evidence of it. There were similarities in the stories they were told, and soon people with machete wounds were searching out RPF bases.[5]

In Kigali on 13 April, there was the sound of heavy machine guns, multiple rockets and artillery fire. An attack on the city by the RPF came from the east and north-east with the main bombardment on the barracks of the Presidential Guard, the most fortified place in the city. The Guard held on, and for the next eight weeks, on this frontline, there would be no more than 100 metres separating the RPF from the Presidential Guard. Once in Kigali, the RPF joined with their troops already in the city, and this battalion's barracks, the CND building, would become their base. It was where RPF casualties were evacuated for prompt medical attention. But the RPF held only a portion of the city. The battle for Kigali lasted three months.

In the weeks to come, the Rwandan army became expert in well-planned and executed withdrawals at night, and whole areas fought over were often found to be empty in the morning. The Rwandan army lacked an established line of defence; if they had advanced on the RPF battalion in the CND building, they could have defeated that single battalion. Instead, the army held back and allowed the RPF to form a firm base, linking up with its battalions from the north.

The Rwandan forces, with a new commander, Major-General Augustin Bizimungu, previously commander of the northern Ruhengeri garrison, had low morale. There had been rapid recruitment in the previous three years. It was the militia which had the strong political indoctrination and an effective command structure, at times intimidating government soldiers at roadblocks.

While the RPF advanced, the images portrayed of them on RTLMC became increasingly horrific. One announcer warned that the Tutsi soldiers were devils who killed their victims 'by extracting various organs … for example, by taking the heart, the liver, the stomach … the cruelty of the inyenzi [cockroach] is incurable, the cruelty of the inyenzi can only be cured by their total extermination.'[6] The radio station described this as a final attack, using the Kinyarwanda word 'simusiga', the same word which would be used to describe the genocide.[7] It was a war which must be waged without mercy, the announcers encouraged.[8] The broadcasters advocated the killing of Tutsi by identifying them with the RPF, and the RPF was going to exterminate all the Hutu. People were encouraged to phone in and reveal where people were hiding. In one broadcast, Valérie Bemeriki read out the names and addresses of thirteen people along with their jobs and even their nicknames, and she urged her listeners to find them. The vehicle number-plates of those who were trying to escape were read on air. Requests from civil servants or militia leaders were broadcast calling for the resupply of weapons, ammunition, or grenades to certain areas.[9]

Dallaire pleaded with New York for permission to neutralize the station: 'It was inciting people to kill, it was explaining how to kill, telling people who to kill, including whites, including me.' On 18 April, the RPF mounted a machine-gun attack on the studios of RTLMC and the broadcasting was stopped, but only temporarily, resuming within hours.[10]

The radio station broadcast that Philippe Gaillard was a Belgian. He was stopped by a gang of Interahamwe but showed them a photograph of his family home in Switzerland, St Pierre de Clages, in the Valais, with the mountains dwarfing a tiny twelfth-century village, explaining that there were no mountains in Belgium. Gaillard went to the radio station and spoke with the announcers. Later, a racist retraction was broadcast stating that Gaillard was too brave, too intelligent and too motivated to be a Belgian.

Gaillard kept in touch with everyone: the announcers at the radio station, the leaders of the Interahamwe, the Rwandan army commanders, and the RPF. 'Dialogue was the cornerstone of our security, more important than protective vehicles or bullet-proof vests which are signs of fear and of aggressive force,' he explained.

On one occasion Gaillard organized a convoy to take 100 wounded out of Kigali to a small hospital some 40 kilometres away at Kabgayi. As the convoy set out, RTLMC began to broadcast that there were RPF hiding in the lorries. Shortly afterwards, the convoy was stopped by a mob of Interahamwe. Gaillard began a furious round of negotiations, driving like a mad man to find army commanders. RTLMC then issued a denial: there were no RPF in the convoy. It moved on. This incident afforded an appreciation of the degree of control exercised by the authorities, using the radio station. The country was run via the airwaves, and RTLMC was clearly the only government institution which operated effectively.

When, early on, the Kigali prefecture asked Gaillard if he would provide petrol for garbage trucks to pick up the bodies in the streets, Gaillard agreed. Later on, the sub-prefect confided in Gaillard that 67,000 bodies had been collected in the trucks.[11]

Gaillard was well informed. He set up an information-gathering unit in the ICRC delegation and instigated twenty-four-hour monitoring of Radio Rwanda, RTLMC and the World Service of the BBC. With an ICRC technical expert and a scanner, he picked up the communications of the Rwandese army and the RPF and listened to the UNAMIR frequency; Dallaire had given him a Motorola with which to keep in touch. The written details of all these broadcasts were compiled and collated. Gaillard kept a large map of Rwanda on his wall, and soon he could show where the next battle in the civil war would be fought.

Each night Gaillard explained to the medical personnel what was happening, and with his map showed them the progress of the civil war. The briefings helped to hold them together, he said. Each night at supper Gaillard read from the one book he had with him, Arthur Rimbaud's *Une Saison en enfer* (A Season in Hell). Gaillard hoped that the poems would have a similar effect to prayer, to calm them. Rimbaud was a friend sitting with them, he said.

On 12 April Gaillard witnessed a miserable spectacle when the interim government fled Kigali in a convoy of cars which set out from the Hôtel des Diplomates. Women and children were crying, ministers were carrying their own suitcases and desperately piling into cars parked in a long line. There was no solidarity; one minister was almost left behind and had to ask a colleague for a lift. The car belonging to another minister ran out of petrol and Gaillard offered him some, explaining to a curious onlooker that a service given might one day be repaid. Gaillard became well known on the streets of Kigali, with his white shirt, jacket and tie. He would chat, cajole and plead for freedom of movement for ambulances. The ICRC administrative co-ordinator, Jean-Pascal Chapatte, later described Gaillard's political finesse, his sensitivity and his talent for negotiation.[12]

On the day the interim government fled Kigali, Chapatte got hold of some Pauilhac 1986 for $5 a bottle, the wine looted from an empty embassy. That night Gaillard dreamed he was alone in a convent in the centre of New York, and New York was in flames.

There were several frontlines in the RPF offensive, and Kigali was divided into RPF and government-held zones. Where there were no soldiers, militia ruled the streets. Neighbourhood boundaries were defined by roadblocks, with their piles of bodies. Thousands of people now decided to leave Kigali and follow the interim government to Gitarama. On Wednesday, 13 April, a week after the genocide began, a column of people, about five kilometres long, moved slowly along the road out of the city.[13] Some rich Rwandans travelled in Mercedes saloons with armed escorts in civilian clothes. A news reporter with Associated Press saw a bulldozer with dozens of people clinging to it and twenty people in the bucket at the front.

When the interim government arrived in Gitarama it brought in its wake Presidential Guard and more than a thousand Interahamwe. It might have been possible to have spared Gitarama from genocide because the prefect there, Fidèle Uwizeye, was opposed to the killing, and had organized the bourgmestres to defend the prefecture. Once the interim government arrived and arms were distributed, however, and with hate-propaganda from RTLMC, opposition was soon destroyed.[14] The genocide spread.

Marcelline lived in the commune of Taba in Gitarama. The Interahamwe rounded up her family and killed all the men. The women were made to dig graves to bury the men, and then threw the children in the graves. 'I will never forget the sight of my son pleading with me not to bury him alive ... he kept trying to come out and was beaten back. And we had to keep covering the pit with earth until ... there was no movement left.'[15]

The debate in the Security Council is often shaped by recommendations from the Secretary-General acting on advice from officials in the secretariat who receive all the cables from UN commanders. When it came to Rwanda no such recommendations were forthcoming. Some of the non-permanent members speculated that either the secretariat had no options at all, in which case it was not up to the task of managing the conflict, or it was overwhelmed to the point of paralysis.[16]

Colin Keating, president of the Security Council in April, complained that the Council needed more information from the force commander, particularly on the consequences for UNAMIR once the Belgian peacekeepers withdrew.

The letter to the president of the Security Council, written in Bonn by Boutros-Ghali and dated 13 April, confirmed the Belgian decision to pull out. It was greeted with consternation by the Council. The letter stated that unless the Belgian contingent was replaced by another 'equally well-equipped', then it would be extremely difficult for UNAMIR to carry out its tasks; in these circumstances, Boutros-Ghali had asked the special representative and the force commander to prepare plans for the withdrawal of UNAMIR.[17] Some of the non-permanent members were surprised. Was this all the Secretary-General had to offer after a week?

The British permanent representative, David Hannay, found the letter far from adequate. The Secretary-General seemed to think, quite bizarrely, that if the Belgians were to stay on, then all would be well. It was not right to give the impression that two battalions could protect the civilian population of Rwanda. The peacekeepers, with their limited capacity, could not protect civilians. If a small military presence was left behind, then it could encourage the parties to move back to the peace deal.

The French delegation wanted to know why the Secretary-General had assumed that Belgian withdrawal would lead to an automatic pull-out for UNAMIR. There was every reason for the Belgians to leave Rwanda, for every Belgian national was a target, but if everyone left then the situation would deteriorate further.

An American representative said it was 'unfortunate' for the Secretary-General to appear to blame Belgium for a total withdrawal; while it was not possible to pull the plug completely on Rwanda, the ambassadors remembered Somalia. The best course was to leave a skeletal group of peacekeepers and pull out everyone else.

Some years later, Boutros-Ghali defended this letter. He explained that he was trying to put pressure on the Security Council to authorize a new force; he had requested the force commander to prepare plan for withdrawal, 'unless we received additional forces'. He said he wanted a strengthened mission and an enforcement operation and that his views were not well received.[18]

The briefing at this meeting on 13 April was given by Iqbal Riza. He offered the ambassadors an update on the progress of the battle for Kigali, and told them that the RPF would not agree a ceasefire. The situation was deteriorating, Riza said. Dallaire was conducting some rescue missions and he continued to try for a ceasefire. There were an estimated 14,000 Rwandan refugees sheltering with the UN and the protection of these people required more resources. But there was a question over how prolonged this protection could be, and the Council must consider whether peacekeeping should involve such tasks. Gambari, for Nigeria, said that the protection of civilians must be of concern and wanted to know if Africa had fallen off the map of moral concern.

The remainder of the 13 April meeting was taken up with a discussion on a draft resolution from Nigeria suggesting that peacekeepers be allowed to 'enforce public order and the rule of law and create temporary state institutions'. The resolution pointed to the thousands of innocent civilians being killed but, although it was circulated among ambassadors, it was never tabled. It stood little chance. A US ambassador, Karl Inderfurth, told them of a strong feeling in Washington that peacekeeping was not appropriate for Rwanda. The Americans would not be pushing in the Council for total withdrawal, but the whole Council should give consideration to the future of the mission.

China disagreed. China was the only country not to have closed its embassy in Kigali, and a Chinese delegate pointed out that there was no immediate danger to the remaining UN peacekeepers. Only the untrained contingent from Bangladesh were in a panic. The others – the sixty Tunisians and the 800 Ghanaians – were doing useful work under the force commander. The Rwandan ambassador, Jean-Damascène Bizimana, a representative of the interim government, had sat impassively throughout all these exchanges. Rwanda had a non-permanent seat on the Council, the right to vote, the right to participate in procedural decisions, and the right to block the required consensus on presidential statements.[19] Bizimana, well-dressed and fluent in French, became an essential element in the interim government's propaganda campaign. He was in a superb position to peddle the interim government line that the killings in Rwanda were part of the civil war. Bizimana circulated a letter on 13 April, written by the interim government's minister of foreign affairs, Jérôme Bicamumpaka, which claimed that the situation in Rwanda was improving and that the presence of UN peacekeepers was helping to stabilize the country. Because of the death of the president, the military and the people of Rwanda had 'reacted spontaneously', attacking those under suspicion, but a new government had been created and was giving great hope to the people.

The prime minister in this interim government, Jean Kambanda, was meanwhile broadcasting on RTLMC to tell the population to search out the enemy, those who 'do not share our opinion'. Kambanda ordered the construction of roadblocks. He distributed arms and ammunition. He ordered, incited and helped other ministers, prefects, bourgmestres and other local officials to exterminate the Tutsi and pro-democracy Hutu.[20] There were seventeen cabinet meetings held by the interim government during the genocide from which directives went to local bureaucrats to 'pacify' their areas – 'pacification' was the word the interim government used to describe the genocide. The very first decision of this interim government, on 8 April, had been to call to Kigali all Rwanda's prefects to ensure that, in the weeks to come, each would obey instructions.[21] A minister was designated for each prefecture whose job was pacification.[22] Prefects passed orders to bourgmestres who alerted councillors who held meetings to inform all residents of 'the work in hand' – clearing their areas of Tutsi. Sometimes the councillors went from house to house to sign up all the young males for 'the work'. Administrative officials in possession of birth and death records knew exactly how many Tutsi lived in each area; during the genocide, they kept track of the dead.

The massacres in Rwanda were the result of a chain of command, the result of a prepared strategy. The genocide was a conspiracy at national level, but without the complicity of the local and national civil and military authorities, the large-scale massacres would not have occurred.

On Thursday 14 April, a Red Cross ambulance was stopped at a roadblock in Kigali and six wounded people were dragged from the back and shot. Earlier that day the same ambulance had passed the same roadblock with no problems, but it was raining then. When it rained, the roadblocks were not manned. But in the early afternoon the sun was shining and armed civilians and soldiers had returned; this time there was a man with a sub-machine gun, and grenades had recently been distributed. The ambulance was in a convoy with two cars carrying wounded people and driven by a Rwandan who worked for the Red Cross. This stretch of road had one checkpoint every 100 metres.[23] There had been a recent RTLMC broadcast that the Red Cross was transporting the RPF disguised as wounded.

Gaillard's fury at the ambulance killings was volcanic and he immediately suspended the collection of wounded from the streets. He gave an interview to a journalist in which he asked what was the point of saving people, only to see them killed. He drove to the radio station. He shared a beer with some of the announcers, and asked them to counter-balance the broadcasts in order to guarantee respect for the Red Cross emblem. Gaillard later spoke with the

ICRC Geneva headquarters and a press release was issued appealing for the Red Cross to be allowed to assist the wounded. There were articles in the western press about the ambulance killings, and this was considered unwelcome attention by the interim government. A retraction was broadcast on RTLMC and in the days to come ambulances were allowed to circulate. Gaillard said: 'The assassination of these wounded allowed us to save thousands more.'

Gaillard went to Nyamirambo on 15 April, south of Kigali, where on 8 April dozens of people had been killed in a church. Several days later hundreds of people sheltering in a mosque were murdered, the massacre preceded by an announcement on RTLMC that Tutsi were hiding there. Nyamirambo had a large Tutsi population; in the months before the genocide started, Tutsi living in other communes had moved there for safety.

Nine days after the genocide started, the news that large-scale killing was taking place was made known to the outside world with a report of a massacre in the parish of Musha, 25 miles east of Kigali. The story appeared in a Belgian newspaper, *Het Volk*, with details later picked up by other western media. Associated Press said that this was the biggest massacre reported so far. An attack had taken place on 13 April in a church in which hundreds were sheltering. The Presidential Guard had kicked in the door, opened fire with semi-automatic weapons, and thrown in grenades. 'Afterwards they attacked defenceless people with knives, bats and spears. There were 1,180 bodies in my church including 650 children,' *Het Volk* quoted the pastor there, Danko Litrick.[24]

At a further informal meeting of the Security Council on Thursday, 14 April, there was a spirited defence of the Secretary-General by another of his senior officials, Alvaro de Soto, assistant secretary-general in the Department of Political Affairs. De Soto told the Council that, although he was touring Europe, the Secretary-General was in constant contact with UN headquarters, the force commander and the special representative. It was not correct to say that Boutros-Ghali was in favour of total withdrawal, but the problem was that the peacekeepers were prevented from carrying out their mandate. The Secretary-General had formulated two options: UNAMIR could remain as it was without the Belgians or it could be reduced. Both options were predicated on a ceasefire.

The delegate for Oman called for written proposals from the Secretary-General. Spain wanted to know why no mention had been made of a possible change in mandate. France thought that any mission in Rwanda would have to serve some useful purpose. The UK thought that the Secretariat should be more precise about the minimum force level which could remain behind. The USA said that what the Security Council needed was a resolution to provide for the orderly evacuation of the mission.

The following day, Friday, 15 April, Willy Claes, the Belgian foreign minister, wrote to Boutros-Ghali to tell him officially that the Belgian peacekeepers were all leaving. He recommended that the whole of UNAMIR be withdrawn. Based on an intimate knowledge of events, the scale of the massacres which peacekeepers were witnessing, together with a deteriorating military situation, there was no alternative and no chance of a ceasefire. By waiting to make a decision, the Security Council was increasing the risks to the soldiers. Claes asked that Boutros-Ghali give the instruction to the force commander to release immediately the Belgian soldiers from UNAMIR.[25] There followed a diplomatic blizzard from Belgium to persuade everyone that the entire mission must pull out at once.

Later that day a disagreement developed between the Belgian diplomats and the officials in the DPKO. Kofi Annan did not favour a complete pull-out, and he argued that this would only make the humanitarian situation worse. Dallaire had faxed a long and urgent wish-list of supplies, including water, fuel, medicine and flak-jackets. The list was so long because the UN's Field Operations Division had no cash and no method for crisis resupply. A Belgian saw the list and joked about Dallaire's optimism.

The next day another cable arrived from Kigali, this time from Major Marec Pazik, one of the Polish peacekeepers who had discovered the massacre at Gikondo and who was now employed as humanitarian plans officer. Pazik was faxing to headquarters details of the people sheltering in the Amahoro football stadium. There were 5,000 people, 2,402 of whom were children under the age of fifteen. The majority were orphans whose parents had been massacred. There was no food. There were two local doctors without equipment or medicine. Twenty people urgently needed limb amputations, 150 people were seriously injured, there were 150 cases of malaria, 115 with serious diarrhoea, 205 people with bronchitis, 32 with dysentery, and 15 with chicken-pox.[26] In the stadium, at a makeshift clinic under one of the spectator stands, they were handing out small sachets of apricot jam. 'It's all we have got,' said someone. 'We have to give them something.'[27]

Just before an informal Security Council meeting, on Friday, 15 April, the Nigerian ambassador Ibrahim Gambari had a private meeting with Colin Keating. He advised Keating to pay particular attention to the views of the force commander and told him that Belgium's reaction was slightly hysterical, due in part to historic and domestic concerns. Keating then met with Belgium's UN ambassador, Paul Noterdaeme, who told him that when the Belgian peacekeepers left, there would be a bloodbath.

UN officials told Keating that peacekeeping was suitable only for the most benign environments and that the council was reaping what it had sown by putting in a force with inadequate equipment, inadequate training and lack of firepower. Without the Belgians, UNAMIR was going to be in very deep trouble. Other troop-contributing governments would soon withdraw their troops and UNAMIR would disintegrate. It would be the UN's most ignominious failure.

At the informal meeting that day Gambari made a plea for reinforcements. However weighty the advice from Belgium, he said, the ambassadors must realize no other country had withdrawn its troops – not Ghana, not Bangladesh. The peacekeepers had a vital role to play protecting the population and promoting a ceasefire. The USA objected. America would not accept any resolution except one which withdrew all the peacekeepers. The UK agreed but thought that a compromise could be reached, leaving a token force behind. The UN could hardly leave two battalions in Rwanda to be slaughtered. Gambari said that the troops on the ground were at least accomplishing something, but the USA was adamant. If a vote were to be taken, based on an 'independent assessment' of the situation in Rwanda, the USA would have no choice but to decide that there was no role for peacekeepers. The Council's primary obligation was to ensure that each UN mission was do-able and the priority was the safety of UN personnel. They adjourned for the weekend.

Details of the Council meeting were relayed to the 'interim government' by the Rwandan ambassador. The next day, 16 April, a Saturday, the 'interim government' held a meeting and, confident of no significant international opposition, it was decided to push ahead with 'pacification' in the south.

On 14 April a group of western journalists was taken by UN peacekeepers from the Hôtel des Mille Collines to the airport to be evacuated. As they prepared to leave the hotel, there were dozens of Rwandans in the lobby, crowding around them and begging to go with them. On the road to the airport the journalists saw houses burned and shops looted and in one place corpses piled in a heap. The journalists flew to Nairobi with some forty Rwanda refugees. Five journalists remained in Kigali.[28]

By now UN headquarters in Kigali had been given a written report from two UN military observers who had been present in Gisenyi when the genocide began. They had witnessed a massacre in which an estimated 10,000 people had died. The news was relayed to New York.[29]

The peacekeepers were now faced with the withdrawal of the Belgian contingent. When Marchal first heard this news he was incredulous. 'Under no circumstances could we leave,' he said. 'This was the point of view I expressed to my superiors until the moment when the political decision was made to leave UNAMIR. Our political leaders should have known that in leaving UNAMIR, we would condemn thousands of men, women and children to certain death.'[30]

On Sunday, 17 April, Dallaire wrote a long and detailed cable to UN headquarters that started with his thoughts on the Belgian contingent: 'These men were our best trained, experienced, equipped and motivated ... even though they suffered heavily with the loss of their comrades.' He then outlined his problems. 'A radical change of key staff at such a critical moment is most distressing and may cause us some serious degradation of control in the force.' Dallaire was pessimistic about a ceasefire. The RPF was adamant that the priority and the precondition of any ceasefire must be the stopping of massacres behind government lines by groups armed with machetes. He described to New York how the killing was the work of some soldiers, gendarmes and groups of militia who were increasingly organizing themselves. In the ranks of the Rwandan government army, Dallaire told New York, the hardliners had pushed aside the moderates: 'The stopping of the massacres may become more and more difficult as the local groups/militia are becoming seemingly bolder ... The ethnic killings are continuing and in fact unconfirmed reports indicate it is even increasing in scale and scope in the areas just ahead of the RPF advance.'

His knowledge about events in the rest of the country was limited, for with the evacuation of UN military observers the mission had lost its eyes and ears: 'New York may very well know more about what is going on than UNAMIR with intelligence information (satellite, EW, etc.) from its members of the situation outside Kigali.'

> Behind RGF (Rwandan Government Forces) lines, the massacres of Tutsis and moderate Hutus and sympathizers with opposition parties is taking place. Bodies litter the streets and pose a significant health hazard. RTLM radio broadcasts inflammatory speeches and songs exhorting the population to destroy all Tutsis ... It appears now that the Presidential Guard initiated the ethnic attacks and then handed this task over to the militia like the Interahamwe ... and then withdrew to Butare and Gitarama. In Kigali, frequent roadblocks are established, ID cards checked and Tutsis executed on the spot ... these massacres have been witnessed from a distance by UN troops.
>
> The militia have displayed drunkenness, drug abuse and sadistic brutality. They do not respect the UN flag, the red cross or any other human symbol. They will not hesitate to stop any convoy and attack its Rwandese passengers or even the UN guards. Without our present rules of engagement we are confronted with the dilemma of enforcing the security of persons under our protection. We have attempted to smuggle out small numbers and have been successful to date but it is only a matter of time until a confrontation occurs.

Dallaire informed New York that he was receiving a torrent of requests from expats who had worked for UN agencies and aid organizations and who had been been evacuated. They wanted the peacekeepers to rescue the Rwandans they had left behind. The people the peacekeepers were asked to find were often in places where there were thousands of people. 'Any attempt to rescue, let alone even identify, the individual will lead to a mob attack.' Most of the large concentrations of people were in militia-controlled areas and the risks of rescue had to be assessed: 'Does UNAMIR risk an armed confrontation, for which we are not equipped, protected or mandated, at considerable risk to the safety of our own troops, to attempt to save these people, or do we leave them for possible extermination?'

With armed confrontation, the threat to the peacekeepers would substantially increase. Future withdrawal of UN troops would have to be undertaken under hostile conditions: 'If this mission is to be changed into a peace enforcement scenario to stop the massacres and rescue threatened civilians, then a change in mandate will be required and the mission must be reinforced with men, weapons and equipment.'

Rescue and protection were more and more dangerous. The commander of the Bangladeshi contingent was under his own government's orders not to endanger his soldiers.[31] Bangladeshi soldiers had run for cover to the Amahoro stadium on day two of the crisis and had refused entry to a group of Belgian peacekeepers. The Belgians were threatened by an angry crowd. The Bangladeshi soliders refused to open the stadium doors and would not even allow Bangladeshis sitting in an armoured personnel carrier to help the Belgians by dispersing the crowd. Later, an internal Bangladeshi report noted: 'When the crisis began discipline deteriorated ... some soldiers refused to obey orders, arguing that ... this was not in a peacekeeping mandate ...exaggerated reports were sent back to the ministry of defence and there was panic ... We saw men crying. Our level of training and motivation for peacekeeping was a shame for us.'[32] Dallaire believed that the Bangaldeshis must be withdrawn. They were a handicap and used precious resources, water and food.

Junior Bangladeshi officers told Dallaire that if Bangladeshi troops were stopped at roadblocks with locals in the convoy, they would hand them over, rather than use their weapons. There was a widespread mistrust of this contingent, and it meant that most of the rescue missions would have to cease; with the departure of the Belgian troops it would become more and more difficult to move around the city.

In his long cable to UN headquarters on 17 April, Dallaire wrote:

> due to the militia and self-defence groups controlling important arteries and areas of the city ...they are a very large, dangerous and totally irrational group of people ... The force simply cannot continue to sit on the fence in the face of all these morally legitimate demands for assistance/protection, nor can it simply launch into chapter VII type of operations without the proper authority, personnel and equipment ... maintaining the status quo on manpower under these severe and adverse conditions is wasteful, dangerously casualty-causing

> and demoralising to the troops ... either UNAMIR gets changes ... in order to get into the thick of things ... or it starts to thin out.

A day after Dallaire sent the cable, Annan and Riza began to argue that since there was no prospect of a ceasefire then they must report to the Council that a total withdrawal of UNAMIR needed to be envisaged.[33]

Dallaire need not have bothered to write this cable. In the first four weeks of genocide, the fact that a systematic and continuing slaughter was taking place in Rwanda was not once discussed at length in Council meetings. Everyone in the Secretariat in New York was preoccupied with the civil war, from the officials in the Department of Peacekeeping, those in the Secretary-General's suite of offices on the thirty-eighth floor, and the during the secret discussions in the Security Council.

There was an assumption that only a massive and dramatic intervention would succeed in Rwanda, and that this was out of the question. The preoccupation with civil war meant that no attention was given to the contribution that the peacekeepers could continue to make, even without reinforcements. Dallaire continued to believe that reinforcements for UNAMIR were the only answer. Stopping the killings was far more important than bargaining for a ceasefire.

Notes

1. Copy in possession of the author.
2. Interview, Ambassador Karel Kovanda, 2 June 1994.
3. Letter from the Permanent Representative of Cameroon to the UN addressed to the President of the Security Council, 11 April 1994. S/1994/420, 12 April 1994.
4. Radio Muhubura, Summary of World Broadcasts. AL/1968 A/4. 11 April 1994.
5. Interview, Paul Kagame, October 1997.
6. *Broadcasting Genocide: Censorship, Propaganda and State-Sponsored Violence in Rwanda 1990–1994.* Article 19, October 1996, pp. 146–7.
7. *Broadcasting Genocide*, p. 101.
8. J.-P. Chrétien et al., *Rwanda: Les Médias du Génocide*, Paris: Karthala, 1995, p. 331.
9. *Broadcasting Genocide*, p. 120.
10. André Guichaoua (ed.), *Les Crises Politiques au Burundi et au Rwanda (1993–1994).* Université des Sciences et Technologies de Lille. Paris: Karthala, 1995, p. 526.
11. Gérard Delaloye and Elisabeth Levy, 'Philippe Gaillard, après Kigali, pouvez-vous encore croire en l'humanité?', *Le Nouveau Quotidien*, 30 December 1994.
12. Frederic Fischer, 'The Season in Hell', *Guardian Europe*, 7 July 1994.
13. Mark Doyle, BBc Radio, 12 April 1994.
14. Human Rights Watch/Fédération Internationale des Ligues des Droits de l'Homme. *Leave none to tell the story. Genocide in Rwanda*, 1999, pp. 270–8.
15. UN Commission on Human Rights, Report of the Special Rapporteur on violence against women, its causes and consequences, Ms. Radhika Coomaraswamy (E/CN.4/1998/54/Add. 1) 4 February, 1998, p. 10.

16. Interviews, Ambassador Karel Kovanda (permanent representative to the UN, Czech Republic), New York, July 1995, and Colin Keating (permanent representative to the UN, New Zealand), July 1995. Michael N. Barnett, Department of Political Science, University of Wisconsin, July 1994. See also M. N. Barnett, 'The UN Security Council: Indifference and Genocide in Rwanda', *Cultural Anthropology*, Vol. 12, No. 4, 1997.

17. *The United Nations and Rwanda, 1993–1996*. The UN Blue Book Series, Vol. 10, New York: UN Department of Public Information, p. 259.

18. Boutros Boutros-Ghali, *Unvanquished. A US–UN Saga*. London: I.B.Tauris, 1999, p. 132.

19. Rwanda had officially put forwards its candidacy as a non-permanent member at the General Assembly of October 1993. Its candidacy had been endorsed at the summit meeting of the OAU in June 1993.

20. The Prosecutor versus Jean Kambanda. Case No. ICTR 97-23-S, Judgment and Sentence.

21. All prefects turned up apart from three, from Ruhengeri, Cyangugu and Butare. The meeting was held on 11 April.

22. In Rwanda there are eleven prefectures, each governed by a Prefect. The prefectures are further subdivided into communities which are placed under the authority of bourgmestres. The bourgmestre of each commune is appointed by the president of the republic, upon the recommendation of the minister of the interior. In Rwanda, the bourgmestre is the most powerful person in the commune. His *de facto* authority in the area is significantly greater than that which is conferred upon him de jure. A bourgmestre was responsible for public order within his commune, with exclusive control over the communal police as well as any gendarmes put at the disposal of the commune. A bourgmestre was responsible for the execution of laws and regulations and the administration of justice, subject only to the prefect's authority.

23. Interview, Didier Grond (ICRC delegate), Geneva, 12 December 1998. The checkpoint was at Myambo.

24. Associated Press, Nairobi, 'Tribes Battle for Rwandan Capital: New Massacres Reported', *New York Times*, 16 April 1994.

25. The letter is dated 15 April 1994 (reference S.1168). Trans. from French. In the possession of the author.

26. UNAMIR created a humanitarian assistance cell (HAC) with six military staff. Major Don MacNeil, a Canadian, was operations officer.

27. Mark Doyle, BBC Radio, 15 April 1994.

28. Donatella Lorch, 'UN in Rwanda says it is powerless to halt the violence', *New York Times*, 15 April 1994.

29. Jacques Castonguay, *Les Casques Bleus au Rwanda*, Paris: Editions l'Harmattan, 1998, p. 134. Interview, Major Brent Beardsley, December 1999.

30. Human Rights Watch/Fédération Internationale des Ligues des Droits de l'Homme, *Leave none to tell the story*, p. 620.

31. Outgoing code-cable. To: Baril, UNATIONS. From: Dallaire, UNAMUR, Kigali, 17 April 1994.

32. Castonguay, *Les Casques Bleus au Rwanda*, p. 133.

33. *Report of the Independent Inquiry into the Actions of the United Nations during the Genocide in Rwanda, 15 December 1999*, December 1999, p 17.

15 · Genocide Spreads

AT Kigali airport, Colonel Luc Marchal hung on with the last of the Belgian peacekeepers for as long as he could, and three times refused the order to evacuate given by General José Charlier, the commander of the Belgian army. Marchal wanted Dallaire to have time for the Ghanaian troops to move to Kigali from the DMZ, in spite of a shortage of vehicles, and dig in.

Marchal wrote to Dallaire, letting him know that he was leaving the battleground under protest and the consequences of it were clear to them all. To desert a brother-in-arms was the worst thing a soldier could be asked to do; it was the nadir of his military career. He wanted on record that, in his estimation, the result of the Belgian withdrawal would be a 'bloodbath'. Thousands of people were going to be slaughtered. To evacuate was scandalous. Marchal was told by the Ministry of Defence that he must keep quiet. Years later his anger was undiminished: 'To dare to take this decision, and then to dare to try to persuade everyone else to adopt the same attitude is inexplicable, inexcusable.'[1] Only weeks before, Willy Claes, the Belgian foreign minister, had visited these peacekeepers and praised them, telling them how vital was their work in Rwanda. Claes said then that he would back them to the hilt.

On 19 April, at 9 a.m. Marchal handed over his command. At 11.30 a.m., and with a final salute, he boarded the plane. The Belgian departure shocked Dallaire.

> I stood there as the last Hercules left … and I thought that almost exactly fifty years to the day my father and my father-in-law had been fighting in Belgium to free the country from fascism, and there I was, abandoned by Belgian soldiers. So profoundly did I despise them for it … I found it inexcusable.

The Ghanaian battalion was redeployed to the airport and Canada kept a C-130 plane flying from Nairobi.[2] Without this source of resupply the garrison would have collapsed completely, for there were times when Dallaire ran out of everything, even food. At one point a Canadian Hercules was sent to Somalia, to Mogadishu, to fly in some Canadian rations. It was able to land only when there was a lull in the fighting; on these occasions it would wait with engines running, for between five and ten minutes, as near as possible to the airport building, allowing those evacuated from Rwanda to make a dash for it. Each time it landed, Dallaire was there. His determination and obstinacy helped to persuade the Canadian government that the mission must not be abandoned.[3]

When the genocide started, Dallaire had been short of water and fuel. There had been no reserve stocks before 6 April, even though the issue came up again and again in his daily reports to UN headquarters. There was no blood bank for the forces, no way of screening or storing blood and no essential drugs. Throughout the genocide, emergency electrical and communications facilities were kept operational by four UN civilian employees who had volunteered to stay behind with troops.[4] Dallaire wondered if the idea in New York was to weaken his mission to the point where withdrawal seemed the most rational action. He refused to consider the thought.

As the Belgian troops prepared their departure the shelling intensified, and two mortar rounds hit the airport. On Tuesday 19 April, thirty shells were fired by the government army directly at the Amahoro stadium, killing forty-five people and injuring hundreds more. The Red Cross and MSF managed to evacuate some of the seriously wounded and distribute food. The RPF had taken control of the area on 8 April, telling Dallaire that because his headquarters was sheltering the prime minister designate, Faustin Twagiramungu, rescued by peacekeepers, then the UN risked an attack from the Rwandan government para-commando unit at the airport. The presence of the RPF prevented the harassment of the people sheltering in the stadium by Rwandan government soldiers, but it encouraged almost constant shelling.

To the outside world, the killing in Rwanda continued to be portrayed as tribal, preordained and impossible to prevent, and although the RPF had called what was happening a genocide on 13 April, the announcement was ignored. The word surfaced again in New York on 19 April, when the executive director of Human Rights Watch, Kenneth Roth, wrote to Keating to point out that the killing in Rwanda was neither random nor inevitable and the atrocities were spreading: 'we urge your attention to the fact that the Rwanda military authorities are engaged in a systematic campaign to eliminate the Tutsi ... the organised campaign has become so concerted that we believe it constitutes genocide as defined by Article II of the Convention on the Prevention and Punishment of the Crime of Genocide.' Roth called on all parties to the convention, including the five permanent members of the Security Council, to take steps to suppress and punish genocide. Roth pointed out that the maintenance of the peacekeeping force was essential to continue safeguarding the estimated 25,000 Rwandans under UN protection. But the fact of genocide was something which no government was prepared to confront. David Rawson, the US ambassador to Rwanda, now back in Washington, was quoted as saying: 'If you get into a stalemate, and trench warfare in which the country totally exhausts itself, and there is anarchy in the countryside, then we could have taken a step backward into Somalia.'[5] Yet in at least one US department, the fact of genocide *was* recognized. According to James Woods, deputy assistant secretary for African affairs at the Department of Defense: 'Never mind that the American press, which was poorly represented anyway, hadn't quite got it right yet, at all, in fact ... there was plenty of evidence around if you'd wanted to use it.' There had been information for a couple of years, Woods said, that extremists in Rwanda were planning to do something like this. 'It was known that this was planned, premeditated, carefully planned, and was being executed according to a plan with the full connivance of the then Rwandan government. This was known.'[6]

For two weeks Rwanda's second city, Butare, had remained untouched by genocide, and thousands of people fleeing the massacres elsewhere, from the prefectures of Kigali, Gikongoro and Gitarama, sought refuge and protection there. The city had a high percentage of Tutsi and in the Butare prefecture Jean-Baptiste Habyalimana was the only Tutsi prefect in Rwanda. Habyalimana was educated in America, and had gained a PhD in engineering. He turned down a good job offer to return to Butare, Rwanda's intellectual heartland, known for its liberal traditions and ethnic tolerance. In Butare, Tutsi and Hutu had lived together for centuries. It was where the National University was located. Under its colonial name, Astrida, it been the administrative capital of Rwanda.

On 13 April RTLMC announced that there were Tutsi hiding themselves among people fleeing to the prefectures of Gitarama and Butare. In response, the prefect of Butare, Habyalimana, to calm the people, ordered that meetings be held throughout the prefecture. Four days later, on 17 April, he was named on radio RTLMC by Valérie Bemeriki and accused of working for the RPF. On 18 April, the interim government dismissed him. Habyalimana was captured at his home and then sent to the headquarters of the interim government in Gitarama, where he was executed.[7]

Jean Kambanda, the prime minister in the interim government, was travelling the country and went to the prefectures of Gitarama, Gisenyi, Cyangugu and Kibuye to incite, encourage and direct massacres. He gave an interview to RTLMC during which he said: 'the population must search out the enemy and this enemy is Tutsi and Hutu who did not agree with our [government] policy.'

Jean Kambanda was in Butare on 19 April at the inauguration of a new prefect, Sylvain Nsabimana, as was the president of the interim government, Theodore Sindikubwabo. These two addressed local dignitaries and gave rousing speeches. Kambanda described what was happening as a 'final' war: 'it must be finished ... the State, the military, the people have decided to wage this war, and to win it.'[8]

The speeches were broadcast by RTLMC.

The next day the new prefect held a meeting at which a discussion took place about what should happen to the 'infiltrators'. There were smaller meetings throughout the prefecture. Some time that morning the first victim was Rosalie Gicanda, the eighty-year-old widow of Mutara Rudahigwa, the ruler of Rwanda who died in 1959.

Interahamwe had been bussed in from Kigali, and were lodged in hotels near Butare airport. The Presidential Guard had arrived and, as in Kigali when the genocide started, the first targets were selected from lists. A witness remembers how on 21 April people were rounded up in Butare: 'I saw them driving groups of people ahead of them, behind came the soldiers with their guns … they took them down to the valley and killed them with nail studded clubs, with hoes and machetes, I heard no shots … only the cries of horror and pain.'

That day, soldiers rounded up students from the National University cafeteria, and those with Tutsi identity cards were taken to the arboretum and shot. Hutu Power students searched the university and pulled Tutsi from their hiding places. Some 600 bodies were later found in a mass grave in the area where the students were taken. In the Groupe Scolaire, the first high school in Rwanda, an estimated 600 orphans and several hundred people were attacked by Interahamwe. The people were separated into two groups on the basis of their identity cards. It is estimated that three thousand people died here. In one massacre in Butare gendarmes fired rocket-propelled grenades into a crowd and used machine guns. After these attacks there was feasting, singing and dancing. Human Rights Watch collated evidence to suggest that in the prefecture of Butare the killing was faster than anywhere else. At several places, thousands of people were killed at a time, in health clinics, in schools, on playing fields, in markets.[9]

The British-based African Rights estimated that in the commune of Karama Gikongoro a total 43,000 people were killed, the killing starting almost immediately after the prefect Habyalimana had been replaced. One witness described how the parish rocked with the deafening explosions of grenades and the shooting which lasted all day inside the church, and in both the secondary and primary schools where people had gone for safety and were crammed in. At first the men tried to fight back, but their only weapons were stones.[10]

It is thought that 100,000 people were killed in large-scale massacres in the prefecture of Butare.

The Secretary-General's report on Rwanda, promised for two weeks, arrived at the Security Council on 21 April. (It is dated 20 April.) It presented no new options, nor did it give a clear picture of the situation in Rwanda, and it contained details which clearly reflected the views of the 'interim government'. The report focused on the civil war, and described 'anarchy and spontaneous slaughter'. It claimed that the killing was started by 'unruly members' of the Presidential Guard, and described widespread killings with both 'political and ethnic dimensions', with deaths in 'tens of thousands', but it did not mention the organized killing of Tutsi and moderate Hutu. The killing of moderate cabinet ministers and of the Belgian soldiers were carried out by 'unruly soldiers'. The report made no mention at all of the efforts of the peacekeepers to protect civilians. Boutros-Ghali clearly believed that the most important task was to obtain a ceasefire. There was no mention of the massacres, which were extensive and organized. This crucial report framed the violence in terms of the breakdown of the peace process. A plan to protect civilians, which had been discussed by officials in the secretariat, was not in the report.

In portraying what was happening in terms of civil war, the report undermined the moral case for military intervention; military intervention in a civil war was presented as totally impractical, for it would lead only to a 'repetition of Somalia'. The first option, an enforcement operation 'to coerce the opposing armies to stop fighting', would need the strongest possible mandate – chapter VII of the UN Charter – and would require 'an immediate and massive reinforcement of UNAMIR'. The report noted that the peacekeepers had performed courageously in dangerous circumstances, but could not be left at risk indefinitely with no possibility of their performing the tasks for which they were dispatched.[11] The report's two other options were either a complete withdrawal or a token group of some 270 UN military personnel to promote a ceasefire and assist in the resumption of humanitarian relief.[12]

The British ambassador, David Hannay, was disappointed. He had expected a choice of options based upon the opinions of the force commander and the Secretary-General's special representative in Rwanda. Hannay dismissed the idea of reinforcements. The Council only had to 'think back to Somalia and think about what you would ask these troops to do'. It was not possible to wage war against the RPF or the Rwandese troops, nor to take over the country and try to deal with two heavily armed groups. If a ceasefire were to be agreed next week, needing military observers, then the UK would give any request for help very serious consideration. The UK opted for leaving a token force and Hannay urged a speedy decision, as did the US delegate. But Nigeria did not. Gambari said that none of the options met with his government's approval, and they must find out the force level needed to protect the 14,000 people presently sheltering under the UN flag. Was the UN to do nothing to help civilians?

There was a recess that night during which a group of ambassadors from the non-permanent Council members were briefed by the Secretary-General's Canadian military adviser, Maurice Baril. Baril came from the same French

Canadian brigade as Dallaire and had been in daily telephone contact with him. Baril quietly described to the ambassadors the conditions under which the peacekeepers were living and told them there was not a military commander in the world who would leave a force exposed in such a way. Dallaire was trying to feed 25,000 desperate Hutu and Tutsi fugitives living in internment camp conditions. Most of his soldiers were 'exhausted, confused and questioning the responsibility of their superiors' and constantly in fear. The Bangladeshi government was warning that unless the safety and security of their troops were assured with reinforcements and heavy equipment, including APCs, then they would immediately be relocated to a neighbouring country. There was already desertion, with Bangladeshi soliders leaving by road.

The military situation was hopeless. The RPF was advancing south, and against determined resistance. The Rwandese army was strengthening its position near the airport and blocking the runway at night. Dallaire, with the means at his disposal, was unable to defend the airport from a determined attack. The airport was the only lifeline, as the roads were lined with ambushes from both sides, especially at night. Every hour of delay in taking a decision about evacuation, said Baril, was an hour closer to losing the airport.

Afterwards, Keating said that he believed that if the Council had left the Bangladeshi peacekeepers in Rwanda, then most of them would have voted with their feet anyway, and in utter chaos. Without the strength of the Belgian contingent, UNAMIR was unsuitable for anything other than a benign environment. Keating argued that with a total pull-out, no one would get back in again. If a small contingent was left, it could later be built upon. A UN presence would symbolize continued concern and help preserve the Council's reputation. Keating had learned that Dallaire was willing to take action to save lives and that a small number of troops, in particular from Ghana, were willing to stay in Rwanda. Their existing mandate – resolution 872, which stipulated that UNAMIR maintain security in Kigali – was sufficiently flexible to allow for whatever robust action Dallaire thought necessary.

At around 10.30 p.m. on 21 April, the fifteen ambassadors filed wearily from their informal discussion room into the Security Council chamber to vote resolution 912. It was their first decision on the genocide and under its terms the majority of the peacekeepers were withdrawn, leaving behind a small group with the force commander 'to mediate between the two armies and facilitate human relief ... to the extent feasible'.

The resolution was tailored exactly to fit a situation in which a civil war had resumed. It spoke of 'large-scale violence' which endangered the safety of the civilian population. Baril telephoned Dallaire to tell him that he could give the order to evacuate. At first light the evacuation began, and within two days most of the peacekeepers were gone.

Of the eventual Security Council resolution vote that night to withdraw the troops, a decision which the press would call one of the most ignominious in UN history, Keating said: 'It was not a resolution that went forward with any enthusiasm on my part. But I am still convinced it was the only decision.'

In New York, a UN press release explained that the mandate for UNAMIR had been 'adjusted' and the Council had now 'authorized a force level of approximately 270' in order to secure a ceasefire, to assist in the resumption of humanitarian relief and to 'monitor and report developments'.

Six days after the decision to pull out from Rwanda, on 27 April, the Council authorized an increase in the strength of UNPROFOR of up to 6,550 additional troops. The Serbs had been testing the Security Council and Nato resolve. Gorazde was filled with some 60,000 people, one-third of whom had fled to the town from surrounding villages. Because of its location in Europe, and its echoes of the Holocaust, Bosnia commanded front-page news. Many intellectuals and public officials both in America and Britain lobbied hard for enforcement measures by the UN to stop the carnage. It was the carving up of Bosnia which would be seen as the UN's ultimate humiliation, not Rwanda.

In a clearly illegal act, Dallaire and his deputy, Brigadier Henry Kwami Anyidoho, commander of the Ghanaian troops, defied the Security Council and 456 men remained. It was a minimum option. Dallaire had asked for a residual force of 1,200, but the Council had agreed only 270. Dallaire gave everyone the option of leaving. Those who decided to stay believed that Dallaire was right, and that they did have a viable role. 'We believed in Dallaire', said one of them later, 'and we believed in this mission.' The residual force comprised mostly Ghanaians, plus forty Tunisians.[13]

In spite of the near hopelessness of it all, and even after the main force had pulled out, Dallaire was continually badgered by telephone calls from UN employees in New York and Geneva, asking for the peacekeepers to go and look for and rescue contacts or friends who were missing, people connected to various UN agencies or embassies who had earlier been abandoned. The peacekeepers were wary. After one successful rescue mission, and after evacuating a group of people on a Canadian C-130 on 21 April, the Kenyan authorities had sent the people back to Kigali from Nairobi. There were forty-seven of them, returned for failing to have a visa or passport. The peacekeepers' anger and despair were palpable. 'Each rescue mission poses a direct threat to the lives of UNAMIR soldiers,' cabled Dallaire to New York. 'Our efforts cannot be wasted in such a way.' His peacekeepers were constantly asked to do more to help expatriates, missionaries and Rwandans who were missing.

> My force was standing knee-deep in mutilated bodies, surrounded by the guttural moans of dying people, looking into the eyes of children bleeding to death with their wounds burning in the sun and being invaded by maggots and

> flies. I found myself walking through villages where the only sign of life was a goat, or a chicken, or song-bird, as all the people were dead, their bodies being eaten by voracious packs of wild dogs.[14]

The stench in the city worsened. Polish peacekeeper Major Stefan Stec described the smell of rotting bodies as so bad that it was like living on top of rotting meat. There were thousands of unburied bodies in the streets of Kigali and a large number of scavenging animals – rats, birds and dogs – were spreading disease.

Rwanda's countryside was littered with dead and on the border with Tanzania the Kagera river was full of the mutilated bodies of men, women, children and babies. Some people had been dismembered. There were reports of body parts stacked neatly, instances where the militia had joked about cutting the Tutsi down to size by chopping off their hands and feet.

Laetitia Ugiriwabo, aged ten, said:

> Some people dressed in uniforms and carrying guns came into the church. They asked everybody to come out with their arms in the air ... They made us sit in the sun and then searched people for money. They separated the boys from the women. They ... removed baby boys from their mothers' backs ... Then they macheted the men, including the babies right in front of us ... they brought a tractor to take the bodies away.

In Gikongoro prefecture, in a parish called Murambi, a large-scale massacre began at dawn on 21 April. Thousands of people were urged by Catholic priests to shelter in a technical school on a hilltop at the end of a narrow road. The priests said that all Tutsi would be safe, but Rwandan soldiers surrounded the school. The water supply was cut. When the massacre began, the Interahamwe went from building to building, throwing grenades through windows. People outside were beaten or slashed to death. There were sixty-four classrooms full of people. The killing lasted several days and thousands perished.

A survivor recalled: 'She said, "Ah, you have given birth to another Inyenzi" ... and she picked up a stick and killed my child.'

On 22 April a second road convoy of the ICRC reached Kigali from Burundi. It carried doctors and nurses and medical supplies. Elsewhere, in Gitarama prefecture, two ICRC delegates had begun caring for 100 people and two more ICRC teams had entered Rwanda from Zaire, one going to the Gisenyi area, and the other to Cyangugu where delegates were hoping to gain access to 5,000 people in a stadium surrounded by Rwandan police and militia. These people had initially sought refuge in the cathedral and were then herded into the stadium, and there were reports that sixty people, pulled out from the crowd, had been executed. There were reports from missionaries that some 10,850 people had been killed in Cyangugu town. In a press release on 20 April, the UNHCR reported that 16,870 people had been killed in nine villages around Cyangugu. A Hutu man in Cyangugu, who opposed the CDR, was killed by having parts of his body cut off.[15]

On 23 April, Mark Doyle, a journalist with the BBC who had won Dallaire's respect through his persistence, reported that up to 100,000 people had been killed in Rwanda in the past eighteen days. That day, the world's dilemma was laid out in a *New York Times* editorial which began: 'What looks very much like genocide has been taking place in Rwanda ... The wider horror is that the world has few ways of responding effectively when violence within a nation leads to massacres and the breakdown of civil order.' The editorial described how the Security Council had 'thrown in the bloodied towel', and, however unsettling, the pull-out of the peacekeepers fairly reflected the unwillingness of most UN members to recruit a force big enough to stop a genocidal conflict. Most troubling of all was the uncertain fate of thousands of Rwandans who sought the protection of UN peacekeepers. All of them could now be slaughtered. 'Yet what other choices really exist?' Somalia had proved ample warning against plunging into an open-ended 'humanitarian mission'. American diplomats argued that keeping a UN presence, however reduced, was better than nothing. The editorial continued:

> But it is scant comfort to Rwandans who in good faith sought UN protection ... the horrors of Kigali show the need for considering whether a mobile, quick-response UN force under UN aegis is needed to deal with such calamities.
>
> Absent such a force, the world has little choice but to stand aside 'and hope for the best'.[16]

On the Burundi–Rwanda border, a British emergencies officer with Oxfam, Maurice Herson, telephoned his headquarters in Oxford. He was desperate. He had worked out that the current reported death toll of 100,000 was hopelessly misleading. Herson had spoken with people who were escaping into Burundi, and had jotted some figures on the back of an envelope. His conclusion was that perhaps half a million people had been murdered in three weeks. He said he did not want to use the word genocide, but it was appropriate.

The following day, Tuesday, 26 April, Herson called again, more agitated. The UN was going to do nothing, he said, that much was clear. Even if it did, it was too late. Everyone would soon be dead.

There was a serious discussion in Oxfam. Could Herson be right? Was it genocide? And if it was genocide, what should they do with such information? The press officer, John Magrath, thought they must go public, for it would at least provide a moral and legal stick with which to beat the Security Council.

There then came a call from Tanzania, from Alfred Sakafu, Oxfam emergencies officer. He told Magrath that hundreds of bodies were clogging the Kagera river flowing from Rwanda. Magrath wrote a press release using the word genocide, but did not send it. He wanted to talk with an Oxfam employee in Kigali whom he believed might still be alive.

That day in New York, Keating had a meeting with a representative of MSF-Belgium who told him the story of a medical co-ordinator, Dr Rony Zachariah, who two days ago had made the decision to abandon the University Hospital, Butare.

On the night of 22 April, about forty wounded male Tutsi patients had been taken away by Interahamwe and soldiers and killed behind the hospital. Their bodies were later removed by prisoners supervised by soldiers. In the night all Tutsi patients had been brutally removed from the wards to make room for wounded Presidential Guard who had been flown to Butare by helicopter from the fighting around Kigali. Zachariah had tried to ensure the security of his patients by negotiating with a military captain who was responsible for welfare of the Presidential Guard but shortly after this discussion around 170 wounded Tutsi, among them children, were taken out in groups and either beaten or hacked to death. Three nurses were taken. One of them was a Hutu but she was seven months pregnant and married to a Tutsi. 'She apparently had to be killed because her baby would be Tutsi at birth,' Zachariah had reported. 'I tried to intervene between the soliders, but they told me that these people were on their list.' He heard one of the soldiers say, 'This hospital stinks with Tutsi. We must clean up.'[17]

Zachariah had returned to Brussels determined that the perpetrators must be judged for this crime. The representative from MSF-Belgium had pleaded with Keating for help for Rwanda. Keating remembers that the word genocide was used.

On the following day Keating received a letter from the RPF's New York representative, Claude Dusaidi, a former teacher in Canada. Dusaidi had not given up hope that the West would send reinforcements. He believed that, so far, the Council had failed to grasp the principle involved. His letter told Keating that a carefully planned campaign was under way to exterminate the Tutsi ethnic group. It continued: 'When the institution of the UN was created after the Second World War, one of its fundamental objectives was to see to it that what happened to the Jews in Nazi Germany would never happen again.' The international community was legally obliged to act under the 1948 Genocide Convention. The letter was copied to Boutros-Ghali and later, from the RPF office in Brussels, the second vice-president of the RPF, Denis Polisi, sent Boutros-Ghali a list of the names of the people thought to be responsible, asking that an international court be created to put them on trial.

Meanwhile, in Washington every attempt was being made to avoid the word genocide. On 28 April at a press conference, a State Department spokeswoman, Christine Shelley, was asked whether what was happening in Rwanda was genocide. Shelley said:

> The use of the term genocide has a very precise legal meaning, although it's not strictly a legal determination. There are other factors in there as well ... When in looking at a situation to make a determination about that, before we begin to use that term we have to know as much as possible about the facts of the situation ... This is a more complicated issue to address, and we're certainly looking into this extremely carefully right now. But I'm not able to look at all of those criteria at this moment.

One of the journalists present, Alan Elsner of Reuters, said that, looking back on it, it sounds utterly ridiculous: 'These were all kinds of artful ways of doing nothing,' he said.[18]

In Oxford that day, 28 April, Oxfam issued a press release. Its headline read: 'Oxfam fears genocide is happening in Rwanda.' There was a flicker of interest in the press, but not a lot because there was another story now grabbing the headlines. Suddenly, thousands and thousands of people were pouring out of Rwanda into Tanzania. This was the fastest exodus the world had ever seen. Whole communities were on the move, not fleeing a genocide, but fleeing the RPF advance. And in each community there were groups of Interahamwe. Unlike the people who had been fleeing into Burundi, these people had no wounds. At first, the Tanzanian officials had disarmed them and machetes were piled high at border posts.

That day in Oxford, Magrath, noting the numbers of journalists who were covering the South African elections paving the way for a new multi-racial parliament, dryly recorded in his diary: 'The South African elections were over and all the crews were diverted to Tanzania – the refugees became the story, not the genocide.' While the genocide took place in Rwanda, the number of reporters never rose above a maximum of fifteen. In South Africa, in early May, there had been 2,500 accredited press.[19]

Quite possibly aware that the attention of the world could shift to their direction at any time, Hutu Power attempted to reactivate a civilian 'self-defence programme', ostensibly to fight the RPF. Unlike the militia which had been controlled by political parties, the defence groups in each commune were intended to be under the control of local administrators. Perhaps Hutu Power wanted more control over the killing, making sure there were sufficient weapons, and that monitoring at the roadblocks continued. These local groups could hunt Tutsi in less accessible sites than churches and schools.[20] In Kigali RTLMC proclaimed that 5 May was 'clean-up day'. It was the day they were going to bury Habyarimana, and the day when there were to be no more Tutsi left in Kigali.

Dallaire warned headquarters that he feared a new round of massacres, and that the people under UN protection would be targeted. A programme was broadcast on RTLMC to the effect that Dallaire was an RPF accomplice who had helped RPF soldiers infiltrate Kigali. There were fears that he was being undermined from within Rwanda. The French were putting pressure on the Canadian government to remove Dallaire from command, and there was a more sinister aspect, with the RPF claiming to have intercepted the communications of the Rwandan army revealing a plot to kill Dallaire, a plot which had the support of a member of Jacques-Roger Booh-Booh's staff. There were also RPF intercepts revealing unscheduled meetings between Booh-Booh and government army officers.

Then Ottawa telephoned UNAMIR HQ to say that a friendly government had warned that Dallaire's life was at risk. Senior officers in UNAMIR assumed that this friendly government was the USA. If US intelligence knew this, what else did they know?[21] Canadian army command ordered Dallaire not to leave headquarters without an escort.[22]

On 30 April, in an interview reported by Reuters, Dallaire said that unless the international community acted, it would be unable to defend itself against accusations of doing nothing to stop genocide.[23] Later, headquarters, in a coded cable, questioned his use of the word. Research undertaken afterwards by Human Rights Watch would show that by now the large-scale massacres were almost over.[24]

The Security Council finally addressed the question of genocide on 29 April, after Keating, whose presidency of the Security Council was over at the end of the month, proposed a presidential statement recognizing the fact. Keating believed that if the Security Council were to admit that this was genocide, then under the terms of the 1948 Genocide Convention all but three member states – Djibouti, Nigeria and Oman, which had not signed the convention – were legally bound to act. Keating was supported by Argentina, Spain and the Czech Republic. The latter's ambassador, Karel Kovanda, had already confronted the Council with the fact of genocide at an informal meeting a day earlier, telling ambassadors that it was scandalous that so far 80 per cent of Council efforts had been spent discussing withdrawing the peacekeepers, and 20 per cent trying to get a ceasefire in the civil war. 'It was rather like wanting Hitler to reach a ceasefire with the Jews,' he told them. What was happening in Rwanda was genocide, conducted by the interim Hutu regime. Yet the Council avoided the question of mass killing. There were objections to Kovanda's outburst and afterwards, he says, British and Americans diplomats quietly told him that on no account was he to use such inflammatory language outside the Council. It was not helpful.

A draft of Keating's proposed presidential statement was submitted to the

Council. It included the paragraph:

> the horrors of Rwanda's killing fields have few precedents in the recent history of the world. The Security Council reaffirms that the systematic killing of any ethnic group, with intent to destroy it in whole or in part constitutes an act of genocide as defined by relevant provisions of international law ... the council further points out that an important body of international law exists that deals with perpetrators of genocide.

The draft warned the interim government of its responsibility for immediately reining in and disciplining those responsible for the brutality.

There were objections. The British ambassador, David Hannay, did not want the word genocide to be used, and argued that were the statement to be used in an official UN document, then the Council would become a 'laughing stock'. To name this a genocide and not to act on it would be ridiculous. Nor did America want the word used, and China argued against it. The Rwandan ambassador said that the civilian deaths were the result of civil war and he was ably supported in this by the French-influenced ally, Djibouti, whose ambassador said later that he was against the statement because it was 'sensationalist'.

The debate went round in circles. Keating, whose term as president would end the following day, tried the somewhat desperate measure of threatening a draft resolution, tabled in his national capacity. This would require a vote, and a vote was always taken in public. This would expose the positions of each country to public scrutiny. In the end, a compromise was reached. Thanks to the drafting ability of the British, known for framing resolutions with mind-numbing ambiguity, a watered-down statement was issued, and while the statement quoted directly from the Genocide Convention, it did not use the word genocide.

> The Security Council condemns all the breaches of international humanitarian law in Rwanda, particularly those perpetrated against the civilian population, and recalls that persons who instigate or participate in such acts are individually responsible. The Security Council recalls that the killing of members of an ethnic group with the intention of destroying such a group in whole or in part constitutes a crime punishable by international law.

The statement recognized that the massacres were systematic, although it did not identify the targets, but it did describe how 'attacks on defenceless civilians have occurred throughout the country, especially in areas under the control of members of supporters of the armed forces of the interim government of Rwanda'. To satisfy French demands that massacres had also been conducted by the RPF, it went on: 'The Security Council demands that the interim government of Rwanda and the Rwandese Patriotic Front take effective measures to prevent any attacks on civilians in areas under their control.' The statement appealed to all states to refrain from providing arms or any military assistance to the two sides in Rwanda and reiterated the call for a ceasefire. It provided that the Secretary-General 'investigate serious violations of human rights law'.[25]

The statement was finally voted at 1.15 a.m. on Saturday, 30 April. 'We ended April exhausted but hopeful that the first few weeks of May would bring action to reinforce UNAMIR with a real force capable of doing what Dallaire had been urging,' Keating said.

On the day of this debate, Boutros Boutros-Ghali recommended a reversal of the decision to withdraw. In a letter to the Council he suggested that they reconsider resolution 912, which had mandated a reduction in the force levels of UNAMIR. Boutros-Ghali told them that the force commander reported a further deterioration in Kigali. This was a humanitarian catastrophe. He urged them to consider what action, including forceful action, was necessary to restore law and order and to put an end to the massacres:

> Such action would require a commitment of human and material resources on a scale which the member states have so far proved reluctant to contemplate. But I am convinced that the scale of human suffering in Rwanda, and its implications for the stability of neighbouring countries, leave the Security Council with no alternative but to examine this possibility.

His letter was greeted with stunned silence. In the secretariat, staff were again surprised by his failure to suggest options to the Council. Options for action had been discussed at length by officials, and with the force commander. Why Boutros-Ghali failed at this stage to guide the Council has never been explained.

In answer to Boutros-Ghali's call for more forceful action, in a largely unnoticed press release issued in New York, the RPF announced that the time for UN intervention was past. The genocide was almost complete. The RPF demanded the removal of Booh-Booh, insisting he be replaced with someone more competent. The RPF said that Boutros-Ghali should urge the international community to ostracize the perpetrators of massacres.

The RPF leadership found it unbelievable that the 'interim government' was given legitimacy when two Hutu Power fanatics had been openly welcomed in Paris on 27 April; Jérome Bicamumpaka, the foreign minister in the interim government, and Jean-Bosco Barayagwiza, the leader of the CDR, were received by the president, François Mitterrand, and had meetings with the prime minister Edouard Balladur, and Alain Juppé, minister of foreign affairs.[26] According to Gérard Prunier, a political scientist advising the French Ministry of Defence, frantic efforts were made at this time by officials in the government to 'save their allies'. Prunier says that the French government was secretly delivering ammunition to the Rwandan army.[27] This was later denied. According to French officials, there were no legal and official deliveries of arms after 8 April.

The RPF later learned that the governments of France and Egypt had hosted high-level talks with members of the interim government and appeared 'to be master-minding the current proposal for the deployment of a UN intervention force as a result of those talks'. The RPF wanted both Egypt and France to be censured by the international community.[28]

The president's widow, Agathe Habyarimana, was living in a luxury apartment in Paris. She made an official visit to Cairo from 17 until 23 June, when she was accorded full diplomatic honours and given the Salon d'Honneur at Cairo's airport.[29]

It was business as usual for Hutu Power, whose most important allies were France and Egypt. Throughout the genocide, with money looted from government coffers, the extremists resupplied their stocks of weapons on the open arms market. There are letters and invoices, bank statements and money transfers, a paper trail to show that, once the genocide was under way, $13 million Rwandan government money passed through the Banque Nationale de Paris. Money was also transferred from the government system to Rwandan embassies in Washington, Moscow, Kinshasa, Bonn and Tokyo and to the Rwanda consulate in Pretoria.[30]

On 10 April, four days after the genocide began, the newly installed interim government made contact with Mil-Tec, a company with offices in London, to order $854,000-worth of arms and ammunition; later, the interim government paid a total of US$4 million to this company for arms shipped on 18 April, 25 April, 5 May and 20 May.[31]

In the murky depths of arms trafficking, the paper trail always ends up off-shore, and Mil-Tec was incorporated in Douglas, the Isle of Man, with a correspondence address in Hove, East Sussex. It bought and flew weapons to Hutu Power from countries all over the world. As an off-shore company it was exempt from a UN arms embargo imposed by the Security Council on 17 May.[32] Under British law, UN arms embargoes are enforced by means of statutory instruments and on 24 June 1994, when the arms embargo statute was drafted by government lawyers, they failed to include the crown dependencies in the enabling legislation.[33] Thousands of rounds of ammunition, bombs and grenades were flown by Mil-Tec from eastern Europe and from Israel.[34] As far as is known, not one single British-manufactured weapon was shipped, so no export licences would have been necessary. The arms did not arrive in nor did they leave the UK. In Britain, with the shipment of weapons from third countries, there was then no obligation to report arms sales.

The Security Council set up an inquiry into the arming of the former Rwandan government forces.[35] This International Commission of Inquiry was chaired by Ambassador Mahmoud Kassem of Egypt, an appointment made by Boutros-Ghali to collect information and investigate reports relating to the supply of arms to former Rwandan government forces.[36] One arms sale uncovered by this commission concerned Colonel Théoneste Bagosora who, during the genocide in May, had negotiated an arms deal in the Seychelles. The government of the Seychelles had been acting on the basis of an end-user certificate issued by the government of Zaire, authorizing the sale. A Nigerian-registered aircraft carrying arms from Malta to Goma on 25 May 25 1994 included Bagosora among its passengers.

During the genocide, contact between Lieutenant Cyprien Kayumba, chargé d'affaires at the Rwanda embassy in Paris, and Jean-Pierre Huchon, head of the military mission at the French Ministry of Co-operation, was frequent.[37]

Research undertaken by the arms division of Human Rights Watch established that on five occasions in May and June 1994 arms were delivered to the Rwandan government army through Goma, and that these arms came from the French government or French companies operating under government licence.[38] The French government has strenuously denied this.

Notes

1. Interview, Colonel Luc Marchal, November 1999.
2. Canada had forty-five pilots and two CC-130s in Nairobi. These planes, throughout the genocide, transported 6,315 passengers from Kigali and brought in supplies, often to be greeted at Kigali airport by missiles and bombs. They also evacuated the majority of the peacekeepers after the 21 April decision of the Security Council.
3. On 5 June, a C-130 made an emergency departure, forced to take off after a mortar-bomb exploded 400 yards away. The plane was hardly in the air when a second bomb exploded on the tarmac. Then the airport finally closed. Attempts were made to resupply the peacekeepers through Entebbe and then overland to Kigali, through RPF territory, about a ten-hour drive. This was the only resupply and casualty evacuation.
4. The technicians who stayed behind were: Per Einarson from Norway, Richard Gregoive from Trinidad and Tobago, Paul Martin from Australia and Shuji Ashiama from Japan.
5. Donatella Lorch, 'The Massacres in Rwanda: Hope is also a Victim', *New York Times*, 21 April 1994.
6. Excerpt taken from interviews published on Frontline's website for 'The Triumph of Evil'. www.pbs.org/WGBH/Pages/Frontline/shows/evil. Copyright WGBH/Frontline, 1999.
7. Another prefect was killed: Godefroid Ruzindana of Kibungo.
8. Human Rights Watch/Fédération Internationale des Ligues des Droits de l'Homme, *Leave none to tell the story. Genocide in Rwanda*, 1999, p. 456.
9. Ibid., p. 488.
10. African Rights, *Rwanda. Death, Despair and Defiance*. London: African Rights, 1995, pp. 345–51.
11. After the Belgian contingent withdrew, the troop numbers decreased from 2,165 to 1,515 and the number of military observers from 321 to 190.

12. *The United Nations and Rwanda, 1993–1996*. The UN Blue Book series, Vol. 10, New York: UN Department of Public Information, pp. 62–5.

13. Even though the Bangladeshi contingent left, the chief of operations and two other officers of the staff remained with a senior non-commissioned officer.

14. Johnathan Moore (ed.), *Hard Choices, Moral Dilemmas in Humanitarian Intervention*, Oxford: Rowman and Littlefield, 1998, p. 81. See also Human Rights Watch / Fédération Internationale des Ligues des Droits de l'Homme, *Leave none to tell the story. Genocide in Rwanda*, 1999, p. 320.

15. Ibid., p. 216.

16. 'Cold Choices in Rwanda', Editorial, *New York Times*, 23 April 1994.

17. Eye Witness Accounts of Massacres / Human Rights Violations (Chronological Recollection of Events) Butare, Rwanda. April, 1994. Dr Rony Zachariah, medical co-ordinator. Wauter Van Emplem, Emergency desk, MSF-Holland. Unpublished.

18. Excerpt taken from interviews published on Frontline's website for 'The Triumph of Evil'. www.pbs.org / WGBH / Pages / Frontline / shows / evil. Copyright WGBH / Frontline, 1999.

19. Steven Livingstone and Todd Eachus, 'Rwanda: US Policy and Television Coverage', in Howard Adelman and Astri Suhrke (eds), *The Path of a Genocide. The Rwanda Crisis from Uganda to Zaire*. New Brunswick, NJ: Transaction, 1999, p. 209

20. Human Rights Watch / Fédération Internationale des Ligues des Droits de l'Homme, *Leave none to tell the story*. p. 282. Also, testimony of Alison des Forges in Assemblée Nationale, Mission d'Information Commune, *Enquête sur la Tragédie Rwandaise (1990–1994). Book III: Auditions*.

21. Interview, Major Brent Beardsley (staff officer, UNAMIR), December 1999.

22. Jacques Castonguay, *Les Casques Bleus au Rwanda*, Paris: Editions l'Harmattan, 1998, p. 89.

23. Buchizya Mseteka, 'UN agencies deal with Rwanda catastrophe', Reuters, 30 April 1994.

24. Human Rights Watch / Fédération Internationale des Ligues des Droits de l'Homme. *Leave none to tell the story*, p. 211.

25. *The United Nations and Rwanda, 1993–1996*, UN Blue Book series, Vol. 10, p. 271.

26. Gérard Prunier, *The Rwanda Crisis 1959–1994. History of a Genocide*, London: Hurst and Company, 1995, p. 277.

27. Ibid,. p. 278.

28. Statement by the Political Bureau of the Rwandese Patriotic Front on the Proposed Deployment of a UN Intervention Force in Rwanda. RPF. New York, 30 April 1994. Signed by Claude Dusaidi and Gerald Gahima.

29. Letters from the Rwanda embassy, Cairo, to the Department of Protocol at the Egyptian Ministry of Foreign Affairs, 13 June and 24 June 1994. Unpublished. In the possession of the author.

30. The South African arms industry, which until 1994 operated covertly, was being brought under increasing government control. But some individuals involved in the arms trade or the armed forces during the apartheid regime were still active in an individual capacity or in private industry. Their activities included dealing arms and providing mercenaries.

31. Shipping documents show that Mil-Tec used an aircraft registered in Nigeria but leased from a company in the Bahamas to make the deliveries.

32. Mil-Tec was set up as a shell company in February 1993 by BDO Binder in Douglas.

33. A Whitehall committee set up after the Mil-Tec deals came to light concluded that there were no structured arrangements in Britain for ensuring the timely and accurate imposition of embargoes. It found a lack of consistency in implementing embargoes in the UK and its dependent territories – such as Bermuda, Gibraltar and Hong Kong. The Home Office, which is responsible for crown dependencies, was not informed of the embargoes until August 1994, and they had still not been applied by January 1997. The committee found gaps in government controls on arms exports and recommended that all future UN and other arms embargoes should be applied promptly in Britain, the crown dependencies and the dependent territories.

34. Documents reveal the exact amounts paid to Mil-Tec during the genocide. On 14 April, Mil-Tec received US$1,621,901, via the Bank Belgolaise in Brussels and later on 17 May a further US$300,000. From the Cairo embassy, on 19 April, $667,120 was paid to Mil-Tec through the National Westminster Bank; on 26 April, $596,120 was transferred to Mil-Tec, and on 8 May the sum of $130,120.

35. Security Council Resolution 1013, 7 September 1995. International Committee of Inquiry (Rwanda).

36. The other members of the commisison were: Inspector Jean-Michel Hanssens (Canada), Colonel Jürgen G. H. Almeling (Germany); Lieutenant-Colonel Jan Meijvogel (Netherlands); Brigadier Mujahid Alam (Pakistan); and Colonel Lameck Mutanda (Zimbabwe).

37. Human Rights Watch/Fédération Internationale des Ligues des Droits de l'Homme, *Leave none to tell the story*, p. 662.

38. Human Rights Watch Arms Project, 'Rwanda/Zaire: Rearming with Impunity'. Vol. 7, no. 4, May 1995.

16 · The World Shuts the Door

TOWARDS the end of April, a logistician with MSF-France, René Caravielhe, watched as a young boy slowly approached the ICRC hospital. The boy had bare feet and he was wearing a dirty Coca-Cola T-shirt and ragged trousers. He was not crying, but he looked sickened. The boy told Caravielhe that there had been a massacre not 500 metres from the hospital and two children could still be helped. The boy told Caravielhe where the place was but would not go himself.

When Caravielhe and a colleague reached the spot they found a gang surrounding the bodies of a family, and spitting on them. Caraviehle later wrote the following description:

> Jean de Dieu, eleven, was curled up, a ball of flesh and blood, the look in his eyes was a glance from nowhere … without vision; Marie-Ange, aged nine, was propped up against a tree trunk … her legs apart, and she was covered in excrement, sperm and blood … in her mouth was a penis, cut with a machete, that of her father … [nearby] … in a ditch with stinking water were four bodies, cut up, piled up, their parents and older brothers.
>
> We took the two children in our arms and we were about to put them in the car when a jeep came past, full of men with weapons, and they started to laugh sadistically. The fact that we had children in our arms did not temper their aggression, and we had to go through the same sort of palaver as usual … There was a torrential downpour which was fortunate, and we were allowed to put the children in the car and we left for the hospital … [one day] another word will have to be coined more terrible than the word horror, in order to describe this sort of thing … this sort of thing was a daily experience for volunteers still in Rwanda. To get back to the hospital we had to go through roadblocks where there were children, grenade in one hand and a machete in another.[1]

After several days, Jean de Dieu told them his age. He explained that boys and men had put their penises in his mouth and then they had beaten him. He had watched while these men killed his parents and hurt his sister. Marie-Ange came out of her coma some days later. She refused to eat or drink but she did find the will to live, probably because she was among other children.

Caravielhe ended his dispatch with the words, 'the laughter of children, although they are amputees, is the strongest medicine in the world'.

On Saturday, 30 April, Dallaire travelled to Byumba, 80 miles east of the city where he had a two-hour meeting with the commander of the RPF, Major-General Paul Kagame. Dallaire carried a ceasefire proposal from the 'interim government' which provided for a return of both armies to the positions of 6 April.[2]

Kagame was scathing. This whole idea, he said, had been devised by the French at a recent and secret meeting in Kampala with the 'interim government'. 'You are the representative of the UN here,' Kagame said bitterly. 'You know who's doing what and who says what.'

Dallaire said that the time might have come for UNAMIR to be reinforced. Kagame told him it was too late; it would be an empty gesture. Only the RPF could put an end to the massacres. Nothing should be allowed to slow his advance. If UN peacekeepers came between the RPF and the government troops, then they would be treated as the enemy and engaged. Kagame said that his aim was to save as many people from the killing machine that had been set up in the interim government's killing zone. This whole thing was the UN's fault for failing to provide the right mandate at the right moment. The RPF had consistently brought to the attention of the international community the alarming preparations for these massacres. Everyone had been warned.[3]

The RPF was gaining ground, infiltrating men and matériel into Kigali at night and slowly and systematically expanding their area of control. The RPF drove government forces back into their camps, seizing key terrain and dominating key cross-roads. Dallaire described it in a cable to New York: 'The blitzkrieg nature of their offensives as was seen in the first days of the war has slowed and has been methodical in its application with the focus of their main effort the strangling and capture of Kigali.'

By Sunday 1 May Rwanda was back near the top of the foreign news schedules, but only because of the flood of Rwandans into Tanzania. A quarter of a million people had crossed a border in twenty-four hours. On the front page of the *New York Times* officials in the Clinton administration were reported to be examining ways of 'helping to organize and pay for military intervention in Rwanda by neighboring African countries'. The idea was at a preliminary stage.[4]

On 1 May in Butare, Rwandan soldiers, convalescing in a local hospital, slaughtered twenty-one children, the survivors of other massacres, and thirteen Rwandan Red Cross workers trying to protect them.[5] The children had been segregated by their killers into Hutu and Tutsi. The killings were reported in the western press together with a story about how UN peacekeepers had tried unsuccessfully to escort sixty people from the 300 who were trapped at Hôtel des Mille Collines in Kigali.[6] This was Kigali's best hotel. The people sheltering there were mostly well-connected Tutsi and pro-democracy Hutu. When Uwilingiyimana had been murdered on 7 April, her five children had been brought here. A dozen soldiers and militia turned up looking for them, telling everyone that each door in the hotel would be blown apart until they were handed over. Only a Senegalese peacekeeper, Captain Mbaye Diagne, persuaded them otherwise and they had left. The children were evacuated that night in a French convoy. Switzerland accepted them as refugees.[7]

For weeks, people trapped in the hotel came under constant threat. The manager, Paul Rusesabagina, was once told by an army officer to get everyone out of the hotel in thirty minutes. Rusesabagina asked where the people would go and he was told that this was not his problem. Using the one working telephone line Rusesabagina made calls to contacts in the army and the threat was lifted.[8]

On Tuesday 3 May it was decided that peacekeepers should escort to the airport people from the hotel who had been offered asylum in Belgium. As the convoy was prepared by Ghanaian peacekeepers, the Interahamwe got wind of the plan, and RTLMC broadcast the names of Tutsi – some of them well-known – who were on the convoy. Barely a mile into the journey at a check-point manned by Presidential Guards the convoy was stopped and everyone in the first car was ordered to get out and sit on the road. The luggage was looted. Then François-Xavier Nsanzuwera, who was a Hutu and Rwanda's deputy attorney-general, was rifle-butted to the floor. He remembers how the peacekeepers with the convoy had sought protection in their vehicles.

'They beat everyone very badly … some young women suffered very serious injuries … they slapped children who cried,' remembered Nsanzuwera.[9] Then Interahamwe turned up and one of them shot at Nsanzuwera but missed and one bullet hit a Presidential Guard. There was chaos. The prefect of Kigali intervened and ordered the convoy to return to the hotel.[10]

Although the hotel was the most high-profile hostage site, there were other places too where Tutsi sought sanctuary. In Kigali, where an estimated 20,000 people were trapped, thousands took refuge in two Catholic churches, St Paul and St Famille, and in the Hôtel Méridien and the King Faisal hospital (the hospital was no longer functional). They were hungry, dirty and desperate. Each night people from these places were snatched by the Interahamwe. In the early morning on 15 April, at the St Famille church, the Interahamwe and Presidential Guard came to select 120 men and boys one by one, calling out their names from lists. They were taken outside and shot. Most victims were political activists, businessmen, students, or young men who looked like Tutsi.[11] In another incident on 16 June, some sixty teenage boys were chosen – two boys who turned out to be Hutu were released and then two more chosen in their place – and the boys were herded to a pit outside the church compound to be killed. This was described to a UN observer by a priest. When the observer relayed the news at UNAMIR headquarters, an RPF colonel there for talks, Frank Mugambage, had wept.

Four days later the peacekeepers mounted an operation to try to evacuate some of the thousands of people sheltering in the St Famille church. When they arrived there was a scramble for the buses and trucks. There were horrific scenes with people clubbed by government soldiers who insisted names be read from a list. People pleaded to be rescued. One small boy, no more than five years old, ran past the guards and leapt on to a flat-bed truck as it drove away. The onlookers cheered.

Major-General Paul Kagame met western journalists at Rusomo on the Tanzanian border on Wednesday, 4 May; they asked him about a ceasefire. Kagame told them that the 'interim government' was no more than a 'clique of murderers' and that a ceasefire was impossible unless there was an immediate end to the massacres, the Presidential Guard was dismantled and the hate radio closed down.

Kagame had stopped looking at the massacre sites because he feared their effect on his actions. The soldiers of the RPF were discovering that their promised land had the foulest stench, and was mostly empty. Flocking to their bases were Tutsi, children and women, with terrible machete wounds. The world had never appeared more hopeless or helpless, he said later.[12] 'All those claiming to be civilized had turned their backs,' he said. 'I knew that we were alone. We would have to sort out the problem. I developed contempt for those people in the world who claimed to stand for values of moral authority.'

The magnitude of the killing was becoming evident. There were bloated and mutilated bodies clogging the Kagera river. At the border with Tanzania, at the Rusomo Falls where the river was as wide as the Thames, a body a minute passed under the bridge. 'Hundreds and hundreds must have passed down the river in the past week and they are still coming,' one report described. 'A terrible genocidal madness has taken over Rwanda. It is now completely out of control.'[13]

With the scale of the killing now apparent and with continued demands that something be done, in the first week in May Boutros Boutros-Ghali assumed a higher profile. Having publicly called for reinforcements at the end of April, he now appeared on American television, on an ABC 'Nightline' programme, interviewed from Geneva by Ted Koppel.[14] Koppel started the programme with the words: 'Tonight, Rwanda. Is the world just too tired to help?' Koppel reminded viewers of the thousands of deaths of the recent past – in former Yugoslavia, in East Timor, in Angola, in Burundi, in Tajikistan and Nagorno-Karabakh. Rwanda, he said, had the misfortune to come at the tail end of a particularly noxious stretch of history. There was a film clip of President Clinton, who, on that day when asked about Rwanda, had said: 'Lesson number one is, don't go into one of these things and say, as the US said when we started in Somalia, "Maybe we'll be done in a month because it's a humanitarian crisis" ... Because there are almost always political problems and sometimes military conflicts, which bring about these crises.'

A letter had been sent to the president from nine representatives from the House African Affairs Subcommittee, asking for strong support for an active US role – short of committing US troops. In London, Oxfam held a vigil and delivered a letter to Prime Minister John Major calling the killing a genocide and comparing the slaughter with that in the killing fields of Cambodia.

Before the 'Nightline' interview began, Boutros-Ghali told Koppel that a modest reinforcement of 5,000 troops could have prevented the slaughter. This surprised Koppel, who remembered that, only a week before, the Security Council had decided to withdraw soldiers from UNAMIR. On air, Boutros-Ghali explained to Koppel some of the problems involved in obtaining troops for Rwanda. He had written letters to heads of state all over the world asking for troops. Koppel asked him why it was taking so long. Boutros-Ghali explained that there was a general fatigue, and that there had been the same reaction to requests for troops for all peacekeeping operations. Rwanda, however, required intervention. He added: 'because it is a question of genocide ... I am sure that we have the capacity to intervene.'

Ted Koppel: 'You appealed to the Security Council the other day?'

Boutros-Ghali: 'Yes, Friday ... '

Ted Koppel: 'For direct intervention ... You got absolutely nowhere with them.'

Boutros-Ghali: 'We have to repeat the appeal ...'

Later in the interview Boutros-Ghali said that if troop offers came from African countries, then this might encourage other nations to help. But the leadership on action over Rwanda was with the Security Council. It was up to the major countries, the permanent members of the Security Council.

The next day in Washington, the position of the Clinton administration became clear at a press conference given by national security adviser, Anthony Lake. Lake explained that America could not solve other people's problems. Nor could America build their states for them.

> When I wake up every morning and look at the headlines and the stories and the images on television of these conflicts, I want to work to end every conflict. I want to work to save every child out there. And I know the president does, and I know the American people do. But neither we nor the international community have the resources nor the mandate to do so. So we have to make

distinctions. We have to ask the hard questions about where and when we can intervene ... these kinds of conflicts are particularly hard to come to grips with and to have an effect on from outside, because basically, of course, their origins are in political turmoil within these nations. And that political turmoil may not be susceptible to the efforts of the international community. So, neither we nor the international community have either the mandate nor the resources nor the possibility of resolving every conflict of this kind.[15]

This press conference marked the publication of the first ever comprehensive review on US policy towards multilateral peace operations. The review, months in preparation, and post-Somalia, was known as presidential decision directive no. 25 (PDD-25) and it set strict limits on future US involvement with the UN, which from now on was going to depend on certain criteria: whether or not US interests were at stake, whether or not there was a threat to world peace, a clear mission goal, acceptable costs, congressional, public and allied support, a working ceasefire, a clean command and control and a clear exit point.

Rwanda failed every criterion bar one: that the USA would consider contributing to a UN peacekeeping operation if there was 'urgent humanitarian disaster coupled with violence'.

The directive reflected most strongly the view from the Pentagon where it was considered that there was only one mission for an army: to fight and win its nation's wars. The former chairman of the Joint Chiefs of Staff, General Colin Powell, when once asked about a UN standing army, had replied: 'As long as I am chairman of the Joint Chiefs of Staff, I will not agree to commit American men and women to an unknown war, in an unknown land, for an unknown cause, under an unknown commander, for an unknown duration.'[16] Rwanda was the first UN operation to come up against the presidential directive.[17]

In Kampala on the day of the press conference, President Yoweri Museveni of Uganda accused the interim government of Rwanda of using genocide to eliminate the opposition. It was a criminal band, not unlike the Nazis, Museveni said, and if people understood what was going on in Rwanda, then the whole of the international community would hunt down the perpetrators.

Dallaire sent a cable to headquarters on 6 May saying that the civil war was intensifying. The RPF had launched a major attack against government forces in Kigali and had bombed the city centre. The Canadian transport plane had been forced to take off within minutes of touching down.

The RPF shelling seriously worried the 'interim government'. The prime minister, Jean Kambanda, broadcast over the radio to call for mass mobilization. 'We have men, munitions, a united government, a united army and we have to win,' he said. Everyone must be armed, Kambanda said, and added that weapons were a main priority for the government even if this prevented the 'normal importation of goods'. Kambanda was speaking from the safety of Kibuye, 70 miles from Kigali. A month earlier, in Kibuye prefecture, there had been a quarter of a million Tutsi. By the time Kambanda made this broadcast, more than 200,000 of them had been killed.

In New York, a month after the genocide started, and still with no options presented to the Security Council, the president of the council for the month of May, the Nigerian ambassador Ibrahim Gambari, wrote to Boutros-Ghali asking for 'contingency planning' with regard to the delivery of human assistance as well as support for the displaced people in Rwanda.

At a meeting of the Council on 6 May, a group of non-permanent members – Spain, New Zealand, Argentina, the Czech Republic – presented a resolution calling for reinforcements. But British and American diplomats told everyone that future action in Rwanda must be taken primarily through the efforts of African countries, and David Hannay said that in his opinion the Organization of African Unity (OAU) had a 'key role to play'. Boutros-Ghali had approached the OAU, and had consulted with Hosni Mubarak, the president of Egypt, who was going to be the next OAU chairman. Boutros-Ghali had written to Salim Salim, the OAU secretary-general, requesting that African states contribute troops. Salim Salim had replied to Boutros-Ghali's letter, pointing out that because of the magnitude of the Rwandan tragedy, efforts must be made under UN auspices, with all that implied in terms of political engagement and resource commitment. 'This has been the practice in other situations of dire need elsewhere in the world. It must not be set aside in the case of Africa,' wrote Salim Salim.

By the first week in May there were delegates from the ICRC in five locations in Rwanda – in Kigali, Byumba, Gisenyi, Kabgayi and Kibungo – trying to alleviate the suffering of thousands of sick and wounded people trapped and surrounded by Interahamwe and Rwandan soldiers. The president of the ICRC, Cornelio Sommaruga, spoke with Gaillard. Then he wrote an article for the *International Herald Tribune*, condemning the press and governments for a failing to give Rwanda the attention it warranted and saying that all states had a responsibility to act. This was unprecedented criticism.[18]

Gaillard travelled to Kabgayi where 30,000 people were trapped, people who had fled from massacres all over Gitarama. The ICRC was providing emergency medical care, and a sous-delegation had opened on 12 May. The town was known as the Vatican of Rwanda but now people were crammed into the primary and secondary school, and a health centre. There was no clean water or food. About a dozen people a day died from starvation and the corpses were bloated and unburied. A foul stench was everywhere.

'Every day soldiers came to the camp to take away Tutsi to kill … at night soldiers went through the classrooms looking for victims … it was terror time … in addition to killing people they came to take girls and women to be raped and afterwards they were brought back,' a survivor recalled.

There was a hospital nearby treating wounded government soldiers. Some of those convalescing would come to the camps to kill Tutsi for sport. Once the militia took victims away in stolen Red Cross vehicles.

A graphic description of Kabgayi was provided by Sam Kiley of *The Times*. Kiley interviewed a Franciscan priest, Father Vieko Curic, described as the only white man south of Kigali. The priest was trying to get food for the trapped of Kabgayi and had negotiated his way through thirty roadblocks on his road journey from the border with Burundi. Curic had seen hillsides literally covered with bodies. He reckoned that at least half a million people had been killed.[19] Kiley interviewed also Pauline Nyiramasuhuko, minister of the family and women's affairs in the 'interim government'. An MRNDD stalwart, she had, according to witnesses, played a part in the massacres in Butare. Nyiramasuhuko told Kiley that basically the Rwandans were a peaceful people but that the militia had been armed so as to weed out Tutsi extremist infiltrators sent by the Rwandan Patriotic Front. The Tutsi plan, she said, was to exterminate all the Hutu. Kiley then met Colonel Augustin Bizimana, the minister of defence. Bizimana told him that people had been afraid that they would be wiped out by the Tutsi and RPF infiltrators. Many innocent people had been killed, Bizimana claimed, including Tutsi who supported the interim government, and Tutsi who had never even heard of the RPF. The armed forces were beginning to gain control of the militia. 'It is very difficult to end these hatreds,' he said.

Gaillard had tried to persuade ministers in the interim government to go to see Kabgayi for themselves: 'They [the interim government] were disorganised, they were powerless and incapable of putting a stop to the murdering madness of systematic massacre they had helped to organize … some of them.' The poor of Rwanda were the damned of the earth, he said for they had accepted, like manna from heaven, the racist insanities pouring over the airways.

A tentative recognition of the genocide came in the first week of May when the UN human rights commissioner José Ayala Lasso, in a press conference in Geneva, said that he was 'inclined to accept' it. Lasso was going to Rwanda to see for himself, to talk to as many people as possible and to gather information.[20]

Lasso had been human rights commissioner since the day before the genocide began, 5 April. This was a newly created post. The idea of having a commissioner was approved during the World Conference on Human Rights held in 1993. It was an idea promoted by the Clinton administration, supported by aid agencies and intended to give human rights a higher profile. The commissioner occupied the most senior position in the UN with regard to human rights. Lasso, an Ecuadorian diplomat appointed by Boutros-Ghali, had no human rights background.

Lasso spent two days in Rwanda, 11–12 May, during which he met Bagosora and Bizimungu. Bizimungu told him the UN had an important role in Rwanda, and he assured Lasso that he would do all he could to ensure that 'hostages' were freed. The problem was that he did not control the militia. Lasso and Bizimungu together visited those trapped in the Hôtel des Mille Collines. Bizimungu stood in the lobby and assured everyone, in the presence of the UN's most senior human rights official, that they would soon be freed. Bizimungu explained that the killings in Rwanda were due to spontaneous anger at the death of the president. Lasso also met Kagame. Kagame told him that the entire international community should be calling for an end to the killings. In an appeal on Radio Rwanda, Lasso said both sides must cease hostilities and allow 'the population to go to the destination of their choice'.

All this Lasso put into a report on his return. He had appealed to both sides to avoid human rights abuses.[21] This was a human rights tragedy. There had been 'wanton killing' of more than 200,000 innocent civilians. The Lasso report noted all the relevant international human rights instruments to which Rwanda was a party, including the Convention on the Prevention and Punishment of the Crime of Genocide.[22] He was no more specific than this.

A clearer grasp of reality and an impassioned plea for Rwanda came from the MSF-France doctor, Jean-Hervé Bradol, who in April had worked in the ICRC hospital with Gaillard. Bradol was back in Paris, certain that what Rwanda needed urgently was military intervention, not to stop civil war but to stop genocide. Bradol appeared on the French nightly news, on TF1, and gave a moving interview to explain that the killing in Rwanda was not the result of a civil war. The killing was a political act, a deliberate and planned extermination. Never in its history had MSF been witness to killing on such a scale. The attempts to portray what was happening as ethnic was an affront to the victims. The French government bore a special responsibility for having armed and trained the perpetrators. The newscaster Patrick Poivre d'Arvor, seemingly surprised, ended the interview describing what was happening in Rwanda as a 'veritable genocide'.[23]

MSF-France was to launch a press campaign a few days later, buying space in *Le Monde* to print an open letter to President Mitterrand saying that doctors could not stop a genocide and that France should immediately take action to stop genocide and protect the population of Rwanda.

The Security Council, having requested a further report from Boutros Boutros-

Ghali, waited a week for it to arrive. When it did, on 13 May, it contained details of Dallaire's original plan, which was to airlift a standing brigade into Kigali, for some 5,500 well-armed and trained soldiers to protect civilians at risk, and provide security for humanitarian operations. This was a minimum viable force, Boutros-Ghali told the Council, and for such an operation to work, the troops had to be highly mobile. The operation would be called UNAMIR II, and would require sixteen helicopters and teams of military and civilian police. The key to success was speed of deployment and it was intended that the troops be airlifted as soon as the Council authorized the resolution. The longer the delay, the greater the risk of not achieving its purpose. Protected sites would be created to be patrolled and monitored by peacekeepers. The airport would become a neutral zone under the control of the UN. The operation would begin the with immediate dispatch to Kigali of 800 soldiers from the Ghanaian battalion who had been evacuated to Nairobi when UNAMIR was reduced, and were currently languishing in an aircraft hangar, but these troops had to be provided with the protection of APCs. If countries which provided troops for this operation could provide already formed infantry brigades, this would mean that deployment could be rapid.[24]

There were immediate complaints about this plan from the American diplomats. Madeleine Albright, the US ambassador, was now championing the new presidential directive on peacekeeping and in accordance with this directive her staff said the plan for Rwanda was inadequate and lacking in field assessments. There must be more detailed preparations, a clearer concept of operations, a breakdown in the costs, and an idea of the duration of any mandate. The Americans even suggested, albeit discreetly, that the plan, rather than a serious strategy for a realistic and do-able mission, was a public relations exercise by Boutros-Ghali. The relationship between Boutros-Ghali and the Americans, which had worsened over Somalia when Boutros-Ghali had insisted that American troops make arms seizures, was deteriorating further. Boutros-Ghali was openly critical of the Security Council for 'shocking behaviour' and for meekly following the US lead in denying the reality of the genocide. The USA, he said, benefited from the strong support of Britain. Boutros-Ghali was particularly scathing about Albright. He said she was always waiting for instruction from Washington. 'As the Rwandan genocide continued, she was apparently just following orders,' he wrote later.[25]

Boutros-Ghail later said the blame for the inaction over Rwanda rested with America. The US had spent a billion dollars a day overall during the Cold War, but was now prevailing upon other governments to withhold relatively trivial sums to stop genocide.[26]

There had been desperate attempts in May in the UN's Department of Peacekeeping to find troops and equipment for Rwanda. If armoured personnel carriers could be found, then the Ghanaian battalion could return to

Kigali. UN officials sent urgent requests for APCs to forty-four member states known to have spare military capacity. On 28 May a call came from an official in the Pentagon to say that the USA had forty-eight APCs in storage in Germany. If the UN wanted them, the Americans would be willing to lease them for $4 million. The USA already owed the UN more than one billion dollars in back dues. As this was the only offer, UN officials started negotiations to have the APCs moved at once. The Pentagon then insisted that only when the lease was signed could the transport of the equipment begin, and then it would take two weeks to get the APCs to Uganda, which had the nearest large airport. The Pentagon organized its own transport to get the APCs from storage in Germany to Uganda – at an extra charge to the UN of $6 million. When the equipment arrived at Entebbe there were no heavy machine guns or radios, rendering them useless in terms of a self-defence capability.

There would be problems finding people trained to use these older pieces of equipment. The UN came under a barrage of criticism for incompetence and waste in its procurement of equipment, yet it was later discovered that a commercial contractor would have delivered the APCs to Entebbe for much less than the Americans charged. Three months later, in August 1994, the APCs were still in Entebbe. There were no trucks large enough to transport them to Rwanda.[27]

On 25 May during a press conference, Boutros-Ghali told reporters that the real responsibility for Rwanda lay with the Security Council: 'My role is to respect the decisions and the resolutions of the Security Council. I can suggest different solutions, but the decisions are taken by the Security Council.' When asked how he felt as a human being when seeing piles of corpses he said:

> I will try not to be emotional … Let us recognize that this is a failure … not only of the UN but also of the international community. All of us are responsible for this failure. I have tried. I was in contact with different heads of state and I begged them to send troops … I failed. It is a scandal. I am the first one to say it and I am ready to repeat it.

A genocide had been committed, he said.[28]

By now Boutros-Ghali had sent two senior officials to Rwanda, ostensibly to try to get negotiations going between the Rwandan government forces and the RPF; Iqbal Riza, the assistant secretary-general in the Department of Peacekeeping Operations, and Major-General Maurice Baril, the Secretary-General's military adviser who visited Rwanda between 22 and 27 May. When they came back to headquarters they wrote a report in which they described 'a frenzy of massacres' with 250,000 to 500,000 people killed in a systematic slaughter. There was little doubt that this was genocide. The report pointed out that the two primary tasks of the peacekeepers were to assure the security of as many locations as possible where people were sheltering and to provide necessary security in order to get humanitarian relief to these sites, even without a ceasefire.[29] On 30 May the Secretary-General made a report to the Council: 'We must all realise that we have failed in our response to the agony of Rwanda and thus acquiesced in the continued loss of life.'[30]

Dallaire said he often felt as though the ghost of Gordon of Khartoum was watching over him, for no one and no supplies were coming at all. 'Dying in Rwanda without sign or sight of relief was a reality that we faced on a daily basis for several desperate weeks,' he said.[31] The possibility of Dallaire having to fight his way out of the country was a very real and very desperate option that was prepared for, and nearly executed, on at least two occasions.[32]

The tiny garrison ran out of all supplies at one point and they packed up. There was pressure from New York again for them to pull out but Dallaire kept on repeating that it was not an option. Annan and Riza respected his position and were prepared to listen to him; one of the his officers said that, no matter how hard anyone tried, there was nothing the international community could do to budge him. Dallaire once said that his greatest weapon in Rwanda had been obstinacy.[33]

The work continued. The fighting between the RPF and government forces divided Kigali and there were meetings between UNAMIR, the Rwandan army, the gendarmerie and the RPF to try to guarantee the safety of the imprisoned people. There were efforts to broker temporary ceasefires or truces, even for the shortest duration, to allow the rescue of civilians. Sometimes the peacekeepers were too late; one mission in early May to rescue a UN employee in hiding with her five children and five orphans was too late. All of them were dead. Neighbours described men with machetes in civilian clothes as the perpetrators.

The people sheltering in Kigali became hostages to be traded. The RPF was holding thousands of Hutu prisoners. In one successful operation, peacekeepers escorted 300 Tutsi, exchanging them for 200 Hutu. Gerry McCarthy of UNICEF, who had come to Kigali as part of a four-man joint UN–agency cell,[34] recalled that during one of these exchanges in which 200 Tutsi teenage boys were rescued, a group of Tutsi children had been left behind in a carpark. They were quickly surrounded by Interahamwe. McCarthy and colleagues negotiated their rescue. It took them more than an hour.[35]

The first official recognition that the peacekeepers might have to take action to defend the people in their care came only after the Security Council had approved a new resolution, 918, in the early hours of 17 May. The resolution was welcomed as a landmark, for it finally authorized 5,500 troops for UNAMIR. In reality it was a sham. No equipped troops were available for Rwanda, and, even if there had been, there was no airlift. Nor was there an agreed plan for what they would do when they got there. On the night resolution 918 was voted, Keating wrote to his capital: 'As you will see, the US has essentially gutted the resolution … in reality the expansion is a fiction.'[36]

When the American historian and Rwanda expert Alison des Forges heard about resolution 918 she was elated. She says she managed to speak to a friend in hiding in Kigali, a Tutsi who worked for the US embassy, to tell him that at last the Security Council had authorized reinforcements. He pleaded for the troops to hurry. The day after her call the militia came for him. They came back again the following day and killed his wife and baby. Des Forges, desperate to know how much longer Rwanda must wait, called Kovanda. Kovanda broke the news that there was little likelihood of anything happening for three months. 'I threw up my hands in horror,' she said. 'It was unacceptable: human lives were being lost. Why not tomorrow?'[37]

Dallaire believes that if the troops mandated in resolution 918 had been speedily and effectively deployed, tens upon tens of thousands of people could have been saved. But the resolution was conditional; as a first step, and on American insistence, 150 military observers were to be sent. Both British and American diplomats had argued that before troops went to Rwanda, the views of the two armies must be sought and a ceasefire brokered. In favour of resolution 918 the American ambassador, Karl Inderfurth, said: 'This council has struggled to formulate a response that is both appropriate and effective … to ensure its success, we want to bring the end and means of the council's resolutions into balance.' He explained to the Council: 'The key to the problems in Rwanda, is in the hands of the Rwandese people. In Rwanda, this means that the killing – by all parties – must stop.'

Dallaire said he knew that, with resolution 918, Rwanda had been abandoned. The world had shut the door.

It has been claimed many times that there were no troops available to go to Rwanda. This is inaccurate. The government of Ghana had agreed to increase its battalion strength in Kigali to the original 800 soldiers. Without APCs, though, the troops would be unprotected, immobile and ineffective.[38] Ethiopia offered an 800-strong battalion and Malawi promised an infantry company. Offers of troops also came from Senegal, Nigeria, Zimbabwe, Zambia, Congo, Mali, Malawi and Tunisia. But all these countries wanted equipment for their troops and wanted the costs to be underwritten by the UN. Given the state of the UN finances, help for Rwanda quite obviously depended on western states. There were no offers.[39]

Throughout May the Americans blocked effective action for Rwanda by arguing against the plan, devised in the first days by Dallaire, of airlifting a brigade to Kigali. Instead, the Americans wanted the creation of safe havens on the borders of Tanzania and Zaire. Military experts from Washington turned up at UN headquarters to argue the merits of the safe-haven idea with

Kofi Annan. Safe zones were cheaper to create, they argued, and would require fewer soldiers. If the safe-haven idea were to be accepted, then the USA would be prepared to contribute to the costs. The idea was to establish safe havens in areas were there was no civil war, and no killing. There could be buffer zones along the frontier to keep people safe. Dallaire said that this outside-in approach would not work: the people most at risk would be killed before they reached the safe havens and those on the border were not necessarily those at risk. Keating said the situation was surreal: 'While thousands of human beings were hacked to death every day, ambassadors argued fitfully for weeks about military tactics.' The Americans kept arguing against 'wasting money' on failed missions.[40]

Just before the vote on resolution 918, on 16 May, the minister of foreign affairs in the 'interim government', Jérôme Bicamumpaka, appeared before the Security Council.[41] Bicamumpaka, already accorded full diplomatic honours in Paris at the end of April, made the most of his appearance, and in an address to the Council he claimed that systematic massacres in Rwanda were being carried out by the RPF as part of a plot co-ordinated by the Ugandans to seize power. 'It is said that some RPF fighters eat the hearts of men they have killed in order to become invincible,' he said. The apocalypse had happened in the wake of an inter-ethnic war which had 'unleashed the animal instincts of a people afraid of being enslaved once again'. His government condemned every massacre, no matter who the perpetrators.[42]

There has never been an adequate explanation why Bicamumpaka was allowed to speak, nor any reason given as to why, for the duration of the genocide, a representative of the 'interim government', Jean-Damascène Bizimana, was allowed to sit as Rwanda's ambassador in a non-permanent seat. Hannay explained later that there was no procedure for getting rid of him.[43]

Bicamumpaka's shameful speech on 16 May contained the assurance:

> One of the prime tasks of the government of Rwanda is to ensure the peace and security of its people ... the government took strong measures to stop inter-ethnic violence ... messages calling for peace were broadcast over the radio.. the President of the republic, the prime minister and members of the government crossed the country, holding meetings calling for peace.

He assured the Council that the peacekeepers in Rwanda were 'a buffer force'. Their continued presence was the only way to ensure a ceasefire.

Keating was outraged and described Bicamumpaka as the mouthpiece of a faction, not the representative of a state, who had given a shameful distortion of the truth. Hannay regretted 'the tone and the content' of Bicamumpaka's speech. 'We would have wished to see a condemnation of the atrocities that have taken place, many of them in parts of the country controlled by that government, in a less perfunctory manner than was done,' he said.

Kovanda, the Czech ambassador, thoroughly briefed by Human Rights Watch, directly challenged Bicamumpaka by reeling off a list of known massacres sites and giving an estimated casualty figure for each one: 4,000 in Kibeho; 5,500 in Cyahinda; 2,500 in Kibungo. The list went on. Kovanda said that in a sports stadium in Cyangugu, thousands of people were held captive and each day victims were pulled from the crowd: 'All reports indicate that these atrocities have been committed by Hutu cut-throats – and seldom has this word been so literally the right one – against their Tutsi neighbours.' Some would argue, said Kovanda, that there must have been Tutsi atrocities against Hutus. Human rights groups had assiduously sought direct evidence of massacres in territories controlled by the RPF. So far, they had found very little such evidence. 'This situation is being described as a humanitarian crisis as though it were ... a natural disaster,' he said. The massacres were committed on the orders of people close to Habyarimana and at the instigation of a hate-radio, known for its incendiary broadcasts. The massacres were the work of Rwandan government forces, the militia and the gendarmerie. 'In the view of my delegation, the proper description is genocide.' Kovanda told the Council that the priority was not a ceasefire but saving the lives of thousands of civilians. The French ambassador, Jean-Bernard Mérimée, told them that the only way to resolve the crisis was to obtain a ceasefire within the framework of the Arusha agreement.

As the RPF steadily advanced, Bagosora was seen less in Kigali. He is known to have made a trip to the Seychelles in May to buy weapons, but no one doubted who was in charge. Dallaire said that whenever he attempted to establish communications with the Interahamwe leadership for ceasefires and humanitarian operations, the most sure and effective conduit to them was Bagosora. The Interahamwe was responsive to directions received from him.[44]

Gaillard met Bagosora once, by chance, during the genocide. Gaillard told him to do what was necessary to stop the killing. Civilians were being slaughtered, while all the time he was losing the war. 'Monsieur the delegate,' answered Bagosora, 'if I wanted to, I could conscript 50,000 new men.'

Once, after leaving the Ministry of Defence, Gaillard's car was caught up in the fighting and he had run for cover behind a pillar on the front porch of a house. Mortars sliced through the trees. Stopped later by the Interahamwe at a roadblock, he was asked to take one of their injured, a man with a bullet in his back, to hospital. Gaillard put the man in the front seat of his car. The seat was soaked with blood. The medical team operated and some days later Gaillard saw the man in the out-patients room. 'We picked up the debris of genocide,' said Gaillard. 'First the Tutsi and then little by little there were Hutu wounded.'

An Interahamwe had once told Gaillard that the Kalinga, a sacred drum and a symbol of the Tutsi kings' supremacy, had passed into different hands. From the Kalinga were hung the genitals of those killed in the conquered Hutu kinglets. Gaillard was sickened. Some of the atrocities witnessed in Rwanda would never be seen by the rest of the world. Gaillard agreed with this self-censorship of the media.

There were war wounded to treat, people with injuries from shelling and landmines, their limbs blown away. Hutu and Tutsi survivors in the hospital slept side by side, talked with each other, worked together in the laundry and the kitchen, and dug holes in the garden to bury the dead. Eight houses were requisitioned, and the hillside was full of the white flags of the Red Cross. Only the children in the compound were spared any work.

Near the frontline, the Rwandan government army stationed heavy weapons behind the hospital. The RPF wanted Gaillard to move the hospital but he refused. Shelled several times, Gaillard pleaded with both the RPF and the Rwandan army to spare the hospital. On 25 May, two Rwandans were killed when a shell landed in the compound. Gaillard remembers a baby, aged just one month and a half, with shrapnel wounds to the face. Another child received serious injuries. The hospital was shelled again in June when two bombs fell in the emergency room, killing seven and injuring a dozen more. 'I kept insisting that the Rwandan staff who work in this hospital were both Hutu and Tutsi,' said Gaillard.

Then on 19 May, a Swiss doctor, Pierre Gratzl, travelling on the road from Kigali to the south, received shrapnel wounds to his stomach. Gratzl was in the lead vehicle of a convoy which was going to a hospital in Kabgayi and he fell on a frontline between the two armies. With shelling it was impossible to evacuate him and Gaillard asked Dallaire for help. It was the only time he did so. Dallaire went himself and a Tunisian APC followed later. The road was the major exchange route for the Rwandan government forces out of Kigali, with the RPF and the 'interim government' holding the high ground on either side. Kagame once relieved and shot a battalion commander who did not comply with a truce for a particular convoy.

Gratzl underwent a major operation later that day, but the ICRC stopped using the road even though it was the principal resupply route. On 21 May, 7.2 tons of medical aid reached Kigali but after that there were no more convoys, not until Kigali fell to the RPF on 4 July.[45]

By mid-May the RPF was in control of almost half the country, from the north-west to the south-eastern corner, with the 'interim government' and its army retreating east but managing to hold on to western Kigali, with hilltops around the city under RPF control. When the RPF seized Kabuga, 10 miles east of Kigali, it had opened the way for an offensive against the main government army barracks at Kanombe, and the airport on the eastern side of the city. On 20 May, while the fighting continued for control of the capital, thirty patients were killed when a mortar bomb hit the King Faisal hospital, where thousands of people were sheltering. At least twelve mortar-bombs hit UN headquarters.

Where the 'interim government' and the Rwandan army were in control, the militia had created a dense network of roadblocks. Escape for Tutsi was virtually impossible. On 22 May, a nun and eleven novices, who had escaped from Kigali and were on their way to Kabgayi, arrived in Kamonyi where they were caught, thrown into a pit and shot.

There were thousands of people trapped in sites around the country: there were 38,000 people being held in Kabgayi; 3,000 at a stadium in Gitarama; 5,500 in a stadium in Cyangugu; 1,700 at Mibirizi; 400 at Sahngui, near Cyangugu; and 60,000 at Runda, near Kigali.[46]

The Kamarampaka stadium near the cathedral in Cyangugu was full of people. Men and boys were regularly taken away by soldiers and militia to be killed. On 11 May, militia and the military took hundreds of people from the thousands trapped at the Cyangugu stadium into the countryside by bus and then murdered them. When delegates from the Red Cross had first arrived in Cyangugu on 20 April they had found 884 malnourished children needing special treatment. There was no food. There was one water tap. There were 7,889 people at this site; 500 of those needed urgent medical help. Two ICRC delegates and a nurse went there every day and distributed food and opened a pharmacy. A safe water supply was later ensured by an ICRC water engineer who came from Geneva.

The people in the stadium were later moved to a camp at Nyarushishi which had been used for refugees from Burundi who had come to Rwanda in October 1993. Like everywhere else, soldiers ostensibly guarding the refugees worked closely with the Interahamwe who roamed the camp, abducting people. At Nyarushishi it is thought that most of the 10,000 refugees were saved from slaughter only because the gendarmes were under the command of Colonel Innocent Bavugamenshi.

On 13 May, Dallaire received a telephone call from Washington, from Senator Paul Simon (Democrat, Illinois), a member of the Senate Committee on Foreign Relations, and chairman of the Subcommittee on African Affairs. Simon had received information – he does not recall whether it came from the State Department or the CIA – to the effect that in Rwanda hundreds of thousands of people were being killed. With the ranking republican on the committee, Senator James Jeffords (Vermont), Simon placed a call to Dallaire. 'We asked what could be done to stop what was still in the initial stages,' Simon explained. 'Dallaire told us that if he could get 8,000 troops quickly he could put an end to it. Dallaire was very concerned about stopping the killing.' Dallaire indicated to the senators that 5,000 troops was his minimum requirement, but that these troops would be spread too thinly because the killing had spread to other parts of the country. Such reinforcements would need a mandate to stop the massacres, protect civilians and facilitate the delivery of humanitarian assistance. Simon remembered Dallaire as a compassionate, sensitive and sensible military commander.

Immediately after this conversation, Senators Jeffords and Simon wrote a letter to the White House, hand delivered, with a copy to the State Department, asking for the USA immediately to request the Security Council to approve sending troops to Kigali to stop the senseless slaughter. 'Obviously there are risks involved but we cannot continue to sit idly by while this tragedy continues to unfold,' the letter continued. The failure of the international community to take decisive action had served to embolden the extremists; delay or simply doing nothing were not acceptable substitutes for a foreign policy of leadership. Human life was at stake, and swift and sound decision-making was needed.

There was no reply. Ten days later, Simon telephoned the White House but failed to speak with Anthony Lake at the National Security Council. Simon was told by another White House official that there was no public support for US participation in such an operation. 'This might have been accurate,' said Simon five years later, 'but this was a question of leadership, a case in which you have to build a public base.'

Clinton did not officially reply for twenty-seven days and then, on 9 June, he wrote to say that he was in full agreement that there should be action. He listed all those things his administration had done already to alleviate the crisis: the administration had taken action in 'ensuring an effective UN peace-keeping force'; the administration had supported a UN resolution to authorize up to 5,500 troops for Rwanda and to reintroduce a full mechanized battalion and UN military observers as soon as possible. 'We have been contacting foreign governments to urge their rapid participation in the peacekeeping mission … a number of countries had responded positively to these contacts,' the letter said.

The USA had offered financial, logistical and material support, including fifty APCs; the USA was 'working with the UN to ensure that this force is effective, protects the maximum number of Rwandans at risk and meets the conditions set forth in my recent directive on peacekeeping'; the USA had sponsored a UN resolution to impose an arms embargo; the USA had committed more than US$50 million in humanitarian assistance for Rwanda, by far the largest of any donor, to ameliorate the crisis among the refugees on the borders with Tanzania and Burundi; the USA had strongly supported a negotiated settlement; Clinton's senior officials had been in almost daily contact with the leaders in the region to support diplomatic efforts for a ceasefire. The president wrote: 'I have spoken out against the killings … we have called for a full investigation of these atrocities.' These initiatives, he claimed, had helped to relieve some of the suffering of the Rwandan people and supported a 'rapid introduction of an effective UN mission to protect people at risk'.

The RPF advance continued and the army took control of the airport at dawn on Sunday, 22 May, when 200 government soldiers fled their positions. Later that day the Kanombe barracks fell. The next day the RPF was in control of the presidential palace. Hundreds of government soldiers were now leaving the city, together with a column of people stretching for 20 miles on the road to Gitarama. The latest exodus would soon account for some 300,000 people, fleeing to Gitarama and beyond, clogging the roads, the Hutu fleeing an RPF advance.

On the last day of May, Captain Mbaye Diagne, from Senegal, the military observer who had helped to protect the children of Uwilingiymana in the Hôtel des Mille Collines and who was known for his fearless rescue missions, was killed by a shell. Gerry McCarthy of UNICEF later described how Diagne had single-handedly saved Tutsi, bringing scores of people to safety from various hostage sites around the city.

Diagne was the twelfth peacekeeper to die since the crisis began.[47] He had been driving a clearly marked UN vehicle, and was killed by an RPF mortar at an army checkpoint on the frontline as he was negotiating, with banter and extravagant cajoling, his way back to UN headquarters, carrying a message from the government-held part of the city to the force commander in an attempt to allow refugees to cross the front line. Some six soldiers had been the target and Diagne's car had effectively shielded them from the blast. Afterwards, Dallaire's deputy, Brigadier-General Henry Anyidoho from Ghana, spent time with the peacekeepers. 'We tried to talk to both sides,' he said quietly, 'but they just don't seem to be listening.' They suspended rescue attempts.

Peacekeepers wept as Diagne's body, wrapped in the blue sheeting used for refugee huts, there being a lack of UN flags, was carried to a plane. Diagne, one of them said, was the bravest of them all.

The overcrowding in the ICRC hospital reached crisis point in June. Gaillard wanted to transfer patients from his hospital in the government-held zone to the King Faisal hospital on the opposite hill in Rugenge. The King Faisal was a modern and purpose-built hospital, now serving as a camp for thousands of people who had fled to the zone controlled by the RPF.

A Dutch doctor with MSF, Eric Vreede, who arrived in Kigali in mid-June, described the King Faisal as a hospital on three floors built to take 300 beds, but filthy and crammed with people. There was no water and no sanitation, but a logistics expert from the ICRC had managed to create a clean area in the hospital containing 100 beds, a couple of wards and one operating theatre. A transfer of patients was to be made across Kigali from the ICRC hospital. Dallaire negotiated a two-hour ceasefire and parked one of his two APCs at a crucial roundabout en route, with the other near the King Faisal. Those patients considered fit to travel, both Hutu and Tutsi, were put in the back of a lorry. Gaillard led the convoy.

Some days later the ICRC hospital was again inundated with wounded. James Orbinski, a Canadian physician with MSF, remembers hundreds of wounded people, so many needing medical help that they were laid out on the street outside. Orbinski took part in a road-side triage, treating as many as possible of those who were likely to die without immediate medical care. Orbinski said that the ditches ran with blood.

There was a woman, a victim of genocide, whose entire body had been rationally and systematically mutilated with a machete. Her ears had been cut off. Her face was carefully disfigured, and a pattern was obvious in the slashes. 'She was one among many, living an inhuman and indescribable suffering,' Orbinski recalled. There was little he could do for her other than try to stop the bleeding. The woman was aware that there were people in a similar condition all around her. There were only six doctors in the ICRC-MSF team. Orbinski had faltered. 'She knew and I knew,' Orbinski said, 'that we were completely overwhelmed'. And then the woman had released him from his own inescapable hell. She had looked up at him and said to him in the clearest voice he had heard: 'Allez, allez … ummera, ummera-sha' (Go, go, my friend, find and let live your courage).[48]

The medical teams continued trying to alleviate the overcrowding in the ICRC hospital. On 27 June, forty-five more wounded arrived safely at the King Faisal. Other convoys tried to reach it but it was not always possible. The journey entailed crossing a bridge that spanned a valley; the bridge was exposed and was the most terrifying and dangerous place.

At the end of June, just before the RPF took Kigali, one of the convoys of wounded was stopped on the bridge by Presidential Guards. Gaillard argued in vain as one of them climbed into the back of the lorry to 'inspect the wounded'. A crowd gathered and started shouting 'Inyenzi!' Some brandished machetes. Gaillard jumped in his car, drove like a mad man to the Ministry of Defence, waited for piece of paper with a stamp, and then drove back to the bridge and showed the guard the paper. Gaillard watched while the guard radioed headquarters and was told to let the lorry through. The convoy moved off. When it reached the other side there was an RPF roadblock. The RPF soldier insisted on inspecting the wounded. Among them in the back of the lorry, the soldier found his brother.

Gaillard travelled with Dallaire and a group of peacekeepers north to

Buymba. Their convoy was stopped at a roadblock and Gaillard remembered chatting with an Interahamwe. The man looked dejected and exhausted. He was filthy, meagre and unshaven. He asked where Gaillard was going and Gaillard said to see Paul Kagame. 'Tell him to stop the war. We want to discuss everything,' the Interahamwe had said.

On 2 June the RPF took control of Kabgayi. In anticipation of their arrival, government soldiers and Interahamwe went on a killing spree before fleeing themselves. For many of the RPF soldiers, the sight which greeted them in this small and beautiful town near Gitarama was unforgettable. Kabgayi and its beautiful Roman Catholic seminary, the home of the bishop, had been turned into a hell.[49] There were 30,000 people trapped in the town and 200,000 displaced people in the area.[50]

On 9 June, RPF soldiers shot the Catholic Archbishop of Kigali, Vincent Nsengiyumva, who had been Agathe Habyarimana's confessor and a member of the MRNDD central committee.[51] When the 'interim government' had left Kigali, he had gone too. Killed with him were the Bishop of Kabgayi, Thaddee Nsengyumva, the Bishop of Byumba, Joseph Rusindana, and ten priests. The RPF claimed that the killings were carried out by young Tutsi soldiers recently recruited who disobeyed their orders to hold the clerics in protective custody. Some two years later, a letter was sent to Pope John-Paul II by a group of priests to explain that the clerics who were killed in Kabgayi were not in a state of grace for either their faith or their charity. The letter accused the murdered priests of collusion with the genocidal regime.[52]

Although the RPF saved tens of thousands of people from extermination, rumours of summary executions by the RPF began to spread and soldiers from the RPF were accused of committing a number of war crimes.[53] RPF soldiers discovering the fate of their families and friends took part in revenge killings. Sometimes the Interahamwe used the civilian population as a shield to protect them against the RPF. The killing of civilians by the RPF was said to be scattered, irregular and limited.[54]

On 12 June, the interim government was pushed out of Gitarama and ministers fled once more, this time to the Lake Kivu town of Kibuye, and then further to the Hutu Power stronghold of Gisenyi, the northern heartland. For the extremist ideology, it seemed its days were numbered.

Then two days after the fall of Gitarama the French government announced that it was sending troops to Rwanda to protect populations threatened with extermination. President François Mitterrand said there was not a moment to lose. The massacres must be stopped.

Notes

1. René Caravielhe, 'Dans le témoignage, l'horreur', 13 April–19 May. MSF Info. No. 30, May–June 1994. My translation.

2. The other conditions were an end to the massacres, a return for all displaced people and an acceleration in the creation of the transitional government.

3. Jacques Castonguay, *Les Casques Bleus au Rwanda*, Paris: Editions l'Harmattan, 1998, p. 166.

4. Paul Lewis. 'U.S. Examines Way to assist Rwanda without troops. Direct action rejected', *New York Times*, 1 May 1994.

5. Human Rights Watch/Fédération Internationale des Ligues des Droits de l'Homme, *Leave none to tell the story. Genocide in Rwanda. 1999*, p. 494.

6. Peter Smerdon (Reuters), 'Rwanda refugees trapped and orphans massacred', *Independent*, 4 May 1994.

7. André Guichaoua (ed.), in *Les Crises Politiques au Burundi et au Rwanda (1993–1994)*, Université des Sciences et Technologies de Lille, Paris: Karthala, 1995, p. 696.

8. African Rights, *Rwanda. Death, Despair and Defiance*, London: African Rights, 1995, p. 719. The incident was on 18 April.

9. Ibid., p. 723.

10. A group of forty Tunisian peacekeepers was responsible for the security at the Hôtel des Mille Collines under their company commander Major M'fareng Belgacem, an air defence artillery expert. When the genocide was over Dallaire paid tribute to the bravery of these men. Nsazuwera would describe the UN protection of the hotel as 'wholly inadequate'.

11. African Rights, *Rwanda. Death, Despair and Defiance*, London: African Rights, 1995, p. 689.

12. Interview, Paul Kagame, Kigali, October 1997.

13. Richard Dowden, 'Sweet sour stench of death fills Rwanda', *Independent*, 7 May 1994.

14. 'Nightline' (ABC), 4 May 1994. Transcript 3378.

15. White House, press briefing. Policy on Multilateral Peacekeeping Operations, Washington, DC, 5 May 1994. Transcript by Federal News Service, Washington, DC, document number WL-05-01, 5 May 1994.

16. Ivo H. Daalder, 'US Policy for Peacekeeping', in William J. Durch (ed.), *UN Peacekeeping: American Politics and the Uncivil wars of the 1990s*, Henry L. Stimson Center, New York: St Martin's Press, 1996, p. 42.

17. The unclassified text of the presidential decision directive was released as 'The Clinton Administration's Policy on Reforming Multilateral Peace Operations' (White House, Washington, DC, May 1994).

18. Cornelio Sommaruga, 'For Urgent Action to stop the Massacres in Rwanda', *International Herald Tribune*, 5 May 1994.

19. Sam Kiley, 'Tutsi Refugees face choice of starvation or being murdered', *The Times*, 14 May 1994.

20. 'Press Briefing by the High Commissioner for Human Rights, Mr. José Ayala Lasso, Regarding his mission to Rwanda. 6 May 1994.' UN Information Service; for use of the UN Secretariat only.

21. UN Commission on Human Rights, *Report of the UN High Commissioner for Human Rights, Mr. José Ayala Lasso, on his mission to Rwanda 11–12 May, 1994* (E/CN.4/S-3/3) 19 May 1994.

22. After the genocide, Lasso appealed for 147 human rights observers to be sent to Rwanda. Two months later, by September, there was only one, an Irish national, Karen Kenny. She had no phone, no car, no way even to make a recording of an interview, and after two months she resigned.

23. '20 heures' (TFI), 16 May 1994. Patrick Poivre d'Arvor.

24. The United Nations and Rwanda, 1993–1996. UN Blue Book series, Vol. 10, New York: UN Department of Public Information, 1996, pp. 277–82.

25. Boutros Boutros-Ghali, *Unvanquished. A US–UN Saga*, London: I.B.Tauris, 1999, p. 136.

26. Ibid., p. 141.

27. Linda Melvern, *The Ultimate Crime: Who Betrayed the UN and Why*, London: Allison and Busby, 1995, pp. 19–20.

28. 'Transcript of Press Conference by Secretary General Boutros Boutros-Ghali held at headquarters on May 25, 1994' (SG/SM/5297/REV.1). Press release.

29. *Report of the Independent Inquiry into the Actions of the United Nations during the 1994 Genocide in Rwanda*, 15 December 1999, p. 25.

30. *The Blue Helmets: A Review of United Nations peacekeeping* (3rd edn), New York: United Nations, 1996, p. 285.

31. Jonathan Moore (ed.), *Hard Choices: Moral Dilemmas in Humanitarian Intervention*, Oxford: Rowman and Littlefield, 1998, p. 82.

32. Ibid., p. 80.

33. Interview, Major-General Roméo Dallaire, London, November 1994.

34. These four were: Gerry McCarthy and Roger Carter, consultants for UNICEF; Pierre Honorat, World Food Programme; and Gregery Alex 'Gromo' of the UN Development Programme.

35. Interview, Gerry McCarthy, December 1999.

36. New Zealand Mission to the UN, New York, Fax. 17 May 1994. Subject: Security Council: Rwanda.

37. Interview, Alison des Forges, New York, July 1994. Transcript. 20/20 Television.

38. These Ghanaian troops arrived in Kigali on 15 August after the genocide was over, but only in late October 1994 did some small-arms ammunition arrive for them. Tents, night-vision aids, radios and defence stores did not come until much later.

39. Nigeria was an obvious candidate as one of Africa's foremost military powers but it was preoccupied with events in Liberia, where it was leading a West African intervention force sponsored by the Economic Community of West-African States. Troops from Nigeria, Mali and Zambia arrived in Rwanda in October as part of UNAMIR II.

40. The estimated budget for UNAMIR II was $115 million for six months, or slightly under $20 million a month. UNAMIR I cost $10 million a month. Boutros-Ghali, in order to get around this problem, had suggested a voluntary fund of some $80 million but no UN members came forward and the USA was not keen on the idea.

41. Not until 15 July did the USA close its Rwandan embassy in Washington and order diplomats to leave the country in five days. At the same time it began steps to remove Rwandan representatives from the Security Council. 'The US cannot allow representatives of a regime that supports genocidal massacres to remain on our soil,' President Bill Clinton said.

42. Security Council. S/PV.3377. Monday 16 May 1994.

43. Interview, Sir David Hannay, London, 9 November 1999.

44. Human Rights Watch/Fédération Internationale des Ligues des Droits de l'Homme, *Leave none to tell the story*, p. 228.

45. Between 6 April and 23 May, the food supplies which the ICRC provided for Rwanda were as follows: 254.84 tons by air and 1,744.2 tons by road. Medical supplies: 677,76 tons by air and 1.25 tons by road. Water and sanitation equipment: 26.5 tons by air, none by road. Other equipment amounted to 1.6 tons by air. All supplies were initially sent from Nairobi to three locations in neighbouring countries – Bujumbura in Burundi, Ngara in Tanzania and to Kabale in Uganda. From there road convoys or planes took it to Kigali with some supplies provided for a Red Cross team in Cyangugu.

46. UN Commission on Human Rights, *Report of the UN High Commissioner for Human Rights, Mr. José Ayala Lasso, on his mission to Rwanda 11–12 May, 1994.*

47. A Ghanaian soldier was killed in the Amahoro stadium when a mortar round was fired at refugees.

48. The Nobel Lecture given by the Nobel Peace Prize Laureate 1999. Médecins Sans Frontières, Dr James Orbinkski, Oslo, 10 December 1999.

49. According to the Vatican, three bishops and nearly 250 priests, nuns and missionaries were killed in the genocide.

50. The ICRC hospital at Kabgayi was moved, under orders from the RPF, to Nyanza and then at the beginning of July the patients were moved once more, many of them dying en route for Rilima in the Bugesera where the extraordinary convoy arrived on 5 July.

51. Guy Theunis speculates that the archbishop may have had a change of heart for he remained behind in Kabgayi, knowing that the RPF was approaching, when he could have left and gone with the interim government to Murumba and then Gisenyi. See Guichaoua (ed.), *Les Crises Politiques au Burundi at au Rwanda.*

52. Colette Braeckman, *Terreur Africaine. Burundi, Rwanda, Zaire: les racines de la violence*, Paris: Fayard, 1996, p. 82.

53. Human Rights Watch/Fédération International des Ligues des Droits de l'Homme, *Leave none to tell the story. Genocide in Rwanda*, 1999, p. 692–735. A UNHCR report apparently found evidence of an unmistakable pattern of killing and persecution by the RPF. Few have seen the document. Named after its principal author, Robert Gersony, it was rumoured to contain a section which stated that the RPF had murdered 30,000 Hutus in revenge killings between July and September 1994. From now on there would be talk of a double genocide in Rwanda.

54. Gérard Prunier, *The Rwanda Crisis, 1959–1994. History of a Genocide*, London: Hurst and Company, 1995. See also report on the situation of human rights in Rwanda, submitted by Mr. R. Degni-Ségui, Special Rapporteur of the Commission on Human Rights, under paragraph 20 of commission resolution E/CN.4/5.3/1 of 25 May 1994.

17 · For Valour

THE French offer to the Security Council of a humanitarian operation for Rwanda was enthusiastically welcomed by the Secretary-General. Boutros-Ghali explained to ambassadors in the Council that the French mission for Rwanda would be similar to the one undertaken by the Americans in Somalia. Boutros-Ghali took a keen interest in the resolution to authorize the French force and argued that the French were acting out of 'bitter frustration with the US obstruction'. He later wrote: 'the swift UN intervention that I had recommended to the Security Council would have been far preferable.'[1]

For some diplomats, Boutros-Ghali's decision to support reinsertion of the French military into a conflict which France had done so much to fuel was unspeakable. Boutros-Ghali said he had no choice. France was the only country that had offered anything for Rwanda and at no cost to the UN. America was refusing to pay its UN debt and reluctant to incur peacekeeping bills. The French would be providing troops *and* picking up the bill.

France made desperate diplomatic attempts to get endorsement from its European allies and support from African states for Operation Turquoise. Only Senegal and Chad between them would send a few hundred soldiers to join the French, and Congo and Niger about forty soldiers: Mauritania sent four doctors. The French troops would not be wearing blue berets and although France said it would not act without UN endorsement, before the Council had a chance to meet, an advance team of French troops had already arrived at the Zairean border airfield of Goma on 20 June, to make preparatory plans for an intervention force. France had begun to position its forces in central Africa on 16 June.[2]

The Security Council quickly endorsed the French plan and the intervention was authorized on 22 June in resolution 929. The mission was to be co-ordinated by the Secretary-General, and would last no longer than sixty days. By then, it was hoped, a reinforced UNAMIR II would be operational. The Council only narrowly accepted France's offer, for not everyone believed that this was a purely humanitarian exercise. Five states abstained: Brazil, China, New Zealand, Nigeria and Pakistan. The New Zealand ambassador, Colin Keating, had urged instead that member states provide resources for a reinforced UNAMIR.[3]

The US Ambassador to the UN, Madeleine Albright, voted in favour of the French plan. Albright told the Council that it should be flexible enough to accept imperfect solutions – which this was. The French plan was a way of bridging the gap before the 5,500 troops authorized for a reinforced UNAMIR II arrived, and Boutros-Ghali was warning that this could take another three months. The tragedy, said Albright, continued to unfold before their eyes.

The resolution authorizing the French mission gave their troops a chapter VII mandate allowing 'all necessary means', the use of force. The French were to secure humanitarian areas and protect displaced people and the relief workers helping them. The idea, according to French military officials, was to set up security zones to protect fleeing refugees and to prevent warfare between the Rwandan military and the RPF from spreading into Burundi and Tanzania. With the news of the French arrival, the Rwandan government army increased in confidence. Dallaire stopped the rescue missions.

Outside the Council chamber in New York the RPF representative, Claude Dusaidi, told journalists that the sole purpose of the French mission was to save the perpetrators of genocide. France was part of the problem. Dusaidi was shocked and angry.

There was criticism of Operation Turquoise elsewhere. *Le Monde*'s reaction was to warn of a fiasco. There was a growing outcry over French support for the Habyarimana regime and stories appeared in the newspapers about France's involvement in Rwanda. In *Libération*, on 14 June, a letter was printed from Jean Carbonare, president of the French charity Survie, which even accused the French intelligence services of running Rwanda in league with the Rwandan army. France had known for years what was going on. *Libération* printed a story based on an interview with a member of a Hutu Power death squad who was claiming that he had been trained by French instructors.[4]

At the news of French intervention, Dallaire was incredulous. It immediately weakened and endangered his own mission. He cabled New York: 'UNAMIR had been waiting for expansion to help stop massacres … the ineffective reaction to meeting the critical needs of the mission has been nothing less than scandalous … this has directly led to the loss of many more Rwandese lives.'[5] The French deployment would further reduce the chances of another country donating either troops or equipment to UNAMIR. There were serious problems. UNAMIR would be in the middle, with the French operating out of Goma, Zaire on the western frontier, and the UN peacekeepers mostly confined to Kigali, in the centre of Rwanda, with the front line of the RPF and Rwandan government forces in between them. The decision had placed a chapter VI force between a chapter VII force and one of the belligerents.

Dallaire believed that the real reason the French were intervening was to stop the RPF taking the whole country. They wanted to split Rwanda in two, like Cyprus. At one point there was a suggestion that the French land in Kigali. Dallaire told New York that if his peacekeepers were ever intended to become subordinate to French command, then he would resign.

Kagame's reaction to French intervention was to call the plan treacherous. It was an act of war. Kagame was quoted in *Le Figaro* on 25 June: 'You have armed and trained the Presidential Guards; you have accepted that the Presidential Guards armed and trained, in front of you, the Hutu extremists.' Kagame announced that Kigali would be able to absorb far more body-bags than Paris.

The French, however, had a Security Council mandate. And with their imminent arrival, the RPF became immediately hostile to UNAMIR. The lives of the Franco-African peacekeepers from the Congo, Senegal and Togo, whose countries had initially considered providing troops for the French operation, were now at risk from the RPF.[6] There were ninety of these officers. As French-speakers they had provided invaluable liaison between UNAMIR and the government army and were vital for information-gathering. They had come to Rwanda originally with an OAU mission, had solid contacts and knew the country well. They had played a key role in the protection of civilians in the Hôtel des Mille Collines.

Dallaire's only option was to evacuate them, but before he did so many were beaten up by the RPF. His deputy, Brigadier Henry Anyidoho, was given the task of escorting them safely out of Rwanda, through RPF-held territory to Uganda, where they were going to be picked up by Bell 212 helicopters in the Mirama hills and flown to Entebbe. But no sooner had they left Kigali on 21 June than they were stopped at the first checkpoint. An RPF second lieutenant said that all bags must be searched, for they would not be allowed out of Rwanda with anything more than their military kit.[7] The convoy was diverted to the airport and only after a thorough search of their luggage were they allowed to continue.[8] Some weeks later Dallaire travelled to Nairobi to present medals to these officers before final repatriation to their home countries.

Twenty-four hours before French troops were due to land, Dallaire received a telephone call from New York asking him if he would co-operate with Operation Turquoise. The French commander, General Jean-Claude Lafourcade, had set up an inter-service headquarters. A meeting took place eight days after Operation Turquoise had begun. Lafourcade had everything Dallaire had needed, including a chapter VII mandate. He had 2,500 troops, under the Commandement des Forces Spéciales (CFS), 100 armoured vehicles, a battering of heavy mortars, eight Super-Puma helicopters and four Jaguar fighter bombers, four Mirage ground-attack planes and four Mirage jets for reconnaissance.[9] There were nearly 300 soldiers from French special forces. France spent 1 per cent of its annual defence budget on Operation Turquoise for its sixty-day duration. It was an awful lot of military power for what was strictly a humanitarian operation.

Operation Turquoise officially began on Thursday, 23 June, when the French, accompanied by a truckload of Senegalese troops, crossed into Rwanda from Zaire at Bukavu. French soldiers conducted patrols in the prefectures of Gisenyi, Kibuye, Cyangugu and Gikongoro, all of which were controlled by the 'interim government'. There were huge French flags to welcome them and in Cyangugu their vehicles were garlanded with flowers. RTLMC broadcast from Gisenyi that the French had come to help them to fight the RPF and would be giving them weapons. The radio called on Hutu girls to put on their frocks to welcome the French.[10]

The French maintained that its soldiers had come to rescue civilians but as Gérard Prunier has revealed in a book about the crisis, the first draft plan drawn up in Paris was for the French to enter through Gisenyi, in north-western Rwanda. One French journalist was told by a Hutu in Gisenyi: 'We never had many Tutsi here and we killed them all at the beginning without much of a fuss.' Prunier had pointed out to the French government that there were no Tutsi left alive to be paraded in front of the TV cameras as justification for intervention. An initial plan, which was presented at the UN by French diplomats, showed that the French had wanted a zone of control from the north and south-east to Kigali and south-west to Butare. This was where the Rwandan government forces had troops and supplies. When shown this plan, Dallaire reportedly said he did not want the French in Kigali; if the French wanted to help they should provide support for UNAMIR.[11]

In Paris, Prunier argued that French troops should go to south-western Rwanda at Cyangugu and rescue the people trapped in the camp at Nyarushishi.[12] And so, accompanied by journalists, French troops went further south, to two steep hillsides on a tea plantation at Nyarushishi, in the prefecture of Cyangugu, to the camp where 8,000 people were sheltering. When the terrified people first saw the French soldiers, they assumed they had come to kill them. Of an estimated 55,000 Tutsi in this prefecture, only 10,000 were left alive and 8,000 of those were in the camp of Nyarushishi. 'Where were you in April?' someone asked a French soldier.

By deciding to go to Nyarushishi, the French tried to appear neutral. At the same time, in a less well publicized move, French officers paid a courtesy call on the 'interim government' at the Hôtel Méridien in Gisenyi and brought them supplies and equipment. Here the roadblocks were decorated with French flags and whole schools lined up by the side of the road to cheer. The commander of the Rwandan government troops, Major-General Augustin Bizimungu, declared that his forces would soon launch an offensive against the RPF.

A week after their arrival in Cyangugu, on Thursday, 30 June, a group of

French soldiers made the sickening discovery of 400 sick and frail Tutsis slowly emerging from a forest in Bisesero – the remnants of some 10,000 Tutsis from this region. Some of these people had been on the run since April and for the past ten days had been under constant attack from militia and soliders. There had suffered appalling wounds. There were few women and children among them because they had not been able to run fast enough. The area was littered with hundreds of bodies. 'This is not what we were led to believe,' an French officer said. 'We were told that the Tutsi were killing Hutu.' Survivors emerged from months in hiding, creeping out from under sheds, inside cupboards and attics, and there were stories emerging of how some brave Hutu sheltered them at risk to their lives. 'We have not a single wounded Hutu here, just massacred Tutsi,' said a French soldier.

On Friday, 1 July, with the RPF poised to take Kigali, and ten days into the French operation, the French informed Boutros-Ghali of their intention to establish a humanitarian safe zone in south-western Rwanda where the population could be protected from the 'fighting'. This was a departure from the mandate, but the French argued its own interpretation of resolution 929, and the plan received the support of the Secretary-General. Boutros-Ghali argued that with a tide of refugees fleeing the RPF advance, in these conditions France's only options were either to withdraw its troops or to establish a safe humanitarian zone.[13] With his endorsement, the French went ahead and by 4 July had established a major base six miles from the RPF army's advanced line, manning it with paratroopers with heavy artillery. In drawing a line around south-western Rwanda, and declaring it a safe humanitarian zone, the French hoped to link what they were doing with the protection afforded the no-fly zone in northern Iraq. But the decision by the French to create a safe zone, an area comprising some 20 per cent of the country, was considered to be illegal under international law, particularly with French commanders announcing that the RPF would be excluded from the safe zone by force. The French prime minister, Edouard Balladur, later told a meeting of the Security Council that everyone could see that without such swift action the survival of an entire country was at stake and the stability of a region seriously compromised.[14]

There are reports that the French and the RPF clashed in early July as the RPF neared Butare. Eighteen French soldiers were said to have been taken captive by the RPF, and after negotiations between the RPF and Paris they were released the following day. There was no publicity.[15]

The immediate effect of the French humanitarian zone was to provide a secure retreat for the Rwandan government army and the perpetrators of genocide – military, militia and civilian. French commanders maintained that because of limits to their mandate they could not arrest or detain anyone in their zone, whether or not they were war criminals. Neither did they attempt to disarm the thousands of civilians who flooded the zone. The militia were still armed to the teeth. Nothing was done to stop the continuing pro-genocide transmissions of RTLMC from within the zone.

There is a divergence of opinion about French achievements during the sixty days of Operation Turquoise. Prunier writes that the importance and efficiency of the French mission were exaggerated for propaganda purposes. There are varying claims in the number of Tutsi saved by French soldiers. The French military claim that Operation Turquoise saved some 17,000 people, but Prunier maintains that when all the people at the Nyarushishi camp are taken into account as well as people picked up elsewhere, then the figure is more like 10–13,000.[16] The French failed even to prevent massacres continuing in the zone.[17] The only French casualties of Operation Turquoise were soldiers who suffered from shock and trauma at what they had seen.[18]

At dawn on Monday, 4 July, when the Rwandan army abandoned positions, the RPF took Kigali. After three months the city was quiet. The Presidential Guard had held the RPF at the Kacyiru roundabout and now the elite force retreated, scurrying north to the Hutu Power stronghold of Ruhengeri. Before their departure a Rwandan officer telephoned Philippe Gaillard to thank him and the other ICRC delegates for helping with their wounded.

Gaillard left Rwanda the next day. As usual he did not say goodbye at the delegation, but he did have a last supper with Dallaire, whom he considered to be very courageous.[19] Gaillard gave Dallaire an ICRC badge, and jokingly said that Dallaire had no right to wear it but that it was appropriate that it belong to him. He returned the UN Motorola that Dallaire had loaned him. Dallaire gave Gaillard the UNAMIR ribbon he wore on his shirt, as he thought Gaillard deserved a medal.

The Red Cross mission that Gaillard, as chief delegate, operated in Rwanda must rank as one of the most extraordinary of the twentieth century's humanitarian missions. For the duration of a genocide there was some provision of emergency medical help. In Kigali, when the RPF took the city, there were 2,500 people living in the ICRC compound.[20] Gaillard later estimated that between 10 April and 4 July the ICRC had looked after 9,000 injured in Kigali and that a further 100,000 people had been saved because of the work of ICRC delegates elsewhere in the country. In Kigali there had been 1,200 surgical operations, and hundreds of people were treated from the back of ambulances. Some 25,000 tons of food had been distributed. Water engineers repaired the Kigali hydraulic stations and those in Ruhengeri, Gisenyi and Butare.[21] Gaillard considers such an achievement to be no more than a drop of humanity in an ocean of blood.

Gaillard left Rwanda saying he would never go back. He concluded modestly: 'There were no deaths among the ex-pats and that was a miracle … neither were there casualties among our Rwandan collaborators. No armed militia ever entered our compound to threaten anyone although the Interahamwe often came to my office to talk to me.' Some months afterwards he made a speech in Geneva in which he paid tribute to the people in Rwanda who were moderate, who had been open to persuasion, and who had been 'desperate about the assassins among them'. Gaillard described people prepared to save lives, particularly the lives of children, at great personal risk. There had been officials in the prefecture at Cyangugu, said Gaillard, who with patience and persuasion, and in spite of all the pressure they were under, tried to save the 8,000 people at the camp at Nyarushishi. The courage and exceptional vision of these people had put a flower of humanity in what they had all known was a veritable national charnel-house.[22] 'In this century,' Gaillard said, 'the worst memories for humanity are our two world wars and Pol Pot, who killed between two and three million in Cambodia. Now there is Rwanda, a country of seven million people of which one million have disappeared.' In an outspoken interview for a Swiss newspaper, Gaillard said that there had been a degrading of the values of society: 'It is terrible to see that in Europe we give power to the dishonest, and to cynics, people who put their own personal interests before the common good.'[23]

Gaillard considers that Dallaire's experiences were worse than his own. Dallaire lost twelve men, ten of them in the most atrocious circumstances.[24] Hutu Power put a price on his head. And he was abandoned by his own organization, for the UN had not even organized food for its own force, let alone for the displaced people under its protection. The ICRC had supplied food to the people at the Amahoro stadium. Dr James Orbinski of MSF had been shocked at the state of the peacekeepers, astonished that they were obliged to limit their rescue attempts for lack of petrol. Their headquarters was constantly shelled and Orbinski retained the deepest respect for Dallaire's courage and for all he tried to do. 'His tenacity and sheer drive to maximize the impact of UNAMIR was extraordinary. He was left high and dry.'

In one of his last cables to UN headquarters, Dallaire wrote:

> What we have been living here is a disgrace. The international community and the UN member states have on the one hand been appalled at what has happened in Rwanda while, on the other hand, these same authorities, apart from a few exceptions, have done nothing substantive to help the situation … the force has been prevented from having a modicum of self-respect and effectiveness on the ground … FC [Force Commander] acknowledges that this mission is a logistical nightmare for your HQ, but that is *nothing* [*sic*] compared to the living hell that has surrounded us, coupled with the obligation of standing in front of both parties and being the bearer of so little help and credibility … UNHQ, and sovereign countries, with few exceptions, have solidly failed in providing any reasonable/tangible/timely support to the expanded

> UNAMIR so far. The APCs are still in Entebbe, we don't have water ... although Rwanda and UNAMIR have been at the centre of a terrible human tragedy, not to say Holocaust, and although many fine words had been pronounced by all, including members of the Security Council, the tangible effort on the ground to meet the minimum viable operational needs ... had been totally, completely ineffective.
>
> We have no food/fuel/water stocks, we have no operational vehicles in theatre, we have no spare parts, we have *no* logistics support as the contractor has not been hired, we have no water supply. What is worse, we have no sign of the situation getting better in the near future.

Within a few days of the fall of Kigali, and with the army approaching the Hutu Power strongholds in the north, thousands of people, incited by the hate-radio, took to the roads to flee. RTLMC broadcast to the 'Hutu Nation' to warn people to take refuge in Zaire, for the RPF were devil-like fighters and were going to kill them all. There were thousands of people on the move, and the ICRC, MSF-France and Oxfam all predicted that such a massive movement of people was a disaster in the making. On the roads there were soldiers in lorries, people in cars, on bicycles, on foot with cows and chickens, and surrounded by drunken Interahamwe who were 'organizing' an exodus. Some 700,000 people were converging on the north-eastern border with Zaire, between Lake Kivu and the volcano of Nyiragongo.

On 14 July, the Rwanda exodus began. On the Zaire–Rwanda border was Samantha Bolton in Goma for MSF-France, as public information officer. Bolton described the amazing sight of watching the arrival of the people: 'It was a silent line, a long, long black line of people, all of them walking silently, like machines.' All day people poured into Zaire. 'It was as though the whole country was emptying,' said Bolton. 'We had known for two weeks that these people were coming.' Bolton called the BBC and CNN and told them 'the floodgates of Rwanda have opened'. In two days, about a million people crossed into Zaire, dwarfing the previous refugee record set in April when Rwandans fled to Tanzania. 'If they stay here,' Bolton wrote in her diary, 'thousands among them will die.' No one could cope. Oxfam and MSF started to distribute water but people were dying of dehydration and exhaustion. Bolton accurately predicted a cholera outbreak.[25] Among the buses and the cars and the cattle, according to some, they carried what remained of Juvénal Habyarimana, the body parts reportedly collected from the crash site.

The military crossed the border, bringing with them artillery, mortars and at least four anti-aircraft guns and anti-tank weapons. The chief of staff, Augustin Bizimungu, denied that his men were abandoning the fight. The prime minister, Jean Kambanda, said: 'We have lost the military battle but the war is by no means over because we have the people behind us.'

Kambanda was right. Two million people left the country. In Tanzania there were an estimated 500,000 at a camp called Benaco and 200,000 refugees had fled to Burundi. An estimated one million people had passed into Zaire at Goma and 200,000 more into Bukavu.[26]

In Rwanda there were 600,000 refugees in Gikongoro, a further 800,000 in Cyangugu and 300,000 in Kibuye and in these prefectures aid agencies were commencing relief distribution, hoping to avoid a similar exodus to the north-west. Sixty per cent of the Rwanda's population was now either dead or displaced.[27]

The flight of the Hutus into Zaire, into camps at Goma and Bukavu, broke all refugee records, for it was the fastest and largest exodus ever recorded. The horizon was black with people and a remote rural corner of Zaire was turned into a giant camp. Hundreds of thousands of people settled on a barren plain surrounded by volcanoes, without food, water or shelter. Thousands died in appalling suffering in filthy overcrowded camps, walking in a mud of choleric vomit and diarrhoea, for the volcanic rock was as hard as concrete. People died from exhaustion, others from starvation, cholera or dysentery.[28] There were an estimated 4,000 orphaned children. In one camp, boys were paid by French troops to collect the dead, ready to be tipped into vast graves. In other places the corpses sat among the living.

The exodus into Zaire would finally push Rwanda to the top of the international agenda and by the end of July there were some 500 journalists and technicians in the Goma area, and scores of satellite transmission dishes at the airport. In stark contrast with the reporting of the genocide, within three days of the exodus into Goma, there was a media frenzy.

One journalist wrote:

> The slaughter in Rwanda may have been an expression of the bestiality of man, but what is happening in Zaire today is surely the wrath of God. Epidemics of biblical proportions sweep the land. Water is poison ... The dead are everywhere ... It is as if Mother Earth herself did not want to accept the remains of the Hutu refugees from Rwanda.

His piece was accompanied by graphic photographs.[29] The catastrophe made for extraordinary television pictures.

From now on there would be a blurring of the perception of events, so that the plight of the refugees became confused with the war and the genocide. Here was more suffering in what appeared to be a long and complicated story. For Oxfam, Anne Mackintosh, the charity's regional representative for Rwanda, Burundi and Kivu (Zaire) from 1991 to 1994, who was caught up in it, said the genocide was overshadowed by the refugee crisis. Refugees were not, as some journalists and aid agencies stated, fleeing the genocide; they fled with those who perpetrated it. 'Suddenly everyone was there,' she wrote.

'Yet only a year before Oxfam had even had to pay journalists to visit Rwanda and Kivu, and help them place their stories, simply to ensure some serious coverage in the British media of the region and its latent conflicts.'[30] Gérard Prunier notes the convenience of the confusion between the genocide and the refugees for French policy-makers. By now Operation Turquoise soldiers were on every television screen, trying to alleviate the suffering in Goma.[31]

Amid an uproar of public outrage at the agony in these camps, the American administration decided on a major response costing $300–400 million, with up to 4,000 military to reinforce hundreds of US civilian, and mostly independent, relief workers, together with a massive airlift. It took just three days, once the orders had been issued by the White House to the Pentagon, for the first American troops to be on the ground and distributing fresh water to the refugees. The US military was under strict orders not to become involved in operations that could evolve into or be seen as peacekeeping, to limit its action to narrow technical humanitarian tasks and to leave as soon as possible. In Goma, US soliders moved about in convoys of vehicles with heavy machine guns and wore helmets and flak-jackets at all times. All US military personnel had to be back to the secure military compound by nightfall.

On 22 July, President Clinton described the refugee camps as the worst humanitarian crisis in a generation. In Goma, said Clinton, one refugee was dying every minute. There were accompanying briefings with J. Brian Atwood, appointed Clinton's special representative to Rwanda, declaring that 1,200 tons of food a day was needed, on top of 3.8 million litres of clean water – more than twice the food that was needed in Somalia at the height of the famine.

A political military adviser in the State Department, Tony Marley, described America's response to Goma as resulting from the 'CNN factor', that a certain level of media coverage prompts action by governments. Marley also perceived a sense of guilt on the part of those who had obstructed any US action, or any US response, to the genocide. 'People had known what was going on earlier, but had done nothing,' Marley claimed.[32]

In five months, from mid-July to the end of December, the UNHCR estimated that $1 million a day was spent on relief efforts for Rwandan refugees.

Dallaire believes that in the case of the refugee camps in Goma, precious resources were wasted in fuelling a charade of political conscience-cleansing by the developed states in deference to the media and their constituencies.[33]

Notes

1. Boutros Boutros-Ghali, *Unvanquished. A US–UN Saga*. London: I.B.Tauris, 1999, p. 140.

2. J. Matthew Vaccaro, 'The Politics of Genocide: Peacekeeping and Rwanda', in William J. Durch (ed.), *UN Peacekeeping, American Politics and the Uncivil Wars of the 1990s*, Henry L. Stimson Center, New York: St Martin's Press, 1996.

3. Security Council (S/PV.3392), 22 June 1994.

4. Stephen Smith, 'Rwanda. Un Ancien des escadrons de la mort accusé', *Libération*, 21 June 1994.

5. Boutros-Ghali, *Unvanquished*, p. 139.

6. Jonathan Moore (ed.), *Hard Choices, Moral Dilemmas in Humanitarian Intervention*, Oxford: Rowman and Littlefield, 1998, p. 81.

7. They were told to produce invoices for electronic equipment.

8. Henry Kwami Anyidoho, *Guns Over Kigali*, Accra: Woeli Publishing Services, 1997, pp. 77–8.

9. Vaccaro, 'The Politics of Genocide'.

10. Human Rights Watch/Fédération Internationale des Ligues des Droits de l'Homme, *Leave none to tell the story. Genocide in Rwanda, 1999*, p. 678.

11. Ibid., pp 671–2.

12. Gérard Prunier, *The Rwanda Crisis 1959–1994. History of a Genocide*, London: Hurst and Company, 1995, pp. 281–7.

13. *The United Nations and Rwanda, 1993–1996*, UN Blue Book series, Vol. 10, New York: UN Department of Public Information, 1996, p. 55.

14. Security Council (S/PV.3402), 11 July 1994.

15. Mel McNulty, 'France's Rwanda Débâcle', *War Studies*, Vol. 2. No. 2, Spring 1997, p. 16.

16. Gérard Prunier, 'Operation Turquoise: A Humanitarian Escape', in Howard Adelman and Astri Suhrke (eds), *The Path of a Genocide. The Rwanda Crisis from Uganda to Zaire*, New Brunswick, NJ: Transaction, 1999, p. 303.

17. Human Rights Watch/Fédération Internationale des Ligues des Droits de l'Homme, *Leave none to tell the story*, pp. 679–81.

18. McNulty, 'France's Rwanda Débaâcle', p. 18.

19. Philippe Gaillard, *Rwanda 1994: La vraie vie est absente (Arthur Rimbaud) Cycle des Conférences les Mardi de Musée. M. Philippe Gaillard, délégué du CIRC, chef de délégation au Rwanda de juillet 1993 à juillet, 1994* (unpublished).

20. Hundreds more people had been buried in the gardens, many without names, only numbers.

21. By July there were the following ICRC operations in Rwanda: there was a seven-strong medical team in Bukavu working across the Zaire border in Cyangugu and helping those who had escaped the massacres in the Nyarushishi camp in the hills; there was a five-strong medical team in Gikongoro; there were two ICRC delegates in Rutanan. A delegation in Kabgayi was displaced because of the fighting. In Kigali there were ten delegates when the city fell.

22. Gaillard, *Rwanda 1994*.

23. Gérard Delaloye and Elisabeth Levy, 'Philippe Gaillard, après Kigali, pouvez-vous encore croire en l'humanité?' *Le Nouveau Quotidien*, 30 December 1994.

24. The twelve were ten Belgian peacekeepers on 7 April; Captain Mbabye Diagne, of Senegal, who died of a mortar-bomb on 31 May; Private Mensah-Baidoo, of Ghana, who died of a mortar shell on 9 May.

25. Samantha Bolton, 'J'ai vu arriver le choléra', *Le Nouvel Observateur*, 28 July–3 August 1994.

26. Larry Minear and Philippe Guillot, *Soldiers to the Rescue. Humanitarian Lessons from Rwanda*. Paris: Development Centre of the Organization for Economic Co-operation and Development, 1996, p. 63.

27. *The International Response to Conflict and Genocide: Lessons from the Rwanda Experience*. Joint Evaluation of Emergency Assistance to Rwanda. Copenhagen, March 1996, study 3, p. 43. On 24 July, the UNHCR reported 2.1 million refugees and 1.4 million displaced within the French zone, and 1.2 million displaced in the rest of the country.

28. An estimated 20,000 people died of cholera, a disease easily treated with a simple remedy costing less than 50p a day. Oral rehydration salts replace the vital mineral and fluids lost in violent diarrhoea and vomiting.

29. Robert Block, 'A Week in Goma', *Independent on Sunday*, 31 July 1994.

30. Anne Mackintosh, 'Rwanda: beyond "ethnic conflict"', *Development in Practice*, Vol. 7, No. 4, November 1997, p. 466.

31. Prunier, 'Operation Turquoise', p. 303.

32. Excerpts taken from interview published on Frontline's website for 'The Triumph of Evil', www.pbs.org/WGBH/Pages/Frontline/shows/evil. Copyright WGBH/Frontline, 1999.

33. Moore (ed.), *Hard Choices*, p. 72.

18 · Starting from Zero: 18 July 1994

THE last Hutu Power stronghold in Rwanda fell on 18 July, and Kagame declared the civil war was over. The next day in Kigali a broad-based government of national unity was sworn in comprising the representatives of all political parties apart from the MRNDD. Twelve of the eighteen ministers were Hutu. The president was Pasteur Bizimungu, the oldest of the RPF Hutu. A new position was created for Paul Kagame as vice-president.

There was no triumphant victory. The country had been ransacked. There was not a penny in the public coffers. There were no offices intact, no chairs, no desks, no paper, no telephones, nothing at all.

The streets of Kigali were almost empty. From a previous population of 300,000, there were 50,000 people left and half of these were displaced.[1] Their condition was disastrous, and they lacked adequate food and clean water. Outside the capital, whole families and communities had been destroyed. Livestock had been killed and crops laid to waste.[2] Everywhere there were ditches filled with rotting bodies. The people had been terrorized and traumatized. The hospitals and schools were destroyed or ransacked. Rwanda's health centres, one in each commune, were ruined. The stocks of basic drugs and health supplies had been looted. Water supply lines were non-operational. Qualified staff had been killed or fled the country, including most of the teachers. An estimated 250,000 women had been widowed. In the whole country there were six judges and ten lawyers. There were no gendarmes.[3]

At least 100,000 children had been separated from their families, orphaned, lost, abducted or abandoned.[4] Most of Rwanda's children had witnessed extreme forms of brutality and 90 per cent of them had at some point thought they would die.[5] Most children felt they had no future. They did not believe that they would live to become adults. More than 300 children, some less than ten years old, were accused of genocide or murder. An estimated 300,000 children were thought to have been killed.[6]

Rwanda was divided, this time into victims, survivors, returnees and perpetrators. It was as though in 1945 the Jews and the Germans were to live together in Germany after the Holocaust, under a Jewish-dominated army, and with roughly a third of all Germans outside the country.

We will never know the number of victims in the genocide. The million figure is agreed by Gaillard, based on information gathered while the genocide unfolded. This figure was also provided by Charles Petrie, vice-co-ordinator of the UN Rwandan Emergency Office, who said on 24 August 1994 that he did not think the figure of one million dead was an exaggeration.[7] For reasons which remain obscure, the figure now generally accepted is 800,000.

In a report for the Commission on Human Rights, special rapporteur René Dégni-Ségui estimated that between 200,000 and 500,000 people had died. He reached this conclusion at the end of two months of killing, and said that he thought it was far lower than the actual figure, adding that some observers thought the figure nearer one million.[8] A commission of experts, established by the Security Council to investigate the genocide, reported on 9 December 1994 that 500,000 unarmed civilians had been murdered.[9]

Hutu Power remained a threat, its adherents determined to continue their genocidal policies. From Zaire, and with the active support of the Zairean government, it did not take long for a plan to be devised to reconquer Rwanda. Part of a long-term strategy to destabilize the new government in Kigali[10] was to carry on killing Tutsi – the people known as 'rescapés', those who escaped the genocide – in order to provoke the government in Kigali to retaliate against Hutu in Rwanda, thereby driving a wedge between the new government and the people and shifting attention away from the genocide. There would be a 'guerrilla phase', estimated to cost US$6.3 million in arms and ammunition. The second phase, that of open classic warfare, would be decided when the guerrilla phase came to an end.[11] The total cost of invasion was estimated at $50 million.[12]

The former militias were by now integrated into the regular army forces. Young recruits poured in from the refugee camps and the total number of soldiers under Hutu Power command soon reached 50,000.[13] Among the flood of refugees who had poured out of the country there had been some 30,000 soldiers and militia. The state structure had fled too, and there were local officials as well as the national leaders. Military camps were established along Lake Kivu at Manunga.

Before leaving the country, people had looted it. They took all government property and anything which could be moved: corrugated-iron sheets, window frames, door handles. Whole factories were dismantled and taken into exile along with every working vehicle.[14]

In the refugee camps, aid workers saw at first hand how local officials and the militia established their authority and control. There were gangs with guns, grenades and machetes. Some 4,000 murders took place in Goma in the first month of the exodus. Killings, threats, extortions, rape and thuggery were common. The Hutu Power ideology was as entrenched as ever with people openly expressing the view that it was correct to kill Tutsi.

The refugees spread over a network of 60 miles of roads, probably the largest group of fugitive murderers ever assembled, all fed and sheltered by the aid agencies while Hutu Power made profits from refugee commerce, monopolizing the distribution of international aid, and creating a growing trade in purloined humanitarian provisions. There was even tax collection, the money quickly diverted into arms purchases. Richard McCall, chief of staff of the US Agency for International Development, described the camps as 'an unfettered corridor for arms shipment'. Goma settled down into a state within a state, a new 'Hutu land' carved out in Zaire.

In September 1994, a joint mission from the UNHCR and the government of Zaire considered separating the militia from the rest of the refugees. The UNHCR worked out that some 100,000 people would have to be moved – members of the militia and their families. The problems of identifying and relocating these people were immense. In November some of the aid agencies threatened to withdraw from the camps, for the people in them were no more than hostages, denied the right to return to their homes, denied equal access to aid and a guarantee of basic human rights. Some aid agency staff did walk out. MSF-France stated that the diversion of humanitarian aid by the same people who orchestrated the genocide, the lack of effective international action regarding impunity, and the fact that the refugees were held hostage, presented a situation which was contradictory to the principles of humanitarian assistance. A plea was made by the agencies to the UN Secretary-General to deploy a UN security force in the camps. But the Security Council dismissed a secretariat plan which provided for 10,000–12,000 soldiers to separate the former political leaders, military and militia.[15] In any event, only one troop contributor, Bangladesh, came forward.[16]

While aid poured into the refugee camps in Zaire, and while Hutu Power rearmed and retrained, in Kigali there was nothing but debt. In October 1994 France lobbied against the new regime in all the international institutions, trying to block aid from the European Union, and arguing that money should be paid only when the refugees outside Rwanda returned to their country. Nor was it possible for Kagame to find the $4.5 million needed for World Bank debt repayment arrears which had accrued since the genocide began. The main preoccupation of the donors was that the RPF was breaching the Arusha Accords and that there should be elections. But most of the moderate Hutus were dead. The new government considered it a mockery to insist they negotiate with killers in order to form a broad-based government. There was nothing to negotiate; no one to negotiate with, apart from mass murderers.

The main financial donors, however, insisted on negotiation as a prerequisite to aid. The World Bank had earmarked $140 million for Rwanda but wanted $4.5 million first in arrears; under the rules, new loans are not allowed unless other debts are paid, and the new government owed the World Bank

US$6 million in arrears.[17] The new regime would have to repay money borrowed from international financial institutions, money that had been spent on the genocide. Having provided substantial assistance for the refugees, donors now held back, waiting until the new regime had 'established its credibility'.[18]

In November 1995, the Egyptian Office of Military Intelligence wrote to the Rwandan government to demand one million dollars, due at the Crédit Lyonnais bank in London, part payment for weapons under the arms contract signed in March 1992.[19] The debt was eventually paid.

Notes

1. US Agency for International Development. Bureau for Humanitarian Response. Office of US Foreign Disaster Assistance. Situation Report No. 4, 25 July 1994.

2. Nigel Cantwell, *Starting from Zero: the Promotion and Protection of Children's Rights in Post-genocide Rwanda, July 1994–December 1996*. Florence: UNICEF and International Child Development Centre. 1997.

3. Francoise Bouchet-Saulnier, *Mission Rwanda Juriste*, MSF, p. 4.

4. Rwanda Emergency Programme. Progress Report No. 1, UNICEF, Kigali, Reporting Period: May 1994–March 1995.

5. Cantwell, *Starting from Zero*, p. 46.

6. The UK Committee for UNICEF, *Annual Review 1994/1995*, p. 5.

7. 'Rwanda toll could top 1 million', *Guardian*, 25 August 1994. The UN Rwandan Emergency Office (UNREO) was created by the UN Department of Humanitarian Affairs and UNDP to co-ordinate relief efforts. See also Jean-Paul Gouteux, *Un Génocide secret d'état. La France et le Rwanda 1990–1997*, Editions Sociales, 1998, p. 104. While the percentage of Tutsi in Rwanda was officially 9 per cent, research by the UNDP showed this figure to be nearer 20 per cent.

8. UN Commission on Human Rights, Report on the situation of human rights in Rwanda submitted by Mr. René Dégni-Ségui, Special Rapporteur, under paragraph 20 of resolution S-3/1 of 25 May, 1994. (E/CN.4/1995/7) 28 June 1994.

9. *The United Nations and Rwanda, 1993–1996*. UN Blue Book series, Vol. 10, New York: UN Department of Public Information, 1996, p. 415.

10. Report signed Col. Gasake. For the attention of the FAR Commander. Goma, 12 May 1995.

11. Memorandum Presented by the Rwanda Armed Forces (in exile) for the Liberation of Their Country. Signed: Major-General Augustin Bizimungu. Chief of Staff. Goma, 1 June 1996.

12. Report signed Col. Gasake. For the attention of the FAR Commander. Goma, 12 May 1995.

13. Wm Cyrus Reed, 'Guerrillas in the Midst', in Christopher Clapham (ed.), *African Guerillas*, Oxford: James Currey, 1998, p. 140.

14. Ibid., p. 139.

15. Eventually, the issue of camp security was given to the UNHCR and the UNHCR contracted with the Zairian government to provide an elite force to police the camps. It took until the end of January 1995 before the Zairian Camp Security Operation was agreed, and the UNHCR signed a deal whereby Zaire would provide troops and the UNHCR would pay for salaries, food and health care, and the troops would liaise with an inter-

national group of civilians who had police and military backgrounds. By the end of April, the contingent from Zaire had reached 1,500. As a result, the killing and thuggery were reduced but the core problem was not addressed.

16. *The United Nations and Rwanda, 1993–1996*, pp. 80–3.

17. Mark Huband, 'France blocks Rwanda aid in cynical power game', *Observer*, 10 October 1994.

18. Larry Minear and Philippe Guillot, *Soldiers to the Rescue. Humanitarian Lessons from Rwanda*. Paris: Development Centre of the Organisation for Economic Co-operation and Development, 1996, p. 66.

19. Office of Military Intelligence. Section of Military Attachés, Foreign Department to Rwandese Ambassador in Cairo. Dated 12 January 1995. Signed Mohamed El Shahat Abdel Kader, head of the Section of Military Attachés.

19 · The Genocide Convention

THE failure of the international community to act while one million people in Rwanda were slaughtered was one of the greatest scandals of the twentieth century. But there was nothing secret about it. There were no sealed trains or secluded camps in Rwanda. The genocide was broadcast on the radio. Conclusive proof that a genocide was taking place was provided to the Security Council in May and June while it was happening. A report from the Commission on Human Rights concluded that the massacres were planned and systematic. There was a determination to destroy Tutsi. 'No one escapes ... not even new-born babies ... the victims are pursued to their very last refuge and killed there.'[1]

For the first time in possession of overwhelming proof of genocide, the Council thought of one action: to create a committee of experts to 'evaluate the evidence'.[2] That evidence was contained in an interim report in October 1994 which concluded that although both sides of the armed conflict had perpetrated serious breaches of international humanitarian law and crimes against humanity, there existed a mass of evidence that the extermination of the Tutsi and moderate Hutu had been planned months in advance. There had been a 'concerted, planned, systematic and methodical nature of ... criminal acts' committed by government soldiers and the Hutu militia against the Tutsi. Racial propaganda had been disseminated on a widespread basis; posters, leaflets and radio broadcasts had dehumanized the Tutsi as snakes, cockroaches and animals. There had been training camps where men had been indoctrinated in hatred against the Tutsi minority and given information about methods of mass murder. There were ample grounds to prove that the genocide convention had been violated between 6 April and 15 July.[3]

More evidence arrived. It was grim and detailed. There was a provisional list of massacre sites. There were more than six sites in the towns of Gitarama and Cyangugu. At Nyundo, three septic tanks had been used to try to get rid of 300 people. In Nyarubuye there was no burial and there the bodies were strewn about courtyards and alleys, piled upon each other in the classrooms of the parish school and in the church. Yet no real investigations had begun. As early as May the RPF in Rwanda had called for an international tribunal to punish the guilty. Only arrests could end the cycle of violence. Others lobbied the UN Secretary-General to create a tribunal. However, it took until 8 November 1994 before the Security Council voted to create the International Criminal Tribunal for Rwanda.

In view of the enormity of the genocide and the continuing questions surrounding what had happened, Kofi Annan, who was then Secretary-General, announced in March 1999 that an independent inquiry be set up to establish the facts.[4] Nine months later the inquiry issued a report that blamed everyone: the Secretary General, the secretariat, the Security Council, and the membership of the UN.

On the role of Secretary-General Boutros Boutros-Ghali, it concluded diplomatically that he 'should have done more' to argue the case for reinforcement. Under the UN Charter the Secretary-General had a responsibility and the opportunity to bring to the attention of the Council issues requiring action. He could have had a decisive influence on decision-making with the capacity to mobilize political will. Yet Boutros-Ghali was absent from New York during much of the key period. The UN's report says: 'the Secretary-General cannot be present at every meeting ... and although Boutros-Ghali was kept informed of key developments ... the role of the Secretary-General is limited if performed by proxy.' These statements sit uneasily together.

Boutros-Ghali lives in Paris now, and is secretary-general of Francophonie, the grouping of French-speaking countries. He also heads an international panel on democracy-building created by UNESCO (the UN Educational, Scientific and Cultural Organization). In an interview shortly after the UN report on Rwanda was published, Boutros-Ghali angrily blamed the Americans for what had happened. He revealed that during the genocide he had private meetings individually with the ambassadors of America and Britain, Madeleine Albright and David Hannay. To each ambassador he had urged action to stop the killing in Rwanda. Boutros-Ghali described their reaction: 'Come on, Boutros, relax ... Don't put us in a difficult position.. the mood is not for intervention, you will obtain nothing ... we will not move.'

The Americans, liable for the lion's share of the peacekeeping bill, were adamantly against UN intervention, but were happy for the French to take action since they were willing to pay for it themselves. The Council, Boutros-Ghali said, was adequately informed: 'Everybody knew that the people coming from Uganda were Tutsi and the people in power were Hutu and that it was a war between Hutu and Tutsi. We did not need to tell them that, it was evident. What was not evident was that there as a plan of genocide'.[5] The Council had meekly followed the US lead, he said.[6] Had the Council created the UN stand-by force which he had suggested two years earlier, then the genocide might never have taken place. His own failure was to convince member governments to act. 'But believe me,' he said, 'I tried.'[7]

So why *did* the Security Council fail to act? Colin Keating, the permanent representative for New Zealand, and the president of the Security Council in April 1994, once described the Council as a bunch of diplomatic amateurs. 'The UN was not ready to deal with all this,' Keating said. The Security Council was not equipped at ambassadorial level to address professional military issues and the situation in Rwanda cried out for military and technical advisers to sit together to discuss what the options were. No one had listened to Dallaire. The Council had a right and a duty to know the details in order to decide the issues. In the end, politicians had to be made accountable by their own publics.[8]

Even before Rwanda, Keating had lobbied for a change in the system of secret and informal consultations held by the Security Council, for he did not believe that it was an appropriate way of working. Keating had suggested that the informal consultations be filmed on closed-circuit television so that at least other UN members could watch the secret proceedings, a proposal not well received by the permanent five. The argument persisted that 'proper discussions' could not take place in public.[9] The fact that the Council was unaccountable was a recipe for disaster, said Keating. At one point, on 29 April, Keating had threatened to hold the debate about genocide in public in order to shame those ambassadors for their refusal to name it a genocide.

No one can know how humanitarian intervention will work out. If it ends in disaster, then those who take the decision to sacrifice soldiers to save citizens have to answer for it. In 1994 the politicians were determined to conduct casualty-free interventions and, with a lack of public awareness because of the inadequate press coverage, there were no choices given and no risks were taken. There was no moral outcry about genocide and this made it easier for politicians to claim that the hatred in Rwanda was impervious to military intervention and that public opinion was not prepared to pay the price of casualties. And so, like the Jews, the Tutsi were abandoned to their fate.

The Rwandan genocide should be the defining scandal of the presidency of Bill Clinton. Rwanda had been an issue requiring leadership and responsibility, as Senator Paul Simon had reminded Clinton in his letter of 13 May 1994. But the administration took the easy option and failed to push the moral boundaries; there were no votes to be gained advocating help for another collapsed African state. Africa was less important since the end of the Cold War. The recent example of Somalia had shown the risks of intervention.

For three months the Clinton administration played down the crisis and tried to impede effective intervention by UN forces.[10] The secretary of state, Warren Christopher, avoided the issue altogether. Senior officials in the department put Rwanda low on the agenda for fear, according to the Washington director of Human Rights Watch, Holly J. Burkhalter, of another Somalia.

Christopher continued to distort the reality of Rwanda as late as 24 July 1994, when he told a television programme that there had been a 'tremendous civil war' in Rwanda and that the USA had done all it could to try to support the UN, but that it was not a time for the USA to try to intervene.[11]

There was even reluctance to take the slightest action, such as jamming the hate-radio, RTLMC, which could have saved lives. The question was raised several times in May during daily video conferences. The Defense Department's official response was always that jamming the broadcasts was technically and legally impossible, and it was properly the decision of the State Department or the National Security Council. At the National Security Council, neither Don Steinberg, senior director for Africa, nor national security adviser Anthony Lake formulated a policy other than to do nothing.

According to James Woods, deputy assistant secretary of defense, the fact of genocide was known as early as the second week.[12] Recalling the misery of that time, Woods said: 'I think it was sort of a formal spectacle of the US in disarray and retreat, leading the international community away from doing the right thing and I think that everybody was perfectly happy to follow our lead – in retreat.' Everyone knew the true nature of what was going on; no official in the American administration could claim not to have known. Yet in 1998 that is precisely what Clinton did when he visited Kigali and offered a *mea culpa* excuse:

> All over the world there were people like me sitting in offices, day after day after day, who did not fully appreciate the depth and speed with which you were being engulfed by this unimaginable terror.
>
> The international community, together with nations in Africa, must bear its share of responsibility for this tragedy, as well. We did not act quickly enough after the killing began … we did not immediately call these crimes by their rightful name, genocide.
>
> Never again must we be shy in the face of the evidence.

The decision-making process within the government of Prime Minister John Major leading to British policy on Rwanda in 1994 will doubtless remain a mystery. There is secrecy in government and a lack of interest in the media.

The only glimpse into British government thinking is afforded in a letter sent on 7 July 1995 by the Foreign and Commonwealth Office (FCO) to an international inquiry. In this letter, written a year after the genocide ended, the FCO said it did not accept the term genocide. The FCO was inclined to see a discussion of whether or not the massacres constituted genocide as 'sterile'.[13] The Foreign Office approach was characterized from the outset by a determination to play the matter down and, for a body which once regarded Africa as its area of special interest, an almost deliberate ignorance. To begin with, it maintained that it did not know what was going on in Rwanda, which was not in the British sphere. This is an extraordinary claim from a permanent member of the Security Council, with responsibilities as a veto power, a country which had voted in the Council to create a mission for Rwanda.

David Hannay, the UK permanent representative at the UN, confirms that the British were 'extremely unsighted' over Rwanda. There was no British embassy there. There were no British interests. Rwanda was a long way down the list of priorities and the telegrams about Rwanda, received from British embassies in Brussels, Paris and Washington, were not treated as high grade. At the time a large amount of time and resources was being channelled into the problems of Bosnia, and in trying to disarm Iraq. The staff at the British mission in New York were overstretched.

Hannay says the information coming from the secretariat was insufficient; he complained about the inadequate briefings available to the Security Council. Boutros-Ghali controlled the flow of information to the council, Hannay said, allowing only those officials with his permission to brief ambassadors. In all the discussions held about Rwanda before the genocide began the focus had been on how to implement the Arusha Accords. Hannay said: 'Events proved we were looking in the wrong direction, and that the Secretariat was telling us to look in that direction.' He had seen none of the force commander's cables from Rwanda because the Council was not meant to be involved in the day-to-day running of peacekeeping missions.

Even so, Hannay is convinced that there was nothing the UN could have done to prevent the genocide in Rwanda, not with a Hutu-led government intent upon it. Even had the Security Council recognized the killing as genocide, it would not have saved any lives. Hannay said that he was not a lawyer and was therefore not in a position to decide whether or not what was happening was genocide. 'We knew a lot of Tutsi were being killed by a lot of Hutu,' he said. The Council could not conjure up troops and although he believes that Dallaire did a fantastic job, Hannay remains deeply sceptical of Dallaire's belief that 5,500 troops could have prevented much of the slaughter. In any case, to have mounted an enforcement mission with so few troops was totally against American military doctrine.[14]

Some years later, in December 1998, in a BBC Radio 4 interview, Hannay talked specifically about the Genocide Convention in relation to Rwanda: 'nobody ever started to say and who will actually do the intervening and how will it be done.'[15]

In the House of Commons there was no attempt to address the issue and the government was preoccupied with the civil war. After nearly five weeks of genocide and more than 500,000 victims, Mark Lennox-Boyd, the parliamentary under-secretary of state for foreign and Commonwealth affairs, told the House in a written answer on 9 May: 'There are estimates that more than 200,000 people may have perished in the recent fighting in Rwanda. It is a horrific and tragic civil war where we will probably never know the true figure of those killed and injured.'

A debate in the House on Rwanda did not take place until 24 May when Tony Worthington, MP (Labour, Clydebank and Milngavie) expressed shock that so little attention had been paid to Rwanda. 'It is inconceivable that an atrocity in which half a million white people had died would not have been extensively debated in the House,' Worthington said. The press in Britain, had a terrible tendency to dismiss the events as tribalism. 'Genocide is certainly involved', Worthington told the House. Britain was a signatory to the Genocide Convention. 'Has there ever been a clearer example of genocide?' he asked. Lennox-Boyd replied that Rwanda had had a tragic history of ethnic-political violence since independence. The UN had to operate with the consent of the opposing factions.

The Labour Party waited until May before putting pressure on the government to act, and then only because Oxfam telephoned the office of David Clark, shadow secretary of state for defence. Clark called for the UN and the OAU to organize an immediate deployment of forces to try to end the mass killing of civilians and appealed to Malcolm Rifkind, the secretary of state for defence, that the 'advice and expertise that our armed forces possess could be made available to the UN'.

On 23 May Rifkind wrote back to say that troops for Rwanda would 'probably come from regional forces in Africa'. The UK, wrote Rifkind, 'has not been asked to provide any personnel for the operation'. It was an extraordinary sentence for Rifkind to write.[16] Only a few days earlier, Britain had voted in the Security Council to authorize more troops for Rwanda and at the time officials in the secretariat were making desperate efforts to find soldiers. Annan said that every UN member government, with spare military capacity, had received a fax with a list of urgently needed troops and equipment.

So was military intervention by Britain simply impracticable? The British army has two main units that can be rapidly mobilized for deployments overseas, each occupying a very different niche in low- to mid-intensity combat capabilites: the Fifth Airborne Brigade and the Special Air Service (SAS). The level of readiness of the Fifth Airborne Brigade, the only airborne and air-trained brigade in the British army, is routinely set at five days and fewer in a crisis. The brigade consists of two battalions of parachutists plus a command structure – a total of about 5,000 men. (It was to be integrated into a NATO rapid deployment force.) The SAS, described as a precise cutting tool for political policy, is an elite force for covert military operations.

In July 1994 Britain's minister for overseas development, Baroness Lynda Chalker, visited Kigali. She met Dallaire and she asked him what he needed. Dallaire had shown Chalker his list of basic requirements, which by then had been faxed around the world. 'I gave her my shopping list,' he remembered.

'I was up to my knees in bodies by then.'[17] Britain had previously promised Dallaire fifty 4-ton four-wheel drive trucks but they had not materialized. On a BBC2 'Newsnight' programme about Rwanda, Baroness Chalker later blamed Dallaire's lack of resources on 'the UN' which, she explained, ought to 'get its procurement right'.

Only after the genocide was over, and in response to the massive flight of people from Rwanda, did Britain become more generous. Chalker called the refugee tragedy the most ghastly in living memory, a replay of the Middle Ages, and on 28 July Britain offered military assistance in the form of 600 personnel from the Royal Electrical and Mechanical Engineers (REME) to repair the large number of unroadworthy vehicles which belonged to Dallaire's mission, a field ambulance and a field squadron of Royal Engineers to repair roads and drill wells.

Dallaire's only offers during the genocide, as a matter of record, were fifty trucks from Britain, a promise from Italy of one C-130 aircraft plus crew, and six water trucks, a signals squadron plus aircraft from Canada, from the USA fifty armoured personnel carriers, leasehold, and from Japan, US$3 million towards the cost of equipment.[18]

The only government to act during the genocide was France. Both France and Belgium were more centrally involved in the affairs of Rwanda and both countries, stung by criticism of their actions, have held inquiries into the circumstances of the genocide. The Belgian Senate studied documents from within the government system, both confidential and secret, from foreign and defence ministries. Nineteen documents described a Machiavellian plot to terminate the peace process and destabilize the country. Two documents made specific references to genocide.

The Belgian Senate report of December 1997 ran to 1,000 pages and one of its more explosive revelations was the fact that the Belgian ambassador to Rwanda, Johan Swinnen, had warned two years before the genocide: 'a secret command exists which is planning the total extermination of the Tutsis in order to resolve, once and for all, the ethnic problem and to destroy the Hutu opposition.'[19]

In France it took four years to inquire into the events in Rwanda and then only after increasingly frequent accusations that France had been complicit in the genocide. The French inquiry was called a Mission d'Information Parlementaire, a parliamentary information mission. It was ground-breaking, for in the forty-year history of the Fifth Republic there had never been parliamentary scrutiny of the country's role in African policy. It was traditionally an area shrouded in mystery and run from the president's office.

The evidence against France was damming. France, of all the countries in the Security Council, possessed the most detailed knowledge of what was going on in Rwanda; the French had helped to arm the regime, and French soldiers were intimately involved with the Rwandan military, training the militia and helping to train the Presidential Guard. When the genocide began, French soldiers had helped to evacuate Hutu Power extremists, giving many of them, including Agathe Habyarimana, a military escort to the airport.

The Rwanda scandal left no part of French political life unscathed, for at the time of the planning and the execution of the genocide, France was in a left–right co-habitation between a socialist head of state, François Mitterrand, and a Gaullist prime minister, Edouard Balladur.

The French parliamentary inquiry promised much. It was to have access to all relevant diplomatic telegraph traffic and to interview all civil and military personnel involved in decision-making over Rwanda. But because, as its title suggested, it was purely a mission to gather information, there were no judicial procedures, nor did it have the legal authority of a commission of inquiry. When, in the first few days, four former ministers testified together, the tone was set. They were Edouard Balladur, Gaullist prime minister between 1993 and 1995, and three of his ministers, François Léotard, who was minister of defence, Alain Juppé, who was minster for foreign affairs (later prime minister) and Michel Roussin, minister of cooperation. Balladur, who assumed office in March 1993, a year before the genocide took place, was indignant at suggestions that France was as deeply involved as reports had suggested. Only very limited quantities of French arms had been shipped to the Hutu regime; to his knowledge, no more deliveries were made after a French arms embargo was imposed on 8 April 1994. There was a campaign against France, he said, and an attempt to discredit the only country which had tried to act to stop the genocide.

In December 1998 the French National Assembly produced its report. It shed no light at all on the mystery of who, on 6 April 1994, shot down the president's plane. The French report repeated rumour, speculation and intrigue and to date the most basic facts have still to be established. If France knows of a direct link between those who ordered the downing of the plane by missiles, and those responsible for giving the orders to eliminate the political opposition, then it has not made the information public. The French government claims not to have conducted an inquiry, although France lost three nationals, the crew of the jet.

Widely considered a whitewash, the report maintained that all French politicians, all military officers and civil servants and anyone involved in any way with Rwanda had all said that French policy was intended to encourage political reform, and ensure a respect for human rights – as well as to avoid a military victory by the RPF. In this case, French policy was clearly based on the assumption that Arusha could work.

Kofi Annan, and the officials who worked with him in the Department of Peacekeeping Operations, clearly believed the opposite, for they have since maintained that, whatever happened, the peacekeepers could never have overcome the fundamental problem – that the extremists did not want reconciliation with the RPF.[20] But they do concede that once the genocide had started, had Kigali been reinforced, then the militia would have been intimidated.

Mindful of their careers, only privately will those involved in the DPKO lay the blame on the Security Council. One of them said that there had never been any hope of reinforcements. 'If we had gone to the council at the beginning to ask for reinforcements,' one of them said, 'we would have been laughed out of the chamber.' Even when genocide was evident to the whole world, the governments had failed to act. 'And you don't cure cancer', said one of them bitterly, 'with an aspirin.'[21]

There had been years of cut-backs and job losses in the secretariat, and the UN was bankrupt and had been in crisis management for as long as anyone could remember. Scores of officials spent time juggling funds simply to keep the doors open. There were institutional weaknesses and there was no infrastructure for emergency operations, no contingency planning. With the end of the Cold War the Security Council had mandated a huge increase in UN operations and by the time the genocide took place there were 71,543 peacekeepers in seventeen different trouble-spots around the globe. For an army this size, belonging to any developed nation, there would be thousands of people in support back home. Yet in New York there were about 300 officials coping with logistics for this UN army; there was no genuine peacekeeping headquarters, there were too few planning staff, there was no timely intelligence, no adequate command and control operations room.

In an interview shortly after the genocide took place, Annan said he believed that the time had come for the member states to take stock, and to determine that sufficient resources were made available for all UN operations. Large-scale field operations needed advanced planning, clear mandates, trained peacekeepers, assured financing, an effective and integrated UN command and logistical support. In May 1994 Annan had tried to find equipment for the soldiers made available by African countries. 'Those who were critical did not offer ... the sceptical did not offer, and the silent did not offer. What choice did we have?' The UN had been asked to do too much with too little.

'Nobody should feel he has a clear conscience in this business,' said Annan. 'If the pictures of tens of thousands of human bodies rotting and gnawed on by dogs ... do not wake us up out of our apathy, I don't know what will.'

Annan finds it difficult to accept that member states with more intelligence-gathering capabilities than the UN did not know what was happening.[22] No one had the luxury of claiming ignorance.[23] There was a lack of empathy with, and sensitivity to, what was happening in Rwanda. Everyone involved would be harshly judged by history.[24]

There was a time when the sight of a single blue helmet at a checkpoint flying the UN flag was a symbol of peace, security and a determination to impose standards of justice that were understood the world over. The peacekeeper's weapon was not the rifle slung over the shoulder but his credibility; the peacekeeper represented a world community of states and the Security Council's will for peace. After Rwanda that symbol may have been irreparably tarnished. Certainly it will take enormous effort for it ever to regain its potency. That is not to denigrate the individual soldiers of UNAMIR, although criticism was frequent throughout the genocide, and is common today.[25]

This is to lose sight of the remarkable and heroic efforts made by some of the peacekeepers. Jean-Hervé Bradol, MSF, has described how in Kigali, despite the danger to their own lives, peacekeepers had tried to bring help to threatened civilians. James Orbinksi, MSF, paid tribute to their courage and that of their commander. Gerry McCarthy, UNICEF, thought that in the entire UN, Dallaire was the one shining beacon.[26]

Not everyone betrayed the people of Rwanda. The steadfastness of the Ghanaian government allowed its troops to stay, saving UNAMIR from certain collapse. Other countries allowed their soldiers – all volunteers – to stay in Rwanda.[27] Without the Canadian government providing a C-130 for logistics and medical evacuation, the small mission would have been forced to withdraw. There were individuals, including Philippe Gaillard, and others who worked for the ICRC, MSF, and the joint UN–Agency cell, who took extraordinary risks to provide a drop of humanity. It remains incredible to Dallaire that people had been massacred in their thousands almost every day and yet the world remained impassive.

In Rwanda, the anger and bitterness against the UN will last for decades. Hundreds of thousands of victims of genocide had thought that with the UN in their country they would be safe. But in the end the barbarians were allowed to triumph. There is nothing the West can say now to the people of Rwanda to compensate for the failure to intervene in their hour of need. That this genocide should have happened in the dying years of a century already stained by genocide makes it even harder to comprehend.

Only by revealing the failures, both individual and organizational, that permitted it, can any good emerge from something so bleak and so terrible. Only by exposing how and why it happened can there ever be any hope that the new century will break with the dismal record of the last.

Notes

1. Commission on Human Rights. Report on the situation of human rights in Rwanda submitted by Mr. R. Degni-Ségui, Special Rapporteur of the Commission on Human Rights, 28 June 1994.

2. Security Council Resolution 935 of 1 July 1994 mandated the creation of an impartial commission of experts to examine and analyse information concerning serious violations of international law, including genocide. The experts were Astu-Koffi Amega, a former president of the Supreme Court of Togo; Habi Dieng, a former attorney-general of Guinea; Salifou Fomba, a law professor in Mali who was a member of the UN International Law Commission.

3. UN Security Council, The Interim Report of the Commission of Experts on the evidence of grave violations of the international humanitarian law in Rwanda, including possible acts of genocide. UN Document: S/1994/1125, 4 October 1994.

4. The inquiry consisted of a three-man panel headed by Ingvar Carlsson, former prime minister of Sweden, with Han Sung-Joo, former foreign minister of the Republic of Korea, and Lieutenant-General Rufus Kupolati of Nigeria, the former head of the UN Truce Supervision Organization (UNTSO) in Jerusalem.

5. Interview, Boutros Boutros-Ghali, Paris, December 1999.

6. Boutros Boutros-Ghali, *Unvanquished. A US–UN Saga*, London: I.B.Tauris, 1999, p. 140.

7. Interview, Boutros Boutros-Ghali, December 1999.

8. New Zealand Mission to the UN, Statement on 'The Security Council Role in the Rwanda Crisis', by Ambassador Colin Keating, Permanent Representative of New Zealand to the UN, at the Comprehensive Seminar on Lessons Learned from UN Assistance Mission for Rwanda (UMAMIR). 12 June 1996. Unpublished. Copy in possession of the author.

9. Statement of New Zealand to Open-Ended Working Group on the Question of Equitable Representation on and Increase in the Membership of the Security Council. April 1994. Unpublished. Copy in possession of author. Interview, Colin Keating on UN reform, 16 January 1996.

10. A description of what happened within the administration Washington can be found in Holly J. Burkhalter, 'The Question of Genocide. The Clinton Administration and Rwanda', *World Policy Journal*, Vol. 11, No. 4, Winter 1994–95.

11. 'This Week' with David Brinkley, 24 July 1994. Transcript 665. Quoted in Susan D. Moeller, *Compassion Fatigue*, New York and London: Routledge, 1999, p. 296.

12. Excerpts from the interviews on Frontline's website for 'The Triumph of Evil'. www.pbs.org/WGBH/Pages/Frontline/shows/evil. Copyright WGBH/Frontline, 1999.

13. *The International Response to Conflict and Genocide. Lessons from the Rwada Experience.* Joint Evaluation of Emergency Assistance to Rwanda. Copenhagen, March 1996, study 1, fn 101.

14. Interview with Sir David Hannay, London, December 1999.

15. Misha Glenny, 'War Radio', BBC Radio 4, 10 December 1998.

16. This was repeated in the House of Commons on 14 June when, in a written answer, Douglas Hogg claimed that the UK government had not been asked to contribute troops to the UN peacekeeping operation in Rwanda.

17. Interview, Major-General Roméo Dallaire, November 1994.

18. Written answers, House of Commons, 21 July 1994. p. 473.

19. Telex de l'ambassadeur Swinnen du 27 Mars, 1992 in Belgian Senate, *Commission*

d'enquête parlementaire concernant les événements du Rwanda. Report, 6 December 1997, pp. 493–4.

20. Interviews, DPKO, New York, July 1994.

21. Interview, DPKO, 29 March 1996.

22. Interview, Kofi Annan, May 1996.

23. 'Kofi Annan accepte un enquête sur son rôle au Rwanda', *Le Soir*, 27 January 1999.

24. Interview, Kofi Annan, July 1994.

25. An American journalist, Philip Gourevitch, has written how in the summer of 1994 UN troops had killed the dogs feeding off the corpses. Gourevitch noted: 'After months during which Rwandans had been left to wonder whether the UN troops knew how to shoot, because they never used their excellent weapons to stop the extermination of civilians, it turned out that the peacekeepers were very good shots.' Philip Gourevitch, *We wish to inform you that tomorrow we will be killed with our families*, London: Picador, 1998, p. 148.

26. The Canadian government awarded Dallaire the Meritorious Service Cross.

27. Those who stayed behind with Dallaire were, on 25 May 1994, as follows: Ghana 334, Tunisia 40, Canada 11, Togo 18, Senegal 12, Bangladesh 11, Zimbabwe 8, Mali 9, Austria 7, Congo 7, Nigeria 7, Russia 4, Poland 3, Egypt 2, Malawi 2, Fiji 1.

Chronology

1500 It is believed that from 1506 there was increasing unification of the kingdom of Rwanda. A society was created which would be compared with those in European feudal states.

1885 The Berlin Conference agrees that Ruanda-Urundi should become a German protectorate.

1894 The first European, a German, Count Gustav Adolf von Götzen, arrives in Rwanda.

1900 The Missionaries of Africa (White Fathers) found their first mission in Rwanda.

1907 The Germans establish a post in Kigali and a prominent explorer, Richard Kandt, is appointed the first Resident.

1910 The frontiers of the Belgian Congo, British Uganda and German East Africa – including Ruanda-Urundi – are fixed at a conference in Brussels.

1911 A popular uprising in northern Rwanda is crushed by the German Schutztruppe and Tutsi chiefs, leaving bitterness among northern Hutu.

1913 Coffee introduced as a cash crop.

1914 German control strengthens with the introduction of a head tax.

1916 Belgian troops chase out the Germans and occupy both Ruanda and Urundi.

1923 Ruanda-Urundi becomes a mandated territory of the League of Nations under the supervision of Belgium.

1931 *November* King Musinga is deposed by the Belgian administration and replaced with one of his sons.

1933 The Belgian administrators organize a census and everyone is issued with an identity card classifying everyone as Hutu, Tutsi or Twa.

1945 Transfer of the Belgian mandate to a UN Trust Territory.

1946 Dedication of Rwanda to Christ the King.

1948 The Convention on the Punishment and the Prevention of the Crime of Genocide, 1948 voted by the General Assembly on 9 December.

First UN Trusteeship Council visiting missions goes to Ruanda-Urundi and Tanganyika.

1957 Publication of the Hutu Manifesto.

1959 *July* King Mutara Rudahigwa dies in suspicious circumstances.

August–September Political parties are created.

November The Hutus rebel, supported by Belgium, and thousands of Tutsi flee for their lives to Burundi.

Belgium places Rwanda under military rule.

Hutu now favoured by Belgian administrators.

1960 Rwanda's first municipal elections give Hutu a large majority.

1961 *January* The monarchy is formally abolished by a referendum and a republic is proclaimed.

A new wave of violence against the Tutsi. More people flee the country.

1962 Armed attacks by Tutsi exiles from Burundi. There are internal reprisals and 2,000 Tutsi are killed.

Proclamation of the independence of Rwanda.

Gregoire Kayibanda is declared president.

1963 Further armed attacks from Tutsi.

Violence against Tutsi escalates and there are further massacres of Tutsi. A new wave of refugees.

1964 British philosopher Lord Bertrand Russell calls the killing of Tutsi in Rwanda the most horrible extermination of a people since the killing of the Jews.

UN report by Max Dorsinville estimates a few hundred killed and repeats government claims that the culprits will be punished.

1967 Renewed massacres of Tutsi.

1972 Massacres of Hutu in Burundi.

Tutsi are purged from the administration in Rwanda.

1973 A purge of Tutsi from schools and the National University of Rwanda, Butare. More killings of Tutsi.

Coup d'état by Major Juvénal Habyarimana.

1975 Creation of the one-party MRND. France and Rwanda sign a military assistance agreement.

1978 Habyarimana promulgates a new constitution and becomes president of Rwanda after an election in which he is the sole candidate. Hutus are favoured in government.

1979 The Rwandan Alliance for National Unity (RANU) is created in Kenya.

1980 An attempted coup by Colonel Théoneste Lizinde, ex-security chief, and thirty conspirators.

1982 The Rwandan refugee communities in Uganda are attacked. Those who flee to the border are trapped.

1983 Re-election of President Juvénal Habyarimana with 99.98 per cent of the vote.

1986 The government in Kigali announces that Rwandan refugees will not be allowed home because the country is not big enough.

1987 *1 July* Celebrations for twenty-five years of independence.

1988 International conference held by Rwandan refugees in Washington, DC. The RPF is created in Uganda.

Re-election of Habyarimana with more than 99 per cent of the vote.

1989 First meeting of a Rwanda–Uganda ministerial committee to discuss the refugee problem.

The price of coffee collapses.

1990 *July* Habyarimana concedes the principle of multi-party democracy.

September Thirty-three intellectuals publish a letter to denounce the one-party system.

Pope Jean Paul II visits Rwanda.

October The RPF invades Rwanda, starting a civil war. France, Belgium and Zaire send troops.

Rwanda's ambassador to Egypt requests Boutros Boutros-Ghali, minister of state, to help Rwanda obtain arms.

First Egyptian weapons sold to Rwanda.

South Africa starts to sell arms to Rwanda.

Thousands of people, most of them Tutsi, are arrested in Rwanda.

More than 300 Tutsi are killed in Gisenyi.

Structural adjustment programme (SAP) for Rwanda is agreed.

1991 *January* RPF attack Ruhengeri prison.

Massacres of Tutsi take place in the prefectures of Gisenyi, Ruhengeri, Kibuye and Byumba.

A further arms deal is concluded with Egypt.

February Guerrilla attack by RPF in response to massacres.

Summit in Dar-es-Salaam to discuss Rwanda crisis.

March A ceasefire agreement is signed in N'sele, Zaire, under OAU supervision, between the Rwandan government and the RPF but it soon breaks down.

A further arms deal is concluded between Egypt and the Rwandan government.

April A further arms deal is concluded between Egypt and the Rwandan government.

June New constitution adopted bringing in multi-partyism.

A French intelligence report warns that an extremist group surrounding Agathe Habyarimana is encouraging ethnic hatred and is determined to resist democracy.

August Creation of political parties, the MDR, PSD, PL.

September The OAU creates a Neutral Military Observer Group (NMOG) to monitor the border between Rwanda and Uganda.

November A demonstration organized by government opposition brings thousands onto the streets of Kigali.

1992 Boutros Boutros-Ghali takes office as the sixth Secretary-General of the UN.

The UN Security Council meets at summit level for the first time and western leaders promise to equip the UN to deal with crisis prevention.

On and off talks continue between the Rwanda government and the RPF at various locations for over a year and another ceasefire is signed; this one is largely observed.

Assistant secretary of state for Africa, Herman Cohen, convenes an inter-agency forum in Washington to discuss Rwanda.

February Massacres of Tutsi take place in the Bugesera. Radio Rwanda is blamed for incitement by human rights groups.

CDR and MRND militias are built up by Hutu Power supporters.

March Rwandan human rights group link deaths in the Bugesera to local officials.

A further arms deal is concluded between Egypt and the Rwandan government.

April A new government with an increased representation of the opposition.

The president of the World Bank, Lewis Preston, writes to Habyarimana to ask him to stop military spending.

May Violent demonstrations by militia.

Agathe Uwilingiyimana, minister of education, attacked in her home.

Pitched battles between supports of the MRNDD and the PL.

The RPF meets with the OAU in Kampala.

June A further arms deal is concluded between Egypt and the Rwandan government.

August A defector, Christophe Mfizi, reveals that Rwanda is run by a ruthless and greedy oligarchy from the north.

Formal opening of the peace conference in Arusha, Tanzania.

October Professor Filip Reyntjens gives a press conference in Brussels to warn of death squads in Rwanda.

November The planning for a new radio station begins.

Political violence. Hutu extremist militia escalates. Government opponents continue to demonstrate.

Prominent Hutu Dr Leon Mugesera appeals to Hutus to send the Tutsi back to Ethiopia via the rivers.

A further arms deal is concluded between Egypt and the Rwandan government.

December US troops storm Somali beaches – a ground-breaking humanitarian intervention.

1993 *January* The composition of a broad-based transitional government is agreed at the negotiations at Arusha.

More than 300 Tutsi killed in the north-west.

International human rights experts visit Rwanda.

Weapons are distributed to communal police in certain communes.

February RPF launches a fresh offensive and their soldiers reach the outskirts of Kigali. French forces again called in to help.

More than one million people displaced because of the fighting.

March A new ceasefire is agreed.

At the UN Security Council in New York, France suggests the creation of a UN peacekeeping mission for Rwanda.

A human rights report is published revealing that 2,000 Tutsi have been killed since 1990.

A further arms deal is concluded between Egypt and the Rwandan government.

The Security Council passes resolution 814 to restore law and order in Somalia.

April The ICRC warns that because of the displaced people in Rwanda there is the risk of a major humanitarian catastrophe. Famine is imminent.

UN Human Rights Commission, Special Rapporteur on Extrajudicial, Summary or Arbitrary Executions, Bacre Waly Ndiaye, visits Rwanda.

May The Habyarimana regime enters into an arms deal for US$12 million with a French arms dealer.

The Secretary General, in a report to the Security Council, recommends the creation of a UN observer mission for the Rwanda–Uganda border.

June The Security Council adopts resolution 846 creating the United Nations Observer Mission Uganda–Rwanda (UNOMUR).

Brigadier-General Roméo A. Dallaire appointed commander of UNOMUR.

In Somalia twenty-three Pakistani UN peacekeepers are killed during a weapons inspection in Mogadishu.

July A new government is formed with Agathe Uwilingiyimana as prime minister. This results in divisions in within the MDR.

August The Arusha Accords are signed between the Rwandan government and the RPF. Multi-party elections, which are to include the RPF, are scheduled to be held within twenty-two months.

Dallaire arrives in Kigali with a reconnaissance mission to evaluate the possible role of international peacekeepers.

Bacre Waly Ndiaye publishes a report for the UN Human Rights Commission which reveals that in Rwanda the Convention on the Prevention and Punishment of the Crime of Genocide, 1948, is applicable.

September The Secretary-General recommends to the Security Council that a peacekeeping force be provided for Rwanda without delay.

October Eighteen elite US troops are killed in Somalia.

The US Security Council passes resolution 872 creating the UN Assistance

Mission for Rwanda (UNAMIR) which is to help to implement the Arusha Accords. UNOMUR is integrated into UNAMIR.

Dallaire is appointed force commander of UNAMIR.

The Hutu President Melchior Ndadaye is killed in Burundi. Thousands of people flee from Burundi to Rwanda.

Political violence in Rwanda escalates.

November The Organization of African Unity (OAU) Neutral Military Observer Group (NMOG) is integrated into UNAMIR.

The Belgian battalion arrives in Kigali.

The Secretary-General's special representative, Jacques-Roger Booh-Booh, arrives.

A series of killings takes place in northern communes.

December UNAMIR peacekeepers are in place in Rwanda. As part of the Arusha Accords a contingent of RPF troops is deployed in Kigali.

French troops withdraw. A few remain.

Diplomats in Kigali and Dallaire receive an anonymous letter from within the Rwandan army warning of a plan to kill Tutsi in order to prevent the implementation of the Arusha Accords.

1994 *January* Rwanda takes its seat as a non-permanent member of the Security Council.

The Security Council adopts resolution 893 approving deployment of a second infantry battalion to the de-militarized zone.

Investiture of Habyarimana as president.

Transitional government fails to take off, with each side blaming the other for blocking its formation.

Human Rights Watch Arms Project publishes a report on the continuing arming of Rwanda.

The Belgian ambassador in Kigali, Johan Swinnen, warns Brussels that the new hate-radio is destabilizing Rwanda.

Violent demonstration in Kigali by the Interahamwe.

The CIA reports that if hostilities resume in Rwanda up to half a million people could die.

Dallaire informs UN headquarters there is an informer from the heart of Hutu Power who warns that a genocide against the Tutsi is planned.

Dallaire tries to persuade UN headquarters that he be allowed to conduct arms seizures.

February Félicien Gatabazi of the PSD assassinated. Martin Bucyana, the president of the CDR, lynched.

Dallaire warns New York of the deteriorating situation, of weapons distribution, death squad target lists, and pleads for reinforcements.

USA issues a travel advisory for Rwanda.

The ICRC and MSF stockpile medicines and prepare for large numbers of casualties.

Belgian Foreign Minister Will Claes visits Rwanda. Warns Boutros-Ghali that Dallaire needs a stronger mandate. Claes warns the USA that Habyarimana could be playing a double game.

March A joint communiqué is issued by Kigali diplomatic community asking for acceptance of the CDR.

Boutros-Ghali writes a report to the Security Council that the security situation is deteriorating and requests an extension of the mandate of UNAMIR for six months.

2 April Booh-Booh threatens that the UN will pull out unless the peace agreement is implemented.

5 April The Security Council, with resolution 909, renews the mandate for UNAMIR with a threat to pull out in six weeks unless the Arusha Accords are applied.

6 April President Habyarimana and President Ntaryamira of Burundi and a number of government officials returning from negotiations in Tanzania are killed when the plane in which they are travelling is shot out of the sky on its approach to Kigali airport.

7 April Systematic killing begins of opposition politicians, pro-democracy Hutu and Tutsi.

Ten peacekeepers guarding the prime minister are killed in a Rwandan army barracks in Kigali.

RPF troops in Kigali engage Presidential Guard.

Armed militias begin an organized round-up and slaughter of Tutsis and political moderates in Kigali. The violence escalates and spreads.

RTLMC broadcasts that the RPF and the Belgian peacekeepers are responsible for the death of the president.

8 April Telephone lines are progressively cut.

Increasing numbers of people are killed.

Former parliament speaker Théodore Sindikubwabo announces the formation of an interim government and declares himself president.

9 April Interahamwe and Presidential Guard conduct massacre at Gikondo. Evacuation starts of foreign nationals.

The RPF leaves its northern bases and attacks Byumba and Ruhengeri.

Sindikubwabo meets Dallaire and asks him to negotiate a ceasefire with the RPF.

10 April Prisoners are put to work with dust carts picking up bodies.

Ambassador David Rawson closes the US embassy in Kigali.

Massacre at Gikondo.

11 April Dallaire obtains a ceasefire to facilitate the evacuation of ex-pats.

The Belgian peacekeepers pull out of Kicukiro leaving behind 2,000 people.

12 April French embassy closes its doors.

The interim government flees to Gitarama as the RPF moves on the capital.

Claes meets Boutros-Ghali in Bonn to tell him that Belgium is withdrawing soldiers from UNAMIR.

13 April ICRC–MSF convoy arrives in Kigali from Bujumbura with doctors and medicines.

14 April Belgian announces it is withdrawing its troops from UNAMIR.

In Kigali wounded are dragged from a Red Cross ambulance and killed.

18 April An attempt by the RPF to silence RTLMC fails.

The interim government dismisses the prefect of Butare.

19 April The last Belgian peacekeepers leave Kigali.

20 April The last Belgian peacekeeper leaves Rwanda.

21 April The UN Security Council votes resolution 912 to withdraw the bulk of UNAMIR peacekeepers from Rwanda, authorizing 270 to remain.

The RPF takes Byumba.

22 April The Security Council votes to withdraw most peacekeepers.

A second ICRC road convoy reaches Kigali from Burundi.

24 April MSF pulls its medical team from Butare.

Oxfam emergencies officer Maurice Herson telephones Oxfam headquarters to say that genocide of the Tutsi is taking place in Rwanda.

28 April Oxfam issues a press release that the killing in Rwanda amounts to genocide.

28–29 April An estimated 250,000 people stream across the Rwandan border into Tanzania. This is reportedly the largest mass exodus of people ever witnessed by the UNHCR.

29 April A long Security Council debate to discuss the use of the word genocide in a presidential statement. The UK and USA resist the use of the word.

The Secretary-General asks the Security Council to re-examine its decision to reduce UNAMIR.

30 April The RPF takes the Tanzanian border town of Rusumo.

1 May Rwanda is on top of news schedules due to massive exodus of Rwandans into Tanzania.

4 May Boutros-Ghali appears on ABC *Nightline* and says that it is a question of genocide in Rwanda.

5 May The PDD25 presidential directive on peacekeeping is launched.

In Kampala, Museveni accuses the interim government of Rwanda of genocide.

6 May UN human rights commissioner, José Ayala Lasso, says he is going to Rwanda.

13 May Boutros-Ghali suggests to the council Dallaire's original plan to airlift 5,500 troops to Kigali.

Dallaire speaks with Senators Paul Simon and James Jeffords, who write to the White House.

16 May The RPF cuts the road between Kigali and Gitarama.

17 May The Security Council votes resolution 918 approving the deployment of 5,500 troops to Rwanda but no troops are available.

19 May Lasso produces a report which calls Rwanda a human rights tragedy.

21 May An ICRC convoy with medical aid reaches Kigali.

22 May The RPF takes control of the airport and the Kanombe military camp and extends control over the north and eastern part of the country. The government forces continue to flee south in front of an RPF advance.

22–27 May Under-secretary-general Iqbal Riza and the Secretary-General's military adviser, Major-General J. Maurice Baril, visit Rwanda.

23 May The RPF overruns the presidential palace.

24 May The UN Commission on Human Rights holds its third special session to discuss human rights violations in Rwanda.

25 May The UN Commission on Human Rights appoints René Dégni-Ségui as special human rights envoy to Rwanda.

Ghana, Ethiopia and Senegal make a firm commitment to provide 800 troops each to the UN efforts. Zimbabwe and Nigeria make similar commitments soon after.

29 May The RPF takes Nyanza.

31 May The Secretary-General reports to the Council on the special mission by Riza and Baril, recommending that the Council authorize an expanded mandate for UNAMIR.

2 June The RPF takes Kabgayi.

5 June The Canadian relief flight is forced to stop flying relief supplies into Kigali due to heavy fighting around the airport.

6 June Opening of the thirtieth OAU summit in Carthage, Tunisia. The Rwandan government army launch their last major attack against RPF troops in the region of Kabgayi.

8 June The Security Council adopts resolution 925, which extends the UNAMIR mandate until December 1994.

10 June Some members of the interim government leave Gitarama for Gisenyi

11 June Special rapporteur Dégni-Ségui begins a week-long field mission to Rwanda to investigate violations of human rights.

13 June The RPF takes Gitarama.

17 June France announces its plan to the UN Security Council to deploy troops to Rwanda as an interim peacekeeping force. The Secretary-General and the USA support the idea.

21 June First French troops arrive on the Zaire–Rwanda border.

22 June The UN Security Council, in resolution 929, approves the French proposal to dispatch troops to Rwanda under a UN peacekeeping mission.

24 June French military forces are deployed into eastern Rwanda through Goma and Bukavu in eastern Zaire.

28 June The report of the UN Commission on Human Rights Special Rapporteur is published in Geneva stating that the massacres that occurred throughout Rwanda were pre-planned and a systematic campaign of genocide.

1 July Security Council sets up a commission of experts to investigate acts of genocide in Rwanda.

Booh-Booh is replace by Mohamed Shaharyar Khan of Pakistan as special representative.

2 July Boutros-Ghali supports the French proposal for a designated 'safe zone' in south-western Rwanda to protect vulnerable populations in the region.

3 July The RPF takes Butare.

4 July The RPF wins control of Kigali. The RPF leadership states that it intends to establish a new government based on the framework of the Arusha Accords.

5 July The French establish a humanitarian zone in the south-west corner of the country

6 July Canadian relief flights into Kigali are resumed.

7 July Kigali airport reopens.

13 July Ruhengeri is captured by the RPF.

13–14 July An estimated 1 million people begin to flee towards Zaire.

14 July An estimated 6,000 people per hour file into the French safe zone, including members of the militia and interim government officials.

15 July The Clinton administration publicly declares that it no longer recognizes the interim government of Rwanda.

16 July Thirteen ministers of the interim government take refuge in the French safe zone.

17 July The RPF takes Gisenyi, the last Rwandan stronghold of Hutu Power.

18 July The war comes to an end with the RPF defeat of the remnants of Rwandan government troops still in Rwanda.

19 July A new government of national unity is created and announces the end of compulsory identity cards.

22 July Clinton announces that US troops will be deployed to help the refugees.

16 August Dallaire leaves Rwanda. Canadian General Guy Tousignant takes command of UNAMIR, which has 1,624 soldiers.

October An interim report is produced by the Commission of Experts which concludes that a genocide had taken place against the Tutsi.

November UN Security Council adopts resolution 955 on the establishment of an international criminal court for the criminals of Rwanda.

Appendix 1

Background to the Genocide Convention

The Convention on the Punishment and the Prevention of the Crime of Genocide of 1948 was the world's first human rights treaty and it stood for a fundamental and important principle: that whatever evil may befall any group or nation or people, it was of concern not just for that group, but for the whole of humanity. The Convention preceded the Universal Declaration of Human Rights by twenty-four hours and it was the first truly universal, comprehensive and codified protection of human rights. While the Universal Declaration was an affirmation of human rights, the Genocide Convention was a treaty, providing for the judgement and punishment of transgressors. Genocide was legally the gravest violation of human rights it was possible to commit. In the Genocide Convention was enshrined the never-again promise, the world's response to the Nazi Holocaust in Europe and the revulsion at the unspeakable truth of the systematic policy to exterminate the Jews.[1]

Genocide is an attempt to reconstruct the world. The Nazis tried to do it and murdered Jews, intending to exterminate them as people. Nazism used a racist ideology which identified the German people as possessing a distinct identity which was based on blood. Jews, Gypsies and homosexuals were inferior and alien beings who might pollute the people. In genocide, propaganda is used to spread racist ideology and define the victim as being outside human existence – vermin and subhuman. This ideology served to legitimize any act, no matter how horrendous.

The word genocide was coined by a Polish lawyer, Raphael Lemkin, who fled the German occupation and lost his family in the Holocaust. He derived the word from the Greek *genos*, race, or tribe. 'Genocide is intended ... to signify a co-ordinated plan of different actions,' Lemkin wrote, 'aiming at the destruction of essential foundations of the life of national groups, with the aim of annihilating the groups themselves.' Genocide was directed against national groups as an entity, and the actions involved were directed against individuals, not in their individual capacity, but as members of the national group. Lemkin's definition of genocide was published in 1944 before the end of the Second World War in his book, *Axis Rule in Central Europe*.[1] Lemkin was already an expert on the circumstances of the genocide against the Armenians and he had been struck by the universal indifference to the Armenian slaughter, an attitude which he believed had served to encourage Hitler. On 22 August 1939 Hitler addressed his military commanders, a few days before the German attack on Poland, saying that he had placed his formations in readiness 'with orders ... to send to death mercilessly and without compassion, men, women and children of Polish derivation and language. Only thus shall we gain the living space that we need. Who, after all, speaks today of the Armenians?'[2] The world had overlooked the Armenian genocide. It had taken place in a remote part of the world, and there were few accounts written of it, publicized and communicated to the world. It did not attract much attention from writers and intellectuals.

'Genocide is a part of history; it follows humanity like a dark shadow from early antiquity to the present time,' wrote Lemkin. Lemkin believed that genocide could be predicted and that, with an international early-warning system, it was preventable. The more extreme the racism, Lemkin argued, the more likely a genocide. It was Lemkin's definition of genocide that was written into the Genocide Convention and unanimously accepted in 1948 by the UN General Assembly. Lemkin believed that without the protection of international law, no people on earth could be sure of continued existence.

Notes

1. Raphael Lemkin, *Axis Rule in Occupied Europe. Laws of Occupation, Analysis of Government, Proposals for Redress*, Washington, DC: Carnegie Endowment for International Peace, 1944.
2. Michael J. Marrus, *The Holocaust in History*, Harmondsworth: Penguin, 1993.

Appendix 2

Convention on the Prevention and Punishment of the Crime of Genocide, 1948

The Contracting Parties,

Having considered the declaration made by the General Assembly of the United Nations in its resolution of 96 (I) dated 11 December 1946 that genocide is a crime under international law, contrary to the spirit and aims of the United Nations and condemned by the civilized world:

Recognizing that at all periods of history genocide has inflicted great losses on humanity; and

Being convinced that, in order to liberate mankind from such an odious scourge, international co-operation is required,

Hereby agree as hereinafter provided:

Article I

The Contracting Parties confirm that genocide, whether committed in time of peace or in time of war, is a crime under international law which they undertake to prevent and to punish.

Article II

In the present Convention, genocide means any of the following acts committed with intent to destroy in whole or in part, a national, ethnical, racial or religious group, as such:

a) Killing members of the group;
b) Causing serious bodily or mental harm to members of the group;
c) Deliberately inflicting on the group conditions of life calculated to bring about its physical destruction in whole or in part;
d) Imposing measures intended to prevent births within the group;
e) Forcibly transferring children of the group to another group.

Article III

The following acts shall be punishable:

a) Genocide;
b) Conspiracy to commit genocide;
c) Direct and public incitement to commit genocide;
d) Attempt to commit genocide;
e) Complicity in genocide.

Article IV

Persons committing genocide or any of the other acts enumerated in Article III shall be punished, whether they are constitutional responsible rulers, public officials or private individuals.

Article V

The Contracting Parties undertake to enact, in accordance with their respective Constitutions, the necessary legislation to give effect to the provisions of the present Convention and, in particular, to provide effective penalties for persons guilty of genocide or of any of the other acts enumerated in Article III

Article VI

Persons charged with genocide or any of the other acts enumerated in Article III shall be tried by a competent tribunal of the State in the territory of which the act was committed, or by such international penal tribunal as may have jurisdiction with respect to those Contracting Parties which shall have accepted its jurisdictions.

Article VII

Genocide and the other acts enumerated in Article III shall not be considered as political crimes for the purpose of extradition.

The Contracting Parties pledge themselves in such cases to grant extradition in accordance with their laws and treaties in force.

Article VIII

Any Contracting Party may call upon the competent organs of the United Nations to take such action under the Charter of the United Nations as they consider appropriate for the prevention and suppression of acts of genocide or any of the other acts enumerated in Article III.

Article IX

Disputes between the Contracting Parties relating to the interpretation, application or fulfilment of the present Convention, including those relating to the responsibility of a State for genocide or for any of the other acts enumerated in Article III, shall be submitted to the International Court of Justice at the request of any of the parties to the dispute.

Article X

The present Convention, of which the Chinese, English, French, Russian and Spanish texts are equally authentic, shall bear the date of 9 December 1948.

Article XI

The Present Convention shall be open until 31 December 1949 for signature on behalf of any Member of the United Nations and of any non-member State to which an invitation to sign has been addressed by the General Assembly.

The present Convention shall be ratified, and the instruments of ratification shall be deposited with the Secretary-General of the United Nations.

After 1 January 1950 the present Convention may be acceded to on behalf of any Member of the United Nations and of any non-member State which has received an invitation as aforesaid.

Instruments of accession shall be deposited with the Secretary-General of the United Nations.

Article XII

Any Contracting Party may at any time, by notification addressed to the Secretary-General of the United Nations, extend the application of the present Convention to all or any of the territories for the conduct of whose foreign relations that Contracting Party is responsible.

Article XIII

On the day when the first twenty instruments of ratification or accession have been deposited, the Secretary-General shall draw up a *procès-verbal* and transmit a copy thereof to each Member of the United Nations and to each of the non-member States contemplated in Article XI.

The present Convention shall come into force on the twentieth day following the date of deposit of the twentieth instrument of ratification or accession.

Any ratification or accession effected subsequent to the latter date shall become effective on the ninetieth day following the deposit of the instrument of ratification or access.

Article XIV

The present Convention shall remain in effect for a period of ten years as from the date of its coming into force.

It shall thereafter remain in force for successive periods of five years for such Contracting Parties as have not denounced it at lease six months before the expiration of the current period.

Denunciation shall be effected by a written notification addressed to the Secretary-General of the United Nations.

Article XV

If, as a result of denunciations, the number of Parties to the present Convention should become less than sixteen, the Convention shall cease to be in force as from the date on which the last of these denunciations shall become effective.

Article XVI

A request for the revision of the present Convention may be made any time by a Contracting Party by means of a notification in writing addressed to the Secretary-General.

The General Assembly shall decide upon the steps, if any, to be taken in respect of such request.

Article XVII

The Secretary-General of the United Nations shall notify all Members of the United Nations and the non-member States contemplated in Article XI of the following:

a) Signatures, ratification and accessions received in accordance with Article XI;
b) Notifications received in accordance with Article XII;
c) The date upon which the present Convention comes into force in accordance with Article XIII;
d) Denunciations received in accordance with Article XIV;
e) The abrogation of the Convention in accordance with Article XV;
f) Notification received in accordance with Article XVI.

Article XVIII

The original of the present Convention shall be deposited in the archives of the United Nations.

A certified copy of the Convention shall be transmitted to each Member of the United Nations and to each of the non-member States contemplated in Article XI.

Article XIX

The present Convention shall be registered by the Secretary-General of the United Nations on the date of its coming into force.

Sources

The documents obtained during the research for this book are to be placed in a special collection in the Hugh Owen Library at the University of Wales, Aberystwyth. This archive, the Linda Melvern Rwanda archive, will be made available to journalists and researchers. The archive is to be copied and placed in a special collection in the library of the National University of Rwanda, Butare. The archive will include the arms contracts and related correspondence; the minutes of the Security Council's informal and secret deliberations and other unpublished internal UN documents and letters; the Dallaire cables mentioned in the text; the RPF press releases, 1993–94; the correspondence and reports, 1990–94, from G2, military intelligence, the Rwandan government army; the lists of 'reservists', their names and communes, for the 'popular defence' of Kigali; the statute and the list of shareholders of RTLMC; the report of a government investigation into how the genocide was planned and financed based on invoices, import licences, bank transfers, all relevant correspondence, and internal reports of the Banque Nationale du Rwanda; the 1995 plans of Hutu Power to continue the genocide, and to invade Rwanda; the writings of Théoneste Bagosora.

United Nations books and documents

General Assembly

Trusteeship agreement for the Territory of Ruanda-Urundi. As approved by the General Assembly on December 13, 1946.

Report of the Trusteeship Council to the General Assembly. Official Records: Thirteenth Session. Supplement No. 4 (A/1306) 1949.

Report of the Trusteeship Council to the General Assembly. Official Records: Third/Eighth and Ninth Sessions (A/1856) 1951.

Report of the Trusteeship Council to the General Assembly. Official Records: Fourth/Tenth and Eleventh Sessions (A/2150) 1952.

Report of the Trusteeship Council to the General Assembly. Official Records: Ninth Session. Supplement No. 4 (A/2680) 1954.

Report of the Trusteeship Council to the General Assembly. Official Records: Thirteenth Session. Supplement No. 4 (A/3822) 1958.

Report of the Trusteeship Council to the General Assembly. Official Records: Fifteenth Session. Supplement No. 4 (A/4404) 1959.

Report of the Trusteeship Council to the General Assembly. Official Records: Seventeenth Session. Supplement No. 4 (A/5204) 1962.

Question of the Future of Ruanda-Urundi. Report of the United Nations Commission for Ruanda-Urundi established under General Assembly resolution 1743 (XVI) (A/5126), 30 May 1962.

An Agenda for Peace: Preventive Diplomacy, Peacemaking and Peacekeeping. Report of the Secretary-General pursuant to the statement adopted by the Summit Meeting of the Security Council on January 31, 1992 (A/47/277 – S/24111) 17 June 1992.

Effective Planning, Budgeting and Administration of Peace-keeping Operations. Report of the Secretary-General (A/48/1994) 25 May 1994.

Trusteeship Council

Report of the Visiting Mission to the Trust Territory of Ruanda-Urundi under Belgian Administration (T/217), 31 October 1948.

United Nations Visiting Mission to Trust Territories in East Africa, 1957. Report on Ruanda-Urundi (T/1346) 4 December 1957.

Rural economic development of the Trust Territories. Report submitted by the Food and Agriculture Organization concerning land tenure and land use problems in the Trust Territories of Tanganyika and Ruanda-Urundi (T/1438) 19 February 1959.

United Nations Visiting Mission to Trust Territories in East Africa, 1960. Report on Ruanda-Urundi (T/1538) 2 June 1960.

Economic and Social Council. Commission on Human Rights

Report by Mr. B.W. Ndiaye, Special Rapporteur, on his mission to Rwanda from 8–17 April, 1993 (E/CN.4/1994/7/Add.1) 11 August 1993.

Report of the United Nations High Commissioner for Human Rights, Mr. José Ayala Lasso, on his mission to Rwanda 11–12 May, 1994 (E/CN.4/S-3/3) 19 May 1994.

Revised and updated report on the question of the prevention and punishment of the crime of genocide. B. Whitaker (E/CN.4/1985/6) 2 July 1985.

Report on the situation of human rights in Rwanda submitted by Mr. René Dégni-Ségui, Special Rapporteur, under paragraph 20 of resolution S-3/1 of 25 May, 1994 (E/CN.4/1995/7) 28 June 1994. Further reports: 12 August 1994 (E/CN.4/1995/12) and 11 November 1994 (E/CN.4/1995/70).

Report of the Special Rapporteur on violence against women, its causes and consequences, Ms. Radhika Coomaraswamy (E/CN.4/1998/54/Add.1) February 4, 1998.

Security Council

Somalia

Report of the Commission of Inquiry Established Pursuant to Security Council Resolution 885 (1993) To Investigate Armed Attacks on UNOSOM II Personnel Which Led To Casualties Among Them. 24 February 1994.

Rwanda

Interim report of the Commission of Experts established in accordance with Security Council resolution 935 (S/1994/1125) 4 October 1994.

Final report of the Commission of Experts established pursuant to Security Council resolution 935 (S/1994/1405) 9 December 1994.

First report of the International Commission of Inquiry to investigate reports of the sale or supply of arms to former Rwandan government forces in violation of the Security Council arms embargo and allegations that those forces are receiving training to destabilize Rwanda (S/1996/67) 29 January 1996.

Report of the Independent Inquiry into the Actions of the United Nations during the 1994 Genocide in Rwanda. 15 December 1999.

UNICEF

Rwanda Emergency Programme: Progress Report No. 1 / Reporting Period May 1994–March 1995. Kigali: UNICEF.

Rwanda: a phoenix arises. The United Kingdom Committee for UNICEF Annual Review 1994/1995. London: UNICEF, 1995

Cantwell, Nigel. *Starting from Zero: the Promotion and Protection of Children's Rights in Post-genocide Rwanda, July 1994–December 1996*. Florence: UNICEF and International Child Development Centre, 1997.

United Nations archives

Max Dorsinville, *Report of the Officer-in-Charge of the United Nations Operation in the Congo to the Secretary General*. 29 September 1964 (Declassified, 11 November 1999).

United Nations books

The United Nations and Rwanda, 1993–1996. The United Nations Blue Book series, Vol. 10. New York: UN Department of Public Information, 1996 (Contains all the Secretary-General's reports and letters to the Security Council in relation to UNAMIR together with all relevant resolutions.)

The Blue Helmets: A review of United Nations Peacekeeping (3rd edn). New York: UN Publications, 1996.

Comprehensive report on lessons learned from United Nations Assistance Mission for Rwanda (UNAMIR), October 1993–April 1996. New York: United Nations, 1996.

New Zealand Mission

New Zealand Mission to the UN, Statement on 'The Security Council Role in the Rwanda Crisis', by Ambassador Colin Keating, Permanent Representative of New Zealand to the UN, at the Comprehensive Seminar on Lessons Learned from UN Assistance Mission for Rwanda (UNAMIR). 12 June 1996.

US Congress

United States Congress. Committee on Foreign Affairs. House of Representatives. *The Crisis in Rwanda. Hearing before the Subcommittee on Africa*. 103rd Congress, 2nd Session, 4 May 1994.

United States Congress, Committee on International Relations, House of Representatives, *Rwanda: Genocide and the Continuing Cycle of Violence. Hearing before the*

Subcommittee on International Operations and Human Rights. 105th Congress, 2nd Session, 5 May 1998.

US Senate

United States Senate, 'Crisis in Central Africa'. Subcommittee on African Affairs of the Committee on Foreign Relations, Opening Address by the Chairman, Senator Paul Simon, 26 July 1944.

Reports

ADL, *Rapport sur les Droits de l'homme au Rwanda. September 1991–September 1992.* Kigali: Association Rwandaise pour la défense des droits de la personne et des libertés publiques (ADl), December 1992.

Amnesty International, Rwanda: Amnesty International's Concerns Since the Beginning of an Insurgency in October, 1990. March 1991 (AI Index: AFR 47/05/91).

— *Rwanda: Persecution of Tutsi Minority and Repression of Government Critics, 1990–1992.* May 1992.

— *Rwanda: Mass Murder by Government Supporters and Troops in April and May, 1994.* 23 May 1994.

— *AS Call for UN human rights action on Rwanda and Burundi.* May 1994.

Assemblée Nationale, Mission d'Information Commune, *Enquête sur la Tragédie Rwandaise (1990–1994)*, Paris.

Belgian Senate, Commission d'enquête parlementaire concernant les événements du Rwanda. Report, 6 December 1997.

Chossudovsky, Michel and Pierre Galand, *L'Usage de la Dette Extérieure du Rwanda (1990/1994) La Responsabilité des Bailleurs de Fonds. Analyse et Recommandations.* Brussels and Ottawa. Rapport Préliminaire, November 1996.

Fédération International des Droits de l'Homme (FIDH). *Rapport sur la Commission d'enquête sur les violations des droits de l'homme au Rwanda depuis le 1er October 1990.* Paris and New York.

Feil, Colonel Scott R., *Preventing Genocide. How the Use of Force Might Have Succeeded in Rwanda.* Pre-publication Draft, December 1997. New York: Carnegie Commission on Preventing Deadly Conflict.

Genocide in Rwanda. Documentation of Two Massacres during April 1994. Issue Brief, US Committee for Refugees, November 1994.

Human Rights Watch, *Genocide in Rwanda April–May 1994.* May 1994. Human Rights Watch, *Rwanda: Talking Peace and Waging War.* 27 February 1992.

Human Rights Watch, *World Report, 1994.* December 1993.

Human Rights Watch Arms Project, *Arming Rwanda. The Arms Trade and Human Rights Abuses in the Rwandan War*, Vol. 6, No. 1, January 1994.

International Federation of Human Rights (FIDH), Africa Watch, InterAfrican Union of Human Rights, and International Centre of Rights of the Person and of Democratic Development, *Report of the International Commission of Investigation of Human Rights Violations in Rwanda since October 1, 1990*, 7–21 January 1993. See also: *Report of the International Commission of Investigation on Human Rights Violations in Rwanda since October 1, 1990. January 7–21, 1993. Final Reports*, New York: Human Rights Watch/Africa, March 1993.

International Monetary Fund. *Rwanda. Briefing Paper – 1992 Article IV Consultation and Discussions on a Second Annual Arrangement under the Structural Adjustment Facility*. 14 May 1992.

The International Response to Conflict and Genocide: Lessons from the Rwanda Experience. Joint Emergency Assistance to Rwanda. Copenhagen, March 1996. Study I: 'Historical Perspective: Some Explanatory Factors', Tor Sellström and Lennart Wohlgemuth. Study II: 'Early Warning and Conflict Management', Howard Adelman. Study III: 'Humanitarian Aid and Effects', John Bourton, Emery Brusset, Alistair Hallam'. Study IV: 'Rebuilding Post-War Rwanda', Krishna Kumar, David Tardif-Douglin, Kim Maynard, Peter Manikas, Annette Sheckler and Carolyn Knapp. Synthesis Report, John Eriksson (ISBN 87 7265 335). (This study was initiated in 1995 by the Nordic countries, eventually sponsored by nineteen countries and eighteen international agencies. France withdrew its support for the report after examining the draft.)

Minear, Larry, and Philippe Guillot, *Soldiers to the Rescue. Humanitarian Lessons from Rwanda*. Paris: Development Centre of the Organization for Economic Cooperation and Development, 1996.

Reporters sans Frontières. 'Rwanda: Médias de la haine ou presse democratique?' Report of mission 16–24 September,1994.

Segal, Aaron, *Massacre in Rwanda*. Fabian Society, April 1964.

UN, *Report on the Fifth Annual Peacekeeping Mission. 3–11 November 1995*. United Nations Association of the USA, January 1996.

United Nations Association of the USA. United States Contributions to the UN. Fact Sheet. May 1994.

US Department of State. *Annual Report on Human Rights, 1993*.

Watson, Catherine, *Exile from Rwanda. Background to an Invasion*. US Committee for Refugees, Issue Paper. Washington, DC, February 1991.

Papers

Gaillard, Philippe, *Rwanda 1994: La vraie vie est absente (Arthur Rimbaud) Cycle de Conference les Mardi de Musée. M. Philippe Gaillard, délégué du CIRC, chef de délégation au Rwanda de juillet 1993 à juillet 1994*. Unpublished.

Kroslak, Daniela, *The Media in Wartime. International History and International Politics*. University of Wales, Aberystwyth, 1997. Unpublished.

— Evaluating the Moral Responsibility of France in the 1994 Rwandan Genocide. Paper presented to the 23rd annual conference of the British International Studies Association (BISA), 14–16 December 1998. Unpublished.

Mamdani, Mahmood, From Conquest to Consent as the Basis of State Formation: Reflections on Rwanda. Paper presented to the conference Crisis in the Great Lakes Region, organized by the Council for the Development of Social Research in Africa, Arusha, Tanzania, 4–7 September 1995.

Mfizi, Christophe, *'Le Réseau Zéro', Lettre Ouverte à M. le Président du Mouvement Republicain National pour la Démocratie et le Développement (MRNDD)*. Editions Uruhimbi, BP 1067 Kigali, Rwanda, 1992.

Journals

Africa Confidential, 'Rwanda: Civilian Slaughter', Vol. 35, No. 9, 6 May 1994.

Barnett, Michael N., The UN Security Council, Indifference, and the Genocide in Rwanda. *Cultural Anthropology*, Vol. 12, No. 4, 1997.

Blankfort, Lowell, 'Almost a Million dead, Rwanda Seeks Justice', *World Outlook*, 2 December 1995 (UNA-US).

Bradol, Jean-Hervé, 'Rwanda, Avril–Mai 1994. Limites et Ambiguités de l'Action Humanitaire. Crises Politiques, Massacres et Exodes Massifs', *Le Temps Modernes*, No. 583, 1995.

Burkhalter, Holly J., 'The Question of Genocide. The Clinton Administration and Rwanda', *World Policy Journal*, Vol. 11, No. 4, Winter 1994–95.

Clapham, Christopher, 'Rwanda: The Perils of Peacemaking', *Journal of Peace Research*, Vol. 35, No. 2, 1998.

Destexhe, Alain, 'The Third Genocide', *Foreign Policy*, No. 97, Winter 1994–95.

Heusch, Luc de, 'Rwanda. Responsibilities for a Genocide', *Anthropology Today*, Vol. 11, No. 4, August 1994.

Jones, Bruce, '"Intervention Without Borders". Humanitarian Intervention in Rwanda, 1990–94', *Millennium*, Vol. 24, No. 2, Summer 1995.

Leitenberg, Milton, 'Rwanda, 1994: International Incompetence Produces Genocide', *Peacekeeping and International Relations*, November–December 1994.

Lemarchand, René, 'The Apocalypse in Rwanda', *Cultural Survival Quarterly*, Summer/ Fall 1994.

Mel, McNulty, 'France's Rwanda Débâcle', *War Studies*, Vol. 2, No. 2, Spring 1997.

Mamdani, Mahmood, 'From Conquest to Consent as the Basis of State Formation: Reflections on Rwanda', *New Left Review*, No. 216, 1996.

Melvern, Linda, 'The UN and Rwanda', *London Review of Books*, 12 December 1996.

— 'Genocide Behind the Thin Blue Line', *Security Dialogue*, Vol. 28, No. 3, September 1997.

Nshimiyimana, Vénuste. *Prélude du Génocide Rwandais. Enquête sur les Circonstances Politiques et Militaires du Meutre du Président Habyarimana*, Brussels: Quorum, 1995.

Smith, David Norman, 'The Genesis of Genocide in Rwanda: The Fatal Dialectic of Class and Ethnicity', *Humanity and Society*, Vol. 19, No. 4, November 1995.

Suhrke, Astri, 'Dilemmas of Protection: The Log of the Kigali Battalion', *Security Dialogue*, Vol. 29, No. 1, March 1998.

van Hoyweghen, Saskia, 'The Disintegration of the Catholic Church of Rwanda. A Study of the Fragmentation of Political and Religious Authority', *African Affairs*, No. 95, 1996, pp. 379–401.

Books

Adelman, Howard and Suhrke, Astri (eds), *The Path of a Genocide. The Rwanda Crisis from Uganda to Zaire*. New Brunswick, NJ: Transaction, 1999.

Abdulai, Napoleon (ed.), *Genocide in Rwanda*. Africa Research and Information Centre, 1994.

African Rights, *Rwanda. Death, Despair and Defiance*. London: African Rights, 1995.

Anyidoho, Henry Kwami, *Guns Over Kigali*. Accra: Woeli Publishing Services, 1997.

Barnett, Michael N., 'The Politics of Indifference at the United Nations and Genocide in Rwanda and Bosnia', in Thomas Cushman and Stjepan Mestrovic (eds), *This Time we Knew: Western Responses to Genocide in Bosnia*, New York: New York University Press, 1996.

Bowen, Michael, Gary Freeman and Kay Miller. *Passing By. The United States and Genocide in Burundi, 1972*. Special Report. Humanitarian Policy Studies. Carnegie Endowment for International Peace.

Broadcasting Genocide: Censorship, Propaganda and State-Sponsored Violence in Rwanda 1990–1994. Article 19, October 1996.

Boutros-Ghali, Boutros, *Unvanquished. A US–UN Saga*. London: I.B.Tauris, 1999.

Braeckman, Colette, *Rwanda, Histoire d'un Génocide*. Paris: Fayard, 1994.

— *Terreur Africaine. Burundi, Rwanda, Zaire: les racines de la violence*. Paris: Fayard, 1996.

Castonguay, Jacques, *Les Casques Bleus au Rwanda*. Paris: Editions l'Harmattan, 1998.

Chrétien, Jean-Pierre, *Le Défi de l'Ethnisme. Rwanda et Burundi, 1990–1996*, Paris: Karthala, 1997.

Chrétien, Jean-Pierre, Jean-François Dupaquier, Marcel Kabanda and Joseph Ngarambe (Reporters sans Frontières), *Rwanda: Les Médias du Genocide*. Paris: Karthala, 1995.

Clapham, Christopher (ed.), *African Guerrillas*. Oxford: James Currey, 1998.

Destexhe, Alain, *Rwanda: essai sur le génocide*. Editions Complexe, 1994.

— *Qui a Tué Nos Paras?* Brussels: Editions Luc Piré, 1996.

Dorsey, Learthen, *Historical Dictionary of Rwanda*. African Historical Dictionaries No. 60. Metuchen, NJ and London: Scarecrow Press, 1994.

Durch, William J. (ed.), *UN Peacekeeping: American Politics and the Uncivil Wars of the 1990s*. Henry L. Stimson Center. New York: St Martin's Press, 1996.

Fein, Helen, *Accounting for Genocide after 1945. Theories and Some Findings*. International Journal on Group Rights, Vol. 1. Amsterdam: Martinus Nijhoff, 1993.

Guichaoua, André (ed.), *Les Crises Politiques au Burundi et au Rwanda (1993–1994)*. Université des Sciences et Technologies de Lille. Paris: Karthala, 1995.

Gouteux, Jean-Paul, *Un Génocide secret d'Etat*. Editions Sociales, 1998.

Horowitz, Irving, *Taking Lives: Genocide and State Power*. New Brunswick, NJ: Transaction, 1980.

Human Rights Watch/Fédération Internationale des Ligues des Droits de l'Homme, *Leave none to tell the story. Genocide in Rwanda*, 1999.

Karhilo, Jaana, Case study on Peacekeeping: Rwanda. Appendix 2C. Year Book. Stockholm International Peace Research Institute. Oxford University Press, 1995.

Klinghoffer, Arthur Jay, *The International Dimension of Genocide in Rwanda*. London: Macmillan, 1998.

Kuper, Leo, *The Prevention of Genocide*. New Haven, CT, and London: Yale University Press, 1985.

LeBlanc, Lawrence J., *The United States and the Genocide Convention*. Duke University Press, 1991.

Lehmann, Ingrid. A., *Peacekeeping and Public Information. Caught in the Crossfire*. London: Frank Cass, 1999.

Lema, Antoine, *Africa Divided*. Sweden: Lund University Press, 1993.

Lemarchand, René, *Rwanda and Burundi*. London: Pall Mall, London, 1970.

Lemkin, Raphael, *Axis Rule in Occupied Europe. Laws of Occupation, Analysis of Government, Proposals for Redress*. Washington, DC: Carnegie Endowment for International Peace, 1944.

Marrus, Michael, *The Holocaust in History*. Harmondsworth: Penguin, 1996.

Melvern, Linda, *The Ultimate Crime. Who Betrayed the UN and Why*. London: Allison and Busby, 1995.

Moeller, Susan D., *Compassion Fatigue*. New York and London: Routledge, 1999.

Moore, Jonathan (ed.), *Hard Choices, Moral Dilemmas in Humanitarian Intervention*. Oxford: Rowman and Littlefield, 1998.

Newbury, Catharine, *The Cohesion of Oppression; Clientship and Ethnicity in Rwanda, 1860–1960*, Columbia University Press, 1988.

Nshimiyimana, Venuste, *Prélude de Génocide Rwandais. Enquête sur les Circonstances Politique et Militaires du Meutre du Président Habyarimana*. Brussels: Quorum, 1995.

Piollet, J.-B., *Les Missions catholiques françaises au XIXe siècle*. Les Missions d'Afrique, 1902.

Porter, Jack Nusan, *Genocide and Human Rights, A Global Anthology*. University Press of America, 1982.

Gérard Prunier, *The Rwanda Crisis 1959–1994. History of a Genocide*. London: Hurst and Company, 1995.

Reyntjens, Filip, *L'Afrique des Grands Lacs en crise. Rwanda, Burundi: 1988–1994*. Paris: Karthala, 1994.

— *Rwanda. Trois Jours qui on fait basculer l'histoire*. Paris: Editions l'Harmattan, 1995.

Speke, J. H., *Journal of the discovery of the source of the Nile*. London: J. M. Dent, 1969 (1st edn, 1863).

The Treatment of the Armenians in the Ottoman Empire. Documents presented to Viscount Grey of Fallodon, Secretary of State for Foreign Affairs. Preface by Viscount Bryce. London: Hodder and Stoughton. 1916.

Uvin, Peter, *Aiding Violence: The Development Enterprise in Rwanda*. New York: Kumarian Press, 1998.

Vassall-Adams, Guy, *Rwanda: An Agenda for International Action*. Oxford: Oxfam Publications, 1994.

Vidal, Claudine, *Sociologies des passions. Rwanda, Côte d'Ivoire*. Paris: Karthala, 1991.

Wheeler, Nicholas J., *Saving Strangers: Humanitarian Intervention in International Society*. Oxford: OUP, forthcoming.

Radio

War Radio, BBC Radio 4. Presented by Misha Glenny. Producer Marc Jobst. Bristol. 10 December 1998.

Transcripts. BBC Radio broadcasts by Mark Doyle. Kigali and Nairobi. April, May, June, July, 1994.

Television

Excerpts taken from interviews published on Frontline's website for 'The Triumph of Evil'. www.pbs.org/WGBH/Pages/Frontline/shows/evil. Copyright WGBH/Frontline, 1999.

Index

This book is available in the following countries

Ghana

EPP Book Services, PO Box TF 490, Trade Fair, Accra
tel: 233 21 773087
fax: 233 21 779099

Kenya

EAEP, PO Box 45314, Nairobi
tel: 254 2 534020/545903
fax: 254 2 532095

Rwanda

Librairie Ikirezi, PO Box 443, Kigali
tel/fax: 250 71314

Tanzania

TEMA Publishing Co Ltd, PO Box 63115, Dar es Salaam
tel: 255 51 113608
fax: 255 51 110742

Uganda

Fountain Publishers Ltd, PO Box 288, Kampala
tel: 256 41 259163
fax: 256 41 251112